Integrating TCP/IP i•nets
with IBM Data Centers

Integrating TCP/IP i•nets with IBM Data Centers

Anura Gurugé

ADDISON-WESLEY

An imprint of Addison Wesley Longman, Inc.

Reading, Massachusetts • Harlow, England • Menlo Park, California
Berkeley, California • Don Mills, Ontario • Sydney
Bonn • Amsterdam • Tokyo • Mexico City

The publishers offer discounts on this book when ordered in quantity for special sales. For more information, please contact:

Corporate, Government, and Special Sales Group
Addison Wesley Longman, Inc.
One Jacob Way
Reading, Massachusetts 01867

Library of Congress Cataloging-in-Publication Data

Gurugé, Anura.
    Integrating TCP/IP i•nets with IBM data centers / Anura Gurugé.
        p.   cm.
    Includes bibliographical references and index (p.   )
    ISBN 0-201-30991-2 (alk. paper)
    1. TCP/IP (Computer network protocol)   2. IBM computers.
3. Computer networks—Management.   4. Systems engineering.
I. Title.
TK5105.585.G87   1999
004.6'2—dc21   99-35568
                                                                CIP

ISBN 0-201-30991-2

Text printed on recycled and acid-free paper.

1 2 3 4 5 6 7 8 9 10–MA–03 02 01 00 99
First printing, October 1999

To Lisa, Danielle, and Matthew Gordon

Contents

Chapter 2: SNA to SNA-Capable i•nets: SNA's Final Metamorphosis   45

Chapter 3: Differences between SNA Networks and SNA-Capable i•nets   87

Chapter 4: Integrating SNA/APPN with i•nets   123

Chapter 6: User Interface Rejuvenation, Application-Specific Gateways, and Programmatic Access   231

Chapter 7: Network Infrastructure, Management, and New Mainframe Gateways   291

Chapter 8: Pulling It All Together   337

Foreword

The Internet economy is here. The widespread adoption of the Internet has resulted in the network's new, strategic role within corporate America. Today, the network is being used to gain a competitive advantage through applications such as e-commerce, unified communications, and Internet call centers. Cisco's leadership in pioneering this model of networked commerce is exemplified on our own Web site for customers, partners, and employees—Cisco Connection Online. As the driving force behind the global economy, the Internet economy is enabling a "New World" in communications, where the Internet acts as the foundation for transporting data, voice, and video traffic over a single network.

Extending the power and benefits of the Internet to traditional IBM data centers is crucial for companies that want to thrive in the Internet economy. To reap the full benefits of the Internet, enterprises must be able to leverage the wealth of mission-critical information and applications that reside in corporate data centers via the Internet.

As one of the pioneers of Cisco's technologies for IBM internetworking, I remember when industry pundits predicted the death of the mainframe in the early 1990s and scoffed at the thought of integrating SNA into the client/server environment. We now see, however, that the widespread adoption of technologies, such as Data Link Switching and channel-attached routers, has proven the pundits wrong.

The bottom line is that the mainframe remains a critical part of the corporate network. Only a handful of enterprises have integrated the mainframe with the Internet to position themselves for the Internet economy. These enterprises are now well positioned to embark on a voyage to the New World, where data, voice, and video will converge.

Although many enterprises have successfully made the transition, many companies have yet to begin this important migration. According to a recent study by the Gartner Group, less than half of all SNA networks in North America and less than 20% of SNA networks outside the United States have been integrated with Internet Protocol (IP) networks.

This book is a tremendous resource for those who now face the challenge of integrating their SNA and IP networks to leverage the power of the Internet. Anura takes a complex subject and breaks it down by outlining products, technologies, case studies, and solutions to best integrate traditional data centers with the Internet. I've known Anura for a number of years, going back to the days when SNA migration to client servers was just beginning to occur. Anura recognized early on that the mainframe would not cease to exist, but would instead take on a new role in the corporate environment given the adoption of IP as the protocol of choice.

In purchasing this book, you've taken the first step toward leveraging the combined power of the Internet and corporate data centers. The companies that embrace the Internet economy will be the clear winners as we move into the twenty-first century.

Don Listwin
Executive Vice President
Cisco Systems, Inc.

Preface

This book is a concise but comprehensive technical handbook on how to successfully integrate IBM (or compatible) mainframes or AS/400s with Internet technology-based networks—whether they be intranets, the Internet, or business-to-business extranets. It is nonpartisan and vendor-neutral and freely cites, without any bias or prejudice, technology, products, and actual, named case studies from numerous germane vendors. This book was written to help all those who are responsible for ensuring that traditional IBM data centers will continue to play a gainful and pivotal role in the new Internet-dominated world of intranets, e-commerce, remote access across the Internet, Internet call centers, home banking, TCP/IP, extranets, Java, online investment, HTML, and SSL-based security.

Although essentially technical, this book is not restricted to "technocrats." In fact, it can be of considerable interest and use to MIS and networking managers and executives at all levels in corporations that are evaluating how best to empower their traditional data centers by making them i•net-capable—with "i•nets" being a collective term that embraces the Internet, intranets, and extranets. Although primarily geared toward professionals in end-user organizations, the scope and structure of this book are such that it can be of significant value to developers, support staff, and managers of companies on the supply side—that is, enterprises that provide the products and the expertise to integrate data centers with i•nets.

Given its overt data center orientation, echoed in both its title and subtitle, this book is unlikely to be read by somebody who has no experience or interest in mainframes or AS/400s. The typical reader would, at least when pressed, admit to being involved in some capacity with data processing or networking within the so-called IBM (or "Big Blue") world—where the technology, if not the products, has its roots in architectures, methodologies, or concepts fostered by IBM. Although not imperative, it would help if a reader has had some prior exposure to IBM's Systems Network Architecture (SNA), core IBM mainframe software (for example, ACF/VTAM, OS/390), and i•net-related technologies such as Web servers and Java. In addition to a detailed Glossary and a list of Acronyms and Abbreviations, this book strives to describe (at least once) all of the technologies, protocols, and buzzwords that are mentioned within the text so as to ensure that a reader is never left in the dark or in a state of disorientation.

What Is Covered?

This book contains detailed technical descriptions of all promising technologies that can be used to integrate mainframes and AS/400s with i•nets. To the best of the author's knowledge, no currently available technologies have been omitted. The technologies described include tn3270(E), 3270-to-HTML conversion, applet-based 3270/5250 emulation, Data Link Switching (DLSw), application servers, user interface rejuvenation, HPR-over-IP, AutoGUIs, AnyNet, and channel-attached mainframe gateways. This wide spectrum of technology covered is divided into five broad categories: access technologies (for example, applet-based terminal emulation); transport technologies (for example, DLSw); rejuvenation techniques (for example, Auto-GUI); programmatic solutions (for example, application servers); and network infrastructure (for example, channel-attached gateways).

Chapter 1 is a broad-brush and far-ranging introduction to the whole notion of i•net-based enterprise networking. Following an overall, high-level discourse of all of the pertinent technologies, Chapter 4 concentrates on the transport-related options. Chapter 5 is devoted to terminal-oriented access methodologies. Chapter 6 deals with rejuvenation and the programmatic solutions, with all of the network infrastructure-related topics being covered in Chapter 7. Chapter 2 deals with the transition of SNA networks into SNA-capable i•nets; High Performance Routing, the latest and last incarnation of SNA; its role as a transport scheme in i•nets in the form of HPR-over-IP; and the continuing role of SNA-gateways. Chapter 3 examines how SNA-capable i•nets differ from SNA networks when it comes to security, end-to-end routing, resilience, performance, and congestion control. Chapter 8 sets out to coalesce and consolidate all of the themes and technologies discussed in Chapters 2 to 7, with the help of some particularly illuminating case studies.

How Is It Covered?

All of the in-depth technical material appears in Chapters 2 through 7. Chapter 1 serves as a preamble, possibly provocative, justifying the tantalizing technological revolution now at hand. Chapter 8 sets out to prove that this trend is not all theory and that corporations around the world are already benefiting from SNA-capable i•nets.

Each chapter starts off in an introductory mode and gives the reader a high-level overview of what is to be covered in that chapter. Readers who require only a broad-brush outline of the issues involved and the solutions available may find that Chapter 1 and the first few pages of the other chapters together give them that bird's-eye view.

Given this structure, where each chapter starts off with an overview, many topics will appear multiple times within a chapter—typically with incremental levels of detail or refinement. Headings and subheadings are used extensively after the introductory prose to identify and delineate the topics being addressed. Actual case studies—complete with the customer name and adorned with a detailed architectural diagram highlighting all of the pertinent products that constitute the solution—are the highlights of Chapters 4 through 8. In addition, the technical chapters each contain at least a dozen highly detailed figures that illustrate the key topics being discussed, as well as numerous tables that highlight "pros and cons" of a particular approach or summarize all of the major products offering a particular type of solution.

Navigating Through This Book

This book, of course, is structured to be read sequentially. If read in such a conventional way, the issues, options, technologies, and solutions will be presented in a systematic step-by-step manner, replete with detailed figures, named case studies, and summary sidebars whenever applicable. It could, however, be used in "reference guide" mode, where the reader pursues a particular technology or theme—for example, using 3270- or 5250-to-HTML conversion to provide public access to SNA applications over the Internet, or the pros and cons of using a channel-attached tn3270(E) server versus using a mainframe-based server. If you intend to use this book as a reference guide, you can use the Index or the Contents' listings as the optimal means of locating the desired topics. As the book contains more than 100 highly annotated, half- to full-page illustrations, it may also be possible to locate certain topics or themes by skimming through the book and looking at the pictures!

Each section has a margin note that tries to capture the gist of that section in a few sentences. The contents of this margin note will serve as a good indication of what to expect within that section.

Features

The key auxiliary techniques used in this book to facilitate information dissemination are detailed illustrations for every key topic covered, summary tables of pros and cons for each technology described, named case studies, and margin notes for each section that pithily summarize the gist of that section.

Value Proposition

This book provides the reader with a nonpartisan, objective, factual, and accurate technical appreciation of how best to integrate traditional data centers with i•nets. In addition to always describing the pros and cons of a given technology, it includes lists of the leading products related to that technology to give the reader a quick start in terms of trying to source that technology. The book also contains more than a dozen case studies from around the world, featuring names such as General Motors, TransWorld Airlines, Del Monte, and Lafayette Life Insurance. These case studies illustrate how major companies are gainfully using the Internet to minimize their remote access costs while simultaneously extending the reach and scope of their data center applications.

Supplementary Material

A Bibliography at the end of this book lists other germane books and reference manuals. Online information related to the technologies and solutions described in this book may be found at *www.sna-inets.com*, a Web site maintained by the SNA-Capable i•nets Forum, and at *www.inet-guru.com*, which is the author's personal Web site. For information specific to e-commerce and extranet-based business-to-business transactions, visit *www.ezealous. com*, another Web site maintained by the author.

The Last Word

Now you are ready to dive into the contents of this book. For data center professionals, these are challenging times given the i•net-related changes afoot. This book will help you make the transition. It even strives to convey that this transition is bracingly exciting. I hope you enjoy it.

Anura ("SNA") Gurugé
Lake Winnipesaukee, New Hampshire

Acknowledgments

A book like this one on emerging and fast-evolving technologies and market trends is not possible without the active, unstinted help of many generous individuals. During the course of writing this book, I did more than 30 full-day seminars on this topic in the United States and Europe. In the process, I had a chance to meet and talk with hundreds of folks who were in the throes of implementing various i•net solutions. Their insights, opinions, and experiences were invaluable in crafting and refining the themes covered in this book. I thank you all for your kind help, though I cannot mention all of you by name.

The help of others, given their magnitude, does require special mention. Lisa Lindgren, my partner, who was once Cisco's Product Line Manager for its tn3270 server and WebConnect products, was a constant and ready source of valuable information. The detailed product comparison matrices in this book are her work. Lisa also had the unenviable task of proofreading the first draft of this book and correcting my many mistakes. I am indeed indebted to her—without Lisa, this book would have never been completed.

Much gratitude is also owed to David Johnson of OpenConnect Systems, William C. McCain of Novell, Carlson Colomb of Eicon Technology, Jim O'Connor of Bus-Tech, Charles Machalani of Farabi Technology, and Tod Yampel of ResQ!Net, all of whom provided me with large quantities of information—in some cases, on a near daily basis. Without their help, this book would have been bereft of much detail, case studies, and insights.

Special thanks are also due to Don Listwin, the dynamo behind much of Cisco's success, for taking the time to write the Foreword for this book. I first met Don in January 1992 in Washington, D.C., at ComNet, where we discussed Cisco's plans to implement SNA "PU 4" Subarea Routing in its bridge/routers. Within minutes of shaking hands, I dropped a full glass of beer on his lap! We have been friends ever since and Don has always been ready to give me whatever help I needed. Thank you, Don.

Karen Gettman and Mary Hart, my editors at Addison Wesley Longman, were outstanding in their support, help, and above all patience. They deserve permanent halos for persevering with me and for not chastising me for the many deadlines I brazenly missed. Thank you, Karen. Thank you, Mary. If I ever write another book, I promise to do better.

Special thanks are also due to all the brave and hardy folks that reviewed this book:

Marten Bystrom, Carlson Colomb, J. Alan Gatlin, David Johnson, V. C. Marney-Petix, Bob Moore, Andrew Piggott, Brian Pomeroy, and Les Smith

In addition to finding some "howlers" where I was off the mark, they came up with numerous sound suggestions on how I could improve the overall content. Thank you.

Thanks are also due to the following individuals: Greg and Bill Koss, and Larry Samberg (my friends from CrossComm), now spearheading Sonoma Systems; Stephen Clark, Craig Minyard, and Sean Cahill of Open-Connect Systems; Maks Wulkan, Jean-François Levesque, Jacinthe Paradis, Austin Ladd Roberts, Cleve Graves, Lynne Theoret, and Joan Mimeault of Eicon Technology; Cliff Meltzer of Cisco, for his great sense of humor and for buying Nashoba Networks; Richard Tobacco, Patricia Kinney, Kathleen Riordan, Tom Belz, and Jim Goethals, to name a few of my friends at IBM; Tiffany Allesina and Kevin George at Attachmate; Gale Persil and Lisa Smith of Sterling Software; Bill Jones, my "twin" Mark ("MG") Marsh, and Chris Merrill at Interlink; Adrienne King of Motorola; Bob Reason and Julie Estrada at Nortel/Bay; David Holbrook and Kelly McGunagle at Novell; Scott Merrick, Kristin Connor, and Steve Dulaney at WRQ; Tom Robinson at Blue Lobster; Thomas Wirth of Swiss Air Group; Mark Lillycrop of Xephon; B. J. Johnson at Compaq; Darryl Egbert at Lexis-Nexis; Baylus ("Nick") Francis, now at Tavve; Michael Tosko of MCI/WorldCom; Bob Rosenbaum, late of Nashoba but now a relative through our goldens; Guy Hoffman, who dragged me into this arena; Rich O'Hanley and Theron Shreve of Auerbach; Beth Schultz of Network World; "Sir" Ian C. F. Williams of Scotland; Josh Morrison of Enhanced Computer Systems, for keeping my PCs alive; and Lydia and Nathan Torr of Meredith, who shower me constantly with kindness and generosity.

Matthew Gordon, although only six, checked on the progress of this book weekly, as he was very anxious to have another book with his name in it.

He was more demanding and pressing than even the editors. In addition, Matthew and Danielle continued to enrich my life and motivate me. Winston and Maggie, the goldens, made sure that I was not permanently shackled to my PCs and that I got slightly more exercise than winding up my Rolex every couple of days. Lisa's help and support was my sustaining force. Thank you all.

About the Author

Anura ("SNA") Gurugé is an independent technical analyst and consultant who specializes in all aspects of contemporary IBM networking. He has first-hand, in-depth experience in SNA-capable i•nets, SNA/APPN/HPR/AnyNet, Frame Relay, Token Ring switching, ATM, system management, and *x*DSL technologies. He was actively involved with the Token Ring switching pioneer Nashoba Networks. In a career spanning 24 years, he has held senior technical and marketing roles in IBM, ITT, Northern Telecom, Wang, and BBN.

Over the last seven years, Gurugé has worked closely with most of the leading bridge/router, intelligent hub, FRAD, Token Ring switching, and gateway vendors, designing many of the SNA-related features now found on bridge/routers and gateways. He has also helped large IBM customers to re-engineer their old, SNA-only networks. He is the founder and chairman of the SNA-Capable i•net Forum (*www.sna-inets.com*).

In addition, Gurugé is the author of *Reengineering IBM Networks* (1996), the best-selling *SNA: Theory and Practice* (1984), and several other books on SNA, APPN, and SAA. He is also the editor of Auerbach's *Handbook of Communications Systems Management*. He has published more than 250 articles and is the author of the Business Communications Review (BCR) supplements, *BCR's Guide to SNA Internetworking* and *Beyond SNA Internetworking*.

Gurugé conducts technical and sales training seminars worldwide on a regular basis and has conducted one-day workshops for Networld+InterOp since 1992. He publishes a monthly, 16-page *Newsletter on Contemporary IBM Internetworking*. He can be contacted at *guruge@cyberportal.net*.

Intranets and i•nets
The Next Generation
of Enterprise Networks

Everyone currently involved with information technology in any way knows for sure, with either a growing sense of exhilaration or dread, that they are participating, actively or vicariously, in something huge: the Internet-inspired Information Revolution. The scale, momentum, implications, and especially the inevitable end result of this fundamental recrafting of the way that information is presented, disseminated, and accessed are momentous and unprecedented. This movement makes the titanic strides made by the computer industry over the last four decades look somewhat pedestrian in comparison. Information, affecting every facet of life, is being further liberated; one could even say that information as a whole is becoming a commodity. Although it would be foolish to claim that anything could compete with the Gutenberg press in terms of precipitating the spread of information, the Internet, in time, will surely be viewed as a close second.

The influence of the Internet, especially in North America, is pervasive, impinging on everything from leisure, travel, and entertainment to shopping and personal investment. References to the Internet now routinely appear on commercial TV, including programs for preschoolers, magazines, and newspapers—not to mention trailers for movies. Nonetheless, the most profound effects of Internet technology will be felt in the sphere of global commerce: Internet technology, around the turn of the millennium, will bring as much change to commercial-sector computing, in the form of **e-commerce**, as the now ubiquitous PC did in the late 1980s. The systems and networks based on Internet-related technology, however, cannot start from scratch or expect to thrive without links to today's existing information systems. This book explores the options and possibilities that will emerge as today's data centers are seamlessly but synergistically integrated with the emerging i•nets.

The Internet is only second, and a close second at that, to the Gutenberg press in terms of facilitating and furthering the spread and scope of information.

The Internet (and the **intranets** and **extranets** that it has spawned) is changing not only the way that all types of enterprises view networking, but also their basic precepts of information processing and propagation. Intranets—the private, in-house networks built using Internet concepts and technology—have already become synonymous with next-generation enterprise networking. Extranets that interconnect autonomous intranets or provide agents of a company with remote access to the company's hosts over the Internet are being widely discussed as the basis for much of forthcoming intercompany collaboration, whether it be related to order processing, supply-chain management, inventory look-up, joint research, data interchange, or funds transfer. The Internet, in parallel, is developing into the universal, virtual storefront for global commerce. Today's computing systems and enterprise networks must be modified and extended to accommodate this wholesale and hugely popular move toward Internet-technology-centric information management.

To take advantage of this new corporate information model, most mid- to large-size commercial enterprises will have little choice but to somehow integrate their existing data centers with the nascent Internet-technology-based systems. The need for this integration is very simple. Although i•nets (that is, intranets, the Internet, or extranets) and Internet technology such as Web pages irrefutably represent the future, much of current corporate data, in the case of medium to large commercial enterprises, still resides within data centers populated with IBM or IBM-compatible mainframes, minicomputers, or UNIX-based servers. Attempting to replicate the data available on the data center systems on Web servers—let alone trying to port mammoth, decades-old, mission-critical applications from mainframes to Windows NT-based servers—is invariably infeasible, if not futile. The goal is not to abandon the old, but rather to strive for synergy by assimilating it with the new i•net technology. The remainder of this book covers the issues, pertinent technologies, and implementational options for seamlessly incorporating data center application files and databases with emerging i•nets.

1.1 INTRANET: YOUR VERY OWN INTERNET

Intranet—private, in-house information system, for corporate employee use only, built around Internet technology.

Intranets provide most enterprises with their first hands-on experience of the possibilities, limitations, and potentially rich rewards of information systems based on Internet technology. Intranets, by definition, are private, in-house networks. An intranet per se can thus be viewed as serving only legitimate corporate employees. An enterprise that wants external users—whether agents or the general public—to be able to utilize some of the data accessible via the in-house intranet would typically do so by implementing a secure Internet or extranet interface to the relevant data.

The most widely used and cogent technical description of an intranet is that it is a private, enterprise-specific network built using Internet concepts and technologies. An intranet, just like the Internet, consists of a **TCP/IP** backbone, one or more **Web servers**, users on PCs and other workstations using **Web browsers**, and most likely security-enhancing software known as **firewalls** and function-enriching software known as applets written in **Java** or **ActiveX**. In addition, many intranets have a bidirectional gateway to an Internet gateway, as well as data feeds from various external sources, such as financial data or broadcast news, and most likely internal systems as well. If an enterprise supports a data center, then some or all of the data and applications resident on the data center systems should probably be accessible to the intranet users. Figure 1.1 depicts the overall structure of an intranet, and Table 1.1 shows the key components of a typical intranet.

Other descriptions of what constitutes an intranet are less commonly used. Some maintain that any private network, irrespective of the technology on which it is based and the networking protocol it uses, should now be referred to as an intranet. IBM marketing documents show intranets that use IBM's **High-Performance Routing (HPR)**, which is the latest variant of the

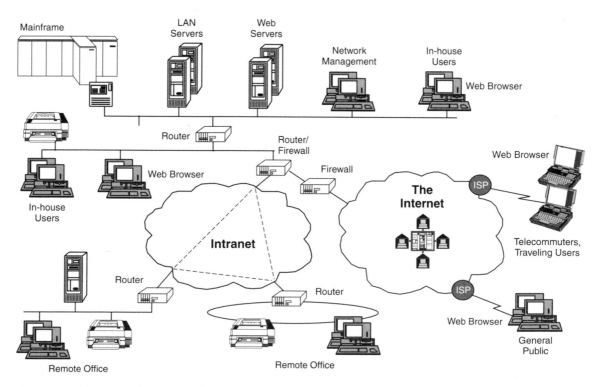

FIGURE 1.1   The general structure of an intranet.

TABLE 1.1 Key components of an enierprise intranet.

Component	Examples
Web server on an NT, UNIX, or possibly mainframe platform	Microsoft Internet Information Server (IIS), Netscape Suite Spot, Apache Web Server, IBM WebSphere
PC and workstation clients with a Web browser	Netscape Navigator, Microsoft Internet Explorer
LANs	Fast Ethernet, Ethernet, Token Ring, FDDI, ATM
Routers	Cisco, Nortel/Bay, IBM, 3Com
Firewalls	CheckPoint FireWall-1, Cisco PIX, IBM's eNetwork
LAN servers	Microsoft NT, Novell, NetWare, UNIX, Linux
Switches	LAN switches (Cisco Catalyst), backbone ATM switches (IBM 8265 Layer 3 switches (IBM 8371)
TCP/IP backbone	Implemented using Frame Relay, ATM, leased lines, or VPN
Internet gateway	Typically realized via a router
Gateway to data center	IBM's Communications Server for NT, Novell's NetWare for SAA

Systems Network Architecture (SNA), as their networking fabric, rather than TCP/IP. To be fair, IBM does acknowledge that the applications and end users of such HPR-based intranets will invariably be TCP/IP-based; as such, these HPR networks will continually resort to protocol conversion, in the form of IBM's AnyNet technology, to transport end-to-end TCP/IP traffic over the HPR backbone. On the other hand, many other marketing and technical documents from IBM describe intranets purely in terms of TCP/IP, without any mention of HPR. Still others claim that an intranet is merely a network-within-a-network—with some interpreting this notion of network partitioning to mean that any intranet is essentially a subset of the all-encompassing Internet.

All of these descriptions, however, agree on the private nature of intranets and differ only in specifying whether an intranet must be based on Internet technology—in particular, on the TCP/IP networking protocol. Given that the term "intranets" was originally coined by the networking press in the mid-1990s to refer to the then emerging genre of Web server-centered and Web browser-accessed private networks, and that most of the large networking vendors agree on the Internet-related roots of intranets, the remainder of this book will adhere to definition of an intranet as being a TCP/IP-centric private network that predominantly utilizes Internet-related technologies such Web servers, Web browsers, firewalls, and SMTP/POP e-mail protocols.

1.1.1 The Tantalizing Lure of Intranets

Intranets are on the ascent. Captivated by the indubitable success of the Internet as a user-friendly, high-volume information disseminator, corporations are rushing to implement intranets in an effort to enhance and simplify their employees' access to data that could make them more productive, competitive, or fulfilled. In 1998, more than 90% of mid- to large-size U.S. commercial enterprises, and more than 60% of their European counterparts already had a production intranet in place. It is anticipated that 1 million intranets will serve in excess of 100 million users worldwide by the year 2000, with nearly all midsize- or larger North American corporations actively using intranets for some part of their day-to-day business. To put this idea into perspective, it is sobering to realize that the most successful commercial networking scheme in the past, IBM's renowned SNA, in its heyday in the late 1980s could lay claim to at most 45,000 networks around the world, including AS/400-only networks running the **Advanced Peer-to-Peer Networking (APPN)** variant—albeit with most of the SNA networks being considerably larger than the average intranet.

> By 2000, at least 1 million intranets will serve 100 million users, or more than 20 times as many SNA and APPN networks as ever existed.

The Internet's resounding success in simultaneously supporting vast numbers of interactive users, transporting huge volumes of data, and presenting information in a user-friendly manner through a visually riveting multimedia Web page format is both legendary and inescapable. Thanks to the popularity of the Internet, the Web browser is slowly but surely emerging to be the first and only universal user interface, or universal client, for PCs—more than 18 years after the advent of the species. Intranets set out to duplicate this success at the corporate level by using the same core technology, albeit with vital enhancements to ensure watertight end-to-end security, all-encompassing management, committed bandwidth, scalability on demand, and guaranteed performance.

The overriding lure of intranets is that they are implemented using highly proven, widely available, readily scalable, and cost-compelling Internet technology. In essence, intranets unashamedly rely on the Internet as a bountiful source for leading-edge but relatively inexpensive technology, an ultra-high-volume and zealously rigorous test bed, an uncompromising technology proving ground, and a fertile incubator for exciting new innovation—for example, voice-over-IP or **Secure Sockets Layer (SSL)**-based security. Intranets, which are intrinsically client/server-oriented in terms of their computing and networking paradigms, and also ideally suited to facilitate the widespread use of low-cost **network computers (NCs)**—especially as a strategic replacement for aging fixed-function terminals such as IBM 3270s or compatibles.

Intranets have another serendipitous and near-priceless attribute: They can be instrumental in expediting the delivery and deployment of new end-user applications. This point has particular significance for the mainframe-oriented, so-called IBM shops, where lead times for new applications are discussed in terms of years, rather than months or weeks. Most enterprises, wherever they call home, cite the inability to quickly develop new applications or extend existing applications to address changing market opportunities as a primary impediment to growth and competitiveness. The beneficial influence that intranets can have on accelerating application development relates to their inherent relationship with Web servers. Multiple factors have transformed Web servers, where necessary augmented by application servers such as IBM's WebSphere, into the optimum and strategic platforms for new application delivery.

For a start, there are Java and ActiveX, the object-oriented and Internet-capable programming languages developed by Sun Microsystems and Microsoft, respectively. Java stresses platform independence; ActiveX touts tight integration with Windows 95 even though it is supported on Macintosh and UNIX systems. Both languages epitomize feature-rich, totally object-oriented, turn-of-the-millennium programming initiatives with built-in support for multithreading as well as protection to control the behavior of program (to obviate invalid memory access, for example). They credibly compete with C++ and with each other in the fight to be today's most strategic and effective means for developing next-generation, Web-oriented applications.

1.1.2   Intranets Expedite Application Delivery

Thanks to Java, ActiveX, and JavaBeans, i•nets are able to promote the rapid and economical development and deployment of new, Web-oriented applications.

Although Java and ActiveX can be readily used outside the context of i•nets, the real power and beauty of these programming schemes lies in their ability to augment Web pages at the client, the server, or both, and to make them truly interactive, informative, and productive. Moreover, given that they are platform-independent (Java, in particular) when it comes to the hardware and operating system, a Web page enhanced by Java or ActiveX will work exactly the same whether it is being displayed on a PC running Windows 95/98, NT, or 3.1, a Macintosh running Apple OS 8, or a RISC workstation running a version of UNIX. The only proviso is that a Java- or ActiveX-capable Web browser must be used. This platform-independent portability aspect of Java and ActiveX, more notably Java, is widely referred to by the colloquialism, "Write once, run anywhere." Since around late 1996, solid Java support has been available with version 3 and above of both Netscape Navigator and Microsoft's Internet Explorer. Internet Explorer has native, built-in support for ActiveX. Netscape Navigator currently supports ActiveX only on Windows platforms, via an optional plug-in provided by Esker S.A. In addition to browsers, Java applets (more precisely, Java applications) can be freely executed on a wide variety of popular operating systems, including IBM's flagship OS/390 for mainframes.

Figure 1.2 provides a high-level view of how the Java Virtual Machine (JVM), which is a component of the overall Java Development Kit (JDK), is

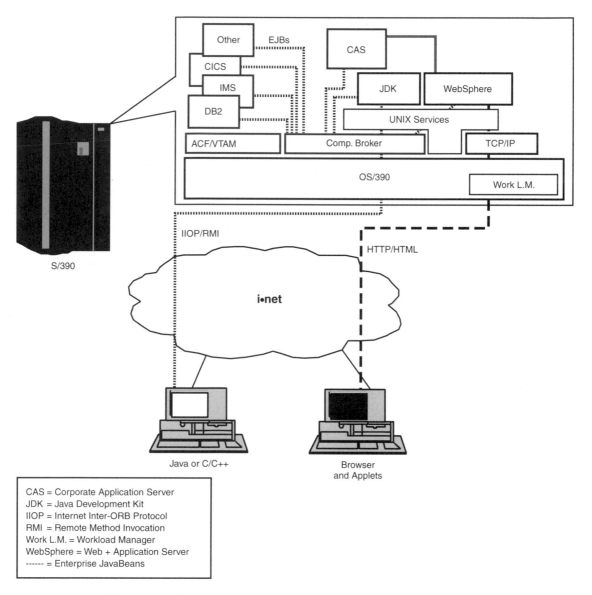

FIGURE 1.2 A high-level view of how the mainframe-resident OS/390 Java Virtual Machine, within the JDK, relates to other components.

implemented with OS/390. Figure 1.3 shows this OS/390 JVM implementation in more detail—in particular, how the compiled Java code is converted to C code for execution.

Thanks to these Web-oriented programming schemes (in particular Java, which currently has a head start because of its larger following of devotees), some corporations are already providing their employees, via their intranets,

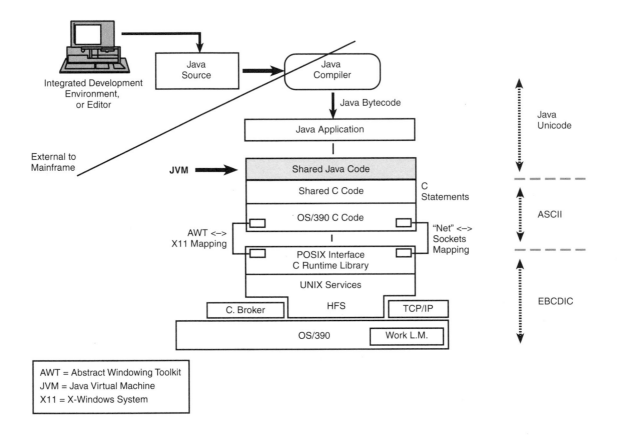

FIGURE 1.3   Details of IBM's Java Virtual Machine implementation on OS/390.   (*Source:* Some Input from IBM.)

highly specialized applications that would not have been feasible or economically justifiable in any other methodology other than Java. Many of the initial Java-based applications have focused on administrative task automation, such as electronic expense report processing and electronic timesheets; electronic benefits management relative to 401(k) tracking or stock option status; and human resource functions à la vacation administration. In the past, these areas may have been poorly served because MIS departments had their hands full just trying to deliver and maintain revenue-related, business-critical applications.

Java has been further fortified through the introduction of the **JavaBeans** and **Enterprise JavaBeans (EJBs)** technologies. These technologies provide a set of standards and application programming interfaces (APIs) to enable Java applications to easily access and reuse other programming components through object-oriented programming techniques. With these JavaBeans methodologies as well as with ActiveX, programmers developing new Web-oriented applications can readily exploit functionality available from other previously developed programming components, including other Java applications, ActiveX applications, or even modules developed in other languages.

In the IBM world, efforts are afoot by several vendors to provide much of the functionality required to programmatically interact with either terminal-oriented, mainframe-resident SNA/3270 applications or mainframe-based relational databases as EJBs modules. Such models will enable Java application developers to provide nearly effortless and transparent access to information from data-center applications and databases, without having to know anything about the actual, mainframe-centric mechanics involved in extracting such data. Obviously, the availability of such sophisticated EJBs modules and equivalent ActiveX components will facilitate the development of increasingly more incisive, elegant, and complex object-oriented applications.

Java and ActiveX, though key, are not the only factors underlying enterprises' ability to deliver new applications more quickly and cost-effectively within the context of Web servers and intranets. Most of today's Web servers are implemented on Windows NT or UNIX systems. Both of these intrinsically cost-effective and scalable systems are noted for their capabilities and tool repertoire that facilitate application development, testing, and deployment. Thus it is not surprising that most of today's programmer community, especially the latest generation of programmers who grew up being Internet-aware, not only want to work on these systems (instead of mainframes or minicomputers), but also prove noticeably more creative and productive when allowed to do so. Thus NT and UNIX, with NT increasingly gaining ground over UNIX despite its poorer scalability, have emerged as today's preferred and strategic platforms for new application development and deployment. Mainframe- and minicomputer-resident applications are now being routinely augmented or even permanently usurped by NT- or UNIX-based applications. Browser-based access schemes that support terminal emulation such as IBM's Host On-Demand, OpenConnect Systems' OC://WebConnect Pro, and Eicon's Aviva for Java, as well as JavaBeans-based application integration, ensure that these NT and UNIX applications can be freely accessed over an intranet or delivered subject to appropriate firewall-governed authorization over the Internet or extranets.

1.1.3   The Lure of Intranets: A Reprise

A multitude of compelling reasons exist as to why enterprises across the world are unequivocally banking on intranets to be their strategic next-generation enterprise networks, including the following:

1. Intranets are based on highly proven technology, software, and protocols (such as TCP/IP, HTTP, and SSL) that have been thoroughly and mercilessly field-tested on the Internet.

2. Intranets, thanks in part to Java, ActiveX, and JavaBeans, provide a tangible and alluring basis for expediting the delivery and deployment of cost-effective and easily maintainable new applications.

3. With the Internet adroitly supporting millions of concurrent users, intranets that use much of the same technology are, justifiably, seen as seamlessly scalable network solutions—capable of easily supporting even the largest enterprise networks, which are unlikely to have more than a few hundred thousand users.

4. The basic building blocks of intranets, such as Web servers, Web browsers, TCP/IP routers, firewalls, and Java development tools, are readily available from multiple vendors and generally run on readily extensible industry standard platforms such as Intel Pentium-based systems. Routers, with their vendor-specific hardware and software, are typically the one major exception to this rule.

5. The overall cost of implementing an intranet is invariably more attractive than the costs associated with alternative computing or networking solutions. Moreover, much, if not all, the intranet-related technology is well on the way to becoming off-the-shelf, commoditized entities, thus ensuring that prices will continue to fall.

6. The Internet, now the habitual sandbox for global academia and intelligentsia, is an unprecedented hotbed of technical innovation. Given the commonality of the base technology, any pertinent or intriguing offerings available on the Internet can easily be made available on intranets. It is worth noting that technologies, such as voice-over-IP, video-over-IP, and data-promulgating "push" technology à la PointCast, all of which are now being advocated for use within intranets, were first developed for use over the Internet.

7. With very little effort, intranets can be seamlessly linked to the Internet via bidirectional and firewall-protected gateways.

8. Once an Internet gateway has been implemented, corporate employees (in particular, road warriors and telecommuters) can gain access to the corporate intranet via the Internet—rather than being able to gain such access only via a dial-in, remote access scheme. In the case of geographically displaced telecommuters, intranet access over the Internet could be very cost-effective compared with long-distance dial-in, allowing them to reach the Internet through a local ISP with competitive, unlimited usage rates—typically in the $20 per month range. The interface to the Internet, usually in the form of a home page, will also enable the public to freely glean valuable information about the corporation, its

products and services, and possibly conduct secure financial transactions. This option is already available at many Web sites, such as
www.schwab.com, www.fidelity.com, www.aa.com, www.fedex.com,
and www.amtrack.com.

9. Intranet technology, due to its Internet roots, is effectively standards-
based and easily extensible. It is continually and proactively nurtured and
enhanced to meet the insatiable demands of the Internet user populace.

10. Because of the spread of multiprotocol corporate networks since the late
1980s, most enterprises already have experiences with, and an installed
base of, bridge/routers that can perform all of the TCP/IP routing functions required to realize a TCP/IP-based intranet.

11. With TCP/IP-based SNMP already being the universal means for managing and monitoring the bridge/routers, intelligent hubs, and LAN
switches needed to sustain existing multiprotocol corporate networks,
network administrators are quite comfortable with the underlying TCP/IP-
centric management scheme of intranets.

1.1.4 The Networking Fabric of Intranets

Intranets are TCP/IP-centric. Consequently, their backbone infrastructure is
typically realized using either established techniques for high-speed routing
or emerging IP-switching methodologies. In the case of the WAN, this IP
routing or IP switching can be done across Frame Relay, ATM, leased-line,
X.25, SMDS, or ISDN-based connections. The typical link speeds for these
WAN connections over the next few years are likely to be in the 56Kbps to
155Mbps range, with the 155Mbps links being based on ATM or SMDS.

Multiprotocol LAN/WAN networks will now coalesce into intranets. TCP/IP will rule the roost with SNA/APPN for some time to come. Intranets will eventually displace other data-oriented corporate networks, and extranets will emerge as the accepted means for business-to-business interactions.

The LAN and campus bandwidth needs of intranets can be easily satisfied through an amalgamation of traditional LANs such as 16Mbps Token
Ring, 100Mbps LANs (in particular, Fast Ethernet), LAN switching, and
ATM at either 155Mbps or 622Mbps. In addition, the nascent Gigabit LANs,
either by themselves or in conjunction with ATM, offer the promise of a
scalable migration path that should be able to accommodate the inevitable
future demands for additional LAN and campus backbones. Figure 1.4 illustrates the synthesis of routing and switching technologies used to implement
the Layer 2 and Layer 3 infrastructure of an intranet.

Intranets can have a secure and bidirectional interface with the global
Internet. This interface with the Internet can facilitate intercompany and, in
some instances intracompany, e-mail; it may also permit intercompany electronic commerce through so-called 'extranet' applications. It could also
provide the intranet users with ready access to the Internet. In addition, this
intranet-to-Internet interface, subject to stringent authentication and firewall-
based security, could be used to provide mobile users and telecommuters with
easy and cost-effective access to their corporate intranet over the Internet.

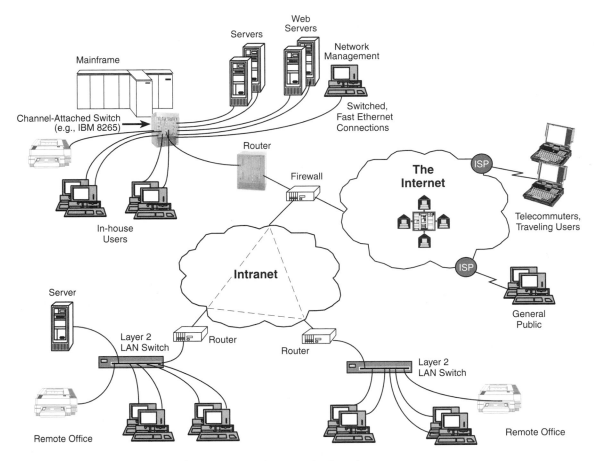

FIGURE 1.4   Using switching and routing to implement a high-performance i•net.

Such Internet-based access can complement and possibly even supplant remote access schemes based on dial-in technologies.

Intranets have effectively become the final embodiment of multiprotocol LAN/WAN networking, which emerged in the late 1980s. Such networks needed to simultaneously support a very potent cocktail of protocols, including TCP/IP, SNA/APPN, IPX/SPX, NetBIOS, AppleTalk, DECnet, Banyan Vines, and OSI. These multiprotocol networks were implemented using bridging or routing methodologies. I•nets as a whole, when the Internet came to the fore, testified to the emergence of TCP/IP as the undisputed winner of the "battle of the protocols." Other hitherto commercially significant protocols, most notably SNA/APPN and IPX/SPX, have now become subservient to TCP/IP, although they are by no means obsolete. OSI, which had been touted for more than two decades as the

universal panacea for multivendor interoperability, has been totally van-
quished by TCP/IP and is no longer even discussed in networking circles.

   With intranets, TCP/IP becomes the overarching basis for the entire network and especially for the WAN backbone. Any non-TCP/IP protocols,
such as SNA, that must be transported end-to-end across the WAN are
accommodated by either becoming encapsulated within TCP/IP message
units or being converted to TCP/IP via a gateway. Chapter 4 examines the
ways in which SNA/APPN traffic can be transported end-to-end across a
TCP/IP-based intranet.

   Over the next few years, intranets will slowly but surely displace all
other data-oriented and video-related enterprise networks. With the maturing
and acceptance of voice-over-IP technology, intranets could even handle
large volumes of voice and fax traffic. Today, most medium to large North
American enterprises have at least two disparate data networks, not counting
their blossoming intranets. They invariably have a bridge- or router-based
multiprotocol network to support their LAN-to-LAN interactions, and another network typically based on aging Front-End Processors (FEPs) and costly leased lines or possibly Frame Relay to handle the flow of mission-critical
SNA/APPN traffic to and from data centers.

   With an increasing number of native LAN applications, LAN-server functions, and new client/server applications rapidly becoming TCP/IP-based,
intranets with their inherent TCP/IP bias become the obvious and strategic
means for facilitating LAN-to-LAN transactions. Thanks to encapsulation
techniques, such as **Data Link Switching (DLSw)**, intranets can also effectively transport non-TCP/IP traffic—including mission-critical SNA/APPN
traffic. Proven protocol conversion technologies, such as **tn3270(E), tn5250**,
or **3270-to-HTML conversion** on the fly, also make it possible for some of
this SNA mission-critical traffic to be in TCP/IP form while traversing the
WAN, with protocol conversion to or from TCP/IP taking place at the data
center. Thus enterprises can start to phase out their stand-alone mission-critical networks within the next couple of years and still have all of their mission-
critical traffic reliably, securely, and efficiently transported across an intranet.
The remaining chapters of this book focus on achieving this transition in a nondisruptive, safe, cost-justifiable, and systematic manner. Chapters 5 through 8
include numerous case studies, replete with the customer name, location, and
an architectural diagram of the preferred solution.

   Intranets can thus adroitly handle all Web-related applications, Internet
traffic, LAN-to-LAN interactions, and even mission-critical transactions.
Consequently, they have the capability and the capacity to become the universal data highway for enterprise data. Technology also exists to permit
enterprise-to-enterprise transactions, such as electronic funds transfers, order
placement, collaborative engineering, and supply-chain management, to occur
between intranets. This inter-intranet data interchange capability, which can

now be realized in a very secure, authenticated, controlled, and audited manner, is referred to as extranet applications. The term "extranet" is sometimes used to describe remote access scenarios where employees of a company (such as insurance agents, automotive distributors, and travel agents) use the Internet, typically through a browser-based access scheme, to execute business with that company. The Lafayette Life Insurance and Royal Jordanian Airlines case studies in Chapter 6 give archetypal examples of such remote access specific extranets.

Figure 1.5 provides a glimpse of the totally mainframe-centric 3270-to-HTML conversion approach adopted by Lafayette Life to provide its 1000 field agents with extranet remote access over the Internet. With intranets destined to become the enterprise data highway, it is inevitable

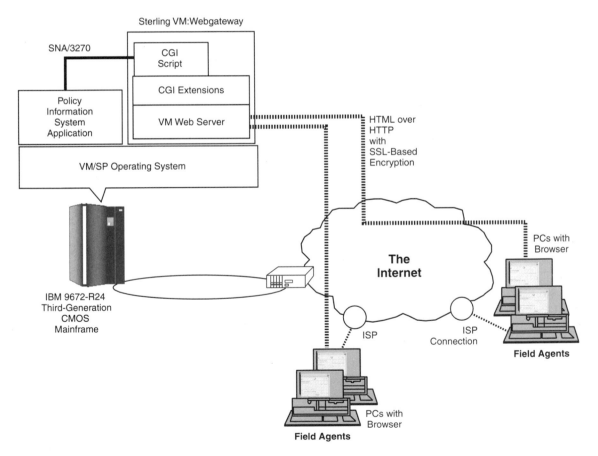

FIGURE 1.5   Mainframe-centric 3270-to-HTML conversion, based on Sterling Software's VM:Webgateway, as used by Lafayette Life Insurance.

that extranets will become an accepted and burgeoning means for inter-enterprise commerce and "agent-to-company" remote access by 2000.

1.2 THE INTERNET CONNECTION

The Internet is the epitome, not to say the pinnacle, of a truly public network. It is not owned by any corporation or a single entity, but rather is a truly egalitarian network for the masses that provides a near-bottomless font of information and an unparalleled means of interaction. An intranet, in marked contrast, is an internal (that is, private or closed user group) network that belongs to a specific corporation. It enables corporate employees and designated agents, such as contractors, to readily access and sometimes manipulate some subset of the corporate pool of data—ideally, based on some prescribed levels of authorization. The corporate data accessible via the intranet will be located on Web servers, Windows NT and UNIX servers, mainframes, and even minicomputers such as IBM AS/400s, as shown in Fig. 1.1. The Internet, on the other hand, allows a corporation to provide public users located across the globe with an enticing electronic billboard or storefront—extremely economically and on a nonstop, $24 \times 7 \times 365$ basis. The Internet is also the basis of e-commerce, the next frontier in worldwide commerce.

The public's interaction with a corporation should always take place via the Internet, not an intranet. The intranet should be purely for in-house use. The Internet, on the other hand, is the port that provides nonemployees with some level of access to a corporation's information resources.

An intranet per se does not (or at least should not) permit the general public to gain access to corporate data. Two primary reasons exist to explain this preclusion. One obviously centers on the security concerns related to the safeguarding of vital corporate data assets, given that much of these data at some point will move across the in-house intranet destined for, or originating from, a corporate employee's PC or workstation. The other reason has to do with the actual provision of physical and logical access. In the past, public access to private corporate networks (the predecessors of today's intranets) was possible only through some form of dial-in mechanism or via an interface from a public packet switching network, such as X.25. Today, things are very different when it comes to intranets.

A very cost-effective, tightly coupled, and clear-cut means of providing external access to the corporate data available on an intranet now exists—the Internet. With intranets being based on standard Internet technology such as Web servers and Web browsers, providing controlled access to a subset of the data sources attached to an intranet, across the Internet, is relatively straightforward. The same methodologies used to permit corporate users to access data over an intranet can be leveraged, albeit with security measures such as firewalls and application-specific authentication, to give external Internet users entrée to some of the data. This concept even applies to data located on mainframes or AS/400s. Technologies, such as browser-based access to SNA or Java-to-data center gateways such as IBM's CICS Gateway for Java, which enable intranet users to reach data-center-resident applications, databases, and files, can be used, without any changes, to cater to Internet users. This ability to utilize the same core data access technology to meet the needs of both internal and external users greatly simplifies the implementation of the overall i•net and the Internet-based access component of the network.

Currently, any legitimate access to corporate data by the general public will take place via the Internet. Thus a fundamental and very important distinction exists between intranet and the Internet vis-à-vis corporate data: an intranet enables employees to gain access to their corporate data, whereas the Internet gives the public at large access to a carefully bounded and controlled subset of a corporation's data bank. In some cases, it would be possible, and even desirable, for members of the public to perform certain transactions across the Internet.

Home banking as is available with BankBoston, online shopping as popularized by www.amazon.com, online investment à la www.schwab.com, online travel reservation as is provided by American Airlines at www.aa.com, and online package delivery tracking as is possible at www.fedex.com are all exciting examples of so-called Internet call centers. They allow customers to quickly and securely perform online transactions across the Web, obviating the need to deal with frustratingly delay-prone toll-free call centers. American Airlines, FedEx, Charles Schwab, Fidelity Investment, and Amazon are also examples of companies that have these toll-free call centers. The Internet can also enable employees who are traveling or telecommuting to gain access to the data that they would normally access via their intranet, provided that their intranets are designed to permit such access, subject to the appropriate firewall as well as in-house user ID/password-based authentication and authorization.

Giving the hundreds of millions of users who routinely surf the Internet the ability to readily and freely view selected corporate data through a registered home page, in the form of a registered domain name and an associated URL, on the Internet has proved to be a great publicity boon for commercial enterprises worldwide. The home page on the Internet in effect provides these companies with a relatively inexpensive billboard that can be easily seen around the globe. Many enterprises now use their home pages as a primary means of advertising. The home page is also becoming a strategic, real-time means for conducting public and, where necessary, investor relations. That is, it is increasingly becoming the most widely seen public visage of a corporation. Figure 1.6 shows an example of a typical commercial-sector home page, in this case that of networking vendor Bus-Tech, Inc.

FIGURE 1.6 A typical commercial-sector home page, in this case that of mainframe channel-attach solution provider Bus-Tech, Inc.

The overall corporate image and even the perception of a company's competitiveness are now becoming contingent on the amount and quality of the corporate, product, service, and even employment opportunity data made available for Internet-based perusal. Fortunately, the potential for tight integration between the in-house intranet and the public Internet makes the task of delivering Internet-accessible corporate data that much easier.

Internet-based access to corporate information, however, is always a two-way street. At the same time that outsiders wish to glean information about a given corporation, employees of that corporation will inevitably be seeking information, over the Internet, about other enterprises—whether they be competitors, suppliers, service providers, or potential partners. The

Internet is also used extensively by most corporations for intercompany e-mail, and by mid- to large-size corporations for intracompany e-mail if they operate in geographically dispersed locations (in particular, overseas offices). Corporations therefore need a reliable, secure, and high-performance bidirectional interface with the Internet for at least five reasons:

- Providing their employees with access to the vast information resources on the Internet.
- Enabling the public to peruse selected corporate data via the corporation's home page.
- Exchanging e-mail with external entities and possibly sending economical intracorporate e-mail between remote sites, especially when multiple international locations are involved.
- Facilitating Internet-based two-way transactions for e-commerce, Internet call centers, online investing, and other purposes.
- Exploiting the bandwidth of the Internet as a highly economical means for achieving remote access, whether it be for remote offices with **Virtual Private Networking (VPN)** technology, telecommuters, mobile employees, or agents. VPN, a means of securely "tunneling" corporate traffic on a point-to-point basis over the Internet, complements the SNA-related access schemes and is discussed in more detail in Chapter 7.

This Internet interface must in some way be integrated with the corporate intranet, if nothing else, to perform e-mail transfers and to enable the corporate intranet users to gain entry into the Internet. Some type of intranet and Internet integration—albeit always with the necessary security measures—is also likely to be a prerequisite for two-way, public interaction applications such as e-commerce, Internet call center functions, online travel reservations, and home banking. In some instances, security concerns may dictate that this integration be loosely coupled, with the relevant data from the intranet being replicated on specially isolated servers to ensure that a level of physical and logical separation exists between the Internet and the intranet.

Most of today's mid- to large-size corporations rely on a router or IP switch, from the likes of Cisco Systems, Nortel Networks, IBM, or 3Com, as their means of managing the interface they require with the Internet. They will typically implement one or more LAN connections, whether Token Ring or Fast Ethernet, from the router or switch into the corporation; they generally use a high-speed WAN connection, such T1, Frame Relay, or ATM, from the router or switch to the **Internet Service Provider (ISP)** or **Network Access Point (NAP)**. The corporate intranet will be connected to the router or switch providing the Internet interface through one of the LAN connections. Routers

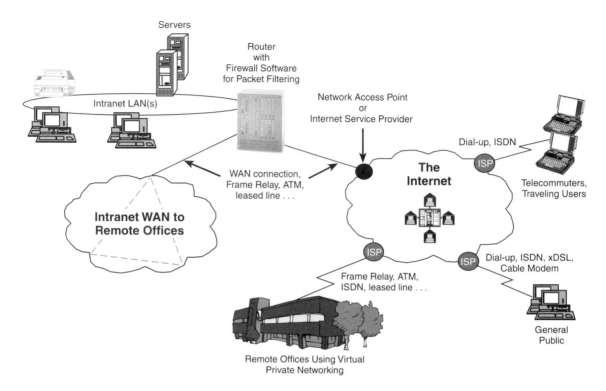

FIGURE 1.7   General architecture of a router-based interface to the Internet.

and switches invariably possess the throughput and some of the desired security features, such as packet filtering and firewall capability, sought by mid- to large-size corporations. Smaller enterprises may initially implement their Internet interfaces using a LAN server with built-in IP-routing software, and a 56Kbps or higher WAN adapter to provide a dial-up, leased, or ISDN connection to the ISP. Figure 1.7 depicts the general architecture of a router-based corporate interface to the Internet.

For commercial corporations, the overriding concern when it comes to providing any kind of Internet interface is that of implementing adequate security measures to thwart unauthorized access to their confidential corporate data. Prescribed policy-based packet filtering by the router or switch providing the connection to the ISP, in parallel with various levels of firewall software-based protection, currently constitutes the primary means of creating a viable defense against unauthorized access. The screened-subnet firewall scheme, for example, can isolate an intranet from the Internet by using two separate routers, each of which provides a firewall capability. Figure 1.8 illustrates the notion of maintaining strictly demarcated data pools based on internal and external Web servers that are isolated from each other via a

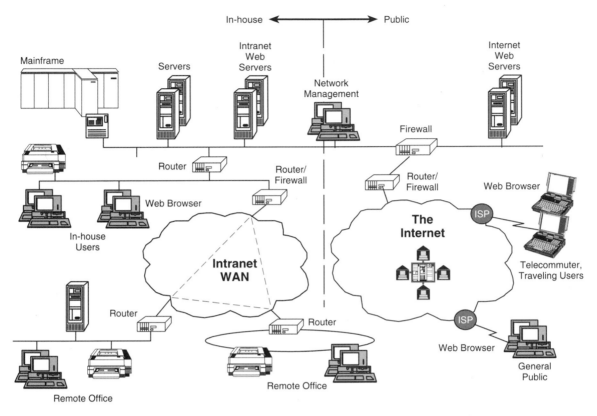

FIGURE 1.8   Keeping the intranet isolated from the Internet.

screened-subnet firewall scheme. It offers just one hint of how a firewall-based scheme may be used to mount a defense against unwelcome intrusion over the Internet.

In some cases, even such firewall-based subnetting is not considered secure enough. In these instances, corporations will typically replicate the necessary data from the intranet on special, highly isolated servers intended just for Internet access. Such replications, which will always result in the data on the intranet being out-of-synch with the data being posted on the Internet, is usually performed on a daily basis, via a batch process automatically executed overnight. Replication, however, is not feasible for some real-time applications, such as online travel reservation, certain types of online investing, and online package tracking. On the other hand, replication, though inevitably cumbersome and costly, will work for applications such as home banking and home shopping.

1.2.1 Immunizing Your Data Center for Internet-Based Access

Replicating relevant corporate data from an internal, intranet-accessible data server to an external, Internet-accessible server, though tedious and time-consuming, is really not a problem if one is dealing with only data resident on Web, NT, or UNIX servers. In most instances, this transfer of data between the two sets of servers can be achieved by copying the pertinent files and Web pages from one system to the other and then updating the affected directories and Web page links on the destination system. Because the source and destination system are likely to rely on the same, or compatible, file structures, software, and utilities, this replication operation is unlikely to be too complicated. Unfortunately, the isolation of the Internet-accessible data by replicating it on an external server will not be as easy, or in some cases even possible, if one is dealing with mainframe- or AS/400-resident data. This issue might be less important except for the fact that nearly 70% of all vital corporate data resides on mainframes or AS/400s in the case of corporations that have relied heavily on data-center-based computing in the past.

Much of the traditional "data center" data can typically be extracted only through the interaction with an application program, such as CICS or IMS, running on the mainframe or AS/400. The format and the structure of the data may also render it highly unlikely that one would be able to just extract it and store it in a "re-readable" manner on the external Web server. Some form of manual or software-utility-based restructuring would be required before data extracted from the data center could be gainfully viewed by Internet users through their Web browsers. A simple restructuring of the data alone may not be adequate, however. In many cases, the data will become meaningful only if they are processed and presented via the business logic embedded within a mainframe or AS/400 application.

In many instances, the primary attractiveness of the mainframe- or AS/400-resident data vis-à-vis an Internet user will be its timeliness, especially when one is dealing with financial, travel reservation, package tracking, or customer-status-related applications. One cannot also assume that the user will realize or appreciate the potential for discrepancy because the data have been replicated. In most instances, the Internet user may not be aware, care, or appreciate that the requisite information resides on a mainframe or AS/400. Consider the Web sites www.fedex.com, www.schwab.com, and www.fidelity.com. Most users interacting with these Web sites are unlikely to have heard of a mainframe or AS/400.

Other impediments could exist as well. Mainframe databases can be huge. Disk space on mainframes is typically discussed in terms of terabytes, as opposed to gigabytes, with a terabyte being 1000 times larger than a gigabyte. Thus, attempting to replicate some or all of the data in such databases on an external Web server could prove to be very costly just in terms of disk

Trying to replicate data to ensure secure Internet access is invariably hampered by the fact that 70% of all corporate data likely resides on mainframes or AS/400s rather than on Web servers, NT servers, or UNIX systems. Such mainframe or AS/400-based data are often intelligible only when processed through business logic embedded within an application. Attempting to bypass the application and extract the data directly from a file or database may prove futile.

space, and impractical given that data movement and file update times, across a LAN from one system to the other, may consume many hours and possibly days. Security, yet again, could be an issue. Mainframes are noted for their sophisticated and highly proven security measures for controlling access to their applications, files, and databases, such as user ID and password-based validation in conjunction with products such as IBM's RACF and Computer Associates' CA-ACF2. Many CIOs or MIS managers may not want certain corporate data, hitherto available only on secure mainframes, to become freely available on Web servers—at least until there is much more proof and consensus that the data security aspects of Web, NT, and UNIX servers match those available on mainframes.

If a corporation does want to make application-dependent, time-sensitive, or hard-to-replicate data-center-resident information available to Internet users (for example, for lucrative e-commerce opportunities), the most realistic means are to adopt a browser-based SNA access scheme or to implement a programmatic application server-oriented solution to enable direct data center access. The technologies available for realizing these Internet-to-data center integration solutions are described, with case studies, starting in Chapter 4. In effect, one would use the same technologies employed to enable the intranet's users to reach data-center-resident applications and data to also permit Internet users to gain access to a selected subset of these applications and data. Although Web-to-data center integration technology is now readily available, the paramount concern for the MIS community is the implementation of security measures to prevent unauthorized intrusion into the data center's assets. Fortunately, the traditional mainframe security facilities, in conjunction with SSL-type security and firewalls, can be gainfully synthesized to provide a formidable, though never infallible, defense against unauthorized access.

Compared with other systems, especially UNIX systems, mainframes are more secure against intruders. Mainframes are rarely, if ever, mentioned in the context of successful hacking missions. Nonetheless, it is imperative to implement firewalls and some form of Web server-based authentication, such as SSL, to provide a first line of defense at the corporation's interface to the Internet against unwanted intruders. Any facilities that provide entrée into the data center, such as the gateways that perform tn3270(E) server functions or an SNA-Web gateway, should remain behind these firewalls and authentication measures. Depending on their assessment of the risks involved, some corporations may choose to implement additional customized user authentication and validation software between the Internet interface and the gateways to the data center to deflect as many unauthorized users as possible even before they have a chance to reach the mainframe-resident security products. Figure 1.9 shows how as many as six levels of security can be implemented with a browser-based SNA access scheme. This notion of having six discrete levels of security is further discussed in Section 8.1.1.

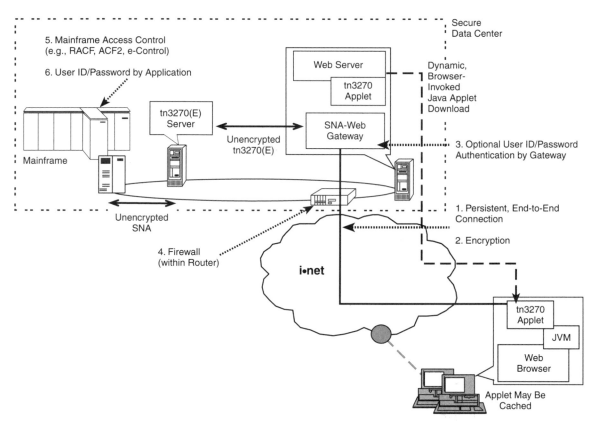

FIGURE 1.9   Up to six levels of security can be implemented with a browser-based SNA access solution.

1.2.2   The Internet as a Global Storefront

In addition to being a high-profile billboard that can be seen from around the world, a corporation's home page can serve as a highly effective, low-overhead, revenue-generating virtual storefront. Given its worldwide reach and relatively low upkeep, this virtual storefront can prove to be an extremely lucrative means of conducting business for both companies and entire industries (such as the mail-order industry). By 2003, e-commerce could generate nearly $1 trillion in revenue. So far, this section has concentrated on the possibilities of permitting the general public to glean information about corporations over the Internet. This form of passive, one-way corporate information dissemination is, in fact, only one facet of the mercantile potential of the Internet.

Information dissemination is merely the tip of the iceberg when it comes to the true commercial potential realizable via the public's ability to freely interact directly with nearly all major corporations over the Internet, around the clock and irrespective of their geographic location. The Internet has, in

Toll-free call centers are an integral feature of contemporary consumer culture but are extremely expensive to run. To minimize the amount of human intervention required, most filter calls via a voice response system. These systems can frustrate callers and considerably prolong the time required to resolve the call. Internet call centers, on the other hand, are quick, responsive, and inexpensive to implement and operate.

effect, brought all of the worldwide commercial entities together to create a mammoth, bustling common market that is open for business 24 hours a day, every day of the year. The coming of age of the new euro currency at the start of 1999 highlighted to many the motive behind the formation of the European Union (EU). The scale of the Internet market, which spans the whole world, dwarfs the enormous EU market, however.

Once a corporation has set up a reliable, secure, and quick-response home page on the Internet, the next step is to expand that system to enable Internet users to conduct two-way call-center-type queries or actual revenue-generating e-commerce. Today, nearly all North American corporations in the service, financial, investment, insurance, travel, mail-order, and high-tech sectors of the market routinely operate call centers to provide support for existing or prospective customers. These call centers, most of which can be reached via a toll-free telephone number, are staffed by highly trained (and thus costly) service representatives. To cut down on costs, many call centers try to screen and handle as many calls as possible via automated voice response systems to minimize the need for service representative intervention and thereby reduce the number of representatives required to staff the call center. Many customers, however, find these schemes, with their often convoluted option selection menus, maddeningly distracting.

Internet-based transaction processing is the obvious, low-cost, and strategic means of reducing call center expenses and shielding customers from the annoying voice response systems. Already, most major companies that operate call center services (especially those in the travel, financial, and package delivery sectors), are offering the option of Internet-based transactions—so-called Internet call centers. Invariably, the Internet-based transaction schemes offer more options and faster service than are possible with the corresponding telephone-based call center. Given that servicing Internet-based transactions is also considerably less expensive than dealing with call centers, many companies now offer discounts in the form of lower transaction fees or other incentives to encourage customers to contact them via the Internet rather than via call centers. For example, with online investment, commissions on stock trades placed over the Web are a fraction of what is charged if that same trade is conducted over the phone. These low commissions for Web-based trading have spawned the notion of "day trading," where people buy and then sell a stock within the space of a very short period of time, because the commission on such trades is now so low as to be negligible.

Over the coming years, a marked increase in Internet-based commercial transaction processing will occur, with a corresponding decrease occurring in call center activity. In many instances, transactions performed over the Internet, such as account balance queries, will not require any human intervention. In other cases, transactions accepted over the Internet can be dynamically fed into existing transaction management systems for the appropriate processing and required output, such as making an airline reservation, trading a NASDAQ stock, or scheduling a parcel pick-up. In a few instances, transactions submitted over the Internet may have to be forwarded to a customer representative for non-real-time validation and processing (for example, submitting a claim for an award or refund).

Irrespective of which of these three distinct ways is used to process a transaction submitted over the Internet, the overall cost of handling that transaction will be considerably lower than if it had to be serviced in real time by a call center representative. The decrease in the volume of transactions handled via call centers will allow companies to minimize call center staffing and equipment needs—and eventually lead to considerable cost savings. Corporations will be able to use the savings to further bolster their Internet-based services (with faster servers, for example), as well as their profitability.

1.3 BUSINESS PROCESS REENGINEERING AROUND I•NETS

About a decade ago, most North American and European corporations undertook torturous business process reengineering programs intended to consolidate and streamline all aspects of their businesses by eliminating duplication, redundancy, unnecessary procedures, underutilization of resources, and blatant waste of material, assets, or time. The end result of this reengineering process, which in some cases spanned quite a few years, was that nearly all corporations that managed to successfully weather the many and far-reaching changes, emerging leaner, meaner, more focused, and more competitive. A key underlying theme of this business process reengineering drive was the innovative leveraging of computer technology to automate as many tasks as possible so as to increase employer efficiency, expedite procedures, and gain faster access to corporate data.

Functions that were being performed manually and perhaps being duplicated in different parts of a corporation were rationalized, optimized, and computerized. Corporate data once fragmented across nonelectronic media (such as ledgers or paper files) and disparate electronic systems were validated, consolidated, and cataloged in data warehouse systems. Certain corporate functions, such as travel services or even data processing, were outsourced; other functions were eliminated altogether. Networked computers began to play a pivotal role in coordinating and managing the information flow as well as the proper functioning of the reengineered processes. The end result of this business process reengineering program empowered PCs and created today's highly computerized business world.

The new and exciting information interchange and online transaction processing opportunities created by intranets and the Internet are now poised

The highly productive business process reengineering effort just over a decade ago was precipitated by the availability of inexpensive computing power— PCs. Today, the sheer pervasiveness, the enticing economics, and the truly global nature of the Internet make it imperative for corporations to reengineer their business processes once again, this time to exploit the tantalizing possibilities of the Internet.

to elevate the business world's dependence on computers to an even higher level. To fully benefit from these i•net-related opportunities, including e-commerce, corporations now must reengineer many of their business processes once more—this time to explicitly accommodate the data retrieval, data transfer, and transaction-processing possibilities opened up by the Internet and intranets.

The compelling possibilities of transitioning much of customer support from costly call centers to relatively inexpensive Internet call centers represent just one example illustrating why corporations now need to reevaluate their ongoing business processes. This time around, they must determine whether they can significantly optimize many of their current customer relations-related business practices by treating the Internet as an extremely cost-effective means of interacting with their customer bases. Enabling customers and prospects to directly perform certain transactions over the Internet, by-passing the need for customer representative intervention, offers numerous advantages. It will indubitably reduce ongoing operational costs, in some instances by quite a large factor. It should also enable corporations to offer expanded services such as new, more specialized options or greater level of details on queries; the minimal "wait" and delay time could bolster user satisfaction as well. In addition, offering broader and faster services through the Internet will increase companies' competitiveness.

The importance of this Internet-induced "competitiveness" aspect cannot be overstated. In essence, a company's Internet-based capabilities will serve as a key differentiating factor relative to other companies offering similar products or services. A company that offers better Internet-based services than its competitors will likely gain more business and be perceived as being more competitive—always assuming, of course, that most of its actual products, services, and financial footing are somewhat comparable to those of its rivals. The danger remains that some unscrupulous entity may be tempted to use an enticing Internet home page as a facade to lure unsuspecting customers by projecting an image that is at odds with its offerings and capabilities. The usual market forces should eventually weed out these charlatans and let the bonafide corporations prosper.

In light of the pervading influence of the Internet, companies now have no choice but to determine how they can reengineer their business processes once again so as to conduct their business better, more efficiently, and "smarter" by exploiting the customer interaction possibilities opened up by the Internet. The Internet, via extranets, can obviously be used to reduce the organization's costs, while simultaneously increasing the speed and efficiency of business-to-business or agent-to-corporation transactions.

Access and direct transactions over the Internet also have the potential of "leveling the playing field" between the various companies involved in the same line of business. The Internet gives the smaller companies, which have fewer sales and marketing resources than their larger counterparts, equal opportunity to that of larger companies when it comes to attracting and conducting business over the Internet. Because the Web server and networking equipment necessary to set up a good home page is relatively inexpensive, larger companies are unlikely to offer an appreciably better level of service than the smaller companies purely by spending more money on their equipment. The best they can do is to provide faster response times by utilizing more powerful systems. Although Internet-based users will no doubt appreciate the rapid processing, response times alone will not compensate for a paucity of capability or options.

This issue of companies becoming significantly more equal when it comes to performing business over the Internet, irrespective of their actual size and standing in the non-cyber world, is yet another pivotal factor that needs to be carefully addressed when reengineering business processes around the Internet. Already, very small start-ups from countries like Israel, the Netherlands, and Canada are exploiting the fact that a good home page on the Internet gives them nearly as much worldwide reach as larger competitors in larger industrial markets.

Complacency when it comes to this issue could prove deadly. Companies must be both innovative and aggressive in determining how they could best exploit the Internet so as to maximize business and customer satisfaction. Just as in the reengineering process of a decade ago, they should carefully evaluate all of their customer- and service-related procedures and practices. This time, however, the focus is on seeing how they can be optimized, expanded, and rationalized through gainfully exploiting Internet-based customer access and transaction processing.

1.3.1   A New Client/Server Model for Business Process Reengineering

The original business process reengineering initiative of a decade ago was highly contingent on the wholesale adoption and deployment of computer and networking technology. This concerted emphasis on technology resulted in a close scrutiny and reevaluation of the then-conventional wisdom pertaining to information management. The outcome of this assessment was that many hitherto "sacred cows" in data center practices were challenged and fundamentally altered to facilitate and expedite the goals of the reengineering initiatives. Fortuitously, this period of business process reengineering and process automation coincided with the ascent of PCs and powerful RISC workstations that ran UNIX. With the availability of much lower-cost systems for data processing, the hitherto dominant role of mainframes in commercial sector computing drew tough questions, and most corporations minimized their investment in mainframes by augmenting them with networked

Until now, client/server methodology has not been a major hit vis-à-vis mainframe-centric data-processing environments. The i•net-based, browser-focused client/server model, however, is changing this irrevocably. Browser-based SNA access and Web-oriented application servers are already proving that the i•net-based client/server model is compelling, highly effective, productive, and economical.

PCs, UNIX workstations, and LAN servers. One could argue that computer technology came of age during the heyday of this 1980s business process reengineering wave.

Despite the overall success achieved by leveraging computer technology to optimize business practices, one much-vaunted computer methodology from this initial business process reengineering era did not live up to expectations, particularly in the mainframe-biased IBM world—client/server computing. In hindsight, one can cite many credible reasons for the disappointment of client/server computing in the IBM world, including the absence of truly standardized platforms, technology, and protocols. The need to reengineer business processes to exploit the Internet and Internet-related technologies provides another opportunity to evaluate client/server computing as it relates to the IBM world and, in particular, mainframes.

Today, the issues pertaining to client/server computing in the IBM world are much different than they were 10 years ago. Thanks to the universal endorsement of intranets, basic building-block technologies such as TCP/IP, browsers, Web servers, HTML, Java, ActiveX, Enterprise JavaBeans, SSL, and firewalls are now not just de facto industry standards; they are the only accepted means for implementing contemporary networks and information-processing systems. Compared to 10 years ago, PC/workstation hardware is also significantly more powerful, capable, robust, and affordable. In addition, Windows NT, Windows 95/98, and UNIX represent stable, feature-rich, and widely supported operating systems for client systems; NT, UNIX, and Linux are the most popular choices for the server systems. By selectively synthesizing all of this available technology, one can now create highly potent contemporary client systems optimized for accessing Web page-based information sources and running Windows, Java, or ActiveX applications.

Web browsers would be the universal user interface, or "Common User Access" as referred to by IBM, on these client systems; TCP/IP represents the only networking protocol they need support. In reality, any of today's Pentium- or RISC-based PCs or workstations running Windows 95/98, Windows NT, or a recent version of UNIX, with the latest release of Netscape Navigator or Internet Explorer, can indeed create this utopian client. Many corporations are already standardizing on such client platforms. In marked contrast to 10 years ago, proven personal productivity software, such as Microsoft Office, e-mail, groupware (Lotus Notes), and networking applications, is currently available for these clients. The "write once, run anywhere" promise of Java (and to some extent ActiveX), coupled with the maturing of object-oriented technology such as CORBA, ensure that new application development and deployment can proceed considerably more expeditiously, efficiently, and cost-effectively than it did 10 years ago. Viable clients, replete with the necessary software, were a major stumbling block then for client/server computing in the IBM world. It is a very different story today, as implementing appropriate client systems for client/server computing no longer poses a real challenge.

Notwithstanding the continual presence of mainframes, the story on the server side also differs markedly from that observed a decade ago—now that intranets have become synonymous with next-generation enterprise networks. With the intranet model, Web servers—whether on the internal intranet or accessed over the Internet—become the primary servers in this new round of client/server computing. The Internet has proved, quite conclusively, that the fundamental networking, data access, and data transfer infrastructure of this client/server model is sound, robust, and extensible. The nascent Java applications, as well as now highly proven browser-based SNA access schemes such as IBM's Host On-Demand, demonstrate quite conclusively that this Internet technology-based client/server model is not restricted just to passive information retrieval. This model also works very effectively for interactive, two-way transaction processing, as well as program-to-program interactions—even with consistent and predictable response times when used in intranets that include committed levels of bandwidth. This development should come as no surprise.

The underlying communications scheme based on TCP/IP sockets that is used by this client/server model is the same as that used to great effect by the UNIX world for more than a decade. This was the networking model that many advocated for client/server computing in the IBM world 10 years ago. SNA, however, was too sacrosanct at that juncture for IBM or the customer base to seriously consider any non-SNA-based solutions. The rampant success of the Internet and the wholesale embrace of intranets, however, have ensured that any lingering blind loyalty to SNA will not undermine the adoption of this TCP/IP-based client/server model.

Nevertheless, one flaw exists in this Internet-inspired, Web server-oriented, client/server model relative to the IBM world: the need for this model to work with other servers, such as mainframes and AS/400s, that do not currently run Web server software. In other words, if this client/server model is to have real use in the IBM world, it must also handle traditional ("legacy") data sources, which may not be based on TCP/IP.

Fortunately, this need for broadening the scope of the servers well beyond just Web servers is not a stumbling block by any means. Proven technology, such as browser-based SNA access, Web-to-mainframe programmatic gateways such as IBM's **CICS Gateway for Java**, and application servers, is already available to smoothly extend the standard i•net client/server model to embrace mainframe and minicomputer data, databases, and applications. Figure 1.10 shows the overall architecture of a browser-based SNA access that uses a Java applet for tn3270(E) emulation, and Figure 1.11 shows the architecture of the CICS Gateway for Java. These two figures illustrate how a browser-based access scheme and a programmatic gateway

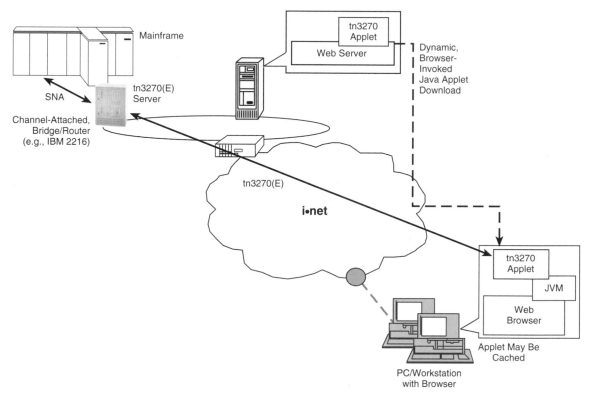

FIGURE 1.10   Overall architecture of a browser-based SNA access scheme that uses a Java applet to act as a tn3270(E) client.

seamlessly extend the i•net client/server model well beyond the information domain of Web servers, despite keeping the client access based on standard browsers and Java.

Extensive in-production use of browser-based SNA access since early 1997, by hundreds of corporations, has shown that the standard i•net client/server model works extremely well with mainframes and AS/400s, as well as with other non-IBM computer systems, such as those from Sun, Hewlett-Packard, Unisys, and Compaq/DEC. These browser-based access implementations have also shown this model can be easily extended to handle the end-to-end security needs of most commercial-sector applications through enhancements such as server-to-client persistent sessions, session-level encryption, and client authentication. Much of the initial client authentication and encryption method negotiation capability used in these implementations was realized using SSL support within the context of TCP/IP or HTTP, or **Secure Hypertext Transfer Protocol (HTTPS)**. In the future, SSL support

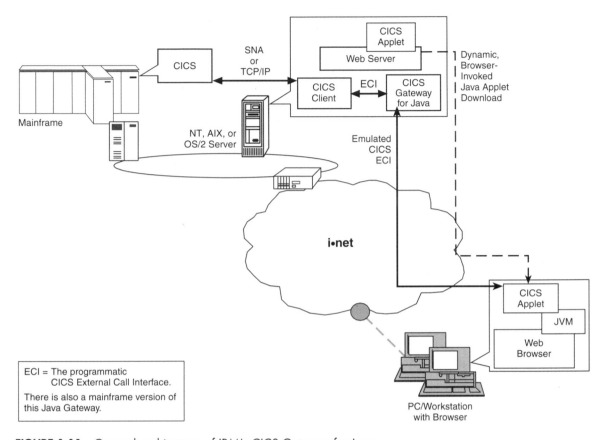

FIGURE 1.11   General architecture of IBM's CICS Gateway for Java.

may be replaced by an emerging standard known as **Transport Layer Security (TLS)**.

The exact mechanics of browser-based access to SNA and Web-to-data center gateways and their ability to work alongside standard Web servers to expand the reach of the normal i•net client/server model are discussed in Chapter 5. At this juncture, it suffices to say that the i•net client/server model appears to work very well relative to the data center access demands of the IBM world—and that this model already has more credibility, backing, and momentum than any previous IBM-sector client/server model. In fact, this model is the first widely accepted, widely supported, general-purpose client/server model to grace the IBM world. Previous attempts, such as IBM's OS/2-centered **Advanced Program-to-Program Communications (APPC)** methodology, invariably failed to capture a widespread following because they were too parochial and technologically inflexible.

A good measure of the ongoing acceptance of this i•net client/server model vis-à-vis the IBM world comprises the initiatives already undertaken to bolster its capabilities and flexibility in handling data-center-related interactions. Already, efforts are afoot to create highly portable Enterprise Java-Beans objects that will turn many of the somewhat convoluted functions associated with interacting with mainframe-resident applications and databases into transparently invocable "commodity" functions. These primarily object-oriented schemes will make the i•net client/server model even more powerful and adaptable within the IBM world. The pertinent object-oriented methodologies are discussed in Chapter 6.

1.3.2   A Notion of a Web Applications Architecture for the IBM World

IBM's 1987 SAA was at least five years ahead of its time. Today, browsers, i•nets, and Java provide all the necessary technology to fulfill the goals of SAA. IBM's new master plan, called NCF, is totally i•net-centric and very partial to Java.

The significance and validity of the i•net client/server model within the context of the IBM world can be fully appreciated by seeing how the model relates to the famous IBM master plan for the automation needs of the initial wave of business process reengineering—in particular, how it relates to client/server computing involving IBM platforms. The master plan unveiled in mid-1987 with enormous hoopla and much chest-thumping was known as **Systems Application Architecture (SAA)**. From 1987 to 1991, SAA was the undisputed and highly vaunted cornerstone of IBM's entire computing and networking strategy. In that time, IBM spent billions of dollars on SAA in terms of product development, created a veritable mountain of documentation, and waged an incessant, high-profile publicity campaign. (The "SAA" in Novell's renowned SNA-LAN Gateway "NetWare for SAA" refers to this architecture and indicates the significance attributed to it at the start of the 1990s.)

SAA's raison d'être was very straightforward and cogent. SAA was a blueprint for a new genre of applications that would be platform-independent, have a common user interface, and work in client/server mode across many different types of networks. In reality, its fundamental flaw was that it was at least five years ahead of its time—especially in the area of truly portable, platform-independent applications. Although the architecture was keenly insightful and topical, in the late 1980s IBM did not have the appropriate technology to make SAA anything other than a "paper tiger." By 1991, the market had lost interest and faith in SAA.

Today, with Java, Enterprise JavaBeans, the browser, and i•nets, all of the building blocks needed to turn SAA into a resounding success are in place. SAA thus gives us a previously validated and once highly accepted framework for providing a sanity check on the viability of the Internet technology-based client/server model. One could argue that the viability of this client/server model is beyond reproach, given its widespread use. Members of the IBM user community, however, are used to having well-defined architectures for their computing models, given that the S/370 Principles of Operations and SNA architectures have served as the bedrock of IBM-centric computing for more than three decades.

An abiding strength of SAA is that most of its quintessential properties, components, and the interrelationship between these components can be very clearly spelled out with a single, very intuitive, diagram. Figure 1.12 depicts the architectural diagram for SAA. The diagram shown in Fig. 1.12 was so "catchy" and user-friendly that it became the icon for SAA. The Common User Access, a novel but much-needed concept in 1987, was a key element of this architecture. At that juncture, however, IBM did not have an adequate solution for PCs running its own OS/2 operating system, let alone one that would also work with other PC operating systems, UNIX workstations, and Apple Macintoshes. The best that IBM could do in 1987 was to publish voluminous style guides and point to the embryonic OS/2 Presentation Services Manager as an example of how things might work. Now, 18 years after the advent of the PC, and 10 years after SAA, we finally have the basis for such a universal user interface—the browser.

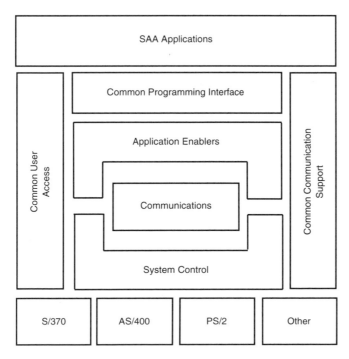

FIGURE 1.12   The famous architectural diagram for IBM's Systems Application Architecture.   (*Source:* Original source is IBM.)

The Common Programming Interface element of SAA included a set of prescribed High-Level Programming Languages and Application Generators, as well as a set of Standard Services for Database Access—namely SQL, Communications, and Presentation. The Presentation Services were to be provided by OS/2's Presentation Manager; the programming languages endorsed were C, COBOL, FORTRAN, and PL/I; LU 6.2 and UNIX's Remote Procedure Calls (RPCs) were the two major communications services prescribed. The Common Communications Support addressed both OSI and SNA. No mention was made of TCP/IP, which was then a totally unknown entity in the IBM world. SAA shocked the IBM networking community by calling for peer-to-peer "Low Entry Networking" (the original name for APPN) and going to great lengths not to explicitly mention Subarea SNA.

Figure 1.13 takes the high-level architectural framework of SAA, as shown in Fig. 1.12, and updates it to reflect 1998 i•net technology. One would have to admit that this updated SAA model has a certain je ne sais

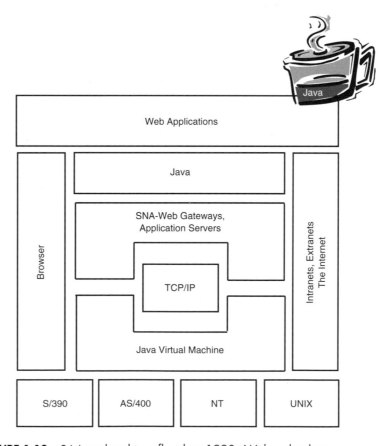

FIGURE 1.13   SAA updated to reflect late 1990s Web technology.

quoi. It definitely shows the role that Java and ActiveX will play in the future in terms of enabling the development of platform-independent, Web-enabled applications that will be accessed via Web browsers and run across i•nets.

IBM's new architecture for i•net-oriented applications is known as **Network Computing Framework (NCF)**. IBM, to its credit, bills it as a "state-of-the-art architecture that exploits the opportunities presented by the Internet." Figure 1.14 depicts the overall architectural composition of NCF and Figure 1.15 shows the components of an NCF client. The important issue in NCF is that IBM, Lotus, and Tivoli, which together make up IBM's software solution delivery arm, are clearly committed to a new, Web-based computing paradigm that is far removed from yesterday's SNA-centric application model.

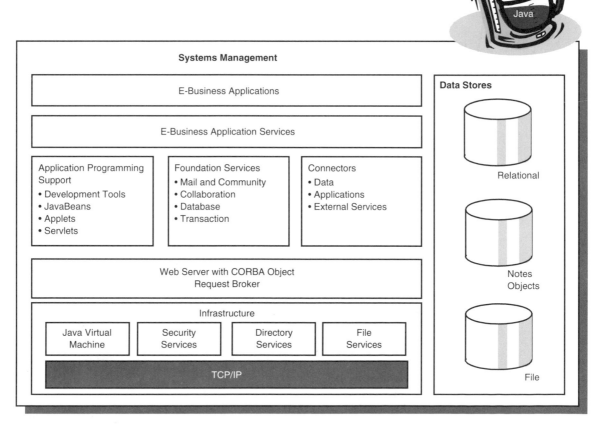

FIGURE 1.14   Overall architectural composition of IBM's Network Computing Framework. (*Source:* Original source is IBM.)

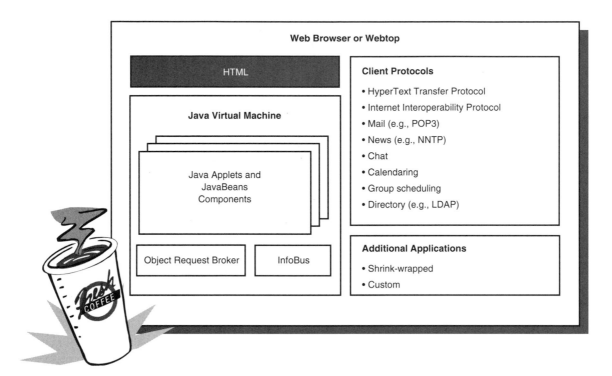

FIGURE 1.15   Components of the Network Computing Framework client.   (*Source:* Original source is IBM.)

At present, the NCF consists of six primary components:

- An open set of set of services, including Directory, File, and Security, as well as a Java Virtual Machine (JVM). JavaBeans, which provides a standards-based set of APIs for extending applications or application components, is supported within this infrastructure as the programmatic means for interfacing with the individual service components.

- A Web browser- and Java applet-based client scheme that addresses universal access, "thin clients," and the "just-in-time" downloading of software based on application requirements.

- A JavaBeans-centric programming model, replete with tools, to build e-business applications using Java and JavaBeans.

- Internet protocols, including HTTP and **Internet Interoperability Protocol (IIOP)**, for interconnecting JavaBeans or other object-based components.

- A set of "Connector" services for providing access to existing data, applications, and external services. These "Connector" services address gateway functionality, such as IBM's CICS Gateway for Java.

- A set of nascent e-business building-block Application Services for expediting the development of new applications. IBM is working on such support services to manage intellectual property and the **Secure Electronic Transaction (SET)** standard developed by Visa and MasterCard in conjunction with IBM.

Figure 1.16 illustrates the overall structure of the distributed, client/server computing model advocated by NCF. The bottom line on NCF is that it, very much like SAA in its day, is a credible, germane, topical, uncomplicated, and perceptive architecture. It is very much in tune with how Web aficionados and i•net application evangelists envision Internet technology influencing and molding the next wave of computing systems.

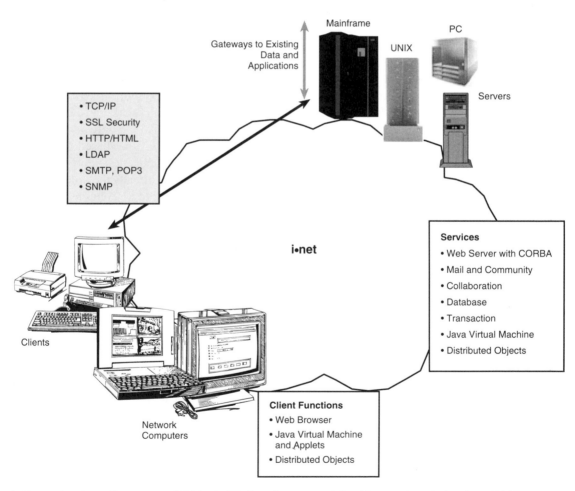

FIGURE 1.16   Overall structure of IBM's NCF client/server model.   (*Source:* Initial idea from IBM.)

NCF, however, differs markedly from SAA in that it is solidly based on existing and proven technology. It is very much a logical synthesis of pertinent and obvious services and technologies. That simplicity and obviousness provide its true beauty and strength.

1.3.3   Application-Centric, Network-Neutral Computing

The new computing model will focus on end-to-end solutions. The i•nets sustaining these solutions will be a "commodity" and will not garner explicit focus as was the case with SNA networks. The network will not take center stage—much like the relationship that exists between air and the human race. Although air is essential for survival, most never give it a second thought. The same will be true of networking. It will be all around, but will not elicit the excitement or emotion that it did in the past, especially in the IBM world with SNA/APPN.

Although not obvious at first glance, NCF contains a very profound and far-reaching message that will have a major effect on how computing systems are regarded and implemented in the IBM world. The hidden message embedded within NCF is the deemphasis of the network and network-related services. NCF, as its name suggests, is obviously a network-oriented framework. If anything, with i•nets, the network would appear to be more important than ever. NCF, however, demonstrates, somewhat subtly, that the network will no longer be an explicit focal point of future systems. Instead, it will be a homogenized commodity—that is, the Internet technology-based, highly standardized i•nets. Although always present, the i•net will remain unobtrusively in the background. Another way to consider this point is to think of i•nets as becoming a corporate utility analogous to the phone system, electricity, or water supply. Rather than continually focusing on the network when dealing with computing issues, corporations will be able to take the network for granted and concentrate on higher-level issues. The new, i•net-based client/server model is, in essence, network-neutral and very application-centric.

In many ways, network-neutral computing is already the order of the day in the non-IBM world. The overbearing influence of SNA has as yet kept the IBM world network-oriented. In the IBM world, it is the norm to talk about "SNA mission-critical applications." Moreover, this trend has been the case for the last 20 years. In essence, applications in the IBM world were defined in terms of the network that was used to access them. Obviously, this definition takes an extremely network-centric view of applications and the computing model as a whole. This network-centric view of computing in the IBM world is now coming to an end in much the same way and in concert with the demise of SNA-only networks. NCF is a harbinger to this very significant change in outlook and very far-reaching paradigm shift.

Moving forward, the IBM world will start to think about computing models and information systems primarily in terms of end-to-end solutions, information content, ease of use, and overall usefulness, rather than in terms of the underlying network used to realize these solutions. The high-capacity bit pipes used to sustain these vibrant, end-to-end solutions will fade into the background, becoming a "commodity" issue. The spotlight will instead fall on applications, application development tools, Web content, and application servers, rather than the network equipment needed to gain connectivity and bandwidth.

This application-oriented focus will force both customers and vendors to address the computing and networking needs of corporations that have relied on SNA for the last 20 years or more in a radically different manner. Within the SNA arena, very little change has occurred in the nature and composition of the application base. The so-called SNA applications, particularly in terms of subsystems like CICS, IMS, and DB2 that serve as application hosting platforms for business-specific applications, have been in place, in more or less the same form, for the last three decades! From a networking perspective, in addition to the protocols and discipline instilled by SNA, all that they required over this very long period of time was end-to-end connectivity, more bandwidth, and support for SNA/APPN vis-à-vis other multiprotocol traffic. Today, this concept is all changing.

Over the coming years, these SNA applications will become merely data sources to a new genre of Web-based applications. These applications, as discussed at length earlier, will most likely run on NT servers and will be based on Java and Enterprise JavaBeans. The networks used by the Web-based applications will take the form of i•nets. SNA, as a protocol, will be restricted to the data center, with gateways such as the CICS Gateway for Java providing the Web-to-legacy liaison. Thus, with the exception of supporting a few legacy devices such as IBM 4700 Financial Systems for a few more years, the mechanics and effort of transporting SNA/APPN traffic across the WAN will not be a cogent issue or a lucrative business opportunity, as it has been for the last 25 years. This change may not seem such a big deal; to those individuals who have spent their entire professional careers dealing with SNA, however, this change is as momentous as changing from a gasoline-powered car to an electric car. The remainder of this book will make numerous references to this theme of IBM-sector computing moving away from being network-centric to become application- and solution-oriented.

1.4   EXTENDING I•NETS INTO THE DATA CENTER

Enterprises that rely on mainframes or AS/400 minicomputers for the bulk of their data processing really have no choice but to integrate their nascent intranets with their traditional data center systems—given that approximately 70% of their vital corporate data is likely to reside on the mainframes or AS/400s as opposed to the new Web servers hosting intranets. For such enterprises, attempting to implement an intranet and a two-way interface to the Internet without the necessary access into the data center would be akin to baking an apple pie with no filling. Fortunately, the necessary technology to seamlessly integrate TCP/IP-based intranets with traditional data centers is now readily available from key vendors such as IBM, Cisco Systems, Oracle, OpenConnect Systems, Attachmate, Eicon, and Wall Data.

For companies that have relied on mainframes or AS/400s for much of their data processing in the past, implementing an intranet that is not tightly integrated with the data center would be akin to baking an apple pie with no filling. I•nets that support data center resources, known as SNA-capable i•nets, are realized through the synergistic synthesis of data-center-specific technologies with standard i•net components.

I•nets that support data-center-resident systems, applications, and data are invariably referred to as **SNA-capable i•nets** because the majority of the mission-critical applications running on the data center systems were developed to be used across SNA, as opposed to TCP/IP, networks. An SNA-capable i•net supports unrestricted SNA/APPN-based application access, printing services, database management, or data transfer across a standard TCP/IP-based i•net, whether it be an intranet, an extranet, or the Internet.

SNA-capable intranets, in addition to using the same components and protocols (such as TCP/IP and HTTP) as standard intranets, include specific technologies to effectively and transparently convert the data-center-related protocols (in particular, SNA and 3270 data streams) to those used within intranets. Some of the key data-center-related technologies that are likely to be found in SNA-capable intranets include the following:

- tn3270(E) servers, possibly in the form of channel-attached off-load servers such as IBM 2216s, Cisco 7500/CIPs, or Bus-Tech NetShuttles that permit PC/workstation users to access SNA applications and print services using TCP/IP-based, low-cost, and readily available tn3270 clients

- SNA-Web coprocessors that permit PC/workstation users to access SNA applications and print services using the standard Web browser, rather than SNA/3270 emulation software such as IBM's PComm Personal Communications program product or Attachmates EXTRA! Personal Client or even tn3270 clients

- Java or ActiveX applets that facilitate feature-rich 3270 or 5250 emulation within the context of Web browsers to deliver browser-based SNA access

- Application servers such as IBM's **WebSphere** and Host Publisher, OpenConnect's Application Server, BEAWebLogic, and Novera jBusiness, which enable a corporation to implement object-oriented, Web-centric applications that have ready access to traditional data center resources in parallel to contemporary data sources such as Web and NT servers

- Web-to-database gateways, such as the OLE Database Provider component in Microsoft's SNA Server version 4.0 and StarQuest's StarSQL, which enable programs running on PCs or workstations with direct access to mainframe-resident relational database systems (most notably DB2)

- **Data Link Switching (DLSw)**, which enables SNA or APPN traffic to be transported end-to-end over the TCP/IP backbone via an encapsulation scheme wherein the SNA message units are encapsulated within TCP/IP packets

- File Transfer Protocol (FTP) for universal file transfer, most likely with a channel-attached off-load FTP server from the likes of Computer Network Technology (CNT) and Apertus; in addition to minimizing mainframe CPU cycle usage relative to FTP, it enables the highly efficient and full-duplex-capable SNA LU 6.2 program-to-program protocol, such as IBM's AFTP offering, to be used between the mainframe and the off-load server

- Cost-effective, channel-attached intranet-to-mainframe gateways such as IBM's 2216s and Cisco's 7200/CPA

Figure 1.17 shows some of the key components of an SNA-capable i•net. It highlights the fact that this type of system enables SNA applications to be easily accessed across the Internet.

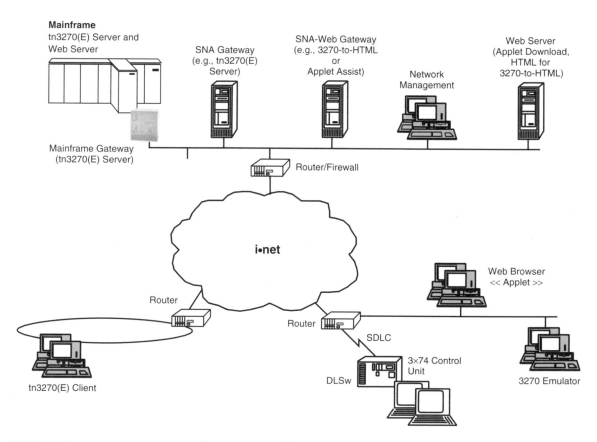

FIGURE 1.17 Primary components of an SNA-capable i•net.

An SNA-capable i•net is realized through the synergistic synthesis of data-center-specific technologies, such as tn3270(E) and DLSw, with standard i•net components. DLSw permits existing "legacy" SNA devices, such as 4700 Financial Systems or 3x74 control units, to be supported across the TCP/IP WAN. Tn3270(E) and browser-based access ensures that PC and workstation users can have unencumbered, but authorized and secure entry into the data center on an interactive basis. Application servers enable new applications, including those written entirely in Java, to have programmatic access to data-center-resident data. Table 1.2 lists the optimum applications for the various data center integration technologies.

SNA-capable i•nets have effectively become the ultimate metaphorphosis of SNA and SNA-related networking. They displace the so-called SNA-capable, multiprotocol networks that began to appear in the IBM space as of the late 1980s. The key difference between the SNA-capable, multiprotocol networks and SNA-capable i•nets is that the former had to support a traffic mix that used a large number of disparate protocols such as IPX/SPX, Net-BIOS, TCP/IP, AppleTalk, and OSI; the latter must concern itself with only TCP/IP and SNA/APPN traffic. In some instances, SNA-capable i•nets may not even have to deal with any native SNA/APPN traffic across the WAN. Traffic to or from the SNA/APPN applications running in the data center is likely to either come from PC/workstation clients that are using TCP/IP à la tn3270(E), or be encapsulated within TCP/IP à la DLSw, at the periphery of the WAN.

SNA-capable i•nets are not contingent on having TCP/IP running on mainframes or AS/400s. Instead, they can be successfully implemented using channel-attached or stand-alone gateways deployed within the data center to perform the necessary TCP/IP-to-mainframe protocol transformations. SNA-capable i•nets will, of course, work with mainframes running TCP/IP, including configurations where the tn3270(E) conversion or even Web-to-SNA conversion is performed on a mainframe. It is worth noting, however, that the rationale for SNA-capable i•nets is to support native SNA applications running on mainframes or AS/400s. In the case of totally TCP/IP-based mainframes or AS/400s, one could essentially link a standard TCP/IP-centric intranet directly to the mainframe or AS/400 without worrying about the need for SNA-specific technologies such as DLSw.

Despite the somewhat complex assimilation of data-center-specific and standard intranet technologies, today's leading SNA-capable i•net solutions are already well-proven, field-tested solutions with more than adequate robustness and resilience to support mission-critical applications. Moreover, they are inevitably tightly integrated and cohesive end-to-end offerings. They set out to excel in delivering the extremely stringent levels of security, manageability, compatibility, performance, and scalability demanded by the very large corporations whose commercial well-being is contingent on the stability and

TABLE 1.2 Optimum scenarios for the various i•net-to-data center integration technologies.

i•net Integration Technology	Optimum Scenario
Transport Technologies	
DLSw	Assimilating existing SNA devices such as 3×74 control units, IBM 4700 Financial Systems, and certain automated teller machines, whether SDLC- or LAN-attached, into an i•net; support for LU 6.2 and LU-LU Session Type 0 across i•nets.
HPR-over-IP	Support for LU 6.2 applications that require SNA "Class of Service" (COS) traffic prioritization end-to-end. Best case: most direct routing when remote end users need to regularly switch between SNA applications running on geographically dispersed data centers. If there is no requirement for end-to-end LU 6.2 COS or direct SNA routing between dispersed data centers, opt for DSLw rather than HPR-over-IP.
AnyNet	AnyNet is no longer strategic. However, if SNA interactions across the i•net are restricted just to data transfers between IBM servers (e.g., mainframe to PC servers running IBM's OS/2), then AnyNet is an inexpensive option because it is bundled in for free with all of IBM's Server software.
Conventional SNA Access Technologies	
ip3270	Easily and cost-effectively integrate existing SNA-LAN gateway configurations, especially if they are based on Novell's NetWare for SAA or Microsoft's SNA Server Gateways, into i•nets by just changing the transport scheme used between the gateway and the desktop 3270 emulators to TCP/IP; if there is a need for LU 6.2 applications at the desktop; or if there are 3270 emulator-specific desktop applications.
tn3270	Medium- to large-scale intranet or extranet scenarios that require cost-effective, standards-compliant 3270-based access (without LU 6.2) through highly scalable mainframe-resident or channel-attached SNA gateways (i.e., tn3270(E) Servers).
New SNA Access Technologies	
Applet based tn3270 emulation	Intranet or extranet scenarios hitherto using SNA-LAN gateways or tn3270 that now want to benefit from the lower software maintenance and software upgrade costs of a "thin-client"-based access scheme. SNA applications whose 3270-centric user interface needs to be face-lifted to present a contemporary look and feel.
3270-to-HTML conversion	Providing the general public with ready access to SNA applications across the Internet. Intranet/extranet query/response (as opposed to data entry) applications that could benefit from an economical, user intervention rejuvenation. Casual access to SNA applications from within intranets/extranets without the users needing to have any SNA/3270-related emulation software or waiting for a 3270 emulation applet download.
Application-specific Web interfaces	Situations where a corporation just needs to Web-enable CICS or IMS as expediently as possible.
Application servers (programmatic solutions)	To develop, in the twenty-first century, object-oriented, Web-centric applications that need access to data center resources.

fidelity of their information systems and the network used to access them. Chapter 4 and following of this book concentrate on the details of the various technologies available for integrating data centers with i•nets.

1.5   THE LAST WORD

I•nets are revolutionizing the way that corporations present, disseminate, and access information. The Internet is becoming both a universal billboard and a global storefront for commercial corporations. It is a highly cost-effective and far-reaching means through which to communicate pertinent corporate information to the masses. Soon the Internet home page will become the defining visage of corporations. The Internet is also an optimum means through which customers can directly interact with corporations and actually perform transactions, bypassing the need for voice response systems or call centers.

In the late 1980s, PCs commoditized computing power and inspired corporations into reengineering their business processes. In the late 1990s, i•nets, with the Internet in the fore, will commoditize information as a whole and galvanize corporations to reengineer their business processes yet again— this time to exploit the considerable information propagation and access potential of i•nets.

Although the Internet permits the public to gain access to certain corporate resources, Internet technology-based intranets are rapidly becoming the basis for next-generation enterprise networks. The lure of intranets is intuitive. An intranet enables a corporation to create its own in-house Internet, replete with applications based on Windows NT, UNIX, Java, and ActiveX. Intranets within corporations that have until now relied on mainframes or AS/400 minicomputers for the bulk of their information processing cannot, nonetheless, flourish in isolation. It is conceivable that as much as 70% of all vital corporate data will reside in the data center, as opposed to the Web servers hosting the emerging intranet. Trying to replicate the data is likely be futile and counterproductive. Consequently, these enterprises have no choice but to synergistically integrate their data centers with their i•nets.

I•nets that can readily access data center resources are known as SNA-capable i•nets. They will usurp and obsolete SNA-only networks. SNA-capable i•nets leverage proven and compelling SNA integration technology, such as Web browser-based access to SNA, tn3270(E), and DLSw, to ensure that SNA can be tightly integrated into TCP/IP-based i•nets without in any way compromising SNA's reliability, integrity, and security. This move toward SNA-capable i•nets is the best opportunity that the IBM world has enjoyed in more than 20 years to "throw out the old and bring in the new" when it comes not just to networking, but also to contemporary standards-based computing and application development.

SNA to SNA-Capable i•nets
SNA's Final Metamorphosis

For the last 20 years, SNA has been a colossal and vital presence in commercial-sector networking. This remarkable domination, however, is now finally and unequivocally coming to an end. Of that there can be no doubt or debate. Most IBM mainframe and AS/400 shops, although inescapably reliant on mission-critical SNA/APPN applications, are inexorably moving toward TCP/IP-centric networks—in particular, toward Internet technology-based i•nets. This move toward i•nets will precipitate what at first appears to be an incongruous dichotomy between data center applications and corporate networking. Despite the forthcoming rapid demise of SNA-based networking, many of today's mainframe- and AS/400-resident SNA/APPN applications will continue to flourish and play a crucial role in successfully sustaining worldwide commerce well into the next millennium. It is highly likely that by 2010 SNA/APPN applications, some of which were initially developed in the early 1980s, will still rule the roost at quite a few data centers around the globe. The rub here is that the access and usage of these SNA/APPN applications will be totally dependent on TCP/IP-based i•nets.

Having SNA/APPN applications depend on a TCP/IP network is not as illogical or convoluted as it may sound. Proven technology for accessing and supporting SNA/APPN applications across TCP/IP networks, such as tn3270(E) and DLSw, has existed for many years. Thanks to such SNA-to-i•net integration technology, an enterprise will still be able to maintain and gainfully exploit its mission-critical SNA/APPN applications even though the native SNA or multiprotocol network hitherto used by these applications will be supplanted by a new TCP/IP-based network. One could even assert that, if not for the availability of such SNA/APPN integration technology, enterprises would not have been able to contemplate and embrace i•nets

SNA applications, buoyed by their mission-criticality, will prevail well into the next century, despite SNA-based networks being rapidly usurped by TCP/IP-centric i•nets.

with such fervor, given that providing unstinted support for mission-critical applications must be the overriding mission of any corporate network. An intranet that cannot provide access to the corporation's mission-critical applications cannot aspire to be the company's true information super-highway. At best, an intranet that cannot embrace existing mission-critical applications will be merely a byway—and such a restricted role is not what is envisaged as the long-term goal for today's rapidly burgeoning crop of intranets.

The ongoing longevity of SNA/APPN applications is not an aberration or the by-product of cavalier and poor planning. SNA/APPN applications prosper because they are mission-critical and will remain so for many years. Although they are now routinely augmented by a new wave of applications based on Windows NT, Web servers, Java, or UNIX, SNA/APPN applications are nonetheless an extremely valuable corporate asset. Today, nearly 70% of the business-critical applications that serve as the life-blood of global commerce are based on SNA/APPN. While the oft-cited corporate adage that "nobody is irreplaceable" may have some merit, this dispensability has definitely not been the case with mission-critical SNA/APPN applications. The loss or malfunction of an SNA/APPN mission-critical application inevitably causes considerable alarm, and in many cases will have a tangible impact on the revenue and productivity of a corporation—even if the downtime was just a matter of minutes. This mission-criticality precludes any easy migration away from SNA applications, even though SNA-only networks based around 37xx communications controllers, APPN network nodes, SNA-LAN gateways such as NetWare for SAA, SDLC links, and other components hitherto used by these applications are now a severely endangered species. The approximately 20,000 SNA-only networks that have been in existence around the world, as well as a similar number of AS/400-centric APPN networks, are likely to be mostly (if not totally) extinct by 2002.

In the case of mission-critical applications, even the slightest change in behavior or results produced can potentially prove catastrophic. Consider the case of large financial institutes that handle transactions that deal with billions of dollars of money transfers and currency exchanges every day. In this scenario, a slight difference in the way that the sixth or seventh decimal point is rounded up or down could add up to hefty variation, one way or another, totaling millions of dollars within a matter of days. When the bottom line can thus be put at significant risk, it takes much deliberation, evaluation, planning, and testing before one can even think about replacing an existing mission-critical application with a new one. Haste and impetuousness are not factors that are normally allowed to play any role when it comes to implementing, modifying, or upgrading mission-critical applications. Instead, the term that most readily comes to mind when dealing with mission-critical applications, SNA, and mainframe-dominated data centers in general is "conservatism."

The installed base of SNA/APPN applications is valued at around $25 trillion. This base is clearly a huge, even monumental, investment. It is, nonetheless, inevitable that all SNA/APPN applications will be replaced by newer, and most likely i•net-influenced client/server applications— for example, by Java clients interacting with a Java-oriented application server such as IBM's WebSphere, OpenConnect's Application Server, BEA WebLogic, or Novera jBusiness 4. This conversion will obviously be costly. Nevertheless, today's object-oriented and highly "visual" development methodologies combined with the ready availability of sophisticated off-the-shelf applications, such as SAP R/3, should ensure that the development costs for the new applications are less steep than they were for the SNA/APPN applications that they displace. In addition, much of the $25 trillion investment in the SNA/APPN application program cache is related to program updating and maintenance costs. Consequently, the overall cost of replacing the entire pool of SNA/APPN applications over the coming decade is unlikely to reach $25 trillion, although it will probably exceed $1 trillion—still a lot of money. In addition to the mission-criticality of SNA/APPN applications, this rather steep replacement cost further guarantees that these applications (much like the Energizer bunny) will keep going, and going, and going . . .

Another factor contributing to the longevity of SNA/APPN applications is the frenzied and hugely costly efforts to ensure that data center applications can cope with the year 2000 and beyond. Some have contended that corporations would use the year 2000 (Y2K) challenge as an impetus to replace their SNA/APPN applications with new ones that, in addition to being able to deal with Y2K, would not rely on SNA. In reality, this envisaged replacement of SNA/APPN applications in preparation for the coming millennium has not happened on a large-enough scale to be noteworthy. Most corporations, quite rightly, decided that it was difficult enough to deal with the Y2K challenge with well-known existing applications without complicating matters by trying to introduce a new crop of applications in a hurry— especially given that they were unlikely to replace all of their applications and thus would still have to update some of their mission-critical programs to deal with Y2K.

The Y2K-related activity has certainly added a few more years to the life expectancy of SNA/APPN applications. Not only has there been a reprieve in the years leading up to 2000, but there will inevitably be another couple of years of hiatus at the start of the decade while MIS departments take a well-deserved breather, take stock of where they are, and try to recoup the monies spent on the Y2K conversion effort.

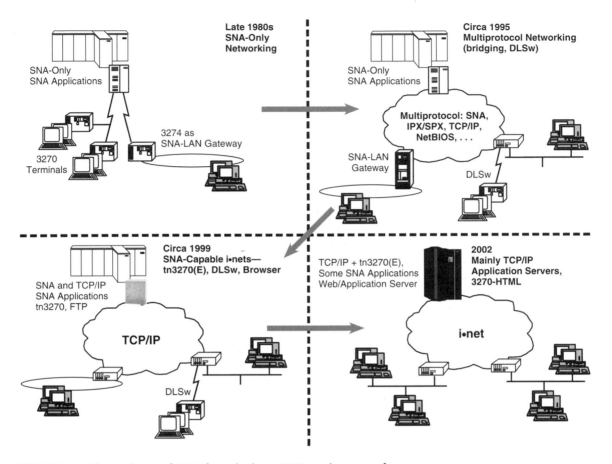

FIGURE 2.1 The evolution of SNA from the late 1980s to the twenty-first century.

Figure 2.1 shows the evolution of SNA from the SNA-only networks of the 1980s to SNA-capable i•nets in the twenty-first century.

2.1 SNA-ORIENTED DATA CENTERS AND TCP/IP-BASED NETWORKS

Although mainframe-oriented networking is undoubtedly becoming TCP/IP-centric, it does not necessarily mean that TCP/IP has already become the preferred networking scheme within mainframes. At the start of 1998, about 60% of mainframes running IBM's MVS or OS/390 operating system were actively using TCP/IP software from IBM or Interlink Computer Sciences to support TCP/IP-based mainframe applications—in particular, tn3270(E) servers or

FTP. Mainframe-resident TCP/IP stacks and applications, however, invariably run alongside the SNA "facilitator" **ACF/VTAM** and a set of SNA-based mission-critical applications. This dichotomous scenario (where the mainframes and data centers are SNA-oriented, and the WAN backbone is rapidly becoming TCP/IP-centric) will not change in the short to mid-term. Most mainframes, though gravitating toward more native TCP/IP applications over time, will remain SNA-oriented well into the twenty-first century.

At least eight somewhat interrelated factors explain why mainframes will remain very much SNA-oriented despite the fact that the networks of which they are a part are becoming TCP/IP-based i•nets. These eight factors can be summarized below:

Business-Critical SNA Applications

The mainframe SNA applications, including subsystems such as CICS, IMS, TSO and DB2, must be sustained because of their mission-criticality, as discussed in detail earlier.

Parallel Sysplex

The new, strategic, and highly cost-competitive IBM mainframes are based on **CMOS** technology. The switching characteristics of CMOS, however, are such that CMOS-based computer circuitry is not as fast or powerful as the circuitry that was possible with the much more costly bipolar technology used in previous IBM mainframe families. Subsequently, the only way that IBM can satisfy the constantly growing demand for mainframe computing power in terms of more MIPS is to offer the CMOS machines in parallel-processing clusters. This factor explains why the CMOS-based mainframes are known as **S/390 Parallel Enterprise Servers**.

This parallel-processing, mainframe-clustering notion can be further extended via a mainframe configuration scheme that is known as Parallel Sysplex. **Parallel Sysplex**, which was introduced by IBM in 1994, permits two or more mainframes or CMOS parallel enterprise servers running MVS or OS/390 to be tightly coupled to permit high-performance, read-write, data sharing and dynamic work load balancing. In 1998, Parallel Sysplex permitted as many as 32 separate mainframes, each with a maximum of 10 processors, to be clustered together to deliver a tightly coupled mainframe complex with more than 2000 MIPS of processing power; all mainframes in the cluster have concurrent read-write access to all of the shared data. Parallel Sysplex can therefore be exploited to provide both scalability and high availability. The fault-resilient, high-availability aspects of Parallel Sysplex are provided via MVS and OS/390 features such as **Generic Resources** and **Multinode Persistent Sessions (MNPS)**.

TCP/IPs dominance in the network will not mean that IBM-biased data centers also become TCP/IP-based. Instead, SNA, APPN, and HPR will continue to be an integral part of intra-data-center and inter-data-center operation.

The Generic Resources facility enables multiple images of the same application, such as CICS, running on separate mainframes or parallel enterprise servers to appear to the end-user population as a single application. Rather than having to log on to a specific application (for example, CICS1, CICS2, or CICS3) running on a particular machine, Generic Resources enable end users to use the generic name for that application (such as CICS). This capability, in addition to facilitating dynamic load balancing across machines, shields new users logging on to the application from the failure of one specific application image, because the logons will be automatically directed to an operational image of the application.

MNPS further extends the nonstop, high-availability aspect of Parallel Sysplex configurations by ensuring that ACF/VTAM mission-critical applications and sessions are not disrupted in the event of any failure within the Parallel Sysplex complex involving a particular copy of ACF/VTAM, the operating system, the application, or even the underlying mainframe hardware. In the event of a failure, MNPS automatically and transparently diverts all existing application sessions to other machines within the Parallel Sysplex complex that are running copies of the affected applications. The read-write disk storage data-sharing capability inherent within Parallel Sysplex configurations, coupled with automatic and extensive transaction "journaling" to disk ensures that few, if any, session-related data are lost during an MNPS cut-over.

The Generic Resources and MNPS features of Parallel Sysplex are currently supported by only APPN and HPR. Until such value-added, high-availability mainframe features are supported across an IP-oriented infrastructure, enterprises, especially if they are committed to Parallel Sysplex-based mainframe configurations, must rely heavily on APPN or HPR for their intra-data-center (that is, mainframe-to-mainframe) and inter-data-center communications. IBM intends to offer increasingly more IP support for Parallel Sysplex function starting in mid-1999.

TCP/IP Off-Load

Current mainframe TCP/IP software, such as tn3270(E) server or FTP, can be somewhat resource hungry. Many enterprises therefore set out to conserve valuable mainframe resources by deploying channel-attached, "off-load" tn3270(E) servers (such as IBM 2216, Cisco 7500/CIP, or Bus-Tech Net-Shuttle) and FTP servers (in particular, CNT Enterprise Connect) that provide all necessary TCP/IP-based services without requiring TCP/IP software or applications on the mainframe. SNA acts between these off-load servers and the appropriate mainframe applications.

The only purpose of tn3270 is to provide TCP/IP-based access to SNA applications and print services. Hence, the use of SNA between the mainframe applications and the off-load tn3270(E) servers is obvious and natural, especially since IBM 2216 can provide approximately 15,000 concurrent tn3270(E) sessions at an all-inclusive, hardware/software cost of roughly $4/user.

With FTP, matters are slightly different because FTP is a native TCP/IP application with no connections to SNA. Therefore one requires a specialized mainframe SNA application that can interact with the off-load FTP server and transfer the required files to and from the mainframe. An IBM-supplied SNA LU 6.2-based utility, known as AFTP, is often used by FTP off-load servers as their mainframe component.

Value-Added LU 6.2 Functions

Some corporations, especially those in the banking and financial sectors, have developed SNA LU 6.2 program-to-program, mainframe-to-PC applications over the last few years that rely on facilities such as end-to-end traffic prioritization based on **Class-of-Service (COS)** and **two-phase commit** to ensure the fidelity of distributed database updates. Like other organizations with SNA mission-critical applications, these corporations are unlikely to have any short-term options other than to continue to use these applications across their i•nets. The only difference would be that they will not be able to use tn3270(E) or browser-based SNA access to support these applications on the i•net, because these SNA integration methodologies are expressly geared for terminal emulation based on the 3270 data stream. Instead, these LU 6.2 applications will most likely be supported using DLSw or HPR-over-IP, given that these techniques can transport any type of SNA traffic, independent of the LU-LU session protocol being used. HPR-over-IP is discussed in detail in Section 2.4.

Mainframe-to-Mainframe and Data Center-to-Data Center Routing

SNA subarea, APPN NN, or HPR NN routing will continue to be the preferred methods for intra-data-center and inter-data-center routing if a corporation has SNA/APPN applications deployed across multiple mainframes or multiple data centers.

MPC Channel Protocol

IBM's latest, and consequently most efficient, flexible, and high-throughput channel protocol, known as **Multipath Channel (MPC)**, is optimized and targeted at APPN- and HPR-based data transfers, even though OS/390 version 2, release 6 also permits IP traffic to be run across MPC. MPC is discussed in more detail in Chapter 7. MPC permits multiple subchannels on separate channels to be grouped together, much like an SNA **transmission group (TG)**, to permit genuine full-duplex data transfers at a minimum throughput of 272Mbps. Many corporations are planning to configure ACF/VTAM to run HPR on the mainframe so that they can eliminate network-to-mainframe bottlenecks by using MPC between their network gateway, such as an IBM 2216 or Cisco 7500/CIP, and the mainframe.

Tighter Security

SNA, in conjunction with products such as IBM's RACF, at present provides more water-tight security and access auditing than is typically possible with contemporary mainframe TCP/IP software. This situation is changing, however.

Higher Throughput

HPR support, which became available with ACF/VTAM version 4, release 4, in mid-1995, provides considerably faster throughput than has been possible

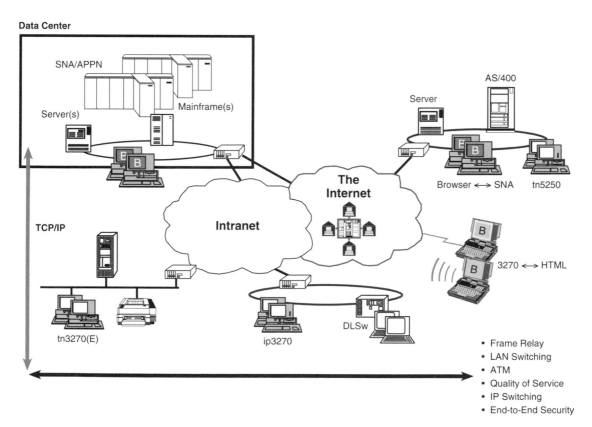

FIGURE 2.2   SNA-based data center tightly integrated with TCP/IP-centric network.

with SNA software in the past. This throughput is especially possible if HPR is combined with MPC for data transfer across channels. Many large SNA shops plan to migrate to HPR on their mainframes to benefit from both the added throughput and the high-availability functions provided by Parallel Sysplex.

These factors will ensure that today's SNA shops have little choice but to maintain some level of SNA, APPN, or HPR networking capability within their data centers for quite a few more years, despite their networks per se becoming TCP/IP-centric. Figure 2.2 illustrates the notion of an SNA-based data center that is integrated with TCP/IP-centric i•nets.

2.2 REASONS FOR THE DEMISE OF SNA-ORIENTED NETWORKING

OSI, which became an official standard in 1982, was historically touted as SNA's most likely vanquisher. In the end, however, the honor of being SNA's nemesis has obviously fallen to TCP/IP, despite the fact that it is nearly as old as SNA. For the record, TCP/IP saw the light of day around 1977, roughly three years after SNA. It is therefore safe to surmise that SNA's downfall has little to do with its vintage per se. Lack of functionality is also not the real issue. HPR, SNA's latest incarnation, is a low-fat, peer-to-peer networking scheme replete with dynamic alternate routing. HPR (described in Section 2.4) can, at least on paper, rival **IPv6**, the latest version of TCP/IP, when it comes to overall capabilities, scope, and features.

Instead, SNA's downfall was precipitated by the fact that LAN-oriented, bridge/router-centric internetworking, the Internet, and now intranets are all uniformly based on TCP/IP. During the early 1990s, when nearly all corporations embraced LAN/WAN internetworking, TCP/IP gained so much momentum, corporate mind share, public acceptance, and overall popularity that even SNA, with its entrenched base of mission-critical applications, could do little to thwart its rapid spread.

The growth of internetworking across the corporate world coincided with the advent of the World Wide Web (WWW), which elevated the Internet from an arcane network to an indispensable public information and entertainment resource. TCP/IP essentially cornered the market from both ends: corporations through internetworking, and the public sector with the Internet. The overwhelming and continued mandate now given to it by the ever-burgeoning popularity of the Internet and intranets is inescapable and highly persuasive. TCP/IP is indubitably the "king of protocols." It has won, conclusively and irrevocably, the "battle of the protocols" over rivals Novel IPX/SPX, NetBIOS, DECnet, AppleTalk, and OSI—but most notably against SNA and its designated heirs, APPN and HPR.

The growth in multiprotocol networking in the early 1990s, followed by the phenomenal popularity of the Internet, was the catalyst for the erosion of SNA's dominance within the enterprise. A complacent and inattentive IBM was caught flat-footed when the tide began to turn—and elected, to its credit, to wholeheartedly embrace TCP/IP rather than attempting to resurrect SNA/APPN.

It would be a huge mistake to think that TCP/IP's current level of approval and acceptance is likely to be a short-lived phenomenon. SNA dominated the last 20 years of commercial-sector networking. The next 20 years belong to TCP/IP.

In theory, the rapid decline in SNA-related networking as of 1996, particularly as it affected wide area networking, should not have caught many by surprise. Since the advent of LAN-based multiprotocol networking (in particular, IPX/SPX, NetBIOS, DECnet, and AppleTalk) in the late 1980s, SNA networks have been steadily losing ground because IBM never provided any compelling solutions for accommodating non-SNA traffic across existing SNA/APPN backbones. Nonetheless, the displacement of SNA/APPN networks by TCP/IP networks remains a source of considerable consternation for the army of data-processing and networking professionals who have enjoyed buoyant, secure, and often lucrative careers thanks to their expertise in SNA. Many of these SNA stalwarts are being forced, in the autumn of their careers, to learn new networking skills or to pursue other careers. Some still hope that SNA might receive a last-minute reprieve and that this talk of its imminent demise will prove as baseless as the obituaries that were being written for mainframes a decade ago.

Although some parallels can be drawn between the challenge to mainframes made by UNIX-based "open systems" and the woes to SNA induced by TCP/IP, the overall dynamics of these two battle royals are very different. For a start, UNIX systems really could not match the raw power and capacity of mainframes, at the right price points, when it came to performing large amounts of commercial transactions. In contrast, TCP/IP's networking prowess and affordability relative to that of SNA are already proven and not in question. Confronted with the assault of its beloved (and cash-cow) mainframes, IBM mounted a concerted campaign to reduce the overall cost of mainframe ownership, which culminated in the breakthrough, CMOS-based parallel-processing mainframe systems that now rival equivalent RISC machines in terms of computing costs. On the other hand, when SNA was under siege, IBM did little, if anything, to try and reverse the tide. Instead, astutely noting the groundswell of support for TCP/IP, it rapidly transformed itself into one of the most ardent advocates of TCP/IP, i•nets, and electronic commerce across i•nets. In a sense, IBM's unstinted endorsement of TCP/IP and i•nets has guaranteed that SNA-only networks will soon be history.

2.2.1   Other Factors Contributing to SNA's Downfall

Given that SNA's downfall can be directly attributed to the ascent of i•nets, one could argue that any kind of postmortem examination is superfluous. Given the enormous power that SNA once wielded over global commerce, its decline in fortune in the face of TCP/IP was more precipitous than one would normally expect. Hence, it is interesting to determine some of the major factors that contributed to the erosion of its power base so as to give TCP/IP an edge. The main factors that collectively undermined the viability of SNA-based networks are summarized below.

Inadequate Support for Multiprotocol Networking

Until quite recently, LANs were IBM's Achilles heel. Although IBM procrastinated on the Token Ring architecture until 1986, by the late 1980s LANs had become the preferred means for PC interconnection and resource sharing within virtually all corporations, independent of their affiliation to IBM or their dependence on SNA for mission-critical application access. At this juncture, IBM believed (somewhat myopically) that the SNA **LU 6.2** program-to-program protocol it had introduced in 1984 would soon become the strategic and optimal means for LAN-based applications—especially given the existing and then very loyal SNA customer base. Consequently, the company worked on the assumption that the new breed of LAN-oriented protocols, including its own NetBIOS, represented essentially tactical, stop-gap solutions. Contrary to IBM's expectations, however, protocols such as IPX/SPX, NetBIOS, AppleTalk, Banyan Vines, TCP/IP, and even OSI—rather than LU 6.2—became the accepted means for LAN-centric file server, print server, program-to-program, and client/server applications.

The spread and popularity of these new LAN protocols caught IBM off-guard. It did not add any extensions to SNA to accommodate and transport these alien protocols. This decision proved disastrous, because corporations were beginning to require LAN-oriented remote office-to-headquarters and remote office-to-remote office interactions. Although a corporation's SNA backbone already had the physical WAN connections reaching out to all of the various corporate sites, SNA's inability to support the LAN protocols precluded the hitherto infallible SNA network from becoming the foundation for the new wave of LAN-based applications. Corporations had no option except to implement a separate bridge or bridge/router-based network for their non-SNA LAN-oriented applications and traffic. During the early 1990s, most SNA shops therefore maintained two separate networks: an SNA network and a bridge/router-based multiprotocol network.

Although SNA/APPN networks continued to shun alien protocols, bridge/router vendors, ably led by Cisco, went to inordinate lengths to provide SNA, APPN, and even HPR support within multiprotocol networks with techniques such as **Source-Route Bridging (SRB)**, **Protocol-Independent Routing (PIR)**, **Remote Source-Route Bridging (RSRB)**, DLSw, and APPN/HPR network node routing.

To be fair, IBM made a few half-hearted attempts to stop the encroachment of bridge/router solutions into the SNA base, such as the software-only

The rampaging popularity of the Internet was bound to take its toll on SNA, but the decline of SNA would have been less precipitous if IBM had done a better job of coping with multiprotocol networking, and if APPN was not so slow in embracing 3270 traffic.

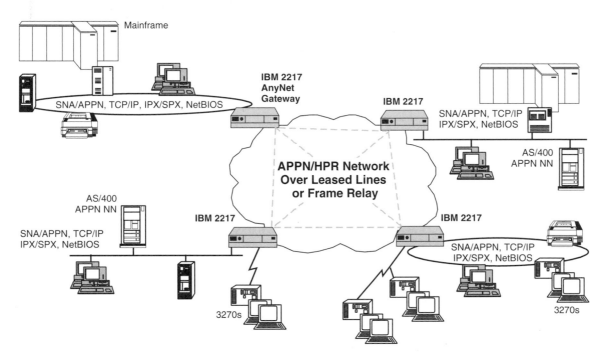

FIGURE 2.3   IBM 2217-based multiprotocol network where SNA/APPN, TCP/IP, IPX/SPX, and NetBIOS are transported across an APPN/HPR WAN.

LAN-to-LAN Wide Area Network Program (LTLW) and the underpowered 2217 Nways MultiProtocol Concentrator. Figure 2.3 shows an IBM 2217-based multiprotocol network where SNA, TCP/IP, IPX/SPX, and NetBIOS are transported across an HPR-based backbone. These isolated attempts to make SNA/APPN multiprotocol-capable, however, were late to market, under-featured, lackluster, poorly marketed, and unprepossessing.

Maintaining parallel networks was costly and unwieldy. The die was now cast. SNA customers began to slowly move their SNA traffic onto bridge/router-based multiprotocol networks from their SNA-only networks. Figure 2.4 depicts a quintessential SNA-capable multiprotocol network. The marked and dramatic improvement in the reliability and resilience of bridge/router-based networks toward the mid-1990s was an added and much welcome catalyst. SNA-only networks were no longer strategic. SNA-capable i•nets are but the final embodiment of this evolution from SNA-only networks to multiprotocol networks.

Inexcusable Delays in Ensuring Comprehensive Support for 3270 Sessions within APPN and HPR Networks

APPN and HPR were both created such that the only SNA sessions that they could support in native mode (that is, without any additional extensions) were

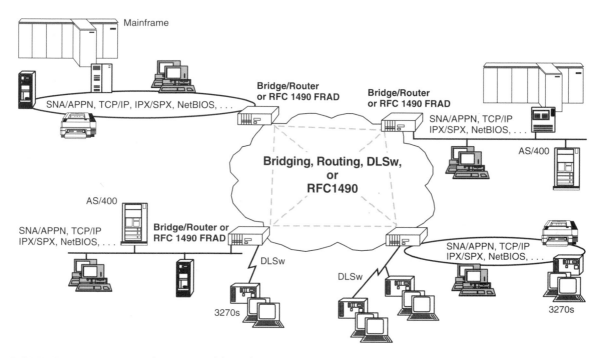

FIGURE 2.4 Quintessential SNA-capable multiprotocol LAN/WAN network based on bridging, routing, or RFC 1490.

LU 6.2 program-to-program sessions. Moreover, because APPN and HPR were both intrinsically peer-to-peer architectures, they did not cater to the mainframe ACF/VTAM-based **SSCP-LU** and **SSCP-PU** "control" sessions that were a cornerstone of hierarchical, mainframe-centric SNA subarea networks. To support traditional SNA traffic, such as 3270 traffic based on the LU-LU session type 2, without any restrictions being placed on the network configuration (such as that all SNA devices must be logically adjacent to a 37xx communications controller), APPN and HPR required an extension referred to as **dependent logical unit server and requester (DLUS/DLUR)**. This lack of built-in support for the traditional SNA session types was unfortunate and imprudent because non-LU 6.2 traffic (in particular, 3270 traffic based on LU-LU session types 2 and 3) remains the predominant form of SNA.

The term "dependent" as it is used in the context of DLUS/DLUR alludes to the fact that LUs that are not type 6.2 are totally dependent on ACF/VTAM on a mainframe for their Directory (session setup) and Configuration (node activation/deactivation) services. In marked contrast, LU 6.2s can be configured to operate independently without being beholden to an ACF/VTAM. Such LUs are therefore referred to as **independent LUs (ILUs)**. HPR and APPN were developed to cater to ILUs.

DLUS/DLUR is essentially a client/server mechanism. DLUS resides within ACF/VTAM on a mainframe. DLUR is either embedded within an SNA device such as an IBM 3174 control unit or is implemented as a surrogate DLUR server in an APPN node (for example, within a bridge/router) and provides DLUR functionality to SNA devices attached to that NN. Figure 2.5 illustrates the architecture of DLUS/DLUR, including the notion of a surrogate DLUR server.

ACF/VTAM had DLUS capability since mid-1994, with version 4.2. The problem was the paucity of SNA devices that had DLUR implemented within them and the delay in the implementation of surrogate DLUR server capabilities within key IBM networking products, such as the 3746-950 communications controller and the 6611 bridge/router. In 1995, only two SNA devices offered DLUR: the IBM 3174 control unit with configuration support "C," release 5 microcode, and PCs running OS/2 with the latest CM/2.

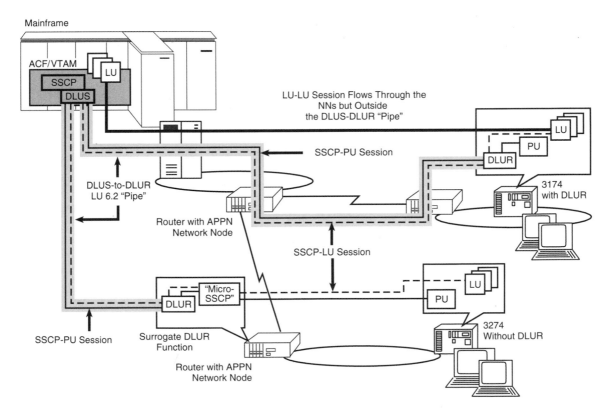

FIGURE 2.5 DLUS/DLUR client/server architecture and the ability of a network node to act as a surrogate DLUR server to an SNA node that does not have DLUR.

If an SNA device, such as a PC LAN gateway (for example, NetWare for SAA) or an IBM 4700 financial controller, did not have built-in DLUR, only two ways existed to deploy it within an APPN or HPR network. It could either be directly attached to a 37xx or be "front-ended" by an APPN or HPR NN containing a surrogate DLUR server. The former option was referred to as the "one-hop away" configuration, because the SNA device had to be logically adjacent to a 37xx. Figure 2.6 illustrates the configuration limitations of an APPN or HPR network, vis-à-vis SNA devices, if the necessary DLUR

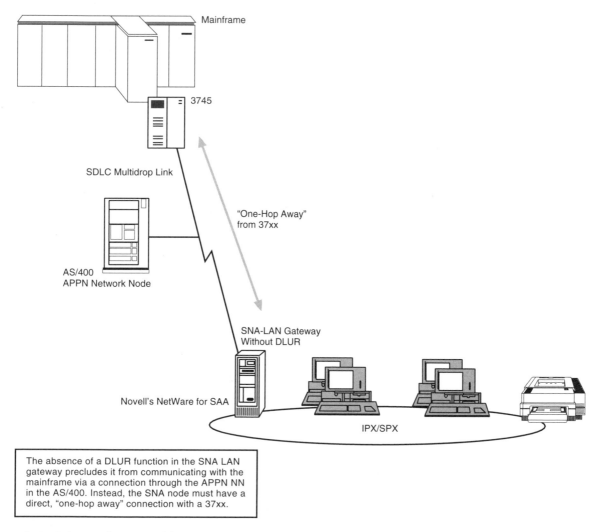

Mainframe

3745

SDLC Multidrop Link

"One-Hop Away" from 37xx

AS/400 APPN Network Node

SNA-LAN Gateway Without DLUR

Novell's NetWare for SAA

IPX/SPX

The absence of a DLUR function in the SNA LAN gateway precludes it from communicating with the mainframe via a connection through the APPN NN in the AS/400. Instead, the SNA node must have a direct, "one-hop away" connection with a 37xx.

FIGURE 2.6 Configurational limitations imposed in the absence of DLUR functionality.

or surrogate DLUR server functionality was not available. The inadequate availability of DLUR curtailed SNA subarea-based WAN backbones from being readily migrated to APPN or HPR, because the configuration limitations related to the SNA devices diminished the attractiveness of these peer-to-peer networks.

Around mid-1996, DLUR and surrogate DLUR server functionality became available on a sufficient range of key networking devices to enable SNA devices to be relatively freely used within any given APPN or HPR network configuration. By then, the tide was changing. Most SNA shops had shelved their original early 1990s plans to migrate to APPN or HPR. Instead, they augmented their solid and proven SNA subarea backbones with bridge/router-based, SNA-capable multiprotocol networking. Many of the bridge/routers used to realize these SNA-capable multiprotocol networks (in particular, the market-dominating Cisco routers) offered comprehensive APPN and HPR NN routing capability. Most SNA customers, however, refrained from using APPN or HPR NN routing on their multiprotocol networks as the means of supporting SNA traffic. Instead, they opted for techniques such as SRB, RSRB, PIR, DLSw, and native Frame Relay encapsulation à la RFC 1490. These bridge/router-centric, multiprotocol networks are now evolving toward becoming SNA-capable i•nets.

APPN and HPR, in Marked Contrast to SNA, Are Patented and Licensed

The original subarea SNA architecture, although invariably disparaged by IBM's competitors as being proprietary, was in reality a very open, public standard. Other vendors did not need a license, or even permission, from IBM to implement an SNA node (for example, a type 2 node or PU type 2), based on the once-readily-available architectural specifications, within their products.

The thriving plug-compatible 3270 control unit industry of the late 1970s would not have been possible if these IBM competitors had not provided the same SNA functionality within their boxes as comparable IBM 3270 control units, without paying any license fees or royalties to IBM. Comten (later NCR Comten) thrived for nearly 10 years by selling a family of plug-compatible 37xx communications controllers, which ran Comten's own NCP software to implement a full-function type 4 SNA subarea node that emulated the SNA subarea routing and boundary functions found within IBM's ACF/NCP software. Comten did not have to compensate IBM in any way for its liberal use of the SNA architecture.

Minicomputer vendors such as Wang, DEC, Data General, Prime, and Apollo enjoyed the same largess from IBM when it came to SNA. Much of the triumph that minicomputers enjoyed in the early 1980s in the *Fortune*

5000 arena derived from their ability to freely and reliably interact with IBM mainframes, IBM minicomputers such as S/36s, and even with each other using SNA.

SNA had by now become a de facto industry standard and a widely used mechanism for multivendor interoperability. It was SNA's success as a proven basis for multivendor interoperability that continually thwarted OSI from gaining ground. By the mid-1980s, SNA was a $20 billion per year industry serviced by hundreds of vendors, although IBM continued to take the lion's share (50%–60%) of this substantial revenue stream.

The original industry standard openness and the consequent near-universal adoption of this architecture by other vendors was key to the popularity and market domination enjoyed by SNA. In addition to direct revenues from SNA-oriented products such as ACF/VTAM, 37xx communications controllers, and 3x74 control units, IBM also benefited from substantial SNA-induced "drag" for its mainframes, minicomputers, service, and software offerings as corporations expanded and enhanced their mission-critical SNA networks. The company, however, was not content. It resented the money that other vendors were making with SNA-related products and services. IBM unastutely lost sight of the pivotal fact that SNA would never have been as powerful and pervasive if it had not been so readily endorsed and supported by a battalion of other vendors.

To control and share in the SNA-related revenues being made by other vendors, IBM decided to institute two far-reaching measures. First, it chose not to make any new extensions to the SNA architecture (for example, the integration of type 2.1 node-resident ILUs with mainframe-based SNA networks) as readily available to the public and other vendors. In the past, documents related to SNA architecture and format information were readily available from IBM at very nominal prices (in the $70 range). Second, IBM patented certain elements of APPN and HPR and then mandated that other vendors pay a license fee, as well as royalties on any units they sold, if they wished to implement an APPN or HPR network node within one of their products. SNA, although not hamstrung by licenses or royalties, was no longer truly open. APPN and HPR were proprietary from their first introduction.

Vendors such as Cisco, Bay, Novell, and 3Com, which wanted to aggressively compete in the IBM networking space, had no choice except to license APPN from IBM and agree to pay royalties. Although most of the leading bridge/router vendors implemented APPN NN routing to show their commitment to SNA-based networking, none aggressively promoted APPN. Cisco, the undisputed market leader in integrating SNA into bridge/router-based, multiprotocol LAN/WAN internetworks, went as far as proposing a TCP/IP-based, "open" alternative to APPN known as **APPI**; in theory, APPI could support APPN end nodes across a TCP/IP backbone that would emulate APPN services and routing.

By the mid-1990s, APPN and HPR faced two major impediments. The paucity of DLUR support constrained its appeal among the SNA customer base. In parallel, the bridge/router vendors, which dominated the IBM networking arena, downplayed the need and attractiveness of APPN and HPR as a WAN backbone protocol. Instead, the bridge/router vendors aggressively promoted open, industry-standards-based TCP/IP networks that would support SNA, APPN, or HPR traffic using DLSw and SNA application access via tn3270(E), tn5250, and browser-based access. IBM's forlorn hope that HPR might still prevail, at least in some SNA shops, as a WAN backbone was finally dashed. In the future, HPR's role, at best, will be restricted to the data center and Parallel Sysplex configurations.

2.3   THE ROLE OF SNA-LAN GATEWAYS WITHIN SNA-CAPABLE I•NETS

SNA-LAN gateways, which come in many different flavors, enable PCs and workstations to access SNA applications. Today's strategic tn3270(E) servers are merely one example of an SNA PU Controller-type gateway.

Since the late 1980s, SNA-LAN gateways, such as Novell's NetWare for SAA, have been used to enable PC and workstation users to access mission-critical SNA applications running on mainframes or AS/400s. The need for such gateways stems from the fact that PCs and workstations do not possess built-in SNA or 3270 terminal emulation functionality. If PCs and workstations are to access SNA applications, they require the services of two SNA-related functional components: SNA nodes and SNA "client" emulators.

Basic SNA functionality, in the form of an **SNA node**—often referred to as an SNA PU—is typically provided in the form of an SNA type 2 or 2.1 node, which will include the SNA PU, LU, and Path Control Network functionality. Today, this SNA node functionality is usually provided by an SNA-LAN gateway, such as NetWare for SAA, or a tn3270(E) server.

One or more SNA "client" applications, or emulators, will work in conjunction with the SNA node functionality. This client application may take the form of either a 3270 emulation for mainframe application access or a 5250 emulation for AS/400 application access. The client will typically include a 3270 data stream, such as IBM PC 3270 IND$FILE capability, or LU 6.2-based file-transfer scheme. In some instances, the client, rather than providing a 3270/5250 terminal interface, will instead offer an LU 6.2-oriented application program interface (API) to facilitate programmatic access to SNA/APPN applications. IBM's PComm, Attachmate's EXTRA! Personal Client, Eicon's Aviva for Desktops, and WRQ's Reflection are examples of traditional 3270/5250 clients. Applets used by browser-based access to SNA solutions, as well as tn3270(E)/tn5250 clients, are examples of the new generation of i•net-oriented clients.

This SNA node and SNA client functionality can be provided to PC/workstation users in a variety of permutations. The primary difference between these permutations lies in the relative locations of the SNA node and the relevant client. In some approaches, the SNA node and the client run together on the PC or workstation. This approach is known as implementing a full-stack SNA node on the PC or workstation. Such full-stack implementations become possible with most of the major SNA/3270 emulation packages, such as IBM's PComm and Eicon's Aviva for Desktops. In this implementation, the PC or workstation "talks" straight SNA. In the context of SNA-capable i•nets, DLSw or HPR-over-IP will be required to support such full-stack SNA PCs and workstations, as the client will most certainly be based on SNA rather than TCP/IP. As a part of the migration toward SNA-capable i•nets, most corporations intend to move away from full-stack emulations to thinner, TCP/IP-oriented client approaches such as browser-based access, tn3270(E), or a plain 3270-only client that communicates over TCP/IP to an upstream SNA-LAN gateway. Figure 2.7 illustrates some of the possible permutations for the deployment of SNA node and SNA client functionality through emerging SNA-capable i•nets.

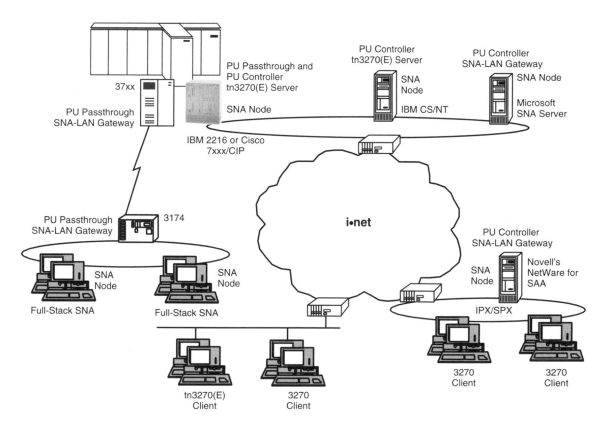

FIGURE 2.7 Some of the primary permutations for SNA nodes and SNA clients.

Today's SNA-LAN gateway solutions can be classified into five distinct categories:

1. **PU Controller Gateways** (for example, SNA Server, NetWare for SAA)
2. **PU Passthrough Gateways** (for example, IBM 3745, IBM 2216)
3. **PU Concentrator Gateways** (for example, SNA Server, Cisco bridge/routers)
4. tn3270(E) Server Gateways (for example, IBM 2216, Cisco 7xxx/CIP, SNA Server)
5. SNA-Web Gateways (for example, OpenConnect's OC://WebConnect Pro, Farabi's HostFront, Eicon's Web-to-Host Gateway)

Two key factors differentiate these five gateway types: the location of the SNA node software that provides the actual SNA functionality, and the protocols used for communication between the client running on a PC or workstation and the gateway. The SNA node software could reside in either the client, as in full-stack SNA, the SNA-to-LAN gateway, or both the client and the gateway. Table 2.1 summarizes functional variations of these five types of gateways.

tn3270(E) servers, although identified separately given their growing strategic significance relative to SNA-capable i•nets, are actually a variant of PU Controller Gateways. The pivotal difference between a tn3270(E) server and a conventional PU Controller Gateway setup is that the former uses an industry-standard client/server protocol (the tn3270 protocol) and the latter solution employs a proprietary, vendor-specific protocol. Most of the leading products used in the past to implement PU Controller Gateways, such as NetWare for SAA and SNA servers, can now also function as tn3270(E) servers, in parallel to acting as PU Controller Gateways. In the case of NetWare for SAA or SNA servers, the same server can simultaneously perform both functions and therefore serve both tn3270(E) clients and traditional emulation clients at the same time.

All three of the SNA-LAN gateway solution types can be found in two very distinct forms: as local, mainframe channel-attached gateways, as with Bus-Tech's NetShuttle, or as remote, link-attached gateways located at the periphery of a WAN. Figures 2.8 and 2.9 show the differences between local and remote gateway configurations. Local gateways act as the interface between a mainframe and the network, whereas remote gateways concentrate on ensuring that PCs and workstations can gain access to the network leading to the destination mainframe or AS/400.

The functionality, as well as the pros and cons of PU controller, PU passthrough, and PU concentrator gateways are discussed in the following

TABLE 2.1 Functional variations of the five types of SNA gateways.

	Contains SNA Node	Protocol to Client PCs	Micro-SCCP Function	Salient Characteristics	Examples
PU Controller Gateway	Yes	IP, IPX, LLC-2, NetBIOS	No	Provides SNA functionality to downstream PCs running 3270 emulators	Novell's NetWare for SAA, Microsoft SNA Server, AS/400, IBM CS/NT
PU Passthrough Gateway	No	SNA	No	Does not provide any SNA functionality, but connects downstream SNA nodes to the mainframe or network	IBM 3174, 3745, 3172, 2216, Cisco 7xxx/CIP
PU Concentrator Gateway	Yes	SNA	Yes	Acts as a "mini-mainframe" and terminates SSCP-PU sessions at the gateway so that the mainframe SSCP sees only the LUs in the various PCs, rather than the individual PUs in each PC	Cisco routers, IBM's CS/NT, Novell's NetWare for SAA
tn3270(E) server	Yes	tn3270	No	Provides SNA functionality and SNA-to-TCP/IP protocol conversion for PCs running tn3270 client software	IBM CS/NT, Novell's NetWare for SAA, IBM 2216, Cisco 7xxx/CIP
SNA-Web gateway	Rarely*	Proprietary or HTML/HTTP	No	Provides 3270-to-HTML conversion, authentication, or applet augmentation	Eicon Aviva Web-to-Host (3270-HTML), OpenConnect OC://WebConnect

*Most gateways do not include an SNA node and rely on an external tn3270(E) server. A few, such as Eicon's Aviva Web-to-Host Server, however, contain a built-in SNA gateway, and hence an SNA node.

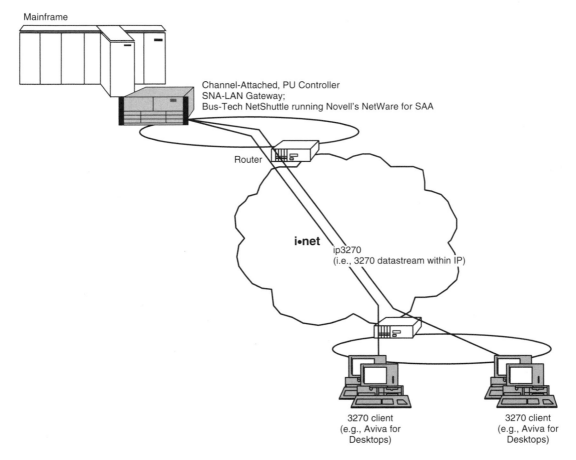

FIGURE 2.8   Local, channel-attached SNA-LAN gateway.

sections. tn3270(E) and SNA-Web gateways are discussed in considerable detail starting in Chapter 4.

2.3.1   PU Controller Gateways

PU Controller Gateways were the first generation of SNA-LAN gateways for LAN-attached (as opposed to coax-attached) PCs and workstations. ("Coax-attached" meant the use of an adapter such as DCA's IRMA card to connect the PC to an appropriate control unit.) These gateways set out to provide the SNA node functionality previously offered by a 3270 control unit—hence the name "controller." PU Controller Gateway setups are sometimes referred to as split-stack gateways, to distinguish them from the full-stack SNA solutions. The term "split-stack" emphasizes that the

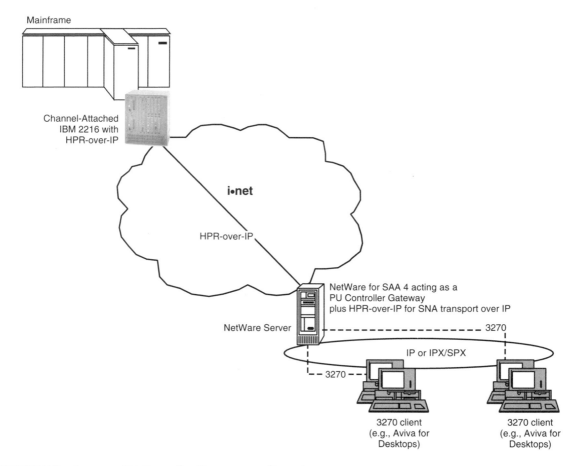

FIGURE 2.9 A remote PU Controller Gateway configuration.

total SNA functionality required by a PC or workstation to access an SNA application is distributed between the SNA node functionality in the PU Controller Gateway and the 3270 client emulation software running on the PC or workstation. Thus a tn3270(E) or tn5250 server is actually an example of a PU Controller Gateway.

With this approach, no SNA functionality is implemented at a client PC or workstation. Instead, the client PC or workstation runs an emulation package that supports 3270 emulation, 5250 emulation, file transfer, or LU 6.2 transactions. This package could interact with the PU Controller Gateway using a protocol such as TCP/IP, Novell's IPX/SPX, NetBIOS, or IEEE 802.2. The only protocol that cannot be used is SNA, because SNA software is not present at the client. In the context of SNA-capable i•nets, TCP/IP would serve as the protocol used between the client and the PU Controller

Gateway. If the client uses 3270 or 5250 emulation, this approach of having TCP/IP as the communications medium between the client and the gateway would be analogous to using tn3270 or tn5250. The only difference between these two approaches involves the exact nature of protocol that is encapsulated within the TCP/IP packets. In the case of tn3270/tn5250, it comprises an open, industry-standard protocol. In other TCP/IP-based, PU Controller-to-client approaches, this protocol will be proprietary. This book will use the terms **ip3270** and **ip5250** to describe scenarios involving a proprietary protocol, albeit encapsulated within standard TCP/IP, to communicate between a client and a gateway.

A key advantage of the PU Controller Gateway approach relates to the elimination of the need to define each LAN-attached device to the main-frame. This consideration is important in a network with a large number of PCs and workstations, especially if not all will access mainframe SNA applications at the same time. Nondedicated access to SNA is increasingly becoming the case, especially with SNA-capable i•nets, as the population of non-SNA applications adopted by enterprises continues to grow. With this type of gateway, only the gateway with 254 (and sometimes even more) SNA Logical Units (LUs) needs to be defined to the mainframe. SNA's addressing mechanism for type 2 nodes has a ceiling of 254 LUs per node. To circumvent this limitation, this type of gateway—like tn3270(E) servers—can emulate multiple separate type 2 nodes within the same piece of software. This type of multinode capability, known as multiple PU support, means that the mainframe requires a PU to be defined for each group of 254 consecutive LU definitions. The gateway provides an LU-allocation mechanism whereby a large population of PC/workstation users can contend, or "bid," for one or more LUs, if and when they are required to interact with a mainframe application.

In addition to minimizing the number of mainframe definitions required, PU Controller Gateways restrict all SNA node functionality to the gateway. Thus they require only a relatively small client running at the PC or workstation. The trend with SNA-capable i•nets is to move toward even thinner and dynamically loadable clients, in the form of applets, that would perform the 3270/5250 emulation. The 3270-to-HTML conversion technique described in Chapter 5 takes this "thin client" notion to another level by just requiring a standard browser at the PC or workstation so as to access SNA applications.

PU Controller Gateways have two drawbacks. First, they do not support SNA on an end-to-end, application-to-client basis. In the case of SNA-capable i•nets, this failure can no longer be deemed a problem, as most corporations now no longer want SNA to provide end-to-end support. Second, this type of gateway cannot support situations requiring full-stack SNA or APPN EN on a client PC/workstation—for example, if the company needs desktop LU 6.2 applications with COS prioritization. PU Passthrough Gateways were developed to eliminate these two weaknesses of PU Controller Gateways.

2.3.2 PU Passthrough Gateways

PU Passthrough Gateways work only with clients that have either full-stack SNA, an APPN EN, or an APPN NN. They can, however, support bona fide SNA devices, such as 3174s, AS/400s, and 4700s in addition to PCs and workstations running SNA/APPN software. This fundamental difference distinguishes Passthrough Gateways from Controller Gateways, as the latter focus on supporting PCs and workstations only.

As its name suggests, the PU Passthrough Gateway relays SNA message units between disparate types of communications media, whether it be LAN ↔ WAN, LAN ↔ mainframe channel, WAN ↔ mainframe channel, or i•net ↔ mainframe channel. A PU Passthrough Gateway transforms only the Layer 2 data link protocol that encapsulates the SNA message.

With the move toward SNA-capable i•nets, the significance of PU Passthrough Gateways will diminish. Initially, many SNA-capable i•nets will, however, require at least one PU Passthrough Gateway. This Passthrough Gateway will connect a mainframe channel and the i•net; examples are a 37xx, 3172, 2216/ESCON, or Cisco CIP. It will sustain SNA/APPN interactions between mainframe-resident applications, with either tn3270(E) servers, PU Controller Gateways, SNA-Web gateways, or downstream SNA devices being supported across the i•net using DLSw. Figure 2.10 illustrates the role of a PU Passthrough Gateway within an SNA-capable i•net.

An SNA-capable i•net will always require a PU Passthrough Gateway as long as legacy SNA-only devices remain within the network or TCP/IP client-to-SNA conversion is performed outside the mainframe. The need for even channel-attached PU Passthrough Gateways will disappear once all SNA-only devices have been decommissioned and PC/workstation access to SNA applications is realized via a mainframe resident tn3270(E) server. Under this scenario, no SNA per se will exist outside the mainframe. Instead, all traffic to and from the mainframe will take the form of TCP/IP messages.

2.3.3 PU Concentrator Gateways

With a PU Concentrator Gateway approach, SNA nodes are implemented both in the gateway and in each downstream client, as shown in Fig. 2.11. A PU Concentrator Gateway appears to the downstream clients as a mini-mainframe. It includes a subset of SNA SSCP functionality, and sets out to capture and control the SNA SSCP-related 'Control Sessions' that must be established and maintained by every downstream SNA device, such as PCs and workstations with full-stack SNA. These control sessions that must be captured and managed are the SSCP-PU and SSCP-LU sessions.

Given that the SSCP function in a PU Concentrator Gateway sits between the mainframe(s) and the actual clients, the real mainframes see only the PU Concentrator Gateways; each has a maximum of 254 SNA LUs corresponding

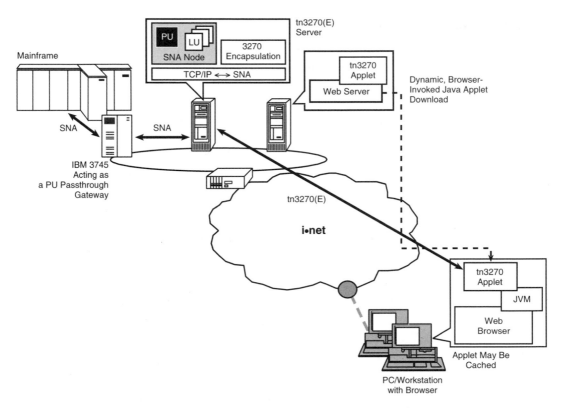

FIGURE 2.10   PU Passthrough Gateway in the context of an SNA-capable i•net.

to the number of SNA nodes it is emulating. The real mainframes do not see the individual downstream clients. In this respect, a PU Concentrator Gateway acts just like a PU Controller Gateway or a tn3270(E) server. In marked contrast to Controller Gateways, however, SNA is the only protocol used between the client and the Concentrator Gateway. In the case of SNA-capable i•nets, this client-to-gateway SNA traffic must be transported across the network via DLSw.

PU Concentrator Gateways provide a contention-based scheme whereby downstream clients can contend for use of the pool of LUs provided by the gateway so as to interact with an application in the mainframe. Thus, unlike in the case of a PU Passthrough Gateway, no end-to-end LU-LU session takes place between an application on the mainframe and the SNA client. Instead, two LU-LU sessions arise: one between the application and the gateway, and one between the gateway and the client. The system can leverage these pooled LUs in the gateway to enable a large number of actual full-stack SNA clients to gain access to a mainframe, without each client requiring a PU definition at the mainframe. The mainframe access takes advantage of

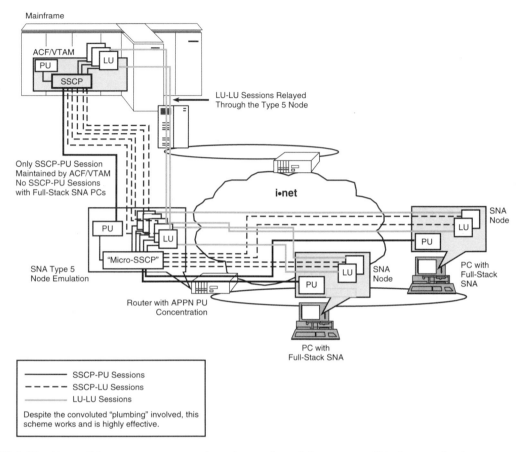

FIGURE 2.11   Using PU concentration to reduce the number of downstream PUs that need to be seen and supported by a mainframe ACF/VTAM.

the LUs defined for the Concentrator Gateway—and 254 such LUs exist for each PU defined within the gateway. In essence, this type of gateway, true to its name, permits a large number of SNA nodes (that is, downstream PUs) to be concentrated—or mapped onto—a smaller number of mainframe SNA node definitions.

This concentration exploits the fact that each SNA type 2 node can support 254 LUs. In reality, a downstream SNA client, especially a PC or workstation, is unlikely to use many more than 10 LUs. Nevertheless, given that each device is a bona fide SNA node, from a mainframe perspective each is no different from another node that does intend to use all 254 LUs. This perception could become an issue in situations where a mainframe PU Passthrough Gateway can support only a limited number of SNA nodes. This situation was once commonplace when trying to use a 3172 as a LAN-to-mainframe gateway.

To accommodate initial memory limitations, IBM restricted the 3172 to supporting only 1020 downstream SNA nodes. In reality, the limitation existed on a per-LAN adapter basis. A single 3172 LAN adapter could support a maximum of 255 SNA nodes. To accommodate 1020 downstream nodes, a 3172 would therefore require its full complement of four LAN adapters. Support for such a relatively small number of SNA nodes could prove extremely restrictive, especially with PCs and workstations running full-stack SNA. Even though each PC or workstation may use only a few LUs, each PC or workstation counts as one node.

PU Concentrator Gateways can overcome such limitations. With PU Concentration, only the gateway node, with a full complement of 254 LUs, would count as a single node, rather than each PC or workstation. If each PC or workstation used only one LU, as might be the case with 3270 emulation, an immediate 1-to-254 multiplier factor would apply. In that case, a 3172, rather than supporting a maximum of 1020 PCs or workstations, could theoretically support the work flow of 259,000 PCs and workstations!

A need may still exist for PU Concentrator Gateways within SNA-capable i•nets to circumvent such gateway capacity limitations. Some of today's channel-attached mainframe gateways (in particular, Cisco 7xxx/CIPs and Bus-Tech NetShuttles) now have built-in PU Concentration so as to support large populations of SNA clients. The need for PU Concentration will, however, diminish as corporations migrate away from SNA clients to TCP/IP clients. For a start, fewer full-stack SNA clients and devices will need to be supported. In addition, tn3270(E) servers and PU Controllers working in ip3270 mode already utilize the full 254 LUs-to-PU mapping scheme, thus obviating the need for further concentration.

2.4   HPR AND HPR-OVER-IP: SNA'S LAST HURRAH

High Performance Routing (HPR) is the latest, and most likely the final, incarnation of SNA. From a technical standpoint, it represents the pinnacle in the evolutionary ascendancy of the illustrious clan of SNA architectures. Unlike APPN, it was intended to inherit SNA's mantle and propagate SNA's heritage of value-added, mission-critical networking into the twenty-first century. HPR is a refreshing new paradigm for SNA-centric, peer-to-peer networking that boasts an impressive list of features, including dynamic alternate routing and anticipatory congestion control, to justify its right to be considered SNA's true successor. Unfortunately, HPR's progress toward inheriting the commercial-sector networking market from SNA fell afoul of the relentless popularity of i•nets, and it lost its mandate to TCP/IP. IBM, however, has not given up on HPR altogether. Acknowledging the ascendancy of IP, IBM is now trying to propagate and promote HPR, in the form of HPR-over-IP, as a strategic alternative to the ubiquitous, but nearly decade-old Data Link Switching.

HPR's primary raison d'être was to serve as a low-overhead, nimble, dynamic, and secure transport for SNA traffic within high-speed, broadband networks—in particular, ATM-based networks. IBM initially positioned HPR in the early 1990s as the follow-on to APPN. In reality, HPR was always much more. This totally new architecture dramatically revamped the networking concepts and capabilities hitherto associated with SNA and APPN networks. HPR was one of the most significant and dramatic meta-morphoses undergone by SNA in its eventful history. Its role in reshaping IBM-centric networking matched that of some of the most noteworthy land-marks in IBM-oriented networking, such as cross-domain routing between multiple mainframes (in 1976), virtual routes and transmission groups (1979), LU 6.2 (1982), and Token Ring LANs (1986).

HPR is a very contemporary, Layer 2-based routing scheme that, in the vein of Frame Relay and ATM, eschews processing and error checking at intermediate nodes. Its total functionality, although extensive, remains con-tained within Layer 2 from an architectural standpoint. This approach repre-sents a major departure from previous SNA and APPN routing schemes, which in addition to taking place in Layers 3 and 4, required considerable table lookups and processing at each intermediate node. It also indicates a major difference between HPR and IP. This aspect of IP is now being adroit-ly compensated for by IP switching or Layer 3 forwarding mechanisms; these mechanisms, in essence, attempt to obviate the need for IP-related Layer 3 processing at intermediate nodes once the end-to-end path for a par-ticular connection has been initially established via traditional IP routing.

HPR also served as the first IBM networking scheme to include nondis-ruptive dynamic alternate rerouting in the event of path failure—hitherto an Achilles heel for APPN, Source-Route Bridging (SRB), and SNA. HPR's dynamic alternate routing is, however, somewhat atypical and very different from that employed by IP. In HPR, a path failure necessitating a reroute can be detected and performed only by one or both end points. Unlike with other dynamic alternate rerouting schemes, the intermediate node that actually experiences the path failure cannot perform a path switch. The inability will delay the amount of time taken before the switch occurs.

In addition, HPR boasts a highly sophisticated congestion control mecha-nism that works by trying to anticipate and avoid congestion from building up within the network, rather than trying to detect and dissipate it after the con-gestion has already occurred. All of these value-added features are seamlessly synthesized and carefully integrated with the user-friendly plug-and-play net-working infrastructure originally pioneered by APPN. This infrastructure includes automatic end-node registration and dynamic location of remote LUs. HPR is, however, not exactly new or untested. The architecture was developed in the early 1990s, and the first implementations of HPR became available in mid-1995 on ACF/VTAM version 4, release 3, and ACF/NCP version 7, release 3. Today, HPR is available on many devices, including the IBM 2216, IBM 2212, IBM 3172, Cisco's bridge/routers, IBM's CS/NT, and Novell's NetWare for SAA.

HPR was meant to be used, in native mode, across LANs, Frame Relay, X.25, SDLC leased lines, or ATM—à la SNA or APPN. Nevertheless, the primary transport mechanism used by HPR will be IP, through HPR-over-IP. Bypassing error checking and error recovery at intermediate nodes is a key precept of HPR. Hence, wherever possible HPR, in marked contrast to SNA's total reliance on session-based protocols, attempts to use a "connectionless" protocol across the links; for example, it resorts to the "no sequence number" Unnumbered Information (UI) frame capability in SDLC rather than to the sequence-numbered I-Frames that are mandatory in SNA and APPN. Although it prefers to restrict error checking to each end of a connection, HPR does, however, offer an option of performing intermediate node error checking and recovery if the links are deemed "noisy" or unreliable.

This preference for lower-layer connectionless protocols is echoed in HPR-over-IP. Instead of using TCP and its guaranteed delivery scheme, HPR-over-IP, in marked contrast to DLSw and tn3270, opts for the unreliable **User Datagram Protocol (UDP)** as its IP-based delivery mechanism. The use of unreliable, connectionless protocols at the link layer does not mean that HPR is remiss in ensuring the end-to-end fidelity and integrity of data transmissions. In fact, it relies on an end-to-end protocol, connection-oriented **Rapid Transport Protocol (RTP)** to realize a highly reliable, in-sequence data delivery scheme between end nodes. The pivotal issue here is that HPR elects to forgo error checking and error correction at each intermediary to generally expedite overall message throughput, working on the assumptions that errors will be relatively infrequent given the very low error rates of today's data links.

In common with APPN, HPR directly supports only SNA LU 6.2 peer-to-peer, program-to-program traffic. Non-LU 6.2 SNA traffic (in particular, 3270 traffic) as in the case with APPN, is supported only via DLUS/DLUR technology. Another trait that HPR and APPN share relates to their inclusion of IBM-patented technology. Therefore, just as with APPN NNs, a license is required from IBM before a vendor can implement HPR-based routing.

HPR is very eclectic and has borrowed many ideas from IP, SNA, APPN, Frame Relay, and IP switching. Connection networks, which are also supported by HPR-over-IP, are HPR's equivalent of IP switching and permit direct, end-to-end communications without the need for continual routing via an HPR NN.

2.4.1   The Highlights of HPR

HPR had a very straightforward and intuitive mission. It set out to eradicate the major weaknesses inherent in SNA, TCP/IP, and APPN, while simultaneously trying to capitalize on their strengths. (Table 2.2 summarizes the strengths and weakness of SNA, APPN, HPR, and TCP/IP.) Consequently, HPR is unashamedly eclectic. In essence, it represents an inspired amalgamation of the best features found in IP, SNA, APPN, and Frame Relay. From

TABLE 2.2 Strengths and weaknesses of IP, SNA, APPN, and HPR.

	Strengths	*Weaknesses*
IP	• Now the wholly victorious and undisputed "king of protocols" thanks to its pivotal role in sustaining the Internet; has the undivided mind share and reverence of the entire industry and market • Dynamic, scalable networking • Open, egalitarian standard • Has been the underlying basis for enterprise multiprotocol networking since the mid-1990s	• Need to move to IPv6 to overcome the increasingly acute address space limitations • Headers and protocols are not as compact as those of SNA • Congestion control needs improving • Not adverse to arbitrarily discarding packets when in a jam
SNA	• Highly reliable, resilient networking scheme based on a hierarchy of end-to-end sessions • Predictable, consistent performance in most instances • Single network could support hundreds of thousands of users • Compact, highly optimized protocols • Used to be a highly open protocol with no patents or licenses	• No longer deemed strategic by IBM, the industry, or the market • No dynamic alternative routing in the event of a path failure • Not a plug-and-play architecture • Hierarchical, mainframe-oriented control scheme • LU 6.2 was too complex
APPN	• Peer-to-peer, mainframe-independent networking • Peerless, plug-and-play networking • Sophisticated multicriteria path selection scheme	• Required DLUS/DLUR for generalized support of 3270 sessions • Patented technology that irked other vendors • No dynamic alternative routing in the event of a path failure • No support for any non-SNA protocols in multiprotocol environments
HPR	• Dynamic alternative routing • Agile, Layer 2-specific routing mechanism • Powerful congestion control	• Required DLUS/DLUR for generalized support of 3270 sessions • Patented technology • No support for any non-SNA protocols in multiprotocol environments • Had already lost moral high-ground to IP by the time it was ready for prime time

SNA, HPR's RTP protocol borrows the notion of session-based interactions that provide reliable communications with predictable and deterministic response characteristics. HPR also shares SNA's concern for congestion avoidance and control, although HPR uses its own state-of-the-art anticipatory scheme, which differs dramatically from SNA's and APPN's window-size-based pacing schemes.

APPN provides HPR with its overall framework and infrastructure. From an architectural perspective, HPR could be viewed as merely replacing APPN's Layer 3-based **Intermediate Session Routing (ISR)** component without altering too much of the remaining architecture. Figure 2.12 compares and contrasts the HPR protocol stack with that of APPN. HPR benefits from APPN's peerless mechanisms for distributed directory-inspired "plug-and-play" networking, as well as COS-dictated traffic prioritization and path selection. IBM, to its credit, manages to maintain these attributes with HPR-over-IP.

Like Frame Relay, HPR performs all of its protocol processing and network routing at Layer 2; in HPR-over-IP, in contrast, the HPR protocols run over UDP (a Layer 4 transport protocol per the OSI Model). The lion's share

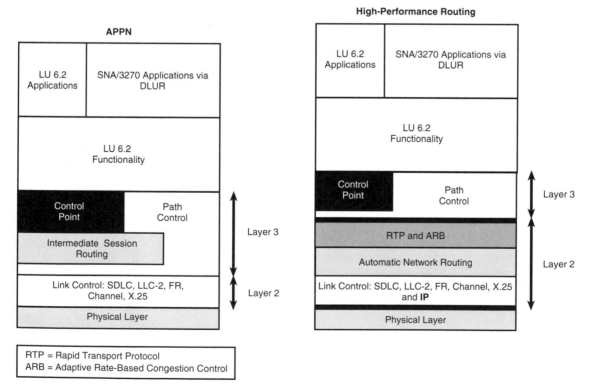

FIGURE 2.12 Comparison of HPR's Layer 2-heavy protocol stack with that of APPN.

of this processing occurs at the start and end nodes, with intermediary nodes doing minimal processing to route HPR packets to their eventual destination.

HPR apes IP in offering dynamic alternate routing. Its alternate routing, however, is executed only on an end-to-end basis and can be instituted by only an end node, rather than an intermediate node that actually detects a path failure. Thus HPR is not as agile and fast-recovering as a scheme that permits intermediate nodes to reroute data over another path when the original path becomes disrupted or overly congested. Relying on the end nodes to recover from a path failure and to establish a new end-to-end route is consistent with HPR's goal of minimizing intermediate node processing, as well as its emphasis on selecting the optimum path based on prevailing COS criteria and network topology. Route failure detection, and the subsequent establishment of a new path, are performed by the RTP components at each end node. Implied within this routing scheme is the fact that HPR, like SNA and APPN, uses a fixed, end-to-end path for a given session, as opposed to endorsing a dynamic scheme where an intermediate node may detect and use a more optimum, newly established route to the destination.

True to a notion held dear in SNA, HPR relies on end-to-end sessions for end-user data transfers. These sessions are built on top of a connectionless routing scheme, such as UDP. Until HPR, connectionless networking—much like dynamic alternate routing—was another networking notion that was totally alien to IBM. HPR's technique of using RTP connections as a guaranteed delivery mechanism on top of a connectionless fabric is essentially what TCP provides as a guaranteed delivery mechanism when it is deployed on top of IP. In the case of HPR-over-IP, RTP acts as the guaranteed delivery mechanism that runs on top of UDP and IP.

The quintessential characteristics of HPR can be summarized as follows. First, all processing is performed at and restricted to Layer 2, as in Frame Relay. In Frame Relay, end nodes carry out much of the processing, with only a bare minimum being performed by the intermediate nodes.

Second, HPR provides nondisruptive, dynamic alternate rerouting in the event of path failure. Only the two end nodes can establish and institute a new end-to-end path for the traffic that needs to be rerouted, however.

Third, HPR relies on a low-overhead, connectionless internode routing mechanism based on a Source-Route Bridging (SRB)-like **Routing Information Field (RIF).** The RIF is prefixed to every HPR message unit and specifies the path to be traversed by that message unit in terms of a hop-by-hop list of link addresses through the various intermediary nodes. The HPR equivalent of RIF is known as the **Automatic Network Routing Field (ANRF).** HPR-over-IP also uses this ANRF routing information.

Fourth, HPR can bypass intermediate nodes having to perform link-level error checking and recovery, as well as message unit segmentation or reassembly. Instead, it employs end-to-end processing.

Fifth, it provides selective retransmission in the form of selective rejections of failed or missing message units, rather than retransmitting all message units between the failed or missing one to the last message unit in the acknowledgment cycle (as is the case with SDLC, LLC-2, or even TCP). This key throughput-enhancing and congestion-minimizing feature is discussed in Section 3.6.

Sixth, the plug-and-play networking of APPN is achieved through the synergistic combination of several independent facilities. The dynamic location of remote LUs takes place via a broadcast search mechanism that is augmented with cache directory entries to preclude repeated searches for previously found LUs. In addition, optional central directory servers can further minimize the number of broadcast searches performed. When central directories are used, source APPN/HPR nodes attempting to locate an unknown LU would first interrogate a central directory server (for example, a mainframe or AS/400). If the central server does not have an entry for that LU, it would conduct a broadcast search on behalf of the source node.

The dynamic registration of end nodes obviates the need to manually predefine the names of all LUs resident in the various end nodes attached to a given HPR NN, as is the case when attaching an SNA peripheral node to an SNA subarea node. [Since mid-1992, with ACF/VTAM 3.4, IBM has offered a feature known as **Dynamic Definition of Dependent LUs (DDDLU)** that belatedly provides dynamic peripheral node LU registration support along the lines of what is available in APPN/HPR.]

The **connection network** concept permits direct end node-to-end node data interchange across LANs, without all traffic being relayed across one or more NNs and without the burden and overhead of each end node having to know the LAN MAC address of the other end nodes. Consider, for example, a network of 50 LAN-attached PCs, where the LANs might be interconnected via bridges or routers. Assume that HPR-based SNA interactions are required between all of these PCs. This setup can be effortlessly achieved through conventional HPR NN routing. Such routing would involve the NN acting as a relay point between the two PCs, despite the fact that the two PCs obviously have a direct communication path with each other through the LAN. One way to eliminate the need for routing of all messages through the NN is to ensure that all PCs know the destination MAC addresses of all other PCs. Defining and maintaining such MAC address lists on every PC can prove cumbersome and difficult even with a small network of 50 PCs. It would be totally infeasible when dealing with hundreds or thousands of LAN-attached PCs.

Connection networks provide an elegant solution to this challenge. Rather than having to know all destination MAC addresses or route everything through an NN node, the NN carries out the routing operation once and then hands over the relevant destination MAC address to the source PC. The

PCs can then talk directly to each other over the LAN, without intervention from the NN. This scheme also obviates the need for the PCs to know the MAC addresses of each other.

In reality, connection networks can be envisioned as **HPR switching,** because the notion is the same as that of Layer 3 switching: Route once, then switch or forward directly to the destination using a Layer 2 address. HPR-over-IP also supports connection networks for both LAN-attached and IP-attached nodes. Thus it would be possible to have direct node-to-node interactions, using the IP addresses of the nodes, once the destination node has been located by an HPR NN node.

The plug-and-play networking also takes advantage of the optional implementation-dependent facility whereby LAN-resident NNs can automatically and periodically advertise their presence via a broadcast message over the LAN.

Seventh, HPR exploits a state-of-the-art, congestion anticipation and avoidance scheme based on a closed-loop feedback mechanism. This scheme, known as ARB, continually measures the rate at which data are delivered to a given receiver across the network and the rate at which the receiver forwards those data to the ultimate end user. If the rate at which data are being received and forwarded to the end user is roughly equivalent to the data transmission rate, the receiver assumes that no congestion exists within the network or at the receiving node. On the other hand, if the receive rate or the forward rate is less than the transmit rate, some congestion may be occurring within the network or receiving node. If HPR detects such congestion, it dynamically lowers the transmission rate until its feedback mechanism indicates that no perceptible congestion remains.

Eighth, HPR boasts a multiple-criteria-based, COS-oriented path selection scheme like that found in APPN. As with APPN, as many as nine physical link-related criteria can be specified for a given path: preferred cost to transmit a byte, acceptable connection cost per minute for a switched connection, desired amount of bandwidth, desirable propagation delay characteristics, physical link security requirements, preferred modem types, and three customer- or network-specified criteria. When one or more of these criteria are specified for a path, HPR endeavors to ensure that all physical links traversed end-to-end by this path conform to the stated criteria. HPR-over-IP continues to support COS for path selection and traffic prioritization. The need to support COS on an end-to-end basis is one of two irrefutable arguments for opting for HPR-over-IP rather than DLSw as the means of transporting SNA/APPN traffic over an i•net.

Ninth, HPR provides dynamic promulgation of network configuration change information between all network nodes via the **Topology Database Update (TDU)** scheme pioneered by APPN. This scheme for automatically adapting to all network topology changes, including the availability of network nodes and the links between such nodes, eliminates the need for human intervention each time an NN or link between NNs fails or becomes reactivated.

Tenth, COS-based, end-to-end traffic prioritization assigns a high, medium, or low transmission priority to the traffic associated with each session in HPR, much like in APPN. HPR-over-IP supports this COS-based traffic prioritization by using separate UDP port numbers, with one port being dedicated to each transmission priority.

Eleventh, HPR offers the optional capability of automatically disconnecting "switched connections" if they have not been used for a predesignated amount of time; inactivity is defined as a lack of session traffic across a given link. This useful feature, which is also available on SNA and APPN, saves switched connection costs by eliminating the possibility of nonproductive switched connections. IBM calls this capability Limited Resource Link Deactivation.

Finally, HPR was originally supposed to support SNA-like parallel link transmission groups (TGs) to facilitate load balancing and safeguard against single link failures. As with APPN, this feature is now inexplicably absent from the official architecture. Certain HPR implementations remain committed to supporting TGs, however. At some point, the architecture will likely be updated to embrace this valuable and quintessential SNA facility. HPR-over-IP does support parallel TGs, where the parallel links are implemented in the form of IP connections.

2.4.2   Thumbnail Sketch of the HPR Architecture

As shown in Fig. 2.12, HPR adds three new functional components at Layer 2 to the APPN network node architecture. In parallel, it replaces the APPN NN Control Point (CP) and the Intermediate Session Routing (ISR) component with an HPR-specific Control Point. ISR, in APPN, handles intermediate routing between APPN NNs. In HPR, this function is performed by **Automatic Network Routing (ANR)**.

In practice, HPR is a replacement for only APPN NNs; HPR functionality per se is not included within end nodes. Instead, HPR NNs work seamlessly with APPN end nodes and type 2.1 peer-to-peer nodes, and use DLUR technology to support SNA nodes. In each of these instances, HPR NNs appear to end nodes as either APPN NN or type 2.1 nodes. HPR NN awareness thus remains restricted to other HPR NNs; it does not extend to the end or peripheral nodes.

The three new Layer 2 functional components that make up HPR are Automatic Network Routing (ANR), Rapid Transport Protocol (RTP), and Adaptive Rate-Based (ARB) congestion control. ANR is a very low-overhead, connectionless routing mechanism for rapidly forwarding message units along a predetermined path. It relies on a RIF, reminiscent of SRB, which is referred to as an ANR Routing Field (ANRF), to denote the path along which a given message unit will be forwarded. Every HPR packet is prefixed by an ANRF that occurs within the Network Layer Header (NHDR) of an HPR packet. HPR-over-IP also relies on this ANRF to determine the end-to-end route through the network.

HPR uses the standard remote LU broadcast search and the COS-based multiple-criteria route calculation mechanisms that were developed for APPN to determine the initial end-to-end path for an HPR-based session. This route is then specified in the ANRF through a series of ANR labels that sequentially identify each intermediate link making up that route. IBM estimates that ANRF-based routing, which is accomplished at Layer 2, will be at least three times faster than the APPN routing scheme. The elimination of "session connector" control blocks should also free up 500 bytes of memory per session at each intermediate node. ANR, as the lowest layer of HPR, also takes responsibility for traffic prioritization. In HPR-over-IP, this traffic prioritization is realized using three separate UDP ports, with one port being dedicated to each of the three priority levels.

RTP, which sits above ANR, is a connection-oriented, end-to-end, full-duplex protocol. HPR uses RTP connections to provide a reliable, in-sequence FIFO (first in, first out) transport mechanism for both LU-LU and CP-CP traffic. RTP also performs ARB-based congestion avoidance data flow control. Its functions, including error recovery via selective retransmission and message unit segmenting/reassembly, are performed only at the end nodes of an RTP connection. The elimination of RTP processing at intermediate nodes is intended to improve the performance of HPR.

RTP, rather than ANR, takes responsibility for the end-user, transparent, nondisruptive dynamic path switching capability of HPR. RTP, however, realizes such dynamic rerouting by substituting a new ANRF in place of the ANRF corresponding to the failed path. Hence, this dynamic alternate rerouting must be performed by an end node, rather than an intermediate node. Four conditions, or triggers, will cause RTP to perform a dynamic path switch:

- The failure of a local link attached to one of the two end-to-end HPR nodes that have an RTP connection between them. No RTP processing is available at intermediate nodes for a given connection.

- HPR NN's receipt of a Topology Database Update (TDU) indicating that a remote HPR link failed.

- Detection of an RTP connection failure, as indicated by repeated timeouts, during an attempted status exchange sequence, which would itself have been triggered by the expiration of a "keep-alive" timer. RTP uses a total of five timers at each end of an RTP connection, with two of them monitoring the ongoing availability of that connection. HPR-over-IP uses a "liveness" interaction, realized using the data link control TEST

HPR consists of three Layer 2-based functional components, including an anticipatory congestion control mechanism. The end-to-end RTP protocol is the glue that holds HPR together and also plays a key role in HPR-over-IP.

command and its response, with a default timer of 10 seconds to monitor for connection failures.

- Request from a human or automated network manager.

When a dynamic path switch is required, HPR solicits the help of its coresident HPR CP to recalculate a new end-to-end path based on the original COS requirements. The HPR CP will attempt to accomplish this task by using the latest network configuration status, as reflected in its Network Topology Database. If an alternative route is located, a new ANRF corresponding to that route is generated. This new ANRF will then prefix all subsequent message units belonging to the rerouted RTP connections.

2.4.3   HPR-Over-IP

HPR-over-IP, which IBM calls Enterprise Extender, is now available on IBM 2216, 2212, and 2210 bridge/routers as well as on IBM CS/NT and Novell NetWare for SAA 4 Servers. Although positioned as a strategic and scalable alternative to DLSw, HPR-over-IP has the edge over DLSw in only two specialized and esoteric applications: direct data center-to-data center routing and end-to-end, COS-based traffic prioritization.

Around 1996, IBM realized that the future of enterprise networks lay with i•nets rather than SNA/HPR-based networks. To accommodate this networking trend and still recoup some of its considerable investment in HPR, IBM introduced the notion of HPR-over-IP, referred to in IBM marketing-speak as Enterprise Extender. HPR-over-IP, which uses UDP on top of IP as its underlying transport mechanism, extends the value proposition of HPR—especially in terms of COS, connection networks, and HPR NN routing—to i•nets (in particular, intranets). In May 1998, IBM submitted an RFC for HPR-over-IP, (RFC 2353). Even within the RFC, HPR-over-IP is explicitly targeted as a scalable and high-availability alternative to DLSw—which happened to be IBM's original method for supporting SNA/APPN for IP in 1992.

HPR-over-IP has two irrefutable and redeeming attributes that give it a distinct edge over DLSw:

- Its ability to perform native SNA routing between data centers across an i•net, thus eliminating two-hop routing or the need to have icons or URLs corresponding to each data center
- Its ability to support end-to-end, COS-based traffic prioritization and route selection

If a corporation does not have a pressing or strictly justifiable need for either or both these facilities, it will be better off opting for the highly proven and widely available capability of DLSw as its preferred means of supporting SNA/APPN traffic across i•nets.

HPR-over-IP is now available on IBM 2216, 2212, and 2210 bridge/routers as well as on IBM's CS/NT and Novell's NetWare for SAA 4 Servers. Figure 2.13 depicts a representative HPR-over-IP network built around CS/NT servers at remote locations and IBM routers. To fully exploit

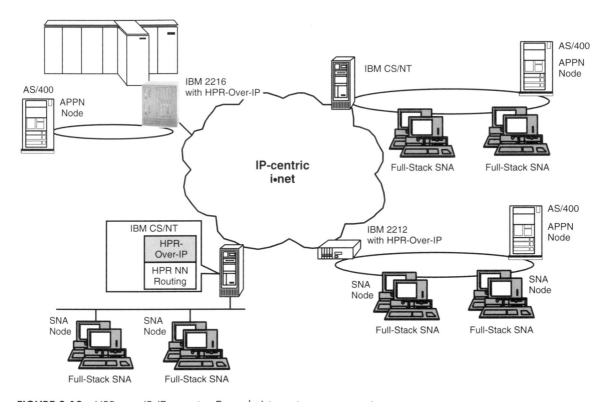

FIGURE 2.13   HPR-over-IP (Enterprise Extender) in action across an i•net.

the power of HPR-over-IP in the type of network shown in Fig. 2.13, especially COS-based traffic prioritization, one needs full-function SNA/APPN emulators at the end nodes, such as IBM's PComm emulator running on PCs.

With RFC 2353, IBM essentially added IP as a viable transport scheme for HPR. As discussed earlier, HPR-over-IP uses UDP as its delivery mechanism over IP. The unreliable nature of UDP, rather than being a problem, is an advantage with HPR because HPR's critical RTP protocol is designed to operate over connectionless transport mechanisms. HPR-over-IP cleverly leverages UDP to explicitly distinguish between multiple destinations within a given node and to realize COS-based traffic prioritization by using separate UDP port numbers to serve message units tagged as being of high, medium, or low priority. (It also allocates a fourth UDP port to handle the ultra-high-priority, network-level messages used by HPR to maintain and manage its overall network configuration.)

The salient features of HPR-over-IP—such as its support for connection networks and TGs—have already been discussed within the overall context of HPR. Details on the implementation of HPR-over-IP appear in RFC 2353. By year-end 1999, HPR-over-IP support should be available on other products—in particular, Cisco and Nortel Networks/Bay routers. At that point, it will indeed be a direct, multivendor-endorsed alternative to DLSw. It is unlikely to have the edge over DLSw, however, unless an enterprise requires SNA/HPR-based data center-to-data center routing or COS-based traffic prioritization. Although scalability was definitely an issue with the original DLSw, DLSw V2 goes a long way toward addressing the scalability issues. as discussed in Chapter 4. Hence scalability is unlikely to be the sole deciding factor between DLSw and HPR-over-IP. The relative merits of DLSw over HPR-over-IP are discussed further in Chapter 4.

2.5 THE LAST WORD

SNA-only networks are now anachronistic and rapidly heading toward extinction. This trend does not, however, mean that the huge base of mission-critical SNA applications will become redundant soon. Instead, these applications will continue to play a major role in sustaining worldwide commerce well into the twenty-first century. Rather than working in conjunction with an SNA network, these applications will be accessed and used over TCP/IP-based i•nets. The enduring longevity of SNA applications in an increasingly TCP/IP-oriented world is not as incongruous as it might first appear. With revenue and profitability at stake, corporations move very cautiously and conservatively when it comes to replacing mission-critical applications. The presence of SNA applications, along with the adoption of Parallel Sysplex, explains why data centers will remain SNA-oriented while the network evolves toward becoming an i•net. The various SNA gateways now available—in particular, tn3270(E) servers, which are a variant of the old PU Controller Gateways, and SNA-Web gateways—will help ensure that end users continue to have access to SNA resources across TCP/IP-based i•nets.

In hindsight, it is easy to see which factors undermined the popularity of SNA. SNA's inability to cogently deal with multiprotocol networking was a major contributing factor. Another issue was the insidious but inescapable spread of the Internet's influence into most facets of everyday life, whether professional or personal. Prior to being unceremoniously swept aside by the sudden ascendancy of i•nets around 1996–1997, HPR had been carefully groomed to be the anointed heir to the once extensive and lucrative SNA kingdom. Architecturally, HPR is the most powerful and compelling iteration of IBM. Its strengths include agile and very low-fat Layer 2 routing; dynamic alternate routing; anticipatory congestion control; elimination of intermediate node processing; and the notion of HPR switching (à la connection networks). Because of the wholesale move toward i•nets, however, HPR's role in the future will likely remain restricted to HPR-over-IP implementations. In this scheme, HPR routing, replete with COS, TGs, and connection networks, will be performed on top of a UDP/IP network. Although a direct alternative to DLSw, HPR-over-IP has a true edge over DLSw only if an enterprise requires SNA/HPR-based routing between data centers or support for bona fide end-to-end traffic prioritization based on SNA/HPR COS.

Despite their seamless support of SNA, SNA-capable i•nets differ from traditional SNA/APPN networks as chalk does from cheese. These differences are discussed in the next chapter.

Differences between SNA Networks and SNA-Capable i•nets

Using a combination of DLSw, fully featured 3270 emulators talking ip320 via SNA-LAN gateways, tn3270(E), tn5250, and browser-based SNA access, it is indeed possible to support any type of SNA interaction or session type across a TCP/IP-based i•net. The full-function emulators in this case could include IBM's PComm, Attachmate's EXTRA! Personal Client, or Eicon's Aviva for Desktops, while the SNA LAN gateway could, for example, be Microsoft's SNA Server, Novell's NetWare for SAA, or IBM's Communications Server for CN (CS/NT). DLSw, which essentially performs LAN-to-LAN transparent bridging over TCP/IP, supports any and all SNA traffic, irrespective of the SNA session type being used. Its function as an end-to-end SNA transport, however, is contingent on having SNA clients or SNA devices downstream of the TCP/IP backbone. In instances where corporations wish to use TCP/IP-oriented clients with their PCs, workstations, and NCs, fully featured 3270 emulators (or "fat clients"), tn3270(E), or browser-based access can be used to ensure unrestricted access to 3270-based SNA applications and print services. tn5250 provides equivalent access to AS/400-centric SNA applications and print services.

This ability of i•nets to easily accommodate SNA traffic and access should not be construed to mean that i•nets are essentially no different from the SNA-only networks that they displace. This, unfortunately, is not true. Some of the characteristics and behavior of i•nets are markedly at odds with those of SNA networks. The key differences between SNA networks and SNA-capable i•nets lie in the following areas:

- Reliability and resilience that could affect high availability
- Security

The ability of SNA-capable i•nets to adroitly support SNA access and SNA traffic disguises the fact that many key characteristics of these TCP/IP-based networks, including reliability, security, and performance, can be very different from those associated with SNA-based networks.

- Application switching and routing between data centers based on SNA-like or APPN-like routing
- Consistent and predictable response times
- Class-of-Service (COS) and traffic prioritization
- Congestion control
- Scalability
- Network management
- Application usage accounting

Most of these differences will certainly be more acute and worrisome in the case of SNA interactions conducted across the Internet than in those performed across an intranet or extranet. Although corporations can and should control the manner in which an intranet or extranet is implemented and operated, they have little, if any, influence when it comes to the functioning of the Internet. The Internet is not just another public network; it is an unregulated, free-wheeling organism that is not owned or controlled by a single, truly accountable entity. The Internet is really anarchy, in the best possible sense of the word, à la networking.

The Internet should never be viewed as yet another example of a public, packet-switching network that is no different than a public X.25 or Frame Relay network. A fundamental and pivotal difference exists between X.25 and Frame Relay public networks and the Internet when it comes to security. Public X.25 and Frame Relay networks are provided by either large corporations or well-known carriers. Once traffic has entered a public X.25 or Frame Relay network, it traverses only intermediate packet-switching nodes that are owned, administered, and managed by the network service providers. It would be difficult (though not impossible) for a hacker to infiltrate these specialized packet-switching nodes so as to intercept and scan the traffic being routed through them—particularly given that these specialized switches typically rely on their own proprietary software kernels rather than using conventional operating systems such as UNIX or Windows NT. In addition, traffic that must travel across multiple public networks, as in international transactions, would be channeled between the networks via secure and well-governed gateways to ensure privacy and data integrity. Consequently, public X.25 and Frame Relay networks offer generally safe and secure means for data transfer with solid and proven track records for safeguarding their clients' data.

The physical links used by these public networks, such as the T1 trunks between the switches, are possibly the most vulnerable components when it comes to security. A hacker with enough motivation and resources (in particular, sophisticated equipment) could, in theory, try to tap into the links using various electromagnetic clamps. In addition, a disgruntled or corrupted employee working for the public network provider could potentially invoke certain diagnostic traces or dumps to obtain access to the data flowing in the network. Both of these security risks apply to all types of networks and systems, however, and the only way to guard against them is to use high-caliber, end-to-end encryption, such as Triple DES encryption. Thus the bottom line when it comes to security on public X.25 or Frame Relay networks is that these configurations have a proven track record of being safe and essentially immune from unauthorized prying of the subscriber data being transported.

IBM acknowledged the relatively high security inherent in public X.25 and Frame Relay networks when it specified the various possible link characteristics for APPN links. The randomness and the data multiplexing that occur on an ongoing basis on a public switched network make it rather difficult for a potential infiltrator to target the traffic belonging to a specific corporation or a given session. In this context, "randomness" refers to the fact that data are continually switched to different links and different paths within the network, whereas "data multiplexing" enables multiple users to share the same physical links. Thus IBM, in the context of APPN link security, classified public switched networks as being more secure than leased lines that were not buried underground or contained in secure conduits that hindered electromagnetic tapping. Interestingly, the highest level of link security cited by APPN was gas-pressurized conduits, where any attempt to break into the conduit so as to tap it would cause a fluctuation in the gas pressure and thereby trigger an alert.

In terms of security, the Internet differs significantly from public Frame Relay and X.25 networks in several ways. Unlike with a public switched network, no one entity runs the Internet. Instead, the Internet is a huge collection of computers, belonging to a myriad of organizations ranging from academic and government organizations to overtly commercial corporations. Traffic traversing the Internet could therefore go across computers and networks owned and operated by many independent organizations. In nearly all cases, Internet users will remain unaware of the exact routes used for their various data transfers—and hence the various computers, networks, and independent organizations involved in performing those data transfers.

This structure is the fundamental problem—but also the enduring beauty—of the Internet. It is a public utility that continues to flourish despite not having a central controlling or accountable authority. Corporations or individuals cannot seek or obtain a charter, contract, or service-level agreement related to their envisaged use of the Internet. Even a mega-ISP, such as AT&T or MCI, cannot guarantee specific availability, privacy, or throughput expectations related to overall Internet usage, because no one has power or jurisdiction over the functioning of the entire Internet. This lack of a financially motivated and obligated controlling authority constitutes the crucial difference between the Internet and a public Frame Relay or X.25 network.

It explains why one cannot demand or expect the same degree of service when it comes to reliability, consistent performance, or security from the Internet as one can from other public switched networks.

3.1 THE AVAILABILITY OF SNA-CAPABLE I•NETS

The reliability of SNA networks is legendary. For many years, corporations have taken for granted that they can expect 99% or even better availability (that is, up time) from their mission-critical SNA networks. SNA subarea networks are the archetypal 24 × 7, nonstop networks. Although SNA's assiduously crafted architecture does play a role in its overall robustness, the real key to the unparalleled reliability and resilience of subarea SNA networks lies in the quality and maturity of the primary products used to implement these networks (such as ACF/VTAM, ACF/NCP, 3745s, mainframes, MVS Operating System, 3174 control units, TSO, CICS, IMS, and DB2). In the late 1970s and early 1980s, the early SNA networks were not nearly as robust as today's SNA networks. In those days, network outages, such as an NCP crash on a channel-attached 3705, might occur on a weekly or even daily basis. This fallibility was to be expected, because most SNA products were new and evolving. Only around 1983 to 1984, some 10 years after the unveiling of SNA, did IBM start to deliver highly tested, proven, and increasingly stable building blocks for high-availability SNA networks in the form of version 2 software releases for both ACF/VTAM and ACF/NCP.

With the move to SNA-capable i•nets, the issue of availability now arises again because much of the proven and bullet-proof infrastructure of existing SNA networks will be supplanted by new TCP/IP- and Web-oriented software and hardware components. Although the overall Internet concept remains proven and solid, the robustness of many of the components needed to implement an i•net, such as Web servers, Web browsers, and applet technology, will mimic that of SNA software during its first decade of evolution. Such problems are not unexpected, given that most Web-related technology was first formulated and formalized only around 1992. Moreover, this technology is evolving rapidly, with multiple vendors aggressively vying to gain a competitive lead by adding more features and capability.

In this area, SNA networks clearly have an edge over i•nets. With SNA, IBM dictated and controlled the innovation process, whether it involved multihost support, transmission groups, LU 6.2, type 2.1 nodes, or SNA Network Interconnection (SNI). The company also set the pace at which new functionality was introduced. The other vendors, true to the notion of plug-compatibility, were happy and willing to follow behind IBM.

With i•nets, or even SNA-capable i•nets, no one technology leader or arbitrator exists for the innovation process. Instead, this area is a competition-driven, high-reward-potential free market. Consequently, some of the product offerings, irrespective of the stature of the vendor, are not nearly as rugged, resilient, and bulletproof as core SNA products, such as ACF/VTAM, ACF/NCP, and 3745s. Corporations that have used LAN-based file servers and mail servers over the last few years know that productivity-disrupting server malfunctions occur on a regular basis—perhaps even as frequently as once per week. It would not be unreasonable to assume that i•net and SNA-capable i•net offerings will likely exhibit similar, but certainly not worse, up-time characteristics. An entire well-engineered SNA-capable i•net will not necessarily fail on a weekly basis, of course. Nevertheless, based on the maturity of current products it would not be unusual to see Web server, Web browser, router, or applet crashes or freezes that affect some portion of the network on a weekly basis. With i•nets in general, irrespective of whether they are SNA-capable, corporations are unlikely to be able to rely on 99% overall up time until after the year 2000.

> SNA-capable i•nets will be hard pushed to match the legendary robustness of SNA networks—at least initially. Means are available, however, to minimize the potential disruption to SNA access.

Another important factor that impinges on the robustness of SNA-capable i•nets is the absence of a highly precise, bits-and-bytes-specific architecture, replete with the exact requirements for node interconnection, as SNA provides. Although IETF-governed standards exist for DLSw, tn3270(E), and tn5250, much of the other compelling technology related to SNA-capable i•nets, at least at present, is vendor-specific. For example, two very divergent methodologies exist for realizing browser-based access to SNA applications: direct **3270/5250-to-HTML** conversion and **applet-based 3270/5250 emulation**. These key technologies are described in detail in Chapter 5.

Even within these two methodologies, significant implementational variations arise. The applet-based emulation, for instance, could use a standard tn3270(E) or tn5250 data stream in conjunction with a conventional tn3270(E) server, or it could be based on a proprietary protocol such as OpenConnect Systems' Java Control Protocol (JCP) between the applet and a vendor-specific Web-to-SNA gateway component. A key justification for such proprietary protocols is that they provide value-added functions such as authentication and encryption—the tn3270(E) standard remains bereft of these security features.

These implementational differences also dictate the various functional components required between a PC client and a mainframe- or AS/400-resident application. In some cases, one could have a three-tier solution that involves a PC-resident tn3270(E)-based ActiveX applet, a mainframe-resident tn3270(E) server, and the mainframe application. In other cases, as many as five separate software components, including a Web server, might be involved in the client-to-application data interchange path. The functional tiers possible with these types of browser-based SNA access solutions are described in Chapter 5. Figure 3.1 shows the functional components involved in a five-tier, browser-based access solution, and Figure 3.2 shows that of a three-tier solution.

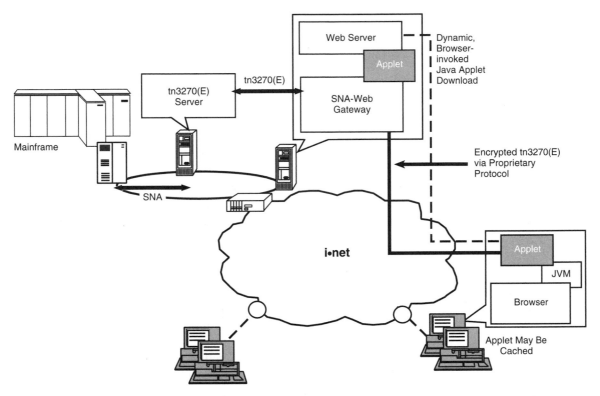

FIGURE 3.1 Browser-based SNA access scheme involving an intermediary SNA-Web gateway and a downloaded Java applet.

With these types of widely divergent vendor-specific solutions, where many vendors rely on key components from still other vendors, one must always be wary of availability-related issues, especially in heavy-load, heavy-stress situations. Nevertheless, it would wrong to imply that SNA-capable i•net technology on the whole is immature or unstable. In fact, many large corporations around the world, such as FedEx, General Motors, Del Monte Foods International, and Lafayette Life, are already successfully using SNA-capable i•net technology, including browser-based SNA access, for daily production use. The purpose of highlighting these availability-related issues is to give corporations a "heads up" that it would be wrong to assume that i•nets and SNA-capable i•nets will be as rugged and robust as SNA networks from day one.

Another way of comparing the reliability aspects and implications of SNA-capable i•nets with those of SNA subarea networks is to consider the lessons learned with bridge/router-based multiprotocol networks—in particular, SNA/APPN-capable multiprotocol networks. The original bridge- or

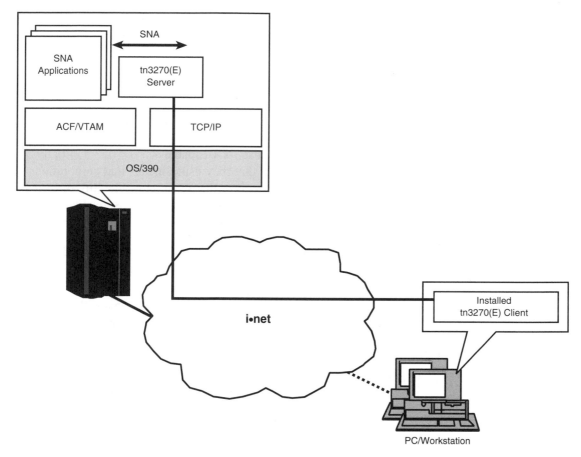

FIGURE 3.2   A tn3270(E) SNA access solution involving the fewest number of components.

bridge/router-based SNA-capable multiprotocol networks, which were deployed around 1991–1992, were prone to fairly regular failures. The norm was 92% up time. Much of the instability of these early networks reflected the newness of the SNA-specific bridge/router software and the haste with which the vendors brought out new releases to garner market attention and share. A parallel scenario is now playing out in the i•net and SNA-capable i•net arenas. Over the 1992–1996 period, however, bridge/router vendors went to great lengths to stabilize their offerings and enhance their reliability and resilience. Today, bridge/router-based SNA-capable multiprotocol networks may offer 97% to 98% up time.

Although still inferior to an SNA network, overall availability is definitely adequate, and the trend in terms of stability and robustness is certainly moving in the right direction. Given that bridge/routers will play a key role in the infrastructure of SNA-capable i•nets, their increasing reliability will certainly ensure that the i•net backbone can deliver up times in the range of 97% or better. This achievement is a very positive and promising start. Just as they did with bridge/routers, the reliability and resilience of the SNA-capable i•net technology will improve over time. Thanks to the lessons learned from the bridge/router exercise, the crucial 5% increase in availability will most likely be achieved in less time than the five years or so it took with bridge/routers.

Knowing from the outset that SNA-capable i•nets will not initially be as fail-safe as the SNA networks that they usurp means that corporations can take proactive measures to maximize the potential availability of their new networks. Some of the key availability-enhancing measures that should be considered for SNA-capable intranets and extranets are as follows:

1. Wherever possible, choose highly proven and widely used products, whose stability has been ascertained via reference checks with other users.

2. Prototype and then rigorously test potential solutions, with as high traffic loads as possible. Make maximum use of hands-on lab testing opportunities now increasingly being offered by most larger vendors so as to stress-test the solution.

3. Ensure that backup access—for example, via dial backup—is available for key remote locations or users to ensure continued data center access, albeit at a possibly lower speed, in the event of a long-duration intranet or extranet failure.

4. Whenever possible, implement redundant, "hot-standby" components, such as tn3270(E) servers, mirror Web servers, and mainframe gateways, so as to minimize disruption and facilitate fast recovery in the event of component failures.

5. If possible, design the intranet backbone with alternate paths between key locations to ensure that traffic can be automatically and nondisruptively rerouted in the event of path or intermediate node (for example, router) failure.

6. Implement one or more high-caliber network management systems on the mainframe or on a distributed platform, such as Sterling Software's SOLVE:Netmaster on the mainframe and IBM's TME 10 NetView on a UNIX platform. Such a system can incisively monitor the operation of the network and give warnings of potential problems, such as a high number of retries on a link that might indicate impending link failure.

7. Obtain realistic but aggressive service-level agreements, with suitable penalties for default, from appropriate service providers (that is, ISPs, Frame Relay providers, equipment maintenance organizations, and so on).

8. Review the health of the intranet or extranet on a weekly basis in terms of its malfunctions, traffic patterns, and response time characteristics so as to analyze availability trends and detect any deterioration of service or quality.

Unfortunately, these measures to enhance network availability apply only to intranets and extranets. As discussed earlier, corporations or individuals have no real control over the availability aspects of the Internet. Nevertheless, some of these measures, such as dial backup, active management of the Internet interface, and even health checks related to Internet access, could be gainfully employed to minimize and mitigate the effect of Internet disruptions or slowdowns.

In the end, however, one must realize that the Internet cannot be treated as a service-guaranteed, mission-critical networking resource. If a corporation does intend to use the Internet for some of its mission-critical applications, such as remote access, it is imperative that the company has adequate bypass mechanisms to redirect traffic and transactions around the Internet in the event of an Internet failure. In some instances, all that may be required in terms of a bypass is access to another ISP or ISP site, because many Internet problems do not affect the entire Internet but are instead localized or ISP-related.

3.2 SECURITY CONCERNS RELATED TO SNA-CAPABLE I•NETS

Just as with reliability, SNA networks and SNA applications are noted for their security. One rarely hears of mainframe-resident applications being hacked across SNA networks. Much of the security associated with SNA networks results from four factors:

1. SNA networks are private networks in which the physical access to the network from terminals or PCs attached to the network is invariably controlled and monitored. In North America, many of these networks, at least prior to advent of Frame Relay around 1995, were built around leased lines.

2. Dial-up access, though possible, is not especially prevalent. Nearly all of today's remote access capability implemented by corporations to cater to mobile users and telecommuters is primarily LAN-centric rather than SNA-based.

3. The intermediate routing nodes in SNA networks, which consist of either 37xx communications controllers running ACF/NCP or mainframes running ACF/VTAM, are difficult to infiltrate. Any attempts at infiltration

   would be contingent on procuring specialized in-house assistance, such
   as the aid of a systems programmer.

4. Access to mainframe-resident SNA applications is governed by highly
   proven security offerings, such as IBM's **RACF**, and protected by individually administered user IDs and passwords.

Because of these factors, security was essentially a nonissue with SNA.
SNA networks were considered to be inherently secure; enough security-
related features were built into SNA, including the option of end-to-end,
LU-to-LU encryption, that most corporations could implement and grow
their SNA networks without expending too much effort or money on security
measures.

In 1990, IBM put forward a comprehensive master plan for total system
management known as **SystemView**. Although SystemView eloquently
addressed nearly all aspects of data center management and operations, it
did not address security at length. SystemView's lack of attention to security-
related matters was not deemed incongruous or even worthy of comment in
the early 1990s, however. In those heady days, before hacking, virus propagation, and network-based attacks on computers had become a past-time,
security concerns had more to do with physical security—that is, controlling
access to computer hardware, printouts, and data tapes—than with worries
about data being intercepted within the network.

Today, with i•nets and the pervading concerns about viruses, computer
sabotage, and network infiltration, this perception has changed drastically.
Security, and in particular network security, is of paramount concern to both
network and data center management.

With SNA-capable i•nets, the security issue has two facets. There is
security for intranets and extranets on one hand and the thorny issue of safeguarding Internet-based transactions on the other. The intranet- and extranet-
related security issues are generally containable, given that these networks
are private; as such, they can be tightly administered, controlled, and monitored. Security issues as they pertain to the Internet, however, open up a
wholly different can of worms.

In the case of intranets and extranets, corporations should take measures
to control physical access to the network just as they did with SNA networks. With the increase in mobile users, telecommuters, and after-hours
online work from home, however, this control is becoming more difficult to
achieve because corporations have no choice but to provide remote access
mechanisms to cater to their off-site workers. The user ID and password
schemes available with LAN network operating systems are obviously the
first line of defense against attempts to gain unauthorized access to the network. These efforts are unlikely to be enough. Corporations should also
evaluate mainframe-based, TCP/IP-specific access control schemes, such as

Interlink Computer Sciences' e-Control, that can grant or deny mainframe application access based on IP addresses, time of day, and TCP/IP socket numbers, as well as user IDs and passwords. In parallel, corporations should implement explicit user authentication systems to verify and validate all attempts to log on to the network.

It is inconceivable that anyone would attempt to implement an intranet or extranet without some form of firewall protection. Firewalls have become the i•net equivalent of a magnetic-stripe badge reader that acts as an access control mechanism. If an intranet will support any form of external access, then one or more firewalls—in hardware, software, or routers—should be implemented to intercept and verify the legality of all packets seeking entrance to the internal network. In the case of Internet-based access to an intranet or data center, a proven firewall solution is imperative to control and monitor ingress into the corporate resources.

In many instances, corporations may opt for an "application-level firewall" or **Proxy Server** to further isolate intranet and Internet traffic. With a proxy server, one can build a logical barrier between the Internet and an intranet such that only copies of messages, as opposed to the original packets, are transferred from one network to the other. This process of transferring only copies of messages between networks keeps internal—that is, corporate-specific—TCP/IP addresses and domain names from being visible to external users. A full discussion of firewall architectures and options is beyond the scope of this book. Under the heading "Security," the Bibliography lists books that provide detailed discussions of firewall-based security schemes.

Although firewalls, authentication schemes, and passwords provide access control, they do not safeguard against data (in particular, sensitive corporate or commercial data) being intercepted and read within the network, especially if these data are traversing the Internet. End-to-end encryption enters the picture here. Although powerful encryption methods were included within the SNA architecture and implemented in some SNA products, such as the IBM 3274 control unit, encryption was not widely used within SNA networks. This reluctance may change when it comes to SNA-capable i•nets. End-to-end encryption should be viewed as an integral part of an SNA-capable i•net architecture, irrespective of whether the i•net involved is an intranet, an extranet, or the Internet.

The good news is that encryption has already become fairly standard fare when it comes to i•nets. Methodologies such as the Secure Socket Layer (SSL) scheme developed by Netscape, **Transport Layer Security (TLS)**, and **Secure HTTP (HTTPS)** permit IP-based i•net interaction to be automatically encrypted on an end-to-end basis. HTTPS consists of SSL being used in conjunction with HTTP. SSL includes a built-in mechanism for client authentication as well as a negotiation process to determine which encryption method should be used. With SSL now enjoying widespread support, it is possible to ensure that data transfers between a Web server and a Web browser are encrypted on an end-to-end basis, thereby thwarting these data from being easily intercepted and interpreted in transit.

Most of the solutions for realizing SNA-capable i•nets support some form of encryption—either standards such as SSL, proprietary versions, or both. Some of the methodologies used in implementing SNA-capable i•nets, DLSw, and tn3270(E) do not as yet provide encryption as a standard, built-in capability. Nevertheless, many vendors offering DLSw and tn3270(E) compensate for this deficiency by delivering proprietary encryption schemes to safeguard the SNA transactions. Encryption tends to be an integral part of most browser-based SNA access schemes that rely on the use of an applet at the client end, such as IBM's Host On-Demand or OpenConnect Systems' OC://WebConnect Pro. The encryption options and capabilities of the various SNA-to-Web integration technologies will be explicitly mentioned in Chapter 5, when these technologies are discussed in detail.

3.3 EMULATING SNA ROUTING WITHIN SNA-CAPABLE I•NETS

Although SNA-capable i•nets will not preclude users from accessing SNA applications running in different data centers, the end-to-end routing could prove far from optimal and very different than what would have been used with SNA or APPN routing.

SNA subarea routing is a much misunderstood notion, even though it has been extensively used around the world for the last 20 years. Even today, some claim that SNA is not a routable protocol, even though some of these critics have used SNA routing, unbeknownst to them, on a daily basis for many years. SNA routing, in its most basic form, provides the mechanism that enables a terminal or PC user to readily switch between SNA applications running on the same mainframe. Even more importantly, it enables a remote terminal or PC user to transparently switch between SNA applications running on multiple, geographically dispersed mainframes without knowing or caring on which mainframe or data center location a particular application is resident. In traditional, mainframe-centric SNA environments, the criterion used for most SNA routing consists of the name of an application, as nearly all of the traffic flows occur between either a terminal end user and an application, an I/O device such as a printer and an application, or, in some cases, two application programs. Hence, an application name—whether it be TSO, CICS, or Payroll—determines the end-to-end, client-to-application path selected and established by SNA subarea routing. Likewise, APPN and HPR routing are governed by destination application names.

SNA subarea routing (or just SNA routing), like any other routing scheme, establishes a path across a network between a given end user and a particular destination—for example, between an end user and an application or between two end users. This SNA routing is realized using SNA-specific constructs, such as **SSCP-LU** and **SSCP-SSCP** sessions, and SNA concepts, such as **Virtual Routes (VRs)** and **Class-of-Service (COS)**. In SNA networks, SNA subarea routing is performed by mainframes running ACF/VTAM and 37xxs or by plug-compatibles running ACF/NCP. Essentially, SNA routing remains the exclusive domain of ACF/VTAM and ACF/NCP. This fixed-path (static) routing scheme is based on manually predefined routes specified via ACF/VTAM and ACF/NCP PATH tables. The fixed route to be used by an SNA session becomes established when the session is initiated and is based on the COS associated with that session.

No other device or product, including IBM's 3746-950 Nways Multiprotocol Concentrator, can perform SNA subarea routing. The IBM 3746-950 and some routers, such as those from IBM and Cisco, can perform APPN or HPR routing; this routing scheme differs from SNA subarea routing, however. The best that today's routers can do with SNA traffic is to route it using non-SNA Layer 2 techniques or to perform APPN NN routing. With the former approach, a bridge or a router transports SNA traffic between an SNA device (for example, a PC or 3174) and an SNA-LAN gateway (in particular, a 37xx) using a Layer 2 routing mechanism such as **Source Route Bridging (SRB)**, transparent bridging, DLSw, or **RFC 1490**-based native Frame Relay encapsulation. SNA works above Layer 2; that is, it remains independent of, and operates above, the Data Link Control layer (whether it be SDLC, LLC-2, or a mainframe channel). Bona fide SNA routing, as performed by ACF/NCP and ACF/VTAM, is best envisioned as occurring at Layers 4 and 5.

SNA routing occurs only between subareas. An SNA subarea is formed around a mainframe with an SNA type 5 node or a 37xx with a type 4 node. ACF/VTAM in a mainframe implements a type 5 node, whereas ACF/NCP in a 37xx implements a type 4 node. Thus SNA routing takes place between 37xxs, 37xxs and mainframes, or mainframes. No SNA routing occurs between peripheral devices, such as 3174 control units, and a 37xx—given that a single link (whether point-to-point, multipoint, or through an X.25/Frame Relay packet switching network) represents the only path between these two types of nodes.

Figure 3.3 shows a quintessential example of SNA subarea routing through a remote 37xx. The remote 37xx in Dallas can act as a two-leg "Y-switch," routing SNA traffic either to New York or Chicago. This routing, based on the specific application program being sought by the end user, will occur on an SNA session-by-session basis. ACF/VTAM in a mainframe will determine the path used by each session when the session is first established. The mainframe on which the destination application resides will determine the endpoint of each session and thus the endpoints of an SNA end-to-end route required to sustain that session. In this example, the relevant applications are CICS/VS in Chicago and TSO in New York.

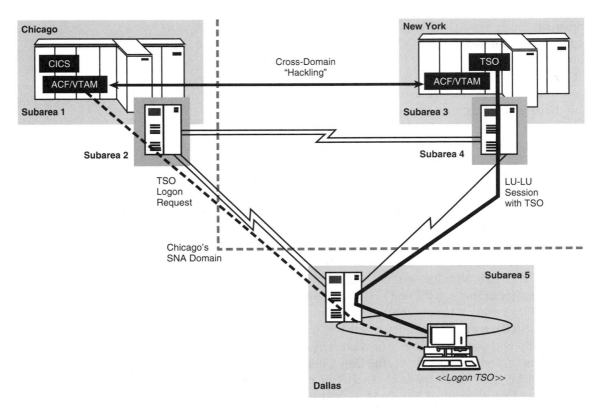

FIGURE 3.3   Quintessential SNA subarea-to-subarea routing.

The route that can be taken from the PC in Dallas to one of the two main-frames consists of, and is specified in terms of, a series of hops between sub-area nodes—for example, the Dallas 37xx to the New York 37xx to the New York mainframe. Once the subarea of the destination application has been located, the appropriate route would be selected from prespecified PATH tables located in the mainframes and the 37xxs, based on a COS associated with that session. Figure 3.4 shows a representative view of the various table lookups required to establish an SNA route.

A TCP/IP-based i•net cannot emulate SNA subarea routing because the WAN network—the so-called cloud—will not contain any subarea nodes. Note that DLSw cannot perform SNA subarea routing. In the context of SNA routing, DLSw is purely a Layer 2-oriented transport and tunneling scheme that essentially performs transparent LAN bridging across IP. It works independently of SNA and remains invisible to SNA. Thus, when an intranet replaces an SNA backbone WAN, one needs a mechanism other than SNA routing to ensure that clients, who are most likely PC users, can

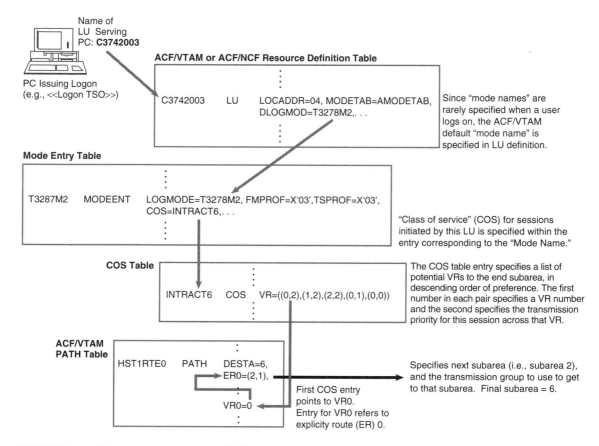

FIGURE 3.4   Table lookups involved in SNA subarea routing.

still reach the requisite mainframe- or AS/400-resident applications. IP routing is obviously the standard and the highly capable routing scheme employed by i•nets. The issue here in the context of SNA-capable i•nets relates to the fact that IP routing is based on a destination IP address, whereas SNA routing is based on application program names.

The good news is that SNA-capable i•nets will not preclude end users from accessing SNA or APPN applications or from freely switching between applications running in different data centers. The problem, however, is that the end-to-end paths used to realize such application access, especially in the case of applications not at the "home" data center, may not correspond to the routes used by SNA or APPN/HPR. Moreover, in some instances, it may be far from optimal. For example, in the Dallas–Chicago–New York scenario illustrated in Figure 3.5, the Dallas–New York route provided by an SNA-capable i•net may be such that all data transfers must be channeled through

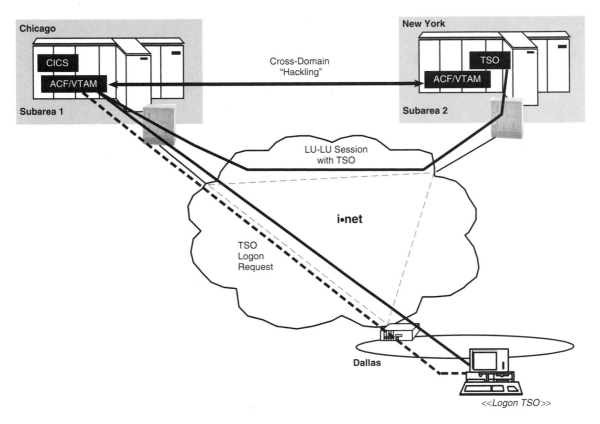

FIGURE 3.5 Two-step routing in the absence of SNA subarea routing.

Chicago, even if direct Dallas–New York links exist within the i•net. The reason for such nonoptimal routing will become clear as the various options for SNA routing vis-à-vis SNA-capable i•nets are discussed below.

Currently, SNA routing can be provided within SNA-capable i•nets in just three ways, as discussed below.

Providing Direct Access to a TCP/IP-to-SNA Gateway at Each Data Center

With this approach, one would implement separate instances of the necessary Web-to-mainframe gateways (such as a channel-attached tn3270(E) server) at each data center or, in some cases, in front of each mainframe. Each gateway will have its own IP address; gateways for browser-based access will also have their own URLs. Each SNA application at the various data centers will then be associated with the IP address, or URL, of the gateway adjacent to the mainframe on which that particular application is running. These SNA application-to-gateway schemes will be configured and set up at each client machine. The setup at client machines will take the form of an icon or book-mark corresponding to each SNA application that must be accessed from that machine. Users will gain access to the SNA applications by invoking the icon or bookmark corresponding to the particular application.

Since the icon or bookmark is set up to route the TCP/IP traffic directly to the gateway serving the host running that application, the path through the i•net need not be circuitous. The actual physical route used may not match the one previously used with the SNA backbone, because the path chosen by IP will obviously depend on the i•net's network configuration and on the way in which the IP routing tables were initially set up and their current status. In marked contrast to the static routing tables employed by SNA, IP relies on dynamically updated and refreshed routing tables. I•nets will also typically have more intermediate routing nodes (in particular, routers), with multiple connections between them, than was the norm with SNA backbones. This meshlike structure of i•nets combined with the dynamic routing and rerout-ing capability of IP can, at least in theory, provide client-to-host paths that are even more optimal than those possible with SNA. This application-to-gateway correlation approach can thus be used to provide efficient SNA routing across i•nets.

The problem is that this routing is realized at a significant, and in many instances unacceptable, cost in terms of administering the various icons and bookmarks corresponding to the gateways at each client machine. With this approach, the manual configuration of the requisite end-to-end SNA routes compensates for the lack of SNA routing within the i•net. In an envi-ronment where most of the clients must access quite a few SNA applica-tions spread over multiple data centers, the administrative effort associated with this approach may be impractical (even with central administration), especially if the application repertoires or locations change frequently. If one is dealing with only four or five applications that reside permanently at a specific data center, this approach is more viable and should be seriously considered, particularly given its potential for delivering optimal client-to-host routes.

Routing All Logons to a TCP/IP-to-SNA Gateway at a Data Center Plus SNA Subarea or APPN/HPR Routing to Locate the Application

This approach is best envisioned as a two-tier routing scheme that involves (1) IP routing within the i•net and (2) SNA or APPN/HPR routing upstream of the i•net at the data center level. With this scheme, standard IP routing is used to forward all logons from a given set of SNA users to a prespecified TCP/IP-to-SNA gateway. In the example described earlier, all logons from

Dallas could be sent to a gateway in the Chicago data center. The gateway will convert the logon to its appropriate SNA format and then forward it to an APPN/HPR NN node (for example, within a router or to an ACF/VTAM running on a mainframe). At this juncture, either APPN/HPR NN or ACF/VTAM-orchestrated conventional SNA subarea routing can be employed to locate the destination application. Thus, in the Dallas–Chicago–New York example, SNA subarea or APPN/HPR routing will ensure that the logons for TSO received from users in Dallas will reach New York.

Once the SNA logons reach the mainframe or AS/400 containing the destination application, the standard SNA or APPN/HPR session initiation and establishment process will commence. At this point, however, one runs into a snag. The end-to-end, LU-LU session cannot be established directly with the actual end user because this end user is using a TCP/IP client and is accessible only via a TCP/IP network. Instead, the destination application and SNA routing software both think that the TCP/IP-to-SNA gateway that forwarded the logon is the location of the end user. Thus the session establishment command—known in SNA as a BIND request—is sent to the original gateway, rather than to the actual end user. In the example, the necessary SNA LU-LU session occurs between TSO in New York and the TCP/IP-to-SNA gateway in Chicago. The TCP/IP-to-SNA gateway will, of course, forward all SNA message units to the user in Dallas and ensure that data from the user are transmitted to New York.

Figure 3.5 illustrates this nonoptimal, bifurcated routing where the SNA routing occurring at the data center level remains oblivious to the IP routing necessary within the i•net to reach the actual end user. Frustration arises because the New York data center also has a TCP/IP-to-SNA gateway and the physical infrastructure exists to channel data directly from New York to Dallas without going through Chicago. When confronted with this nonoptimal, end-to-end routing, an initial temptation is to think that it reflects the selection of the wrong gateway. If the Dallas users were supported by the New York gateway, they would indeed receive optimal, end-to-end routing when they were accessing TSO. When they want to access CICS in Chicago, however, the problem will resurface. CICS will consider the New York gateway, rather than Dallas, as the final destination.

With this single-gateway approach, one cannot avoid the potential problem of nonoptimal routes. If one decides to route the logons to the most appropriate gateway instead, then the routing methodology returns to the multiple icon or URL scenario. The best that one can do with the single-gateway scheme is to ensure that users are routed to the TCP/IP-to-SNA gateway that serves the data center containing the applications that they use most frequently. Then nonoptimal routing will occur only for short durations when users need to access an infrequently used application. This potential nonoptimal routing, which involves multiple data centers, is not a new problem brought about by SNA-capable i•nets. The same problem exists in multiprotocol networks serving multiple data centers when bridging, including DLSw bridging over TCP/IP, supports SNA/APPN traffic.

This routing problem could be overcome through the use of a gateway-to-gateway protocol, in conjunction with enhanced TCP/IP client software that would automatically accept session connection requests issued by a gateway. With this proposed scheme, logons from a given set of users would still go to a prespecified gateway. The gateways in this scenario, however, would maintain tables of the SNA applications they serve. When confronted with a logon for an application that resides in another data center and thus is served by a different gateway, they would forward that logon, using IP routing, to the necessary gateway. The gateway that initially received the logon would also eliminate any TCP connection between itself and the client. After receiving the forwarded logon, the second gateway would establish a TCP connection with the end-user client that submitted the logon. It would then convert the logon to SNA and dispatch it to the necessary mainframe or AS/400. This approach thus has the potential of delivering optimal routing, without requiring the overhead of setting up icons or URLs for every application on each client system.

Currently, no vendors offer this solution. Likewise, no standard exists for the gateway-to-gateway protocol, and the required enhancements to the client software have not been developed. At least one vendor is evaluating this type of approach for possible future introduction, contingent on a strong customer demand for this type of direct routing.

Using HPR-over-IP to Perform Native APPN/HPR Routing Across the i•net

HPR-over-IP (also known as Enterprise Extender) is an alternative to DLSw that is being promoted by IBM and is now available on IBM's 2216, 2212, and 2210 bridge/routers. With this technique, IP-based routers and switches would contain an HPR NN and use HPR routing, rather than DLSw, to transport SNA/APPN traffic across an i•net. The notion of having an HPR NN on an IP router or switch is not far-fetched. Most of the leading bridge/router vendors (such as IBM, Cisco, and 3Com) have supported APPN NN routing on their routers since 1993; some have already upgraded their APPN offerings to HPR.

This approach could provide direct, SNA-oriented routing across the i•net—albeit at a price. This technique is contingent on the end-user client utilizing full-stack SNA on its system, such as IBM's PComm or Eicon's Aviva for Desktops, rather than a TCP/IP client, such as a tn3270(E) client or a Java applet-based emulator. In many ways, this practice runs counter to the way that IBM-oriented networks are evolving. Today, most enterprises want to minimize the cost and ongoing maintenance effort associated with SNA/3270 or 3270 emulation software and migrate toward "thinner" TCP/IP or dynamically downloadable applet-based clients.

HPR-over-IP is also a nascent technology. It is far from being a widely implemented and a readily available standard like DLSw or tn3270(E), although this situation will likely begin to change near the end of 1999. Moreover, considerable functional overlap exists between HPR and IP. HPR, even if stripped of some of its native functionality, such as dynamic alternate routing and anticipatory congestion control, remains a sophisticated, full-function networking scheme that relies on dynamic topology updates and automatic end-user registration processes to deliver its end-to-end routing capability. Consequently, the overhead of running HPR-over-IP will be greater than that if one used IP clients or even DLSw.

Although HPR-over-IP provides key SNA/APPN functionality, including routing and COS prioritization, it carries some costs. This approach requires either full SNA type 2 node stacks or APPN end node stacks on the client systems, and it necessitates the overhead associated with overlaying a full networking scheme on top of that already provided by TCP and IP. The final irony relates to a unique and distinguishing feature of HPR—all of its routing and networking functionality is contained within and restricted to Layer 2. With HPR-over-IP, this Layer 2 protocol is run over IP—which happens to be a Layer 3 protocol. Although this reversing of the functional layering does not prevent HPR-over-IP from functioning, it does highlight the incongruous nature of this approach.

HPR-over-IP should be considered only when the absolute need for optimal SNA/APPN routing or COS prioritization significantly outweighs its client software cost and networking overhead. Otherwise, it would be better from an overall cost and efficiency standpoint to pursue IP client-oriented solutions and use DLSw to support any existing SNA devices, even if the SNA routing is nonoptimal and the SNA COS-based traffic prioritization is sacrificed.

3.4   MAINTAINING PREDICTABLE RESPONSE TIMES WITH SNA-CAPABLE I•NETS

Sustaining consistent and predictable response times when SNA applications are being accessed will be a challenge for i•nets—particularly when the access occurs over the Internet.

Predictable and consistent response times, like high availability, is another hallmark of SNA networks. Many interrelated factors ensure that SNA users can enjoy crisp and relatively constant response times.

First and foremost, most SNA networks were explicitly engineered in terms of bandwidth allocation and configured to meet or exceed prespecified levels of performance. The bandwidth allocation would usually relate to the speeds of the links used, and the configuration aspect would deal with the number of links deployed between subarea nodes. Traffic modeling, as in IBM's TPNS simulator, would typically be used to establish the baseline configuration for the network in terms of the expected throughput and response time criteria.

The SNA network would be iteratively tuned and enhanced on an ongoing basis, using actual traffic volume and response time data collected via tools such as IBM's NetView Performance Monitor (NPM) and the 3174 Response Time Monitor (RTM). Analysis of this information would ensure that the overall performance goals were being maintained. In addition, in SNA-only networks, the SNA traffic did not have to compete with other traffic for bandwidth or network resources. This homogeneity of the traffic involved obviously simplified the modeling, tuning, monitoring, and engineering process of SNA networks. SNA also provided built-in traffic prioritization, in the form of COS, to facilitate the potential customization of response times and overall network performance. It is important to note, however, that such traffic prioritization in SNA subarea networks (as opposed to APPN/HPR networks) was available only between subarea nodes (for example, mainframe-to-3745, 3745-to-3745, or mainframe-to-mainframe).

SNA, reflecting the scarcity and cost of bandwidth in the early 1970s, was developed to utilize remarkably succinct protocols and is parsimonious in its use of headers and responses. Given its penchant for fixed-path routing, this architecture did not employ any periodic updates of routing tables or topology databases, unlike APPN/HPR or IP.

Consequently, SNA is a very efficient networking scheme with minimal overhead. This overall efficiency conserves networking bandwidth for actual end-user data transfers and ensures that network housekeeping-related functions do not impede the constant flow of end-user traffic.*

Another factor that helped SNA networks maintain rapid and regular response times was the interactive and relatively compact nature of most interactions. Even today, networking professionals use a rule of thumb—"120 bytes to the mainframe, and 1200 bytes from the mainframe"—when characterizing the 3270 transactions that still account for the lion's share of SNA traffic that flows across a network. With this type of traffic profile, users do not "hog" a given link or network bandwidth.

These traits and factors, which ensured that SNA networks could deliver predictable and consistent response times to their end users, will not apply to SNA-capable i•nets. For a start, SNA will no longer have exclusive use

---

*One rather trivial exception to this nonstop data-forwarding nature was the **Transmission Group Sweep** process that would occur with multilink TGs between subarea nodes. Each time the sequence numbering used to transmit data frames across a TG reached 4095, it had to be reset to 0. The multiple, parallel links forming a TG would normally consist of a series of SDLC links. Today, it is possible to implement TGs using other types of links, such as Token Ring or Frame Relay.

of the network in SNA-capable i•nets. SNA traffic will have to continually compete for bandwidth and networking resources with non-SNA traffic, such as the downloading of Web pages. In addition, the traffic profile and volume of the non-SNA traffic will be highly variable and unpredictable. The Web page-based interactions, especially those involving Web page or applet downloads, will involve much larger data transfers than was the case with SNA/ 3270 transactions. Just as with SNA routing discussed earlier, corporations that support SNA/APPN traffic across bridge/router-based multiprotocol networks already recognize that delivering acceptable response times to SNA users can be hampered when bandwidth and network resources are consumed by unexpected volumes of non-SNA traffic.

One mitigating factor regarding the availability of bandwidth should be considered. An SNA-capable i•net is likely to have significantly more bandwidth, especially WAN bandwidth, than was the norm with SNA-only networks. The average link speed for SNA/SDLC links remains in the 9600bps to 19,200bps range. In marked contrast, an i•net will rarely have WAN links of less than 56Kbps. This additional WAN bandwidth will, in many instances, compensate for the performance hit incurred by SNA traffic due to the presence of non-SNA traffic.

In the case of an intranet or extranet, a corporation could attempt to model the anticipated traffic patterns of the network and engineer (or even overengineer in terms of bandwidth) the network to deliver the baseline performance levels required to guarantee acceptable response times for all users. In practice, this engineering objective may prove infeasible, as many corporations may not know the scope and magnitude of their nascent Web page-oriented intranet traffic in the beginning. Internet access by corporate employees will also create large fluctuations in the traffic loads flowing within a corporation's internal intranet. The only real option is to increase intranet bandwidth at the LAN level—for example, with 100Mbps LANs and LAN switching— and within the WAN—with T1- to T3-speed Frame Relay or 155Mbps ATM. This scheme would deliver the required performance at least 75% to 85% of the time and accommodate the growing traffic volumes. In reality, the demand for networking bandwidth will likely grow incessantly.

The response times associated with SNA application access across the Internet will be even more difficult to regulate and control given the potential variables involved. For instance, the speed of the link to the ISP may vary for each user. In the case of modem-based connections, the actual speed of this link could differ as much as 30% to 35%, depending on the condition of the dial-up connection or the exact properties of the ISP's modem. In addition, the unpredictable performance profile of the Internet itself can sometimes be exacerbated by traffic-related slowdowns at ISPs.

The bottom line is that the response times for SNA applications accessed across the Internet are unlikely to be as predictable or consistent as those encountered with SNA-only networks. Users may experience a reasonably consistent and acceptable level of performance for some time. This performance may then change without warning for an indeterminate period. In some cases, such variations in Internet performance may reflect sharply increased activity precipitated by a topical event, such as a large swing in the stock market or a breaking, high-profile news story.

If predictable and consistent SNA response times are crucial, as they are for online stock trading, travel reservation, or automated teller machine (ATM) transactions, Internet access to those applications is probably not the right approach to pursue. An intranet scheme based on ISDN or Frame Relay connections to the intranet, where the bandwidth can be more closely regulated, will probably offer a much better option. Internet access, however, may be perfectly acceptable and highly cost-effective for applications that can withstand some variations in response times; such applications might include status queries, data lookups, mainframe e-mail, or even home banking.

The potential response time vagaries of SNA access over the Internet will also affect **Virtual Private Networks (VPNs)**. VPNs permit the Internet bandwidth to be securely used for private corporate transactions, typically to interconnect LANs dispersed across multiple remote locations. These networks, which rely on a combination of hardware or software offerings, provide built-in, end-to-end encryption and the ability to automatically and transparently tunnel traffic that may not be TCP/IP across the Internet. VPNs thus represent a cost-compelling alternative to leased lines or public data networks, such as Frame Relay or X.25, for securing WAN bandwidth for intranets or extranets.

The problem is that the throughput delivered by VPNs depends on the behavior of the Internet. Just as with Internet access to SNA applications, the performance levels could fluctuate unpredictably. Nonetheless, VPNs provide a very attractive solution for delivering WAN connectivity to intranets and extranets—assuming that the applications and people using the VPN-based connections can tolerate some degree of variation in response times. VPNs, obviously, are an ideal means for accommodating data transfers associated with high-volume, non-real-time applications such as e-mail, file transfer, and print distribution.

3.5 GIVING PRIORITY TO SNA TRAFFIC

SNA COS, much like SNA routing, is a misunderstood and often overstated notion. COS, which has been a standard feature of SNA since 1978, permits one of three levels of traffic prioritization—high, medium, or low—to be assigned to traffic related to a particular SNA LU-LU session. It also governs the preferred network routing allocated for the SNA LU-LU session. COS therefore influences the performance characteristics of an LU-LU session both in terms of routing and the relative priority assigned to the traffic flowing on that session.

The often-overlooked limitation of SNA COS is that it has meaning, and is thus applicable, only on a subarea node-to-subarea node basis. ACF/VTAM and ACF/NCP constitute SNA subareas. COS therefore has meaning between a mainframe and 37xx, two 37xxs, or two mainframes. If an SNA network has many subarea nodes (in particular, remote 37xxs) and multiple alternate paths (TGs) exist between these subarea nodes, then COS-based routing and traffic prioritization are highly effective.

Over the last few years, however, an increasing number of SNA networks have lost their remote 37xx-based subarea networks. The WAN capability previously provided by these subarea networks is now realized via a bridge/router-based multiprotocol network or a Frame Relay network that is connected to a channel-attached 3745. Consequently, in many SNA networks COS affects only traffic flowing within the data center or between data centers. The traffic within the data center will move between a mainframe and a channel-attached 3745, whereas the data center-to-data center traffic takes place between 3745s or between mainframes via a channel-to-channel connection.

Contrary to a widespread belief, no COS-based traffic prioritization occurs between a 37xx and either an SNA device, an SNA-LAN gateway, or a PC running a full-stack SNA/3270 emulator, such as IBM's PComm. In this instance, the SNA device might be a 3174 Control Unit or 4700 Financial System; Novell's NetWare for SAA is a good example of an SNA-LAN gateway. Such subarea node-to-peripheral node traffic, in either direction, moves on a first-come-first-serve basis across a single, active physical link.

Thus no explicit SNA-based traffic prioritization takes place between actual end users and the data center in many contemporary SNA networks. This omission is not a major impediment given that much of SNA traffic is interactive and conducted in short bursts. SNA-based file transfers, although growing in popularity, typically do not swamp the interactive traffic because the data transfer over the WAN usually takes the form of 1KB to 4KB blocks that are interspersed with interactive traffic.

APPN and HPR support COS with **Transmission Priority Field (TPF)**-based traffic prioritization between end nodes and network nodes. Because multiple links may exist between ENs and NNs, COS traffic prioritization can be gainfully exploited with APPN and HPR, in much the same fashion as subarea node-to-subarea node prioritization. The fundamental difference between the APPN/HPR scenario and the SNA scheme is that COS works on an end-to-end basis in the former, from an end user at one EN to another end user at another EN or NN. The drawback is that achieving this end-to-end COS-based prioritization requires a full-stack APPN EN, such as IBM's

Although they are invariably proprietary, sufficient traffic prioritization and bandwidth allocation schemes exist to ensure that interactive SNA traffic receives precedence over other types of traffic in intranets and extranets.

PComm, at the client and some form of DLUR support if 3270 sessions are involved.

Traffic prioritization, and especially ensuring that interactive SNA/APPN traffic does not become swamped by high-volume file transfers or large Web page accesses, is a major concern when designing and implementing an SNA-capable i•net. Attempting any kind of prioritization based on SNA COS will at best have limited use, because COS's scope does not extend beyond the subarea. With SNA-capable i•nets, subarea-based WANs become usurped by i•nets, and many PC/workstation-based end users rely on TCP/IP-oriented client software, such as tn3270(E) or browsers, for their SNA application access. (In many instances, the subarea WAN would already have been displaced by a multiprotocol network.) Although Cisco offers a scheme that prioritizes 37xx-to-37xx SNA traffic based on COS/TPF over a router-based internetwork, few enterprises will likely implement SNA-capable i•nets that contain remote 37xxs, acting as SNA concentrators, within the i•net.

Some enterprises, on the other hand, may require APPN COS-based prioritization to accommodate new LU 6.2-based applications that rely on prioritization of different streams of traffic according to their nature and destination. If support for APPN COS is imperative, then HPR-over-IP would be required. Support for COS is one of the few compelling and irrefutable justifications for HPR-over-IP in the context of SNA-capable i•nets. Nevertheless, some enterprises may elect not to pursue this option and instead rely on the additional WAN bandwidth that will typically be available within the i•net to compensate for the lack of COS-based traffic prioritization.

In most cases, the pragmatic need for traffic prioritization within SNA-capable i•nets will boil down to ensuring that interactive interactions, such as 3270 access to mission-critical SNA applications, receive automatic and guaranteed priority over other types of traffic, such as file transfer and e-mail. Hence the prioritization challenge becomes that of isolating various traffic types, whether they be tn3270, DLSw, FTP, or HTTP, and then forwarding certain types ahead of others at every queuing point—in particular, when message units are queued at a router awaiting transmission on a WAN link. Unfortunately, no traffic prioritization standards or conventions exist for i•nets and SNA-capable i•nets. The available traffic prioritization schemes therefore tend to be vendor-specific. Any traffic prioritization will apply only to intranets and extranets. No truly credible ways to ensure traffic prioritization on an end-to-end basis have been developed for SNA access or SNA-based data transfer across the Internet.

The good news is that the major router and switch vendors recognize the need for traffic prioritization and offer a variety of schemes, some more comprehensive and sophisticated than others. For example, Cisco, the unchallenged leader since the early 1990s in integrating SNA into multi-protocol networks, has expended considerable effort in developing various traffic prioritization schemes geared toward the needs of SNA users. Cisco, which also dominates the router market, serves as a good model for the potential traffic prioritization options that could be employed within SNA-capable i•nets. At present, this company provides four traffic prioritization (queuing) schemes within its standard and ubiquitous Internetworking Operating System (IOS) software:

- First-in, first-out (FIFO) queuing
- Priority queuing
- Custom queuing
- Weighted fair queuing

FIFO Queuing

FIFO, as its name implies, does not attempt to give one type of traffic precedence over another. The first packet to arrive at an output point, such as the queue for a WAN link, is the first packet transmitted, irrespective of whether it is associated with an SNA, Web access, file transfer, or e-mail interaction. This scheme, which matches the approach used between SNA peripheral nodes and subarea nodes, works well on noncongested links. Its major shortcoming is that a series of packets sent as a part of a large file transfer can monopolize a link to the detriment of other users.

Priority Queuing

Priority queuing provides one way to circumvent the limitations of FIFO and allocate precedence to certain traffic over others. With this scheme, a network administrator can define queues corresponding to high-priority traffic, medium-priority traffic, normal-priority traffic, and low-priority traffic. The priority assigned to a given traffic flow could be based on the protocol type, TCP port number, message size, MAC address, input adapter address, or other criteria.

In multiprotocol networks, prioritization based on protocol type was meaningful and effective. In SNA-capable i•nets, all of the traffic will be IP in nature—albeit associated with different IP applications such as DLSw, FTP, tn3270(E), **SNMP**, HTTP, and **SMTP**. To be meaningful, prioritization must now be done relative to IP applications. Cisco and other vendors handle this issue by permitting prioritization based on TCP port numbers. There is also the capability to prioritize within DLSw based on criteria such as MAC address or the LU within a given SNA node. Priority queuing, although a significant improvement over FIFO, has a fatal flaw. If traffic tagged as high priority is continually queued such that the high-priority queue is always full, then the only packets that will be dequeued and transmitted will be those in the high-priority queue. The packets in the other queues will languish and will eventually be discarded without reaching their intended destination. A high and consistent volume of high-priority traffic of one type—say tn3270(E)—could therefore monopolize a link and preclude other traffic, possibly including network management-related traffic, from being transmitted.

Custom Queuing

Custom queuing, which is a bandwidth allocation technique, overcomes the inequitable service provision problem of priority queuing by allocating a guaranteed minimum amount of bandwidth, over a given period of time, to the various queues. This technique ensures that higher-priority queues cannot monopolize the available bandwidth at the expense of the lower-priority queues. With custom queuing, even the queue with the lowest priority will receive some amount of bandwidth on a regular basis. Moreover, any bandwidth allocation unused by one queue can be gainfully utilized by another queue to prevent wasting of any available bandwidth. Custom queuing and comparable bandwidth allocation schemes from other vendors represent the most flexible and optimum traffic prioritization scheme, at least for now, for SNA-capable i•nets.

The one drawback of this scheme is that it requires considerable manual preconfiguration of the queue types and the bandwidth allocation per queue. Moreover, for prioritization to work across the network, these definitions must be consistent across all routers involved.

Weighted Fair Queuing

Weighted fair queuing eliminates the need for preconfiguration and automatically applies priorities, or "weights," to different types of conversations. Conversations are classified into one of two groups: those requiring relatively small allocations of bandwidth, such as interactive traffic, and those requiring large amounts of bandwidth, such as high-volume file transfers. Weighted fair queuing attempts to ensure that bandwidth remains sufficient for the conversations that require only small amounts of bandwidth, and that the conversations requiring large allocations of bandwidth can share the remaining bandwidth equitably based on the relative weight of a conversation. When weighted fair queuing is in effect, Cisco routers will automatically classify packets into different types of conversations based on criteria such as TCP port address, UDP port address, IP source/destination addresses, or Frame Relay virtual circuit number.

The bottom line when it comes to traffic prioritization vis-à-vis SNA-capable i•nets is that techniques—albeit vendor-specific options—exist to ensure equitable distribution of bandwidth. The interactive traffic, including SNA/3270 traffic, is therefore able to get precedence over non-real-time, bulk data transfer traffic. These priority schemes are not based on SNA COS—but then SNA COS does not provide prioritization all the way to individual end users. In this respect, techniques such as custom queuing can provide better prioritization between individual SNA end users or devices than was possible within an SNA WAN consisting of just one 37xx serving all remote peripheral nodes. If support for APPN/HPR COS is indeed imperative, the obvious solution is to pursue HPR-over-IP.

3.6   DEALING WITH CONGESTION

Although this feature is not one of its renowned capabilities, SNA has always gone to inordinate lengths to minimize congestion and to avoid having any message units be discarded because of intolerable congestion levels at an end or intermediate node. SNA utilizes a range of mechanisms for controlling and minimizing the danger of congestion, including session-level pacing, Virtual Route dynamic pacing, LU 6.2 adaptive pacing, session quiescing, and Subarea Node Slowdown.

Pacing is the term used by SNA to describe mechanisms whereby a receiving component can regulate the rate at which data are transmitted to it, thereby ensuring that it does not become inundated with data. Pacing relies on the notion that the receiver will send a "go-ahead" acknowledgment when it is ready to receive another series of message units. This type of mechanism can operate when the receiver is willing to accept either a fixed number of message units per acknowledgment cycle or a dynamically varying number of message units depending on the resources available at any given time.

HPR takes congestion avoidance to new heights with a very resourceful, closed-loop scheme known as **adaptive rate-based (ARB)** congestion control. This protocol strives to anticipate the buildup of congestion within a network and immediately slows down transmissions into the network if it detects the possible beginning of congestion.

Overengineering intranets and extranets with excess bandwidth might be the only effective panacea against disruption to SNA access caused by intermittent periods of congestion.

TCP/IP also offers various schemes that can be used individually or in parallel to control congestion, including the **sliding-window acknowledgment process, slowstart**, and the **congestion avoidance algorithm**. Despite the availability of such techniques, congestion control in TCP/IP networks remains less rigorous and less crucial than it is in SNA networks. Moreover, the routers, LAN switches, and even Frame Relay switches used to implement TCP/IP networks, in marked contrast to 37xx communications controllers, cope with unexpected congestion due to heavy traffic loads by arbitrarily discarding traffic packets. Managing congestion by discarding data-bearing packets is an alien and anathemic notion to the SNA/APPN community. Instead, the goal of the various congestion schemes used by SNA, APPN, and HPR is to prevent nodes from suffering buffer depletion because of congestion that would force them to lose or discard data packets. Given this penchant of routers and switches to discard packets as a means of controlling congestion, it is likely that SNA data will, at some point or another, be discarded within SNA-capable i•nets.

Fortunately, discarded SNA/APPN packets within i•nets rarely result in data loss or transaction errors. Higher-level SNA sequence numbers at Layer 3 or Layer 4, as well as application-level transaction numbers, will ensure that any SNA/APPN message units discarded within the i•net are retransmitted. Even a single discarded message unit, however, disrupts end-to-end data flow within the affected SNA/APPN session. This disruption is caused by the retransmission processes that are invoked to recover the lost message unit and resequence the data flow.

SNA, APPN, and TCP/IP do not support the notion of "selective rejects"—the ability to request the retransmission of a single discarded or damaged packet. Instead, they rely on a mechanism that acknowledges the packets up to the first discarded or damaged packet. Consequently, all packets, from the discarded or damaged packet to the end of the acknowledgment window cycle (which could be seven packets or more), are retransmitted. This retransmission occurs even if all other packets following the discarded or damaged one were successfully received at the other end. HPR, in contrast, supports selective rejects.

The retransmittal of previously delivered message units, which obviously increases traffic volume, could exacerbate congestion and lead to even more packets being discarded. The number of retransmissions required will depend on two factors: the size of the original acknowledgment window and the position within this window of the first discarded packet, where the acknowledgment window could be 8, 14, or even 128. If the window size is large and the first discarded packet appeared early in the window, then a large number of packets must be retransmitted—for example, when the first packet in a window of 128 is discarded, as opposed to the seventh packet in a window of 8.

These additional retransmissions could cause other message units within the block that is being retransmitted to be discarded. This development, obviously, would result in even more retransmissions that could worsen the congestion! Moreover, these retransmissions will adversely affect response times, overall network performance, and efficiency, while chewing up expensive bandwidth that could have been used for productive data transfer.

Delays in the in-sequence delivery of SNA/APPN message units as a result of retransmissions invariably lead to erratic response times. When a retransmission affects the data flow of a terminal "interaction," the response time, which might normally be 0.5 second for a given SNA mission-critical application, could suddenly jump to 3.5 seconds or more. The number of retransmissions will, of course, depend on the amount of network traffic and the resultant levels of congestion at the various points within the network. The heavier the traffic load, the greater the chances that one or more nodes within the network may experience buffer-depleting congestion and arbitrarily discard packets. Consequently, the need for retransmissions may occur on a regular and cyclic basis. Terminal operators may experience sudden and dramatic increases in response times every few minutes. Such erratic response times frustrate these users, disrupt their work patterns, and directly affect productivity.

Just as with nonoptimal SNA routing and lack of SNA COS-based prioritization, erratic SNA response times due to retransmissions are not a problem specific to SNA-capable i•nets. This problem already exists in bridge/router-based multiprotocol networks that support SNA/APPN traffic.

The only sure-fire way to minimize the danger of congestion occurring on a regular basis on an intranet or extranet is to model the anticipated bandwidth requirements for the network and then overengineer the network with excess bandwidth to cope with unexpected traffic loads. Though costly, this option offers the only way to minimize erratic performance, especially for the SNA users interacting with mission-critical applications. Ultimately, the justification for the additional bandwidth must be balanced against that of the lost "opportunity" costs. Delays and frustrations when interacting with mission-critical applications will result in lost productivity and decrease the volume of transactions being processed by these applications. In many instances, such "lost opportunity" costs can negatively impact the corporation's sacrosanct bottom line.

Obviously, bandwidth overengineering is applicable only to intranets and extranets. An enterprise could try to improve the performance of its Internet-related transactions by increasing the bandwidth of its link to the Internet—for example, by upgrading the connection to the ISP from 256Kbps to 1.54Mbps. Although this strategy will certainly speed some of the Internet transactions, unexpected and unpredictable congestion, delays, and lost packets will still occur within the Internet that will disrupt SNA application access over the Internet. Consequently, Internet access should not be chosen as the preferred means of access to SNA applications that require crisp and predictable response times.

3.7   SCALABILITY, MANAGEABILITY, AND ACCOUNTABILITY

Scalability in terms of its ability to support hundreds of millions of concurrent users is a trademark of the Internet. This impressive and unprecedented scalability, however, is derived through the synthesis of enormous amounts of computing power spread across many thousands of computers and servers with huge volumes of high-speed networking bandwidth. An intranet, or more particularly an SNA-capable intranet, will not be as scalable as the Internet simply because it is based on Internet concepts and technologies.

The realistic scalability and capacity of a given intranet will be dictated in the main by the power and storage capability of its Web servers, the amount of bandwidth at its disposal, and the volume of transactions involved. In the case of SNA-capable intranets and extranets, scalability will be further gated by the capacity of certain servers and gateways—in particular, tn3270(E) servers and SNA-Web gateways. If the data center routers place limitations on the number of concurrent TCP connections that they can support, it could limit the size and configuration of the DLSw subnetwork because DLSw relies on multiple, active TCP connections between the various routers so as to transfer DLSw-based SNA/APPN data. (Chapter 4 describes the principles of operation of DLSw in detail.) The bottom line is that one needs to ensure that the SNA-related components used to implement an SNA-capable i•net have sufficient capacity to support the necessary number of simultaneous users.

Mainframe- and 37xx-based SNA networks can support large numbers of concurrent interactive users. In the SNA world, networks that handle 30,000 to 40,000 interactive users at the same time are classed as mid-size; only networks that have the capacity to cope with 100,000 or more simultaneous users are deemed to be large. Supporting large numbers of users was not a real problem given the power and the capacities of the hardware involved in SNA networks. A high-end 3745, such as a Model 61A, with a 3746-900 expansion chassis could support as many as 896 low-speed, non-T1 serial ports, or in the case of LAN-attached devices up to 9,999 individual SNA nodes, where a single 3174 or SNA LAN gateway constitutes such a node. Hence, a high-end 3745 might be able to support 50,000 to 100,000 active SNA end users. The move to multiprotocol networks did not dramatically affect the scalability of SNA networks because the data center infrastructure consisting of mainframes, AS/400s and 37xxs was preserved. Moreover, it provided most of the required SNA functionality, albeit in conjunction with distributed SNA-LAN gateways that enabled LAN-attached PCs/workstations to gain access to SNA applications and print services. One major exception was that the TCP connection requirements of the early versions of DLSw curtailed the size of certain networks. Corporations typically circumvented such limitations by using Source Route Bridging, Cisco's Remote Source Route Bridging in non-TCP-based Fast Sequenced Transport (FST) mode, or even APPN NN routing on bridge/routers.

SNA-related scalability will, however, become a more pressing issue with SNA-capable i•nets, particularly with tn3270(E) based access and, in some instances, browser-based access to SNA. All tn3270(E) and some browser-based access to SNA solutions are contingent on the presence and cooperation of a server component. In mid-1999, a single instance of a tn3270(E) server running on a relatively beefy mainframe could support approximately 60,000 concurrent SNA/3270 sessions. The tn3270(E) server implementation running on an IBM 2216 or Cisco Channel Interface Processor (CIP) within a 7500 router can support 15,000 to 16,000 sessions. Given that a Cisco 7500 can accommodate as many as 10 CIPs, it is theoretically possible to support very high volumes of tn3270(E) sessions with this channel-attached solution. Other tn3270(E) servers, including some that run on channel-attached gateways, support considerably fewer sessions.

It is not uncommon for a Windows NT-based tn3270(E) server, such as Microsoft's SNA Server or IBM's CS/NT running on a relatively powerful Pentium II-based PC platform, to support only 4000 or so concurrent sessions. UNIX-based tn3270(E) servers, such as OpenConnect Systems' SNA Access Server, running on mid-size RISC workstations can typically handle 20,000 or so sessions. If an enterprise must support more tn3270(E) concurrent users than are accommodated by a single server, the only real option is to deploy multiple servers. The tn3270(E) client population can be distributed across the multiple servers by either assigning each client to a particular server (with a possible backup server) or using a TCP/IP-based directory server that will dynamically route incoming tn3270(E) to an available router via a load-balancing scheme.

Having multiple servers with sufficient capacity to back each other up also eliminates the potential danger of making a tn3270(E) server become a single point of failure that could disrupt access to mission-critical SNA applications. Some SNA-Web gateways required for browser-based access also place relatively restrictive limits on the number of concurrent users supported. The capacity of a few of these solutions may be as low as 128 concurrent users per Windows NT server; others may support only 256 concurrent users. Other browser-based solutions, and especially those that rely on an applet-based tn3270(E) client emulation, can support as many users as are supported by the tn3270(E) servers, however. The bottom line is that the exact capacities of the various servers used to implement an SNA-capable i•net must be carefully evaluated to ensure that the finished network can handle the necessary number of active users and traffic loads.

The management requirements of SNA-capable i•nets will, obviously, differ greatly from those of SNA-only networks. In the early days, prior to the advent of LANs, SNA networks consisted primarily of serial port-attached SNA/SDLC, SNA/X.25, or 3270 BSC devices. It was then sufficient just to have **NetView** (née **NCCF/NPDA**) on a mainframe to monitor and control the entire network. With the introduction of LANs and hubs, enterprises really had no option except to augment NetView/390 with either SNMP or proprietary management platforms geared toward overseeing the

SNA-capable i•nets will require both TCP/IP- and SNA-oriented management platforms, and possibly TCP/IP management on mainframes. Certain servers and gateways needed to realize these i•nets may not be as scalable as components used to build SNA networks, however.

burgeoning non-SNA-based LAN infrastructure. IBM's TME 10 NetView and HP's OpenView were the most widely used SNMP solutions. The need for and the scope of SNMP-oriented management grew with the move toward multiprotocol networking, because these networks were built around bridges, routers, and switches with TCP/IP-oriented management processes. The growing reliance on SNMP for managing the LAN and WAN infrastructure did not mean that NetView/390 became superfluous. Instead, corporations continued to use NetView/390 to manage ACF/VTAM, ACF/NCP on 37xxs, SNA applications running on the mainframe, and downstream SNA devices such as 3174s and AS/400s.

This need for dual-platform cooperative management—that is, NetView on the mainframe plus an off-board SNMP management system—will not change much with SNA-capable i•nets. The LAN/WAN infrastructure, as well as all of the new Web servers, NT servers, SNA-Web gateways, and even off-board tn3270(E) servers will still require SNMP-based monitoring, control, and administration. Just like multiprotocol networks, SNA-capable i•nets will require NetView-based, mainframe-resident, SNA-oriented management for the SNA components within the network, including the mainframe- or AS/400-resident SNA mission-critical applications. The one key difference relates to the fact that SNA-capable i•nets will most likely also require mainframe-resident TCP/IP-oriented management in parallel to the off-board SNMP manager(s) overseeing the LAN/WAN infrastructure. The reason is that more enterprises are now installing TCP/IP on mainframes along with TCP/IP applications such as FTP, tn3270(E) servers, and Web servers. OS/390, IBM's strategic replacement for its flagship MVS mainframe operating includes TCP/IP software and a Web server (WebSphere) bundled in as standard no-charge components. The TCP/IP stack on the mainframe, and the TCP/IP applications running on the mainframe will both need to be managed in much the same way that enterprises manage ACF/VTAM and SNA/APPN applications running on mainframes. Sterling Software's SOLVE: Netmaster for TCP/IP and Interlink Computer Science's e•Access are two contemporary offerings for mainframe-based TCP/IP management.

The management needs of SNA-Capable i•nets are discussed in more detail in Chapter 7. Figure 3.6 depicts the need for multiple management platforms for monitoring and controlling SNA-capable i•nets.

The ready availability of network usage statistics represents yet another area where SNA-capable i•nets will differ significantly from SNA-only networks. With SNA networks, corporations could rely on the mainframe-resident NetView Performance Monitor (NPM), working in conjunction with ACF/NCP running on one or more 37xxs, to collect actual SNA response time and traffic usage statistics. The NPM data were routinely used for capacity-planning purposes, network fine-tuning, and generating network usage charge-back billing. With the move to SNA-capable i•nets, corporations

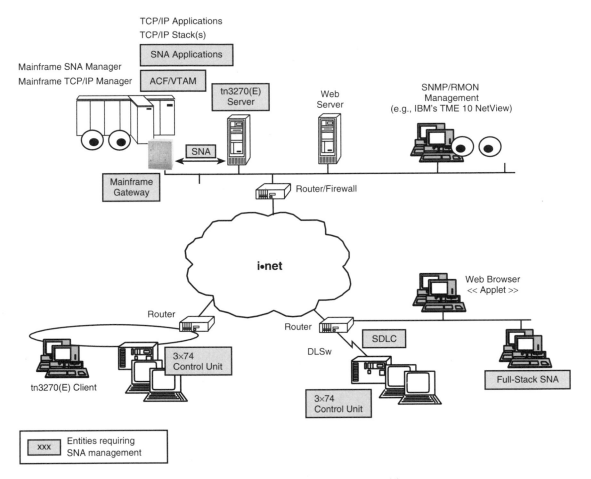

FIGURE 3.6   The need for multiple management systems in an SNA-capable i•net.

could lose much, if not all, of these NPM-based performance and usage accounting data.

NPM is totally dependent on ACF/NCP working in tandem with it to collect the necessary statistics. ACF/NCP, however, runs only on 37x5s. It does not run on the 3746-950 or other IBM mainframe gateways, such as the OSA-2, 2216/ESCON Multiaccess Concentrator, or the 3172 Interconnect Controller. Likewise, it is not supported by other popular non-IBM mainframe gateways, such as Cisco's 7xxx/CIP and Bus-Tech's NetShuttle family. As more corporations displace their anachronistic 37xxs in favor of more cost-effective, i•net-oriented gateways, such as Cisco's 7xxx/ CIP, IBM's 2216/ESCON, and Bus-Tech's NetShuttle, they will lose the NPM-based network accounting statistics.

Moreover, with SNA-capable i•nets, network usage statistics cannot be restricted to just access information related to mainframe SNA/APPN applications. To obtain a true picture of total network usage for an SNA-capable i•net, network managers need to monitor and measure the usage of non-SNA network resources, possibly including Internet access. This type of non-SNA-related accounting lies well outside the scope and province of NPM. To obtain this level of SNA- and non-SNA-related performance and usage data, corporations will have to turn to products such as Legent/CA's NETspy and LANspy.

3.8 THE LAST WORD

Despite their ability to provide unrestricted and unencumbered end-to-end SNA access and SNA transport, SNA-capable i•nets should never be considered as just another variant of an SNA or APPN network. SNA-capable i•nets differ markedly from SNA-only networks in areas such as availability, security, congestion control, SNA routing, and consistent performance. In most cases, the differences will be accentuated when SNA is used across the public Internet, rather than across an intranet or an extranet. The good news, however, is that these differences, though important, are not showstoppers. Other ways and means exist to minimize, circumvent, and even overcome many of the differences. The tide cannot be stopped. SNA-capable i•nets will prevail as the final metamorphosis of SNA, despite having different characteristics from those of SNA-only networks.

Integrating SNA/APPN with i•nets

The lure, the promise, and the scope of i•nets is immense and incontroverti-ble. Nonetheless, for corporations that have hitherto relied on mainframes or AS/400s for the bulk of their data processing, the tantalizing potential of i•nets is marred by one major drawback: TCP/IP-centric and Web server-oriented i•nets cannot natively support the mainframe- and AS/400-resident SNA/APPN applications.

Although they may be augmented by other applications, including in-tranet applications, these SNA/APPN applications and the data accessed through them remain crucial to the ongoing commercial viability of such corporations. In the case of "IBM shops," it is not unusual to find that at least 70% of the vital corporate data resides on mainframes or AS/400s, rather than on Web or Windows NT servers; moreover, much of these data are readily accessible only via the business logic contained within SNA/APPN applications. The types of data located on mainframes and AS/400s are like-ly to include the following: the latest financial records; historic economic data; customer information databases; product information repositories; ser-vice records; customer status entries; product descriptions; product avail-ability dates; manufacturing records; employee records; and corporate assets. In essence, with IBM shops much of their "life blood" information is likely to be located within traditional data centers.

Access to this data-center-resident information cannot typically be real-ized just by expediently installing TCP/IP or a Web server on the appropriate mainframes or AS/400s. This situation is unfortunate because implementing TCP/IP and a Web server on a mainframe or AS/400 is now a relatively easy and inexpensive exercise. Not only do many corporations already have TCP/IP installed on their data center systems, but OS/390, IBM's strategic operating

In IBM shops, at least 70% of the vital corporate data will reside in a traditional data center, and much of these data will be meaningful only when they are processed via the business logic contained within SNA mission-critical applications.

system for mainframes, already has an efficient TCP/IP stack and a proficient Web server, known as WebSphere, bundled in as standard components (see Fig. 1.2 on page 7). In reality integrating i•nets with data centers does not have to be contingent on having TCP/IP or a Web server on a mainframe or AS/400, although their presence on these systems can usually be leveraged to achieve scalable and long-term solutions.

TCP/IP support on the mainframe is a prerequisite for using the TCP/IP interfaces now available on major IBM application subsystems, such as CICS, IMS and DB2. Yet again, having these TCP/IP interfaces alone is not a total solution. Most large corporations will likely have other applications, especially in-house developed applications, that lack TCP/IP capability. Even when a TCP/IP interface exists, as is the case with CICS, there is invariably a need for the appropriate client software component as well as user interface remapping. Chapter 6 looks at some of the major application-specific solutions, particularly for CICS.

Enabling i•net users to access data center resources invariably requires some level of gateway functionality to provide either TCP/IP to SNA/APPN conversion, data format remapping, database compatibility, file conversion, or a combination of these features. The gateway functionality, irrespective of its role, will typically be software-based. This gateway software could be deployed within a channel-attached controller, a channel-attached bridge/ router, or a data-center-resident LAN server. The Bus-Tech NetShuttle running Microsoft SNA Server with its OLE Database Provider, which permits VSAM file manipulation, is one example of a channel-attached controller. An IBM 2216 with its tn3270(E) software feature, which enables TCP/IP clients to access SNA applications, is representative of a channel-attached bridge/router. Novell's HostPublisher running on a LAN-attached PC and performing 3270-to-HTML conversion to permit browser-based access to SNA applications across the Internet would be just one of myriad possibilities when it came to a data-center-resident LAN server that acts as an SNA–i•net gateway.

Such non-mainframe-resident, "off-board" gateways will communicate with the SNA/APPN applications running on a mainframe or AS/400 using standard SNA/APPN protocols. This approach is consistent with the notion of keeping the data center SNA-oriented, even though the network is a TCP/IP-centric i•net, as was shown in Fig. 2.2.

In some instances, the gateway function could be provided within the mainframe—as with a mainframe-resident tn3270(E) server from IBM, OpenConnect Systems' OC://WebConnect Pro for S/390 (which provides Java applet-based access to SNA), or IBM's CICS Web Interface (which performs 3270-to-HTML conversion). If the gateway function is installed on the mainframe, a TCP/IP stack will also be required on the mainframe to enable TCP/IP transactions from the i•net to reach the gateway. The presence of a TCP/IP stack on the mainframe will not mean that no SNA software will reside on the mainframe. As the goal of these gateways is to provide a bridge between i•nets and existing SNA/APPN-based resources, SNA software (such as ACF/VTAM) will invariably be found alongside the TCP/IP software. In that case, the gateway provides the necessary protocol and data conversions between the two environments.

Just implementing TCP/IP or a Web server on a mainframe or AS/400 will not, by itself, solve the i•net-to-data center integration requirements. Some level of gateway functionality, even if it takes the form of a tn3270(E) server, either off-board or on the mainframe, remains a prerequisite. Attempting to bypass the requirement for such gateways by contemplating the wholesale migration of data away from the data center is likely, in practice, to prove futile in most instances. The prospect of replicating or migrating this SNA/APPN-oriented mainframe- or AS/400-resident data on or to other platforms so as to make it i•net-accessible would be a daunting proposition, to say the least. Nevertheless, some have embraced this approach, at least initially, as the only safe option when it comes to providing Internet-based access to corporate data. Many, however, would deem it to be outright infeasible in terms of cost, effort, complexity, magnitude, and potential risk—particularly so given the mission-criticality of the data and applications involved. Indeed, compromising the integrity or the ready availability of mission-critical applications and data has never been conducive to upward career mobility.

Today's mainframe users would likely have already "right-sized" their computing needs wherever possible over the last decade. Moreover they have also, without exception, experimented with various mainframe-oriented client/server schemes. Thus they already know the issues and implications of trying to recreate their mainframe information management and data-processing environment on other non-mainframe platforms. Most have stayed with mainframes, at least to this point, because they realized the impracticality or impossibility of moving to other platforms, whether because of concerns related to scalability, reliability, performance, capacity, compatibility, or even the total cost of ownership. The steadily increasing demand for mainframes and mainframe computing cycles, as attested to by IBM's now highly buoyant financial status, indicates that most of these IBM shops remain inextricably committed to mainframe-based computing. The AS/400 installed base, now more than 300,000 units strong, also continues to thrive despite the popularity of Windows NT-based servers. Hence one does not have the option of postponing the integration of data centers and i•nets and simply waiting for mainframes and AS/400s to be entirely replaced by Web or NT servers.

4.1   I•NET INTEGRATION TECHNOLOGY—
HERE AND PROVEN

The good news is that proven and robust technology, from at least 40 credible vendors led by the likes of IBM, Cisco, Attachmate, Wall Data, Novell, Eicon Technology, and OpenConnect Systems, is now readily available to facilitate data center-to-i•net integration in a seamless and synergistic manner. Consistent with other i•net-oriented solutions, much of this technology is considerably more cost-effective than existing SNA access offerings, such as traditional SNA/3270 emulators or SNA-LAN gateways. Consequently, quite a few enterprises around the world (some of them household names such as General Motors (GM), FedEx, Del Monte Foods International, and TWA) are already gainfully using this i•net-to-data center integration technology on a daily basis for business-critical production use. In addition to these well-known companies, other enterprises currently using this integration technology on a production basis include Lafayette Life Insurance, Ohio State University, the state of Idaho, National Van Lines, Royal Jordanian Airlines, The Chickering Group, Al Rajhi Banking & Investment Corporation (Saudi Arabia's largest bank), and the Cairo (Egypt) Opera House.

Al Rajhi Bank uses **browser-based SNA access** to provide interactive home banking with a highly graphical, Web page-based user interface. Despite this contemporary visage, the actual banking applications being accessed by the home banking consumers are traditional mainframe-resident SNA applications with a standard text-only, green-on-black, 3270 terminal interface. Figure 4.1 shows an example of the type of rejuvenated user interface being employed by this bank. The technology used in this instance to extend conventional Web browser-based access to include mainframe-resident SNA applications is known as **3270-to-HTML conversion**. 3270-to-HTML conversion is performed by a software gateway function. This gateway function accepts the 3270 data stream corresponding to 3270 screen images and dynamically converts the data stream into HTML according to a set of translation rules defined by the customer, the vendor, or both. Graphical elements to be embedded in the HTML-based Web pages, as well as the overall look and feel of the Web pages, are also specified as a part of these translation rules.

3270-to-HTML conversion—or for that matter, any of the other user interface rejuvenation solutions now available in the context of browser-based access to SNA—does not require any modifications to the mainframe-resident SNA applications. All of the browser-based access solutions, including 3270-to-HTML conversion, are discussed in detail in Chapter 5. After the year 2000, 3270-to-HTML conversion is likely to be realized using application servers, as described in Chapter 6.

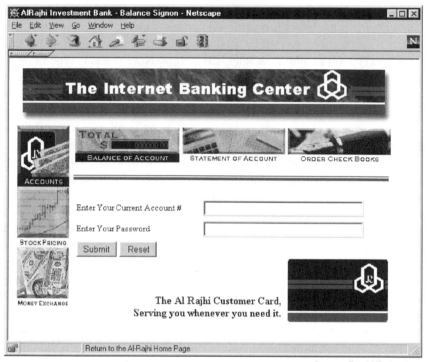

Source: Farabi Technology

FIGURE 4.1 The rejuvenated 3270 user interface being used by Al Rajhi Bank in Saudi Arabia. (Courtesy of Farabi Technology Corporation.)

GM, National Van Lines, and The Chickering Group use browser-based access to SNA technology to provide agents and partners with ready access to mainframe- or AS/400-resident applications or databases across the Internet. Other organizations, such as TWA and Del Monte Foods International, are leveraging this technology to permit employees to access mainframe applications from distant locations across the Internet—in some cases, via satellite links to the Internet. The exact architectures and products used by these enterprises are described in detail in the case studies in Chapters 5 and 6.

These enterprises often use firewalls to provide an initial line of defense between the Internet and their internal corporate networks. Some of the gateways that are used to facilitate browser-based SNA access offer optional user authentication capabilities based on gateway-specific user IDs and passwords. When implemented, this type of gateway-based security will ensure that i•net users cannot reach a mainframe or AS/400 until they have been authenticated by the gateway. The gateway could also limit access to certain

Major corporations around the world, including GM, TWA, and FedEx, are already using i•net–to-data center integration technology, such as browser-based SNA access, to enable employees, the public, or agents to access mainframe applications across the Internet. In many cases, the old 3270 user interface of these applications is being dynamically rejuvenated to be more consistent with the look and feel of contemporary Web pages.

functions, such as printing or applications based on user IDs. Encryption of data sent across the Internet is achieved by these enterprises via product specific encryption solutions or through the use of VPN technology that has end-to-end encryption as a built-in, standard feature. Note that this type of i•net-specific security always represents an adjunct, and never a replacement, for traditional and highly proven data center security measures, such as application-specific user IDs and passwords. Mainframe customers will also continue to use products such as ACF2, RACF, or TopSecret to control and monitor mainframe access.

In the case of nearly all of the companies mentioned earlier, browser-based SNA access across the Internet supplements or displaces previous data center access schemes, such as dial-up connections, remote access servers, leased lines, or Frame Relay interfaces. Invariably, the browser-based access scheme is proving considerably more cost-effective, flexible, and extensible than previous solutions. Once a relatively scalable solution has been implemented at the data center, typically in the form of a gateway, these enterprises can readily accommodate new users without adding or modifying any access capability, especially in terms of hardware or modem connections. Browser-based SNA access gateways running on a PC or UNIX server can currently support from 128 to 20,000 concurrent users. Higher concentrations of concurrent users, as well as redundancy to cope with the failure of a single server, is realized using multiple gateways with a TCP/IP-based directory server that keeps the user load equitably balanced between the multiple gateways.

With the browser-based access schemes implemented by these enterprises, any user or agent who already has access to the Internet can gain access to the data center resources, provided that the user has the correct user ID and password, without the need for any special software or Internet connection. If the data center access occurs via a Java or ActiveX applet, as is the case with the solutions being used by GM, Del Monte Foods International, The Chickering Group, and FedEx, the applet is dynamically downloaded from a standard Web server across the Internet.

4.1.1 The Scope of SNA-Capable i•nets

I•nets that have been enhanced to support data center- or AS/400-resident mission-critical SNA/APPN applications and the data accessible via such applications constitute **SNA-capable i•nets**. SNA-capable i•nets set out to deliver unrestricted SNA-based application access, print services, database management, or data transfer across standard TCP/IP-based i•nets, whether they be intranets, extranets, or the Internet. Browser-based SNA access, which represents a key and strategic technology vis-à-vis SNA-capable i•net, also enables the dated and unfriendly 3270 or 5250 terminal-oriented user interface employed by most SNA applications to be easily rejuvenated—without requiring any changes to the mainframe or AS/400 application.

3270-to-HTML conversion represents one option for realizing browser-based access to SNA. The other option involves the use of an applet-based terminal emulation scheme. User interface rejuvenation—in many cases, with an AutoGUI option that requires no programming, scripting, or customization on the part of the customer—is possible with both approaches.

SNA-capable i•nets need to accommodate an extremely varied and disparate population of end-user devices and functionality. The end-user clients involved could be either SNA/APPN- or TCP/IP-oriented. The universe of end-user types that an SNA-capable i•net needs to support includes the following:

- PCs running various operating systems as well as a gamut of emulation packages ranging from full-stack SNA/3270 emulators, such as IBM's PComm, to strictly TCP/IP-based clients such as a standard Web browser

- Apple Macintoshes with SNA/APPN or TCP/IP clients

- UNIX workstations with SNA/APPN or TCP/IP clients

- 3270 terminals coax-attached to 3x74 control units

- Network computers (NCs)

- Printers

- Minicomputers such as AS/400s and Hewlett-Packard systems

- Remote **SNA-LAN gateways** such as Microsoft's SNA Server, Novell's NetWare for SAA, and IBM 3174s

- SNA-only devices such as IBM 4700 Financial Systems and automated teller machines

- "Legacy" SNA control units such as 3274s or compatibles

- "Legacy" **Binary Synchronous Communications (BSC)** control units still found in SNA networks, despite IBM's attempts since the late 1970s to have these devices replaced by bona fide SNA ones

- SNA or APPN applications running on PCs, workstations, minicomputers, or servers that use LU 6.2 or LU-LU Session Type 0 for program-to-program interactions

The need for accommodating both TCP/IP and SNA clients dictates that SNA-capable i•nets must be capable of offering SNA transport schemes to handle SNA/APPN and BSC clients, as well as SNA access solutions replete with the necessary protocol conversions to support the TCP/IP clients. Figure 4.2 depicts the difference between end-to-end SNA transport and SNA

A typical SNA-capable i•net will require at least one end-to-end SNA transport option as well as an SNA access mechanism. In general, DLSw will likely be the preferred option for SNA transport, with HPR-over-IP having the edge over DLSw only if an enterprise needs either SNA routing to access multiple data centers or end-to-end LU 6.2 COS prioritization from a desktop to a data center.

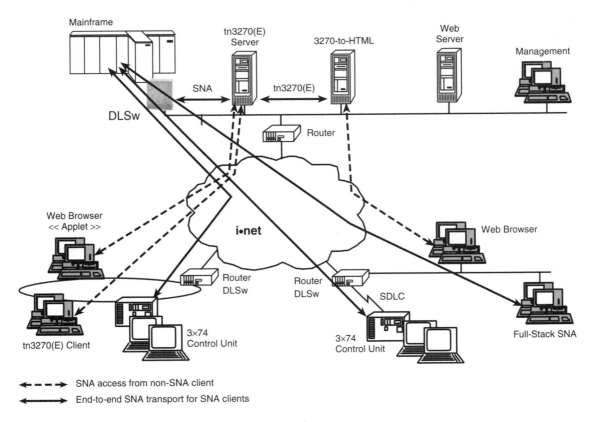

FIGURE 4.2 The difference between SNA transport and SNA access across i•nets.

access for TCP/IP-based clients. The following techniques can be used for SNA transport:

- Data Link Switching (DLSw) and **Desktop Data Link Switching (DDLSw)**
- **AnyNet**
- HPR-over-IP
- BSC traffic encapsulation within TCP/IP à la Cisco's **B-STUN** (BSC Tunneling) or IBM's BSC-over-IP support on the 2216 and 2212 bridge/routers

The prevalent solutions for SNA access through SNA-capable i•nets include the following:

- ip3270 and ip5250—where a TCP/IP transport scheme is used between an emulator, such as Eicon's Aviva for Desktops, and a gateway, such as a traditional SNA-LAN gateway like NetWare for SAA or Microsoft's SNA Server

- tn3270(E) and tn5250
- Browser-based SNA access
- Application-specific Web-to-data center gateways
- Programmatic (or middleware) servers for Web-to-data center integration—also referred to as application servers, corporate application servers, or integration servers

Most SNA-capable i•net implementations will use a combination of these techniques typically with at least one access solution and one transport scheme.

Most networks will most likely need DLSw, at least in the short to midterm, as a foolproof, no exceptions, workhorse scheme to accommodate the installed base of SNA/APPN clients. DLSw support for SNA devices is not contingent on the SNA session types used. Thus DLSw can be used, essentially with impunity, to handle all types of SNA sessions, including program-to-program interactions based on LU 6.2 or LU-LU Session Type 0.

The ability to assimilate LU 6.2 and LU-LU Session Type 0 into an i•net using DLSw is important because much access-related i•net integration technology tends to be highly oriented toward terminal emulation. Thus techniques such as tn3270(E) or browser-based access cannot support PCs and workstations that might be using LU 6.2 for some of their data center interactions. In addition to DLSw, however, AnyNet, HPR-over-IP, and sometimes ip3270 could be used to accommodate LU 6.2. Of these techniques, DLSw is by far the most widely available. As laid out in RFC 1795 and 2166, it is standards-based and readily available on bridge/routers from all major networking vendors, including Cisco, IBM, 3Com, and Nortel/Bay. It therefore has the edge over the other transport options in most scenarios. The only exceptions arise when an enterprise has a need for direct SNA-based routing to access multiple distributed data centers and when it uses LU 6.2 applications that are contingent on SNA COS priority. In these cases, HPR-over-IP should be evaluated as the potential end-to-end SNA transport scheme, as opposed to DLSw.

4.1.2 High-Level Overview of the Pertinent Technologies

SNA-capable i•nets, much like their SNA-only predecessors, will thrive for a long time—most likely well into the second decade of the twenty-first century. Thus it is imperative that enterprises do not allow these i•nets to evolve in an ad hoc manner independent of an overall, predetermined framework that identifies the most germane methodologies for the new network and best addresses the exact requirements of the enterprise in question. SNA-capable i•nets should be explicitly engineered from the

A four-step process should be followed to determine the evolving SNA transport and access requirements of an enterprise and to select the optimal Web-to-data center integration technology that addresses these requirements.

ground up to exploit the optimal set of integration technologies for the needs of a specific enterprise.

The trick to ensuring success when engineering an effective SNA-capable i•net is to rigidly adhere to a four-step process. The first step in this process involves determining all of the SNA access requirements of the entire enterprise, whether terminal, programmatic, or database-oriented—both in terms of the data center applications to be accessed and the equipment to be employed by the end users to access those applications. The second step is to establish the end-to-end SNA transport requirements so as to accommodate SNA-only devices, legacy controllers, and any programmatic SNA clients, such as LU 6.2 applications.

Once the complete set of access and transport requirements has been clearly identified, the third step is to map these requirements to an ongoing timeline stretching from the present to a point three to four years in the future. The spectrum of SNA access and transport needs should now be identifiable as both short- to medium-term tactical requirements and long-term strategic goals. At this juncture, one may realize that ip3270 or tn3270(E) represents a more than acceptable tactical solution during the transition to the TCP/IP-based backbone and that browser-based access with user interface rejuvenation could serve as a subsequent refinement. A similar shift in requirements relative to the time scale may also apply to end-to-end SNA transport. In most instances, the need for SNA transport will diminish with time as the enterprise phases out legacy SNA-only devices.

At this juncture, one should have a requirements list, based on time scale, for the envisaged SNA-capable i•net. The final step in this process consists of an evaluation of the integration technologies available and which best address the identified short- to mid-term, as well as longer-term, requirements.

The remainder of this subsection provides a first-cut, high-level description of all of the various SNA transport and SNA access technologies now available. Each of these technologies is described further in this and the following chapter. The goal here is to become familiar with the technologies so that their best uses can be categorized and discussed.

Technologies for end-to-end SNA traffic transport across an i•net are discussed first.

Data Link Switching

DLSw encapsulates any kind of SNA or APPN traffic, including LU 6.2 traffic, independent of session type, within TCP/IP packets for end-to-end transport across a TCP/IP WAN backbone. Moreover, it provides SDLC-to-LAN conversion so that any serial attached SNA-only device, such as a 3174, can be assimilated into the i•net as if it were a LAN-attached device.

SDLC-to-LAN conversion, using the DLSw capability on remote bridge/routers, eliminates the need for SDLC ports at the data center network-to-mainframe gateway. (Contrary to widespread belief, SDLC is not used across LANs or even IBM mainframe channels. The SDLC equivalent used on LANs in the context of SNA/APPN traffic is 802.2.) DLSw's SDLC-to-LAN conversion facilitates the use of new, low-cost, LAN-centric mainframe gateways, such as IBM 2216s, Cisco 7xxx with CIPs, or Bus-Tech NetShuttles, in place of the costly and now anachronistic 3745 FEPs. DLSw is an IETF standard covered by RFCs 1795, 1434, and 2166 (2166 applies to DLSw version 2.0 enhancements).

Desktop DLSw (DDLSw) is a variant of DLSw that runs within PCs and workstations. It has relevance only if a full-stack SNA/3270 emulator is installed on a PC/workstation. DDLSw acts alongside the full-stack SNA/3270 emulator, ensuring that the SNA message units are encapsulated within TCP/IP, per the DLSw standard, before they leave the PC/workstation. This standard obviates the need for remote bridge/routers to perform DLSw-based TCP/IP encapsulation or deencapsulation. DDLSw, however, is contingent on one or more bridge/routers at the data center end performing the necessary deencapsulations and encapsulations of the SNA traffic flowing into and out of the data center. Note that no DLSw implementations run on a mainframe or AS/400, even though no technical or logical impediments exist to such implementations.

AnyNet

AnyNet converts SNA message units, independent of session type, into corresponding TCP/IP packets for end-to-end transport across a TCP/IP WAN backbone. DLSw encapsulates an entire SNA message unit, including all of the SNA headers, untouched within a TCP/IP packet. In contrast, AnyNet converts the information contained in the SNA Transmission Header (TH) into appropriate fields within the IP header as well as fields within a 10-byte AnyNet header that is appended to each message unit. Consequently, AnyNet transfers slightly less traffic—typically in the range of 12 bytes per SNA message unit—than DLSw. In the context of i•nets, where each Web page is likely to be a few thousand bytes long, most network professionals will not be overly concerned about 12 bytes per SNA message unit, especially when the length of the IP header alone in IP version 6 will be a whopping 40 bytes, or twice as long as the current 20-byte header used by IP version 4 implementations.

Although AnyNet has been available as an X/Open standard since around 1994, it is not supported by any of the major network equipment providers, such as Cisco, Bay, or 3Com. AnyNet conversion is, however, supported by some of the larger SNA/3270 emulation providers, such as

Attachmate and Wall Data. AnyNet also does not support SDLC-to-LAN conversion.

In general, DLSw is likely to be a more prevalent, more flexible, and more potent solution than AnyNet. The one redeeming virtue of AnyNet, however, is that it is bundled, essentially as a no-charge option, into all of IBM's current client and server offerings. Thus, if an enterprise uses PComm or CS/NT on its PCs and has OS/390 with the Communications Server feature on the mainframe, the organization will already have AnyNet in place for end-to-end SNA transport. Even in such scenarios, however, one may find that DLSw is a more satisfactory solution. Bridge/router-based DLSw does not consume mainframe resources for protocol conversion and moreover can exploit all of the TCP/IP routing options and capabilities offered by the bridge/router, including Open Shortest Path First (OSPF)-based, end-to-end routing. AnyNet is not available on bridge/routers or in a stand-alone gateway form. The IBM 2217, which was essentially an AnyNet gateway in a box, was discontinued by IBM in March 1998.

HPR-Over-IP

HPR-over-IP is a direct alternative to DLSw, as described in Chapter 2. With HPR-over-IP, an HPR network node is installed within the relevant bridge/routers in an i•net, and HPR-based routing is performed to convey SNA/APPN traffic across the network.

Technologies for accessing SNA applications running on mainframes or AS/400s from TCP/IP-based clients across an i•net are discussed next.

ip3270 or ip5250

The ip3270 or ip5250 scheme involves running existing 3270 emulators for PCs and workstations, such as Eicon's Aviva for Desktops, in TCP/IP mode. 3270 emulators use a client/server paradigm referred to as "split stack" to denote that the total SNA/3270 functionality required for SNA access is divided between the emulator and an SNA-LAN gateway, such as Microsoft's SNA Server, that is serving multiple client emulators. With this split-stack paradigm, the emulator performs 3270 emulation using standard 3270 data stream, while the SNA-LAN gateway handles all of the SNA/ APPN functionality required for mainframe application access. A variety of different protocols, such as NetBIOS, Novell's IPX/SPX, or 802.2, can be used between the SNA-LAN gateway and a 3270 emulator to convey the 3270 data stream. Another protocol that is widely supported for this emulator-to-gateway communication is TCP/IP. ip3270 and ip5250 refer to such split-stack operation where TCP/IP is used between the 3270 emulator and the SNA-LAN gateway. These options differ from tn3270 and tn5250 in that their 3270 encapsulation, initial handshake, and acknowledgment schemes, although carried out via TCP/IP, are proprietary and gateway-specific; in contrast, tn3270 and tn5250 use open schemes conforming to IETF standards.

The use of proprietary schemes in this instance should not be construed as a major flaw. The ip3270 and ip5250 approach has an advantage in that it rarely requires the installation of new 3270 emulator or SNA-LAN gateway software. Instead, realizing ip3270 or ip5250 can just be a matter of reconfiguring the transport mechanism used between an emulator and the gateway to rely on TCP/IP. The ip3270 and ip5250 approach also has the irrefutable and significant advantage that it provides total support for all terminal emulation functions, emulator customization features, versatile printing capability, LU 6.2, and the APIs used by SNA client applications, such as HLLAPI and EHLLAPI.

tn3270(E) and tn5250

tn3270(E) and tn5250 are IETF industry standards covered by RFCs 1576, 1205, 1647, and so on. They enable PCs and workstations running a TCP/IP client to access SNA applications via a tn3270(E) or tn5250 server. Although some public domain clients are available, enterprises typically use tn3270/tn5250 clients from traditional 3270 emulator vendors such as Attachmate, Eicon, Wall Data, and WRQ. Some tn3270(E) servers are now available on mainframes, channel-attached bridge/routers (such as IBM 2216s), stand-alone bridge/routers (such as IBM 2212s), and PC or UNIX servers.

The fundamental difference between tn3270/tn5250 and ip3270/ip5250 is that the former is standards-based and the latter is gateway-specific. That is, tn3270(E)/tn5250 clients tend to be "thinner" than corresponding ip3270/ip5250 "fat clients," albeit with the thinner clients understandably providing less functionality and flexibility. The lack of support for LU 6.2 and LU-LU Session Type 0 is prime among these deficiencies. On the other hand, tn3270(E) has the significant advantage that highly scalable server implementations are now available on both mainframes and channel-attached bridge/routers. In contrast, no mainframe implementations of the SNA-LAN gateways required for ip3270 exist, and most of the gateways that are available are not as scalable as the tn3270(E) server on a IBM 2216 or a Cisco 7500/CIP. Figure 4.3 shows the possibility of using a mainframe as a tn3270(E) Server.

tn3270(E) and tn5250 now have considerable mind-share within the SNA world, with an estimated 10 million users relying on this technology for their data center access toward the end of 1997. Many of the applet-based, browser-based SNA access solutions, such as IBM's Host On-Demand, WRQ's Reflection EnterView, and Eicon's Aviva for Java, use tn3270(E)/tn5250 as their host communications protocol. This endorsement of tn3270 is also repeated in some 3270-to-HTML conversion solutions, such as Eicon's Aviva Web-to-Host, which offer tn3270(E) as an option for realizing host connectivity.

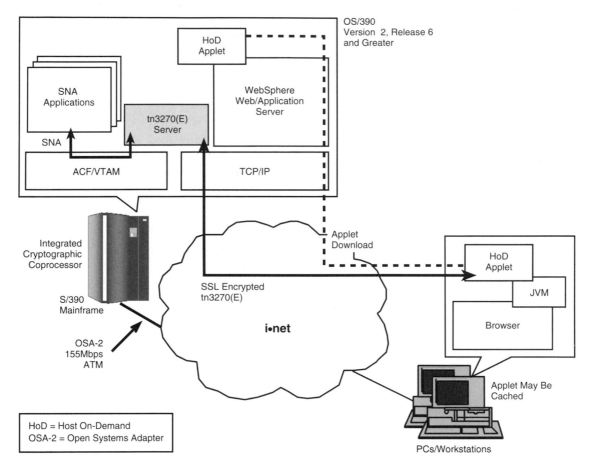

FIGURE 4.3   A high-octane tn3270 solution, replete with end-to-end encryption, based on a mainframe-resident tn3270(E) server and IBM's Host On-Demand.

Browser-Based SNA Access

Browser-based SNA access permits SNA applications running on a main-frame or AS/400 to be directly accessed from within, or alongside, a standard Web browser. It makes SNA applications compatible with the Internet, intranets, and extranets. Browser-based access also provides the obvious answer as to how SNA applications can be easily accessed across the Inter-net—either by company employees who are telecommuting or traveling, by business partners such as dealers and agents, or even more importantly by the general public for applications like home banking and online travel reservations. With SNA-access capability, the Web browser can now become the standardized, **universal user interface** for accessing all types of applications and data—irrespective of whether they are based on SNA,

UNIX servers, the Internet, Windows NT, intranets, or minicomputers. The standardization on such a universal user interface will, in time, significantly reduce user training costs and improve user productivity and satisfaction.

Moreover, browser-based access offers the means and the motivation for painlessly and economically rejuvenating the green-on-black, text-only user interface of most SNA applications. The beauty of facelifting the user interface of SNA applications, as shown in Fig. 4.1, as a by-product of browser-based access is that the mainframe- or AS/400-resident applications do not have to be modified or updated in any way. Instead, the facelift process can be realized using a number of different techniques and tools, including straight-out-of-the-box, completely automated AutoGUI schemes, as an integral part of the SNA-Web conversion processing, as described in Chapter 6.

Three distinct solution families exist for browser-based SNA access: 3270-to-HTML conversion, Applet-based 3270/5250 emulation, and Applet-based emulation with a rejuvenated user interface. With 3270-to-HTML conversion, an SNA-Web gateway intercepts 3270/5250 screens from a main-

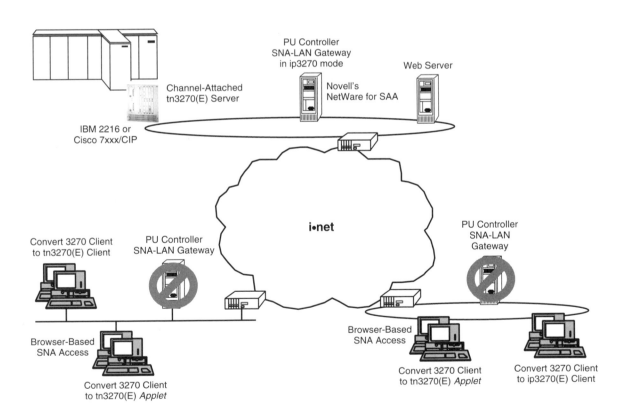

FIGURE 4.4 Replacing remote SNA-LAN gateways with ip3270, tn3270(E), or browser-based SNA access solutions.

frame or AS/400 and then converts the 3270/5250 data stream to HTML-based Web pages. These Web pages are then forwarded to a standard Web server to be sent down to the appropriate PC/workstation user. The Web pages representing what were originally 3270/5250 screens will appear at the client PC or workstation within a standard Web browser, no differently than any other Web page. With 3270-to-HTML conversion, invariably some level of rejuvenation is built-in—even if it consists of only the inclusion of a nonblack background and the rendering of input fields as boxes or trenches.

Applet-based 3270/5250 emulation is, in essence, standard tn3270(E)/tn5250-based data center access with an applet performing the client functions. Although they do not use HTML for their screen rendering, some of the applet-based emulation schemes, such as IBM's Host On-Demand and OpenConnect's OC://WebConnect Pro, enable extensive rejuvenation of the 3270 user interface.

Application-Specific Web-to-Data Center Gateways

Such gateways (for example, IBM's CICS Web Interface) set out to Web-enable specific mainframe or AS/400 applications. They differ markedly from general-purpose, browser-based SNA access solutions in that their scope is always restricted to a single application. Browser-based access for SNA solutions, on the other hand, are application-neutral and will work with any application that has a 3270- or 5250-based terminal interface.

Given their specificity, application-specific gateways really have relevance only if an enterprise has just a few data center applications that need to be Web-enabled and, moreover, if application-specific gateways exist for the applications in question. If an enterprise has many data center applications to be Web-enabled, then it would likely be better off pursuing a general-purpose solution that will work across the board with all of its applications, rather than trying to implement specific solutions for each application.

Currently, application-specific gateways are available for only a few, extensively used, IBM-supplied applications such as CICS and DB2. Thus the lack of coverage when it comes to applications is a serious limitation for this approach. In the case of CICS, however, a surfeit of solutions exists, with IBM alone offering at least five different Web-to-CICS gateways. Nonetheless, the bottom line for application-specific gateways is that their appeal is limited to very few and atypical scenarios.

Application Servers for Web-to-Data Center Interactions

These servers enable new Web-oriented applications, including applications developed using applets, to gain access to data-center-resident applications and data. Browser-based access and tn3270(E)/tn5250 are explicitly targeted at terminal users who require interactive access. On the other hand, programmatic access, which in reality includes the APIs available with ip3270/ ip5250, is aimed at software developers who are creating new applications. These new applications most likely will have contemporary, Web page-like user interfaces that differ dramatically from the green-on-black 3270 screens now used to access data center resources. The programmatic servers will, nonetheless, ensure that the new applications and their users gain ready access to the necessary data center resources—in many instances, without the user ever being aware that some or even all of the data being used are being retrieved from a mainframe or AS/400. In essence, programmatic servers will make data center access transparent to end users.

Technology already exists to establish the SNA/3270-based connection and provide the screen navigation necessary to access applications, databases, or files to be made into reusable objects (even Enterprise JavaBeans). In time, new applications with twenty-first century user interfaces that interact with data center applications via programmatic servers will become the ultimate expression of the 3270/5250 user interface rejuvenation process. Today, a variety of innovative products from IBM/Lotus, Bluestone/OpenConnect, BEA WebLogics, Novera, Interlink, Blue Lobster, and many, many others are available to facilitate Web-to-data center integration based on purely program-to-program communication, as opposed to terminal-based interactions.

4.1.3 Different Horses for Different Courses

Now that all the pertinent SNA transport and SNA access technologies for SNA-capable i•nets have been introduced, it is possible to construct the matrix in Table 4.1 that shows which technologies are potentially applicable to a given category of SNA end-user device.

Table 4.1 does not try to depict how the preferred technology for a given category of end user may change over time. When it comes to implementing SNA-capable i•nets, most enterprises will likely want to initially assimilate their existing SNA/APPN networking infrastructure into a TCP/IP-based backbone, keeping any changes required on the SNA side to a bare minimum. Once this wholesale migration to a TCP/IP backbone has been successfully negotiated, they will seek to explore new technologies that will reduce cost (for example, by eliminating remote SNA-LAN gateways), improve efficiency, and enhance user capability or productivity. Table 4.2 depicts how the preferred Web-to-data center technology for a given category of end user might change over time.

4.1.4 Dismantling Full SNA Stacks

Although the migration process described for most of the SNA end-user categories in Tables 4.1 and 4.2 is relatively self-explanatory, the one category

TABLE 4.1   Technologies applicable to SNA end-user devices.

PCs, Macs, Workstations	Network Computers	SNA-Only Devices (e.g., old 3274s, 4700s)	Remote SNA-LAN Gateways (e.g., Microsoft SNA Server)	Devices That Work in SNA or TCP/IP Mode (e.g., AS/400s, 3174s)
• Browser-based • tn3270/tn5250 • ip3270/ip5250 • Programmatic • File transfer Only if a full-stack SNA/3270 emulator is currently installed: • DLSw • DDLSw • AnyNet • HPR-over-IP	• Browser-based • Programmatic	• DLSw • HPR-over-IP	• Eliminate the remote gateway and opt for ip3230/ip5250, tn3270/tn5250, or browser-based access with data center-resident gateways or servers Until the remote gate way is eliminated: • DLSw • HPR-over-IP	• Convert to IP and then use TCP/IP-based access schemes such as tn3270/tn5250, file transfer, and so on • tn5250/tn3270 • File transfer • Programmatic If the device cannot be converted to TCP/IP or until the conversion is made: • DLSw • AnyNet • HPR-over-IP

TABLE 4.2   Preferred Web-to-data center technologies.

SNA End-User Category	Short-Term Options	Mid- to Long-Term Options
PCs, Macs, Workstations		
A. Running a 3270/5250 emulator	A. ip3270/ip5250 or tn3270(E)/tn5250	A. Applet-based, browser-based access
B. Running a full-stack SNA/3270 emulator	B. DLSw, DDLSw, AnyNet, or HPR-over-IP	B. tn3270(E)/tn5250 or applet-based, browser-based access
C. Already using tn3270(E)/tn5250	C. Stay with tn3270(E)/tn5250	C. Investigate applet-based, browser-based access to benefit from automatic, server-downloaded version updates
D. New software with no SNA/3270 emulation	D. tn3270(E)/tn5250 or browser-based access; possibly 3270-to-HTML	D. Browser-based access In time, all of these browser-based solutions may be based on application server technology as opposed to applet-based emulation or 3270-to-HTML conversion.

TABLE 4.2   Continued

SNA End-User Category	Short-Term Options	Mid- to Long-Term Options
Network Computers	Browser-based access	Browser-based access or programmatic access via application servers
SNA-Only Devices	DLSw or HPR-over-IP	Gradually phase out whenever possible (e.g., replace coax-attached 3270 terminals connected to SNA-only 3x74 control units with network computers).
Remote SNA-LAN Gateways	DLSw or HPR-over-IP	Eliminate the remote gateways in favor of ip3270/ip5250, tn3270(E)/tn5250, or browser-based access with the requisite gateways or servers located in the data center. This scheme eliminates the need to transport SNA traffic across the TCP/IP backbone. Figure 4.4 illustrates how remote SNA-LAN gateways can be replaced by a data-center-based solution that ensures that the remote PCs and workstations have access to the relevant data center applications.
Devices such as AS/400s That Work in Either SNA/APPN or TCP/IP Mode		
A. Bulk data transfers between the devices and systems	A. Use DLSw or AnyNet and continue to perform data transfers in SNA/APPN mode. AnyNet is an integrated feature within the AS/400 operating system.	A. Migrate to a TCP/IP-based file transfer scheme
B. PC/workstation access to the system (e.g., AS/400)	B. DLSw or possibly AnyNet if supported by the client software (e.g., IBM's OS/2) or SNA/3270 emulator	B. ip5250/ip3270, tn5250/tn3270, or browser-based access
C. AS/400-centric APPN network where PCs and workstations with APPN end node software can freely access SNA applications running on different systems	C. HPR-over-IP, DLSw, or AnyNet	C. HPR-over-IP with possible gradual migration to browser-based access

Unless an ongoing need exists for desktop LU 6.2 applications, the idea of persevering with full-stack SNA emulators has little merit. Transitioning to ip3270, tn3270(E), or browser-based access will simplify network operation and generally be much more strategic and forward-looking.

that may require slightly more elaboration is that of PCs and workstations running a full-stack SNA/3270 emulator. A decade ago, enterprises could select one of two distinct options through which to provide PCs/workstations with access to SNA applications. One was the split-stack approach, where a 3270 emulator ran on the PC or workstation and the actual SNA functionality was performed by a remote or data-center-resident SNA-LAN gateway. The other approach was to run a full-stack SNA/3270 emulator in each PC or workstation. IBM advocated the full-stack approach because it ensured that SNA was used end-to-end from the host to the desktop.

To be fair, maintaining SNA on such an end-to-end basis offers several advantages. It ensured that mainframe-resident NetView network management had visibility and control of the desktop. It also meant that SNA's renowned and highly proven protocols for error correction, guaranteed in-sequence delivery, and flow control were available uncompromised all the way to the desktop. If the system used LU 6.2 applications, the full-stack approach provided end-to-end support for COS-based traffic prioritization. With the split-stack approach, in marked contrast, SNA ended at the gateway. If the SNA-LAN gateway was located within the data center, SNA per se never traversed the WAN.

Today, a relatively large installed base of PCs and workstations continues to run full-stack SNA/3270. The fact that most of IBM's popular remote SNA-LAN gateways—in particular, 3174s and 37xxs acting as remote communications processors (RCPs)—worked only in PU Passthrough gateway mode and did not offer a split-stack PU Controller gateway capability encouraged enterprises to adopt full-stack solutions. PCs and workstations running full-stack SNA/3270 emulators can obviously be supported in the context of i•nets using DLSw or HPR-over-IP. DDLSw is also an option, although the merit of performing DLSw encapsulation and deencapsulation at each individual PC or workstation, when it can be carried out relatively easily and efficiently on the fly by a bridge/router for all PCs and workstations at a given site, is highly questionable. AnyNet is yet another option if the emulator supports it or if IBM's OS/2 operating system is being used.

DLSw, DDLSw, HPR-over-IP, and AnyNet can all ensure that the benefits of using SNA end-to-end are maintained more or less intact, despite the use of a totally TCP/IP-centric WAN backbone. The mid- to long-term advantages of persevering with full-stack solutions within SNA-capable i•nets need to be carefully evaluated and rationalized, however. The need for SNA on the desktop once an enterprise has decided to standardize on a TCP/IP backbone is questionable. Given that network management will become increasingly TCP/IP-biased, one can argue that it makes more sense for the desktops to be based on TCP/IP rather than SNA. Most SNA access schemes—with some 3270-to-HTML schemes being the only possible exceptions—provide some level of end-to-end persistent connections to ensure

SNA data delivery integrity and fidelity. Hence, one can debate the need for end-to-end SNA to guarantee in-sequence, orderly data delivery.

Full-stack SNA/3270 emulation software is expensive to purchase and costly to maintain, distribute, and update. A browser-based access scheme, which uses applets for its terminal emulation, will invariably be a considerably lower-cost solution and minimize the software distribution, maintenance, and version control effort through the use of downloadable applets. All of the major full-stack solution providers, including IBM, Attachmate, Wall Data, and Eicon, have already embraced browser-based access and now offer multiple tn3270(E), ip3270, and browser-based products in parallel to their SNA clients. As a result, it seems safe to assume that full-stack emulators will gradually be displaced by TCP/IP access clients such as tn3270(E) or browser-based access solutions.

4.2 DLSW—THE WORKHORSE SNA TRANSPORT SCHEME

DLSw ensures that today's large installed base of SNA devices and control units will be able to communicate with mainframe- or AS/400-resident SNA/APPN applications across TCP/IP-based i•nets—using unadulterated SNA on an end-to-end basis. DLSw works by encapsulating SNA/APPN traffic from SNA devices, irrespective of the SNA session protocol used, within TCP/IP packets. It then routes these TCP/IP packets end-to-end across an i•net toward the relevant SNA destination. DLSw encapsulates all of the SNA headers—namely, the **Transmission Header (TH)** and the **Request/Response Header (RH)**. These headers are left intact and untouched within TCP/IP. Figure 4.5 shows the format of the DLSw encapsulation scheme.

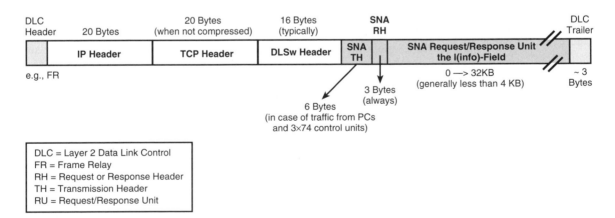

FIGURE 4.5 Format of the Data Link Switching (DLSw) encapsulation scheme.

DLSw is a highly proven and extensively used encapsulation scheme. Since 1992, it has been a highly popular methodology for integrating SNA traffic into multiprotocol networks. It is ubiquitously available on all mainstream bridge/routers, and multivendor interoperability is not an issue because DLSw implementations adhere to an IETF-controlled industry standard (addressed by RFCs such as 1434 and 1795). Although currently the only TCP/IP encapsulation scheme for SNA/APPN of strategic importance, DLSw was not the first or the initially dominant scheme for such encapsulation. That distinction goes to Cisco's **Remote Source Route Bridging (RSRB)**, a proprietary scheme that has now been superseded within Cisco by DLSw or, to be more precise, DLSw+ (standard DLSw with some optional Cisco-specific extensions).

IBM introduced the term "DLSw" in 1992, using it to describe the TCP/IP encapsulation scheme offered on the IBM 6611 bridge/router. IBM submitted a specification of DLSw as implemented on the 6611 to the IEFT in January 1993. It was the genesis of the standards-based DLSw now implemented and promoted by so many vendors, including Cisco. RFC 2166, which was submitted to the IETF in June 1997, covers the "DLSw v2.0 enhancement"—colloquially referred to as DLSw "version 2," with the implementations corresponding to RFC 1795 being classified as examples of DLSw standard version 1.0. The overriding thrust of DLSw version 2 is to improve the scalability of DLSw by reducing the number of DLSw end-to-end TCP connections required within the network. With DLSw version 2, it is possible to have just one TCP/IP connection per remote site, as opposed to the two required in previous implementations. One can also establish a TCP connection dynamically on-demand, when actual end-to-end interactions must be transferred.

DLSw is best envisioned as a LAN-to-LAN bridging scheme over TCP/IP WANs, which in effect performs an optimized Source Route Bridging mechanism over TCP connections. Figure 4.6 depicts the notion that DLSw is merely a transparent LAN-to-LAN bridging mechanism over TCP. DLSw works with any type of SNA traffic. It is thus extremely useful for accommodating SNA LU 6.2 or LU-LU Session Type 0-based traffic within the context of i•nets, given that today's tn3270(E) and browser-based access schemes cannot deal with programmatic SNA access à la LU 6.2 or LU-LU Session Type 0. At present, tn3270(E) and browser-based access schemes support only 3270-centric terminal access based on SNA LU-LU Session Types 1, 2 and 3.

The DLSw based encapsulation and deencapsulation of SNA/APPN traffic, into and out of TCP/IP packets, is typically performed by bridge/routers. A variant of DLSw, known as Desktop DLSw (DDLSw), exists where the SNA/APPN encapsulation/deencapsulation is performed within a PC or workstation. Currently, no DLSw implementations run on mainframes or AS/400s. Consequently, DLSw within a channel-attached bridge/router, such as an IBM 2216 or a Cisco 7500 with a CIP, is the closest point to a mainframe at which DLSw can be invoked.

DLSw is a no-nonsense, LAN-to-LAN bridging scheme performed over TCP/IP. In its latest form, it is scalable and delivers the plug-and-play simplicity of traditional Source Route Bridging—without any downside, such as repeated broadcast searches or multitudes of LLC-2 acknowledgments across the WAN.

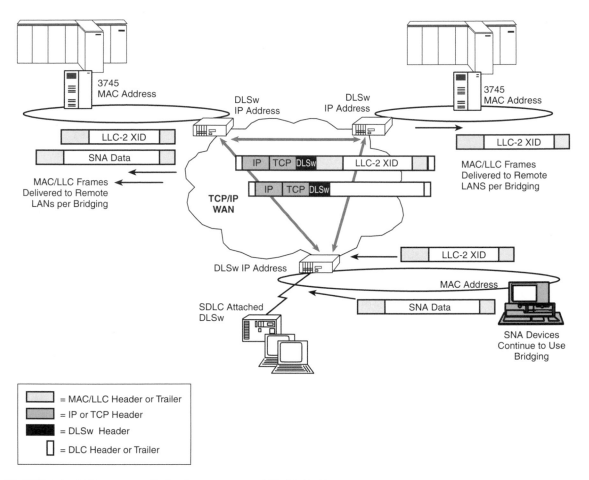

FIGURE 4.6 DLSw essentially bridging across a TCP/IP WAN.

DLSw's ability to effortlessly support all types of SNA/APPN traffic could be easily abused when migrating toward SNA-capable i•nets. DLSw could be used, all by itself, to implement SNA-capable i•nets that consist of existing SNA/APPN networks grafted onto a TCP/IP backbone, totally unchanged, through the extensive deployment of DLSw around the periphery of the TCP/IP backbone. This brute-force, no-SNA-reengineering approach has been used in the past to integrate SNA networks into TCP/IP networks. With this type of DLSw-only network, one would find SNA-LAN gateways downstream of the TCP/IP cloud, with DLSw then being used to transport the SNA output of these gateways across the TCP/IP WAN. Although such networks indubitably work, other strategic techniques, such as tn3270(E) and browser-based access, should typically be employed in conjunction with DLSw so as to build much more effective and efficient SNA-capable i•nets, as discussed earlier.

4.2.1   DLSw—More Than Just a TCP/IP Encapsulation Scheme

DLSw has always been more than just a TCP/IP encapsulation scheme to facilitate SNA/APPN end-to-end transport across TCP/IP WANs. It is an integrated and powerful set of functions that address many SNA-related requirements for i•nets, such as support for SDLC and the elimination of the need to transport LLC-2 acknowledgments across the WAN.

In the context of SNA-capable i•nets, DLSw is invariably viewed as a proven end-to-end SNA/APPN transport scheme that is based on TCP/IP encapsulation. In fact, DLSw has always had more to offer. For a start, it also supports NetBIOS transport through TCP/IP encapsulation. Its capabilities extend even beyond that, however. DLSw is, in effect, an integrated set of core facilities for effectively and efficiently dovetailing LAN- or SDLC-based SNA traffic and LAN-based NetBIOS traffic into a TCP/IP WAN backbone that is built around bridges and routers. The key capabilities found within DLSw's overall repertoire of facilities can be summarized as follows:

1. It provides for the encapsulation of SNA/APPN and NetBIOS traffic within TCP/IP packets and the routing of these packets, using IP routing methodology and protocols, to transport SNA/APPN and NetBIOS traffic between bridge/routers within an i•net; in this case, the i•net consists of dispersed LANs that are interconnected via a TCP/IP-based WAN. The remainder of this chapter does not focus on DLSw's support for NetBIOS traffic because NetBIOS usage is now declining. Moreover, NetBIOS is a LAN server, as opposed to data center, oriented protocol.

2. SDLC-to-LLC:2 conversion enables link-attached SNA/SDLC devices, such as IBM 3174 control units, to appear to, and be treated by, mainframe-resident software as if they were LAN-attached devices. This DLSw-provided SDLC-to-LAN conversion permits SDLC WAN links to be terminated at a remote bridge/router. It obviates the need to bring SDLC connections across long distances and into the data center. Moreover, it eliminates the need for large numbers of SDLC ports on the network-to-mainframe gateway. The remote termination of SDLC links through DLSw permits enterprises to migrate toward LAN-centric, low-cost mainframe gateways, such as IBM 2216 or Cisco 7xxx/CIP channel-attached bridge/routers. This SDLC-to-LAN conversion capability is another valuable and unique contribution of DLSw relative to SNA-capable i•nets. AnyNet and HPR-over-IP do not support SDLC-to-LAN conversion.

3. Local LLC:2 acknowledgment precludes Data Link layer—that is, Layer 2—Receive Ready (RR) acknowledgments associated with SNA message units having to be sent end-to-end across the TCP/IP WAN. This feature minimizes the amount of SNA-related overhead traffic that must be continually conveyed across the i•net.

4. The caching of the exact destination location of MAC addresses and NetBIOS names precludes the need for repetitive broadcast searches to locate this information each time a new SNA or NetBIOS session must be established.

5. A DLSw capabilities exchange scheme allows DLSw-capable bridge/routers to specify which DLSw features they support and the version of DLSw they are using. This feature permits bridge/routers with newer and older implementations of DLSw to coexist within the same i•net.

6. A congestion control mechanism modeled after APPN's adaptive pacing. Pacing, as mentioned in Chapter 3, is a proven SNA protocol that allows a receiving component to control the rate at which it receives data by opening and closing a pacing-specific transmission window. A dynamic pacing scheme, where the window size could vary between a minimum and maximum value depending on the rate of data flow, was included in SNA in 1978 to augment the previously fixed window size pacing system. First LU 6.2 and then APPN included a variant of this dynamic pacing, through which the window size could be dynamically set each time the window was to be open (that is, prior to each new cycle of message unit transmittals). This technique, known as adaptive pacing, provides the most powerful and flexible approach to pacing to date. This congestion control mechanism is available within DLSw to provide end-to-end flow control of DLsw-based traffic.

7. SNMP-based MIB is available for managing the DLSw subnetwork within an overall structure of an i•net.

8. A DLSw circuit prioritization scheme ensures that different sessions using DLSw can be prioritized relative to each other.

Clearly, DLSw embodies a pertinent and powerful set of capabilities for effectively integrating LAN- and SDLC-based SNA/APPN traffic into an i•net. Given the lengths of the IP, TCP, and the 16-byte DLSw header, the overall header overhead of DLSw is considerably greater than that encountered by SNA practitioners—especially so when compared with RFC 1490, which deals with the native encapsulation of SNA/APPN traffic within Frame Relay. Nearly 70% of the header overhead of DLSw relates to the lengths of the IP and TCP headers, however, which is not the fault of DLSw. Moreover, with the move to i•nets, the header overhead of TCP/IP becomes irrelevant.

Scalability was once the other major criticism leveled against DLSw. Addressing this scalability issue is the overriding theme of DLSw version 2.0. Along with the scalability improvements provided by DLSw version 2.0, the overall scalability of DLSw is being enhanced by two other factors. In the past, the number of concurrent TCP connections that could be sustained by the data-center-resident routers was the gating factor when it came to DLSw scalability. Today, bridge/routers, thanks to processor and memory upgrades, can support more TCP connections than they could a few years ago. This factor, even without the DLSw version 2.0 improvements, bolsters

DLSw's scalability. Another important factor that comes into play relates to the number of remote SNA devices and remote locations containing SNA devices, in a given network. This number is diminishing as SNA users move toward TCP/IP clients, obviating the need for remote SNA-LAN gateways and SNA control units.

4.2.2   DLSw's Principles of Operation for SNA/APPN Traffic

With DLSw, the SNA/APPN traffic that must be forwarded from one LAN to another, across an i•net, is initially intercepted by a bridge/router connected to the LAN at which the data originate. Thanks to its built-in SDLC-to-LAN conversion capability, DLSw can treat SDLC traffic as if it were just additional LAN traffic. If DLSw was not being used, this LAN-to-LAN traffic forwarding would normally have been realized using a bridging scheme such as **Source Route Bridging (SRB)** or **Transparent Bridging**. Thus, to intercept SNA/APPN traffic, the DLSw component of the bridge/router needs to masquerade as a standard LAN-to-LAN bridging function. It can identify SNA/APPN traffic by examining the Source Service Access Point (SSAP) value that is included within the LLC portion of a MAC/LLC frame. SNA/APPN traffic will have SSAP values such as X'04', X'05', X'08', and X'0C'.

Correlating the Layer 2 MAC address of an SNA device with the IP address of a DLSw-capable bridge/router attached to the same LAN as that device is a fundamental function that must be performed by DLSw—given that DLSw works with the same MAC-level addresses hitherto used by bridges, which means that no changes need to be made to installed SNA software or devices.

The need to base DLSw on bridging boils down to one fundamental issue: the need for it to be absolutely compatible with SNA/APPN software running on PCs and workstations, LAN attached devices, and mainframe SNA-LAN gateways (such as IBM 3745s and 3172s). SNA/APPN software developed for LAN applications invariably uses MAC addresses to denote destinations. Given the variety, diversity, complexity, volume, and mission-criticality of SNA/APPN applications, DLSw cannot afford to request that this software be modified to accommodate its TCP/IP-oriented requirements. Thus it uses destination MAC addresses as its means (or metric) of locating desired destinations. Consequently, DLSw relies on intercepting and supporting standard LAN MAC frames containing SNA/APPN data. It can therefore be envisioned as a LAN-to-LAN bridging scheme where the bridging-based data transfer takes place across Layer 4 TCP connections, rather than Layer 2 data links.

Note, however, that IP's end-to-end routing is conducted on the basis of destination IP addresses, rather than Layer 2 MAC addresses. Thus DLSw must have an effective mechanism whereby it can correlate a given destination MAC address with the IP address of the DLSw bridge/router closest to that destination. Just as with SRB, DLSw's need to locate a remote destination is triggered when a DLSw-capable bridge/router receives an "off-segment, broadcast search required" TEST or XID LLC command. The destination being sought would be indicated by the command's destination

MAC address. A search process will be initiated only if the destination MAC address does not already appear in the bridge/router's DLSw cache directory.

DLSw does its MAC address-to-IP address correlation by first locating the LAN containing the desired destination, which would typically consist of the MAC address of a mainframe gateway such as an IBM 3745. It accomplishes this task by using a broadcast search, typically conducted over IP using User Datagram Protocol (UDP), via a DLSw-specific search protocol known as CANUREACH/ICANREACH. After locating the destination LAN, the DLSw search protocol identifies the IP address of a DLSw-capable bridge/router that is attached to that LAN. This bridge/router is classed as the destination bridge/router for the destination in question. At the conclusion of a successful CANUREACH/ICANREACH search process, the source bridge/router that initiated the search will create an entry in its search directory that correlates the destination MAC address with the IP address of the destination bridge/router. This directory caching process obviates the need for repeated broadcast searches for the same destination MAC address—as is required with SRB. A bridge/router supporting DLSw must, and will, correlate each destination MAC address that it encounters with the IP address of the corresponding destination bridge/router.

With the initial implementations of DLSw, two DLSw-specific TCP connections had to be set up between a pair of DLSw-capable bridge/routers before conducting a CANUREACH/ICANREACH broadcast search. Once the destination was located, these two DLSw-specific TCP connections between the source and destination bridge/routers provided for full-duplex data transfer, with one connection supporting data transfer in one direction and the other supporting transport in the opposite direction. DLSw version 2.0 eliminates the need for two TCP connections between a pair of bridge/routers involved in DLSw. For a start, a TCP connection is no longer required to conduct a CANUREACH/ICANREACH search. Instead, the search can be carried out, with DLSw-specific multicast addresses, using UDP (a connectionless protocol). To conserve bandwidth, responses generated during the search are sent only to the search originator using its specific unicast address.

After locating the required destination DLSw bridge/router, DLSw no longer immediately sets up a TCP connection. Instead, a TCP connection is instituted only when a need arises for end-to-end data transfer. As noted earlier, two TCP connections between a pair of bridge/routers involved in DLSw is also no longer a requirement. Bidirectional, end-to-end data transfer now occurs across a single TCP connection. The TCP connection is automatically terminated if no data traffic travels across the connection within a predetermined period of time. With version 2.0, DLSw has thus become very parsimonious in its use of TCP connections and sets up TCP connections only when end-to-end data must be transmitted. These efforts to limit the number of concurrently active TCP connections required to sustain a given DLSw environment have significantly improved the scalability of contemporary DLSw implementations.

The combination of multicast addressing with UDP to conduct the broadcast searches enables DLSw-capable bridge/routers to dynamically identify themselves to other DLSw-capable bridge/routers. This dynamic process eliminates the need to manually define the IP addresses of the bridge/routers that will participate in DLSw at each applicable bridge/router, as was the case in the past. This ability to use multicast addressing greatly simplifies and expedites the process of activating DLSw within an i•net and transforms DLSw into nearly a plug-and-play networking scheme. In general, today's DLSw implementations, with their multicast addressing and on-demand TCP connection establishment capabilities, are considerably more flexible, dynamic, and extensible than the somewhat gauche, heavy-handed early implementations of circa 1995.

In mainframe-centric, traditional SNA environments, it may not be necessary for the remote DLSw bridge/routers to establish TCP connections with all of the other remote routers. Given that all of the SNA traffic will typically be going to or coming from the mainframes, it may suffice for the remote bridge/routers to establish TCP connections with only data-center-resident bridge/routers adjacent to the mainframes. This type of DLSw configuration is known as a "home-run" or "hub-and-spoke" setup; the names denote that all of the TCP connections converge into the data center. If APPN or HPR NN routing between multiple distributed network nodes will be used across DLSw, the remote bridge/routers will most likely require TCP connections between them to accommodate the any-to-any routing required with this type of peer-to-peer networking.

Once a TCP connection is established between a pair of bridge/routers, the duo exchanges DLSw capabilities message units. This DLSw capabilities exchange permits them to determine which DLSw facilities each supports and the version of DLSw implemented by each. It also facilitates multivendor interoperability and backward compatibility with older versions of DLSw.

Once the DLSw capabilities at each end have been determined, the DLSw bridge/routers can begin transporting actual SNA/APPN data traffic across an i•net. A DLSw circuit for the SNA/APPN session is set up between the source and destination bridge/routers. The DLSw search process that concludes with the establishment of this end-to-end circuit would typically be triggered off by the issuance of an LLC:2, or SDLC, TEST command by a remote SNA device. Once this source SNA device receives a positive response to the TEST via DLSw, and the end-to-end DLSw circuit has been established, the next interaction will likely consist of a standard, SNA-prescribed Layer 2 LLC:2 XID exchange. At the end of this XID exchange, the SNA devices at each end will establish a Layer 2 LLC:2 connection for guaranteed, in-sequence delivery of message units. Figure 4.7 shows a typical DLSw connection establishment process, leading up to the data transfer stage.

Although the SNA devices establish an end-to-end LLC:2 connection with each other, DLSw does not maintain this connection in its original LLC:2 form across the i•net. Instead, the LLC:2 connections at each end terminate at the DLSw bridge/router. The DLSw bridge/routers then use TCP's reliable transport mechanism to provide a TCP/IP-based "virtual bridge" between the two separate LLC:2 connections at each end, across the i•net. This termination of the LLC:2 connections at each end is a fundamental precept of DLSw. The lack of an end-to-end LLC:2 connection also eliminates the need to transmit LLC:2 acknowledgments across a WAN between the DLSw bridge/routers. Instead, LLC:2 acknowledgments are generated locally

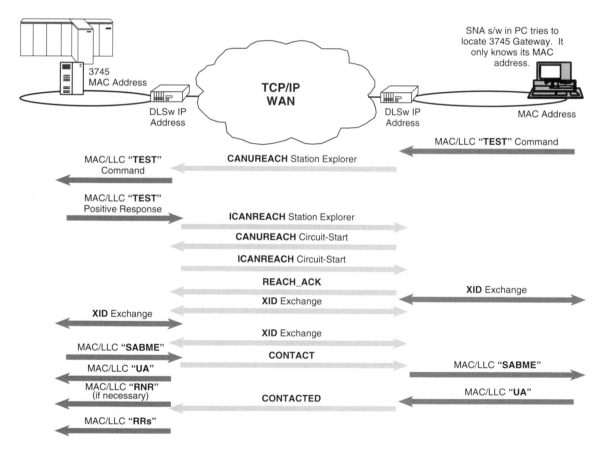

FIGURE 4.7   The DLSw end-to-end connection establishment process.

by the DLSw bridge/routers. This local LLC:2 acknowledgment facility is a quintessential feature of DLSw.

Once the end-to-end DLSw circuit and the two local LLC:2 connections have been established, unconstrained bidirectional data transfer can take place between the SNA source and destination devices. The DLSw bridge/routers intercept all data-bearing LAN frames and extract the data portion (that is, the Information field) from these frames. These data are then placed within DLSw-specific, TCP/IP-based, INFOFRAME message units for transportation across the i•net. An INFOFRAME message unit consists of an I-field "data block" extracted from a LAN frame, such as an SNA PIU message unit, prefixed by a 16-byte DLSw information message header.

Note that DLSw, as shown in Fig. 4.5, does not transport MAC, LLC:2, or SDLC headers across the i•net. This omission is a fundamental and key difference between DLSw and its predecessor RSRB. Not transporting these Layer 2 headers minimizes the header overhead of DLSw. Despite the fact that these Layer 2 headers are not sent across the i•net, they are required for the destination DLSw bridge/router to forward the data it receives to the intended LAN-attached destination SNA device. To cater to this need, the destination DLSw bridge/router creates a MAC/LLC:2 frame at its end to contain the data sent to the destination SNA device. The destination DLSw bridge/router uses a session ID embedded within the 16-byte DLSw header to determine the appropriate MAC addresses and field settings for the MAC/LLC headers it generates.

4.2.3   Pros and Cons of DLSw versus HPR-Over-IP

DLSw version 2.0 effectively addresses some of the limitations of older versions of DLSw—in particular, scalability, overall efficiency, and the amount of manual intervention required to specify the DLSw configuration. Consequently, DLSw now seems very attractive and appealing from an implementation and operation standpoint. Its header overhead might be deemed somewhat excessive vis-à-vis SNA's compact headers, but much of this overhead derives from the IP and TCP headers, over which DLSw has no control.

RSRB had an optional Fast Sequence Transport feature whereby the data transfer could take place without the use of a TCP connection or a TCP header. This scheme, which did not guarantee in-sequence, error-free data delivery, was fast, however, and minimized the bridge/router processing required. Some customers migrating from Fast Sequence Transport RSRB to DLSw have found, not surprisingly, that DLSw is somewhat slower and consumes more bridge/router processing resources. In some cases, an enterprise may need to upgrade to larger routers. The only way DLSw could really address this issue is to offer a nonreliable transport mechanism in a future version, which would run counter to the guaranteed, in-sequence delivery required by SNA/APPN and provided (so far) by DLSw.

Table 4.3 summarizes the pros and cons of DLSw version 2.0.

Table 4.4 summarizes the pros and cons of HPR-over-IP, which was described in Chapter 2, relative to DLSw version 2.0.

TABLE 4.3 Pros and cons of DLSw version 2.0.

Strengths	Weaknesses
• Highly proven • Available from multiple vendors • Based on IETF standards • Proven multivendor operability • Supports SDLC links • Can dynamically locate destination devices • Nearly "plug-and-play" implementation	• IP-based, dynamic alternative routing inherent in DLSw does not provide nondisruptive session handover to another adjacent backup router in the event of a failure to the destination bridge/router, because data transfer is based on end-to-end TCP connections. Hence, dynamic alternative routing only circumvents intermediate link or intermediate node failures. • Does not support SNA- or APPN-based routing in the event that remote SNA/APPN users need to switch between applications running in multiple, geographically separated data centers. In such cases, the routing used may be nonoptimal, as shown in Fig. 3.5. • No DLSw capability on mainframes, even though more enterprises are installing TCP/IP stacks on the mainframe and the use of mainframe-based tn3270(E) servers for SNA access is increasing.

TABLE 4.4 Pros and cons of HPR-over-IP relative to DLSw version 2.0.

Strengths	Weaknesses
• Support for native APPN/HPR NN routing to ensure optimal end-to-end paths for users who must regularly switch between applications running on different data centers or AS/400s • Explicit support for LU 6.2 COS-based end-to-end prioritization • Dynamic location of destination systems • Ability to automatically register end-node resources as well as dynamically deal with ongoing changes to the APPN/HPR topology	• Relatively unproven—the first implementation, from IBM, became widely available only in early 1998 • No explicit support for SDLC • Overhead of running HPR NN routing over IP not justifiable unless an enterprise requires NN routing to facilitate application switching between multiple data centers or needs to support LU 6.2 COS to the desktop

4.3   ANYNET-BASED SNA-TO-TCP/IP PROTOCOL CONVERSION

AnyNet, although as viable as DLSw for end-to-end SNA Transport across an i•net, is a protocol conversion scheme that does not transmit the SNA TH across the TPC/IP WAN. In contrast, DLSw is a protocol encapsulation scheme that transports the entire SNA message unit—TH and all—across the i•ent.

IBM's AnyNet protocol conversion technology is another viable, though possibly not strategic, option for conducting any type of SNA interaction, irrespective of session type, over an i•net. Figure 4.8 illustrates the possibility of using AnyNet to conduct SNA interactions between PCs running OS/2 and a mainframe across a TCP/IP-based i•net. When dealing with SNA transport across an i•net, the AnyNet process is roughly analogous to DLSw in that it just transports SNA data across the TCP/IP WAN. The fundamental and crucial difference between DLSw and AnyNet is that the former is a straight encapsulation scheme whereas the latter is a true protocol conversion scheme.

With DLSw, the entire SNA PIU (including the SNA TH) is encapsulated, untouched, and hence unadulterated within a TCP/IP packet, as shown in Fig. 4.5. AnyNet, in marked contrast, tries not to include the entire SNA PIU within a TCP/IP packet. Instead, it maps the information carried in the SNA TH, such as the destination address, to comparable fields in the IP

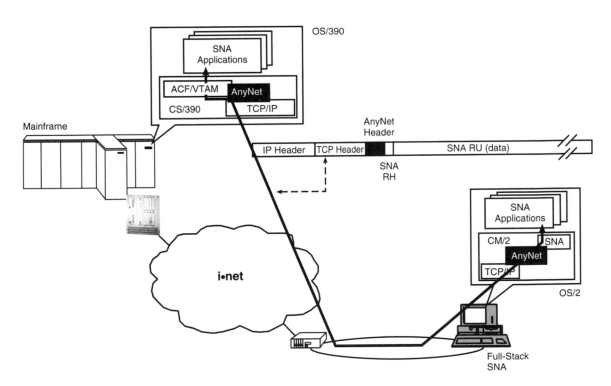

FIGURE 4.8   End-to-end SNA across an i•net using IBM's AnyNet protocol conversion.

header. It also uses an AnyNet-specific header to carry information that cannot be included within the IP header. The SNA Sequence Number Field (SNF) used by SNA's Layer 5 (Transport layer), which is a crucial 2-byte field found within all SNA THs, is included within the AnyNet header. The remainder of the SNA PIU (that is, the RH and the RU) and this AnyNet header are encapsulated within a TCP/IP packet for transportation across the i•net. Figure 4.9 depicts the difference in concept and format between DLSw's encapsulation scheme versus AnyNet's conversion approach.

Whether AnyNet protocol conversion improves upon DLSw's encapsulation scheme in terms of transporting SNA/APPN over an i•net is a highly debatable issue. What should be noted in this context is that AnyNet was not envisaged merely as addressing the need to transport SNA/APPN or Net-BIOS over TCP/IP—which is the express charter of DLSw. The roots of AnyNet technology lie in the Networking Blueprint initiative unveiled by

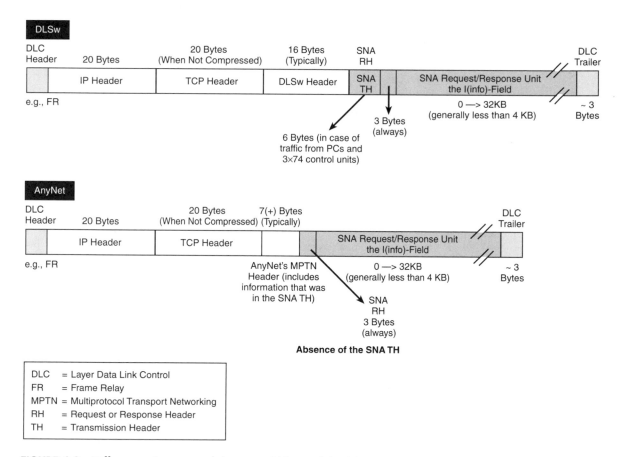

FIGURE 4.9 Differences in approach between DLSw and AnyNet.

IBM in 1992. The Blueprint was an ambitious but perspicacious framework that postulated having network-neutral applications and running SNA/APPN applications across IP, TCP/IP applications over SNA/APPN, and even SNA/APPN or TCP/IP over IPX. The ability to realize this type of "any application over any networking scheme" was addressed by an architectural component referred to as the **Common Transport Semantic (CTS)**. (The CTS architecture is also known within IBM as **MPTN, Multiprotocol Transport Networking**). Comparing AnyNet with DLSw is somewhat inappropriate and unfair, given that AnyNet set out to address protocol conversion and data transport on a global basis rather than focusing on the needs of SNA/APPN transport across TCP/IP.

In terms of overall header lengths, the AnyNet approach, as depicted in Fig. 4.9, appears to be slightly more efficient than DLSw, because it does not include the TH and the typically 7-byte AnyNet header is shorter than the 16-byte DLSw header. The FID-2 THs used by the SNA type 2 and 2.1 nodes, which account for the lion's share of the installed base of SNA remote devices, are 6 bytes long. So are the THs used by APPN nodes. Thus AnyNet's TH elimination scheme coupled with its 7-byte header saves 15 bytes of header per SNA PIU compared with DLSw's encapsulation scheme. This 15-byte saving in header lengths, however, must be offset by the fact that AnyNet's protocol conversion approach will likely require slightly more processing effort at either end.

In practice, the differences in header lengths or processing efficiency are less important than the availability of these two SNA transport options. DLSw is widely available from multiple vendors, including IBM, on full-function, stand-alone, or channel-attached bridge/routers. AnyNet, on the other hand, is not available on bridge/routers. IBM also does not offer a high-performance, stand-alone box that runs AnyNet and that can be deployed more or less like a bridge/router to provide AnyNet services to any SNA device attached to a LAN segment. The closest that IBM comes to offering such an "AnyNet-in-a-box" solution is to suggest that AnyNet software might be run on a PC running a stand-alone OS/2 operating system. Most enterprises, quite correctly, realize that this option is not a scalable, mission-critical solution for high-volume production use. Consequently, DLSw inevitably has the edge over AnyNet when it comes to mid- to large-scale networks.

4.3.1   Brief Overview of the AnyNet Protocol Conversion Process

The AnyNet protocol conversion process, in addition to performing format translations such as changing headers from one format to another, "compensates" for functions used by SNA but not explicitly supported by TCP/IP. It also takes care of mapping SNA destination addresses to IP addresses so as to transport SNA message units, without an SNA TH, across i•nets. AnyNet's "compensation" facility is required because a given transport protocol has its own unique set of functional capabilities.

For example, SNA supports the notion of expedited flows, whereby certain requests within a given session can leap-frog normal-flow requests at all queuing points and therefore reach their destinations prior to normal-flow requests that were sent before them. SNA typically uses expedited flows to send network control requests that may be needed to maintain session integrity. In essence, expedited flow is a means for assigning an ultrahigh priority to specific requests within a given session. TCP does have a so-called urgent mode. It is, however, merely a means of *notifying* the other end that urgent data are being sent across the connection, as opposed to an SNA-like mechanism that actually ensures that urgent data receive precedence over normal-flow data. Thus, when converting SNA to TCP/IP, AnyNet provides a compensation mechanism whereby TCP's urgent mode can be suitably extrapolated to emulate SNA's expedited flows.

In addition to providing functional compensation, AnyNet tackles the issue of directly mapping individual SNA/APPN LU names to corresponding destination IP addresses, rather than using a Layer 2 MAC address to identify the destination device, as is the case with DLSw. AnyNet address correlation, like the rest of the AnyNet conversion process, is handled at the Transport layer, as opposed to Layer 2. AnyNet's architectural name, Common Transport Semantics, attests to this Transport layer orientation. The AnyNet address translation of LU names to IP addresses takes place for the purpose of transporting the data across the i•net to the destination node. At the destination node, the IP transport address will be reconverted to the relevant SNA names and TH addresses per those specified by the transmitter.

MPTN specifies three techniques for realizing address mapping:

- Algorithmic mapping
- Protocol-specific directory
- Dynamic address mapping

With *algorithmic mapping*, an algorithm converts from one address scheme to another. This technique is typically employed when transporting TCP/IP across an SNA/APPN backbone—which is the opposite of what happens in an SNA-capable i•net. The *protocol-specific directory* approach is typically used when transporting SNA/APPN across a TCP/IP network, as is the case with SNA-capable i•nets. TCP/IP networks have **Domain Name Servers (DNS)** that provide them with global, but distributed directory services that dynamically map mnemonic, user-friendly destination names to the appropriate, but totally cryptic IP addresses. AnyNet extends this DNS name resolution capability to embrace SNA destination LU names, converting them to the necessary IP addresses. The *dynamic address mapping* scheme is used when neither of the other two techniques can be gainfully employed to achieve the required address mapping. Its main application is with NetBIOS and IPX, rather than with TCP/IP or SNA/APPN.

The initial AnyNet products were all pragmatic implementations of the Networking Blueprint's CTS architecture. The first AnyNet product, AnyNet/MVS, became available in mid-1993, just a year after the Networking Blueprint was unveiled. AnyNet/MVS, which was initially referred to as the Multiprotocol Transport Feature (MPTF) for MVS/ESA, supported both LU 6.2 across TCP/IP networks and sockets applications across SNA/APPN applications. It included AnyNet code for OS/2 that could be downloaded to PCs running OS/2 from the mainframe. Today, AnyNet protocol conversion appears as a bundled, no-charge option on all of IBM's server software packages, including OS/390, OS/400, AIX, OS/2, and CS/NT. Some SNA/3270 emulator vendors, such as Attachmate and Wall Data, also support AnyNet.

The AnyNet protocol conversion products from IBM come in two distinct forms: AnyNet access products and AnyNet gateways. Access node software is installed in end nodes, such as PCs and mainframes, and provides protocol conversion for applications running on that node. With AnyNet access products, the protocol leaving a device would already have been converted to the transport protocol employed across the network. SNA/3270 emulator vendors, such as Attachmate and Wall Data, offer AnyNet only for PC and workstation access nodes. These non-IBM access solutions, however, work seamlessly with IBM AnyNet implementations—in particular, AnyNet running on mainframes or AS/400s. The end result of AnyNet access running on a PC/workstation is analogous to that achieved with DDLSw, with the exception of the differences in the encapsulation format, in that the SNA traffic leaving the PC/workstation already appears in TCP/IP form before it reaches the LAN.

AnyNet gateway software typically resides in a stand-alone box—usually a PC, now that IBM has discontinued the 2217 (which was, in effect, "AnyNet-in-a-box"). An AnyNet gateway provides AnyNet protocol conversion services to multiple devices that do not contain any AnyNet software. AnyNet gateways can also interconnect SNA networks to each other across a TCP/IP network, in effect providing SNA network interconnection (SNI) over TCP/IP. The need for such esoteric network interconnection requirements is now disappearing as enterprises converge toward SNA-capable i•nets. In general, AnyNet gateways can realize any protocol conversion permutation that can be achieved via the AnyNet access products.

TABLE 4.5 Pros and cons of AnyNet.

Strengths	Weaknesses
• Bundled in, no-charge option within all of IBM's server software packages, including OS/390, OS/400, and CS/NT	• Not available on multiprotocol bridge/routers or in a prepackaged, scalable, stand-alone form
• Protocol conversion scheme has a slightly lower header overhead than the encapsulation scheme used by DLSw	• Overshadowed by the wide, multivendor backing enjoyed by DLSw
• Can identify an individual SNA destination, at a given node, by its SNA LU name, as opposed to the Layer 2 MAC address scheme used by DLSw	• Never aggressively marketed by IBM
	• No compelling advantages over DLSw

Given that IBM does not offer a credible, scalable, stand-alone AnyNet gateway, however, most enterprises remain leery of the long-term strategic implications of production networks based on AnyNet gateways.

Despite its relationship to the Blueprint and its considerable potential for delivering either SNA/APPN- or IP-centric multiprotocol solutions, AnyNet has not achieved major market success. Much of this lukewarm response can be directly attributed to lackadaisical and garbled marketing on IBM's part. With the multivendor impetus around DLSw and its near-ubiquitous availability on bridge/routers, the demand for AnyNet as a means of realizing SNA/APPN over IP has been declining. To compound the woes of AnyNet, IBM is now backing HPR-over-IP with no mention at all of AnyNet.

Table 4.5 summarizes the pros and cons of AnyNet.

4.4 THE LAST WORD

SNA-capable i•nets that seamlessly and synergistically integrate data centers and i•nets now appear poised to become the next-generation enterprise networks, rendering SNA-only networks obsolete. With nearly 70% of vital corporate data being resident within traditional data centers, it would be foolhardy, if not totally futile, to attempt to pursue an i•net strategy that did not ensure that data center resources could be accessed over the i•net. Fortunately, a plethora of proven and compelling data center-to-i•net integration technology exists. These products, from more than 40 separate vendors, address both the needs of end-to-end SNA transport, and those of unrestricted SNA access using TCP/IP-oriented clients.

In many cases, DLSw will likely be the preferred and optimal solution for SNA transport. Both ip3270/ip5250 and tn3270(E)/tn5250 are sound interim solutions for SNA access. Browser-based access, which can significantly minimize software distribution costs and offers extensive user interface rejuvenation capabilities, is an obvious and persuasive mid- to long-term option. When it comes to developing a new genre of i•net-oriented applications, programmatic servers are likely to emerge as the most powerful and flexible solution. All of these technologies, whether transport or access, ensure that SNA/APPN can be tightly integrated into an TCP/IP intranet without compromising SNA's sacrosanct reliability, integrity, and security.

Terminal-Based SNA Access over i•nets

Terminal-oriented, real-time, online transaction processing is by far the most prevalent form of SNA usage. More than 90% of SNA traffic, worldwide, uses 3270 or 5250 data stream and flows between applications and terminals, despite IBM's efforts over the last 15 years to encourage LU 6.2-based program-to-program interactions. The population of terminal users accessing SNA applications continues to grow, especially given the increased home use of data center applications for activities such as home banking, personal travel reservations, and online investing. Consequently, unimpeded terminal-oriented access must be the cornerstone of any credible data center-to-i•net integration strategy.

The SNA application access requirements of PCs and workstations that contain a full-stack SNA/3270 emulator and hence are SNA clients can more than adequately be accommodated with DLSw or HPR-over-IP, as was demonstrated in Chapter 4. The unmistakable trend, however, is toward non-SNA clients—in particular, TCP/IP-oriented clients.

Ironically, too much choice tends to be the major hurdle when it comes to homing in on viable approaches for realizing TCP/IP client-based access to SNA applications across i•nets. Rather than a few somewhat similar alternatives, seven very distinct approaches exist, each with a distinctive look and feel, that can now be used for SNA access. All of these options are persuasively viable and highly proven. The seven choices for SNA access are as follows:

1. Traditional, full-function terminal emulation with "fat clients" using ip3270 or ip5250.
2. Green-on-black tn3270(E)- or tn5250-based terminal emulation, with a tn3270 (or tn5250) client running on the PC or workstation and interacting with a tn3270(E) (or tn5250) server located in the data center.

Heads-down terminal users busily interacting with real-time transaction processing systems epitomizes SNA. Home-based applications, such as home banking, are expanding the base of SNA terminal users. Fortunately, the biggest problem when providing viable terminal-oriented access to SNA applications over i•nets is choosing from the wide range of technologies available.

161

3. Green-on-black terminal emulation, typically invoked via a browser, with a Java or ActiveX applet performing the requisite emulation functions. The protocol used by the applet to realize SNA access could be either standard tn3270(E)/tn5250 to an appropriate data center "tn" server or a proprietary applet handled by a data-center-resident SNA-Web gateway.

4. Browser-based access with a rejuvenated user interface achieved via 3270-to-HTML or 5250-to-HTML conversion, where the data stream conversion is performed by a data-center-resident SNA-Web gateway (such as Eicon's Aviva Web-to-Host Server) that interacts with a standard Web server to send and receive HTML-defined Web pages. Invariably some level of user interface rejuvenation occurs with this on-the-fly 3270/5250-to-HTML conversion approach.

5. Application-specific HTML conversion (such as that provided by IBM's CICS Internet Gateway), where a data-center- or even mainframe-resident SNA-Web gateway uses a programmatic API (as opposed to 3270 interface) to interact with the subject application and performs the necessary conversions to and from HTML. This approach differs from the fourth option in that it is application-specific and typically implemented using a programmatic scheme to interact with the application, rather than relying on just 3270 data stream interception.

6. Applet-based emulation, within the context of a browser, as in the third option, but with a rejuvenated user interface realized with either applets that display the new screen images or software resident on the PC or workstation that accepts the 3270 data stream from the SNA application and then performs the necessary conversions. AutoGUI schemes, such as IBM's ResQ!Net option for Host On-Demand and OpenConnect's AutoVista, fall into this category.

7. Programmatic access or application server-based access, where a new application running entirely on the client or based on a client/server model handles the SNA application access in the background, ensuring that end users see only a new, contemporary application front end. The client software could take the form of an applet. Application-specific programmatic access approaches, such as IBM's CICS Gateway for Java, IBM's WebSphere, and OpenConnect's Integration Server, are included within this category in the context of terminal-oriented access. General-purpose programmatic access solutions are described in detail in Chapter 6.

The availability of so many feasible solutions can pose quite a distraction. Having such a wide range of solutions is also beneficial, however, and should be gainfully exploited. With these possible solutions, one can tailor highly effective and pragmatic configurations, in which the access solutions employed within a given enterprise depend on both the requirements of the end user and the type of i•net across which the access will be conducted. Consequently, it is possible and even desirable to have one set of access solutions for intranet access and another set for Internet-based access.

Implementing multiple access solutions does not necessarily have to markedly increase the maintenance cost and effort related to SNA access. With judicious planning, the overall maintenance and support effort could actually be reduced from previous levels, even when multiple access solutions are employed, because many of the access solutions are "thin client" schemes that eliminate the high cost of installing and maintaining SNA/ 3270 emulation software on individual PCs and workstations. In the case of 3270-to-HTML or application server-based application-to-HTML conversion schemes, all that is required on a PC or workstation is a standard Web browser.

Table 5.1 provides guidelines regarding how the various access solutions may be best deployed depending on the type of i•net across which the access takes place. Note that 5250-based emulation (that is, ip5250 or tn5250) can be substituted for 3270 emulation within this table if the access is to an AS/400 rather than a mainframe.

The bottom line is that an enterprise should not attempt to pick just one supposedly universal scheme for providing terminal-based SNA access over i•nets, particularly if it intends to provide the general public with access to certain SNA applications over the Internet. Access solutions that are appropriate and geared for company employees using an intranet will likely be unsuitable for casual, Internet-centric use by the public. For a start, it would be inappropriate to even contemplate employing a green-on-black terminal emulation scheme for casual, public access. Instead, a browser-based access scheme, replete with a rejuvenated user interface, is a must. In the case of very short duration, query–response-type Internet access involving just a few screen exchanges with the data center, the download time of an applet-based scheme is bound to make the application appear sluggish, unwieldy, and therefore unwelcoming. A 3270-to-HTML conversion or a programmatic approach using an application server will be much more appropriate.

Some 3270-to-HTML solutions, however, do not attempt to provide sufficient end-to-end connection integrity, particularly in terms of guaranteed in-sequence data delivery; instead, they go along with the connectionless page delivery scheme employed by HTTP. Notable exceptions include Novell's IntranetWare HostPublisher and Eicon's Aviva Web-to-Host Server, which go to inordinate lengths to ensure connection integrity. Consequently, many MIS managers are leery of using off-the-shelf 3270-to-HTML solutions, with no end-to-end integrity guarantee, as the basis for certain secure interactions—especially if they involve real-time monetary transactions. Such

TABLE 5.1   Guidelines to deployment of the various access solutions.

	Intranet		The Internet		Extranet	
	Interim	Mid-term	Interim	Mid-term	Interim	Mid-term
Employees						
• Data entry	tn3270(E)	Browser: tn3270(E) emulation			tn3270(E)	Browser: tn3270(E) emulation
• Power user (e.g., programmer)	ip3270	ip3270			Browser: tn3270(E) emulation if ip3270 not already installed on PC	Browser: tn3270(E) emulation if ip3270 not already installed on PC
• Senior management: queries, e-mail, calendar	ip3270	Browser: with rejuvenation or programmatic			Browser: tn3270(E) emulation if ip3270 not already installed on PC	Browser: with rejuvenation
• Professional: less than 2 hours/day mainframe access	tn3270(E)	Browser: some rejuvenation depending on application, or programmatic			tn3270(E)	Browser: some rejuvenation depending on application
• Professional: more than 2 hours/day mainframe access	ip3270	Browser: some rejuvenation depending on application; possibly programmatic			Browser: tn3270(E) emulation if ip3270 not already installed on PC	Browser: some rejuvenation depending on application
• Telecommuter			Browser: tn3270(E) emulation, cached applet	Browser: some rejuvenation depending on application (most likely using applets)		
• Mobile user			Browser: tn3270(E) emulation, cached applet	Browser: some rejuvenation depending on application (applet download time an issue)		

TABLE 5.1 Continued

	Intranet		The Internet		Extranet	
	Interim	*Mid-term*	*Interim*	*Mid-term*	*Interim*	*Mid-term*
• Agent working for the company (e.g., dealership, travel agent)			Browser: tn3270(E) emulation, cached applet	Browser: rejuvenation either with applet or 3270-to-HTML depending on application	Browser: tn3270(E) emulation, cached applet	Browser: rejuvenation either with applet or 3270-to-HTML depending on application
Public						
• Simple query			Browser: 3270-to-HTML	Browser: 3270-to-HTML or programmatic		
• Insecure, multistep query			Browser: 3270-to-HTML with some form of screen sequencing	Browser: 3270-to-HTML with some form of screen sequencing or programmatic		
• Secure, multistep transaction			Browser: applet with rejuvenation or programmatic	Browser: programmatic		

scenarios must be addressed with an applet-based solution that supports both end-to-end persistent connections and user interface rejuvenation, such as OpenConnect Systems' OC://WebConnect Pro. The need for persistent end-to-end connections for certain applications is discussed in Section 5.4.1.

5.1 CASE STUDY: MIXING AND MATCHING SNA ACCESS SOLUTIONS

Gazprom, Russia's premier natural gas company with revenues of approximately $30 billion per year, serves as an excellent case study of a large enterprise that is already employing multiple, disparate, terminal-oriented SNA access schemes across the Internet. Gazprom has a highly dispersed operation, including gas fields, processing plants, and distribution centers, scattered across Russia's vast geography. To deal with this distributed organization, it has multiple regional data centers, each with mainframes running

The beauty of the i•net-related SNA access schemes is that disparate schemes can be used concurrently without schemes interfering with one another. Enterprises therefore have the option of using ip3270 for their power users, applet-based emulation for their data-entry users, and 3270-to-HTML for casual, public access over the Internet.

various SNA applications. Until recently, Gazprom provided PC-based remote access to these SNA applications, across X.25, using Eicon Technology's 3270 emulators; many locations employed dial-up connections to the packet switching network. With the growth of the Internet within Russia, Gazprom decided to move away from X.25 to higher-bandwidth, Internet-based data center access, employing satellite links where necessary to reach ISPs.

Rather than trying to address the diverse needs and usage patterns of its large PC user population with just one SNA access scheme, Gazprom decided to actively evaluate multiple access approaches, on an experimental basis, to determine whether they could deliver more customized solutions. In general, the goal was to establish whether the company could embark on a migration path that would eventually facilitate across-the-board standardization on "thin clients" and browser-based data center access. Figure 5.1 depicts the overall architecture used by Gazprom to evaluate its SNA access options. Gazprom evaluated three terminal-oriented SNA access schemes, two of which were based on products that were in beta-test mode.

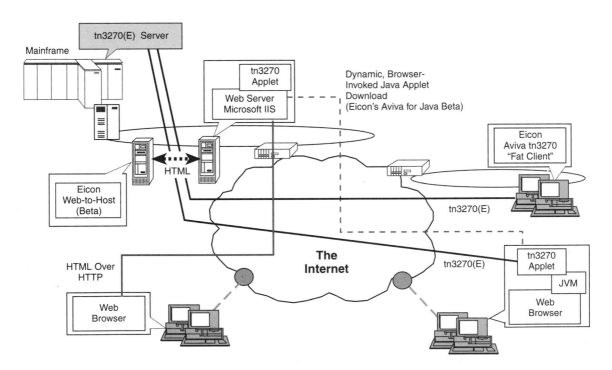

FIGURE 5.1 The beta configuration used by Gazprom to evaluate its SNA access options.

Full-Function, 32-bit, Green-on-Black 3270 "Fat Client" Emulator

This access scheme took the form of Eicon's Aviva for Desktops, with standards-based tn3270 being used to interact with a mainframe-based tn3270 server, as opposed to using ip3270 to a data-center-resident SNA-LAN gateway (another feasible option). (At the time of the Gazprom evaluation, Aviva for Desktops was known as Aviva 8.0.) The full-function clients continue the access regime that was the norm with the X.25 network prior to the move to the Internet. Gazprom, however, is in the process of moving as many PC users as possible toward browser-based access-centric "thin clients." The company recognizes that some of its power users will continue to need some high-end features available only with the full-function client. Thus there is a tacit admission that full-function clients will continue to exist for quite a while, despite the lower cost and software maintenance advantages of "thin-clients."

Downloaded, Java Applet-Based, Green-on-Black tn3270 Emulation

This option relied on a beta-code version of Eicon's Aviva for Java, with the applet talking directly with the mainframe-based tn3270 server. This browser-invoked tn3270 emulation with a Java applet differs from the Aviva for Desktop tn3270 access scheme mentioned above in that no SNA-specific client software must be installed or maintained on the individual PCs. Instead, only a standard Web browser is needed on a permanent basis because the applet is downloaded on demand.

This "thin client" applet-based emulation understandably does not offer the same rich repertoire of functionality as is available with the full-function client, especially when it comes to value-added functions such as graphic capabilities, printing flexibility, and programming interfaces. If the applet set out to match the feature list of the full-function client, its size would grow to be at least an order of magnitude larger, which would considerably increase the time required to download the applet and therefore compromise its viability. Consequently, the applet focuses on providing green-on-black terminal emulation with all of the necessary functionality for conventional 3270 applications, such as data entry, transaction processing, database management, systems programming, system administration, and mainframe application development. Such terminal emulation capability is appropriate for at least 90% of users who are or were using a full-function 3270 client.

Hence, the trend is away from the full-function emulator and toward downloadable applets, as the applet approach obviates the need to install and maintain emulator software on individual PCs. This change provides a huge and tangible advantage to a large and highly dispersed enterprise such as Gazprom.

Moreover, the newer releases of browsers, such as Netscape Navigator 4.0 and Internet Explorer 4.0, offer support for the **Java Development Kit (JDK) 1.1** and permit Java applets to be cached. Cached applets provide the best of both worlds—eliminating the need for continual downloading while simultaneously ensuring the automatic, unattended downloading of any new versions of the applet. Each time a cached applet is invoked, it automatically checks with a predesignated server to determine whether a newer version of the applet has been posted. If it detects a newer version, the user has the option of having it dynamically downloaded. This automatic version-checking mechanism ensures that the software maintenance and version control advantages of applets are not lost if an enterprise decides to cache the applets to minimize the download requirements. ActiveX applets can also be relatively easily cached on Windows 95/98 or Windows NT systems.

3270-to-HTML Conversion Based on a Beta-Test Version of Eicon's Aviva Web-to-Host Server

This product, known as Sunflare, serves only those users who require SNA access for what are essentially status-query updates; such users are not prone to using SNA applications on a prolonged, heads-down, high-transaction-volume basis. This access scheme is totally browser-centric and does not require any other access- or emulation-related software to be installed on or dynamically downloaded to the client. Thus it is ideal for the users who require only casual access to the mainframe applications.

With 3270-to-HTML conversion, SNA screens are converted to corresponding Web pages and then displayed within a standard browser, just like any other Web page. Although 3270-to-HTML conversion can be used on a global basis to apply to all SNA applications and every screen-oriented SNA interaction, Gazprom planned a different strategy. It would limit 3270-to-HTML conversion-based access to certain selected applications. With the Sunflare approach, the transformations to be made when converting the 3270 screen dialogs employed by these applications into corresponding Web pages were defined, programmatically, using visual-programming schemes such as VBScript and JScript. Eicon also provided a set of ActiveX tools to facilitate this programming effort. Other 3270-to-HTML conversion solutions, such as Farabi's HostFront Publishing, permit the screen rejuvenation transformation to be specified via a vendor-supplied scripting system, rather than through a commercial programming package.

Aviva Web-to-Host Server differs significantly from most, if not all, other 3270-to-HTML solutions in that it contains a built-in, full-function SNA gateway, as shown in Fig. 5.1. Thus, with Aviva Web-to-Host Server, one does not need an auxiliary SNA-LAN gateway or tn3270(E) server to achieve mainframe or AS/400 connectivity.

Consistent with a growing trend, Gazprom opted for a mainframe-resident tn3270(E) server rather than an off-board server. The mainframe-resident tn3270(E) server approach is, in reality, a double-edged sword. IBM's latest tn3270(E) servers—such as the one bundled in within Communications Server version 2, release 5, for OS/390—are indeed scalable; IBM claims support of as many as 60,000 concurrent users is possible. A mainframe-resident server is also likely to be more robust and resilient than a PC-centric server. In addition, it obviates the need to manage and monitor an off-board server. The downside, however, is that it requires TCP/IP on the mainframe and utilizes mainframe resources, which are still relatively expensive, to perform a straightforward protocol conversion task that might otherwise be very cost-effectively handled on a channel-attached tn3270(E) server, such as Cisco's 7000/CIP or IBM's own 2216. The IBM 2216 tn3270(E) server implementation can currently support approximately 16,000 concurrent sessions at an extremely competitive price. A Cisco CIP can also support at least 16,000 concurrent sessions, with the added proviso that it is possible to have as many as 10 CIPs within a Cisco 7500.

This case study demonstrates that it is possible to effectively employ multiple i•net-based SNA access schemes at the same time without the various schemes interfering with each other or being mutually exclusive. It also shows that the "thin client," browser-based access solutions can minimize the cost and effort of distributing and maintaining SNA access/emulation software. This minimization in the cost of installing and maintaining client software is the major value proposition of applet-based emulation solutions. The real cost of installing and maintaining SNA client software on individual PCs and workstations can approximate $150 per user per year. When dealing with thousands of users, this amount adds up to become quite a hefty cost. "Thin client" SNA access solutions eliminate this expense. Browser-based access, either via 3270-to-HTML conversion or via an application server-based programmatic approach, is also the optimal way to provide the general public with transparent access to SNA applications.

5.2 SNA ACCESS-RELATED COMPONENTS AND COMPONENT TIERING

Many of the i•net-oriented SNA access schemes require at least one intermediary server between the mainframe and the client, running one or more software components. For example, all of the browser-based access schemes require, at a minimum, the presence of a Web server to download Web pages if 3270-to-HTML conversion is being used or applets if the terminal emulation occurs via an applet. The requisite Web server is likely to reside on an NT or UNIX server, even though it is now possible, especially with OS/390,

Any viable browser-based solution offering access to SNA will likely involve multiple components—typically a minimum of four. A solution that requires five or more components is not necessarily less efficient than one that uses fewer components. A solution with fewer components may not provide encryption, while one with four or more certainly will provide this feature.

to have a mainframe-resident Web server. Non-browser-based schemes are likely to require an SNA-LAN gateway or a tn3270(E) server. Although a company can use a mainframe-resident tn3270(E) server, many enterprises currently opt for off-board servers to conserve mainframe resources, though this trend will likely begin to change by the year 2000.

With the inevitable presence of an intermediary server, the overall architecture of i•net-oriented SNA access schemes tends to remind people of the two-tier and three-tier models used to describe client/server configurations for mainframe environments. Consequently, the terms "2-tier," "3-tier," "2.5-tier," and "3.5-tier" are often employed when discussing the architecture of i•net-oriented SNA access solutions, with 2.5- and 3.5-tier referring to solutions where Web server involvement in the overall end-to-end data interchange process remains limited to downloading a terminal emulation applet. This tiering methodology is misleading and unrepresentative, however, because it counts only the physical boxes involved; it does not account for the actual software components required, particularly at the intermediate server. Moreover, the count focuses on the minimum number of physical boxes required, rather than the actual number that may be required to handle large numbers of concurrent sessions.

Some access solutions may require only one software component on the intermediate server; others may require as many as four. In the box count approach, however, the intermediate server is always counted as one component irrespective of the number of disparate software components it runs. Hence, while some so-called 3-tier solutions may have just three software components distributed between the mainframe, client, and intermediate server, others may involve as many as six, with four of these components running on the intermediate server. Thus the box count approach does not provide a meaningful "apples-to-apples" comparison metric for the various access architectures involved, nor does it accurately depict the actual data path employed by any one solution.

To make matters even worse, all of the multiple server-related software components in a given 3-tier solution may not reside within a single server; they could be distributed across multiple servers. A 3-tier solution, though purporting to reflect the number of boxes involved, may require three intermediate servers—and thus have a box count as high as six! Figure 5.2, which shows the actual architectures of two Java applet-based emulation solutions, illustrates how one solution requires three separate software components running on the intermediary NT server and the other approach uses only two.

Scalability is invariably the reason why the software components may be deployed on separate servers rather than on the same one. Some browser-based access solutions, for example, require a Web server, a tn3270(E) server, and an

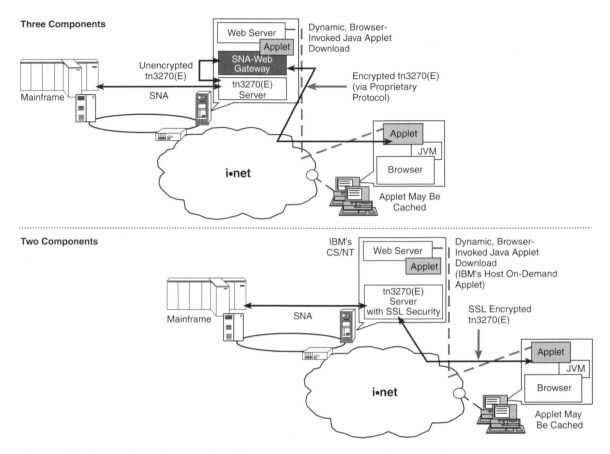

FIGURE 5.2 The number of server-side software components can vary between solutions.

SNA-Web gateway to perform functions such as encryption. Running all of these server components on a single 266MHz Pentium II-based NT server might not provide the concurrent session limits or throughput required by an enterprise. To achieve the required scalability, the organization may be forced to run the Web server on one NT server, the tn3270(E) server on another server, and possibly the SNA-Web gateway on a third server. Under the box count method, this multiple-server configuration would still be classified as a 3-tier scheme.

Counting the actual software components involved in a given access solution is much more logical and germane than the misleading box count approach, and serves as a solid basis for comparing different access architectures. Consequently, the remainder of this book will discuss access architectures in terms of the software components involved, rather than in terms of the minimum number of boxes required. To systematically pursue this software component approach, one must identify and categorize the entire inventory of the various components that may appear in the various access schemes. The following comprehensive list describes all of the SNA access-related components that may be found in an SNA-capable i•net, grouped where appropriate into functional classes.

- *Web server:* to download applets or HTML-based Web pages containing host information that were created using either 3270-to-HTML or a programmatic application-to-HTML approach.
- *Web browser:* if applet-based terminal emulation, 3270-to-HTML conversion, or application-to-HTML conversion is to be used.
- *Client software, other than the Web browser:*
  1. Full-function, 3270/5250 emulator for ip3270 or ip5250 mode operation
  2. tn3270(E) or tn5250 client for tn3270(E) or tn5250 mode operation
  3. Terminal and possibly printer emulation applet, with or without interface rejuvenation capability
  4. Optional AutoGUI applet (such as IBM's ResQ!Net) that works with the terminal emulation applet to provide automatic, out-of-the-box user interface rejuvenation
  5. Programmatic client, which could take the form of an applet
  6. Optional, very small applets downloaded by a few 3270-to-HTML conversion solutions (in particular, Novell's HostPublisher and Eicon's Aviva Web-to-Host Server) to overcome browser-related limitations, such as a lack of direct support for PC function keys or the display of input fields with attributes such as color and highlighting
- *TCP/IP-to-SNA gateway:*
  1. SNA-LAN gateway for ip3270/ip5250 (such as Microsoft's SNA Server), located on a PC server or a channel-attached controller (such as Bus-Tech's NetShuttle)
  2. tn3270(E) or tn5250 server, located on a PC server, bridge/router, channel-attached bridge/router, channel-attached controller, or mainframe
- *SNA-Web gateway:* for applet-based solutions either to augment the applet's functionality, provide security features, or both. Examples include Attachmate's HostView Server, Farabi's HostFront, and OpenConnect's OC://WebConnect Pro. This gateway typically resides on an NT or UNIX

server, although OpenConnect has a version, with integrated TCP/IP-to-SNA gateway functionality, that runs on a mainframe.

- *3270-to-HTML or 5250-to-HTML gateway:* typically resides on an external server, but mainframe implementations are also available. In some cases (for example, with Eicon's Aviva Server), this gateway may contain an embedded SNA gateway to obviate the need to install a separate SNA-LAN gateway or tn3270(E) server.

- *Application-specific Web gateway:* for example, IBM's CICS Internet Gateway or CICS Gateway for Java. The gateway could reside on an external server, as is the case with the two examples cited here, or on the mainframe, as in the case with IBM's CICS Web Interface.

- *Programmatic or application server:* a server-resident component required for certain programmatic access schemes.

Table 5.2 shows which components are used by the most prevalent i•net-oriented SNA access solutions. For the sake of brevity, only the 3270 schemes are included, although all explicit references to 3270 also apply to corresponding 5250-related schemes. The ◆ symbol denotes an integral component required for the entire duration of the SNA access session. The ↓ symbol is used with the Web server if the server's presence is required only during the time that an applet is being dynamically downloaded, or when an applet's version needs to be checked as it is being invoked from a previously cached image. With the applet-based terminal emulation schemes, the Web browser is depicted as an integral component even though most solutions use a separate window from that provided by the browser to display the green-on-black or rejuvenated screen.

All of these access schemes inevitably run their applets on the **Java Virtual Machine (JVM)** provided by the browser, rather than relying on one that may be available within the operating system. As a result, the applet ceases to function if the browser closes down. Consequently, the browser is actually an integral component of the overall solution.

The terminal emulation applet could be made to run on the operating system's JVM. In that case, the applet would be referred to as an "application" because one criterion for being an applet (particularly with Java) is that it be integrated with a browser and a source Web page. A Java application-based terminal emulation, in effect, is really no different from a traditional tn3270(E) client or even an ip3270 client in that it operates independently from a browser. The remainder of this chapter will assume that applets always require the presence of a browser and that any implementations that are applications resemble a tn3270(E) or ip3270 client.

The functional component distribution depicted in Table 5.2 will be used extensively in the remainder of this chapter when discussing the architectual basis of the various access solutions.

TABLE 5.2　Functional component distribution.

	ip3270	tn3270(E)	3270-to-HTML				Applet-Based Terminal Emulation			
			Scheme 1	Scheme 2	Scheme 3	Scheme 4	Scheme 1	Scheme 2	Scheme 3	Scheme 4
Web server			◆	◆	◆	◆	↓	↓	↓	↓
Web browser			◆	◆	◆	◆	◆	◆	◆	◆
ip3270 client	◆									
tn3270(E) client		◆								
Emulation applet							◆	◆	◆	◆
Value-added applet(s)				Optional		Optional				
SNA-LAN gateway	◆			◆	◆			◆		◆
tn3270(E) server		◆	◆				◆			
SNA-Web gateway					◆			◆		◆
3270-to-HTML gateway			◆	◆	◆					
3270-to-HTML with built-in SNA gateway						◆				
Mainframe: SNA-Web with SNA gateway									◆	
Examples	Aviva client talking to SNA server	Attachmate client talking to tn3270(E) server on a Cisco 7000/CIP	Wall Data Cyberprise Host HTML	Novell HostPublisher	Farabi Host Publishing	Aviva Web-to-Host Server	IBM Host On-Demand with or without SSL	Farabi HostFront	OCS WebConnect Pro/390	Wall Data Cyberprise Host Pro

The absence of a built-in security scheme within the tn3270(E) standard has meant that most Java applet-based emulation schemes had to rely on an auxiliary server-side component to encrypt and decrypt the tn3270(E) data flows. IBM and Novell, however, now offer built-in SSL security with their tn3270(E) servers, as an optional, vendor-specific extension.

5.2.1　Additional Components Required for Security

The component permutation matrix in Table 5.2 clearly demonstrates the architectural and implementational variations of the key access schemes; moreover, it shows how multiple disparate solutions can exist within the context of a given scheme. Note that Table 5.2 always includes the client component, but does not show the presence of the SNA application being accessed. If the total number of components participating in a given scheme is to be counted as in the client/server tiering schemes, one must always add one to the number of components included with a given scheme to get the representative total aggregate. In reality, the only true "3-component" solutions available for SNA access across i•nets comprise traditional ip3270 or tn3270(E) schemes. Browser-based access schemes are at a minimum 4.5-component solutions when one factors in the application and the browser.

When considering browser-based access offerings, one should not assume that a solution that requires more components than another is necessarily inefficient and nonoptimal. In many instances, the additional components add value and even make the transactions across a WAN more efficient. Security is invariably the most important feature that may be provided by an additional component, such as an SNA-Web gateway. Although difficult to imagine, the current tn3270(E) standard does not include support for any type of data encryption, reflecting the fact that most SNA access in the past remained confined to secure private networks or commercially operated public networks with some level of intrusion protection. Consequently, some kind of adjunct component is needed to add encryption to tn3270(E) solutions, irrespective of whether an applet or a traditional client is being used.

Claiming that SSL will be used for authentication and security does not always satisfy the need for an additional security-related component. SSL works only on a client/server basis. Typically, the client is a Web browser and the server is a Web server. Today, all major Web servers and browsers support SSL, but this SSL support is restricted to Web pages flowing between the two. A terminal emulation applet, which works in conjunction with a browser, does not use the browser-Web connection to exchange data between its window and the tn3270(E) server. The only exception is an optional feature in Client/Server Technology's Jacada product, which allows the Java applet to talk to the Jacada server through the Web server using HTTP and a proxy servlet component. The architecture of Jacada's HTTP-based access is shown in Fig. 6.16.

An applet-based emulation scheme therefore needs SSL or another encryption scheme that can operate independently of the Web server and browser. The data-center-side support for the applet-specific security, whether SSL or another scheme, is usually realized using an SNA-Web gateway component or a security "wedge," such as WRQ's Proxy Server for Reflection EnterView 2.0, in front of the tn3270(E) server. Figure 5.3 shows the architecture used by WRQ, replete with its Proxy Server component, to provide encryption. Note that WRQ uses Transport Layer Security (TLS) as opposed to SSL, and that the Proxy Server, which is written in Java, is shown executing on a mainframe to highlight that mainframes with OS/390 represent viable Java platforms. The applet itself will perform the client-side encryption/deencryption.

The need to have a separate component to realize encryption for tn3270(E) is, however, changing, even before the extension of the tn3270(E) standard to include a security mechanism. IBM and Novell have taken the initiative to add SSL-based security to their tn3270(E) servers as vendor-specific extensions. Thus the tn3270(E) server function in IBM's Communications Server family (which includes CS/NT, CS for OS/390, and CS/AIX)

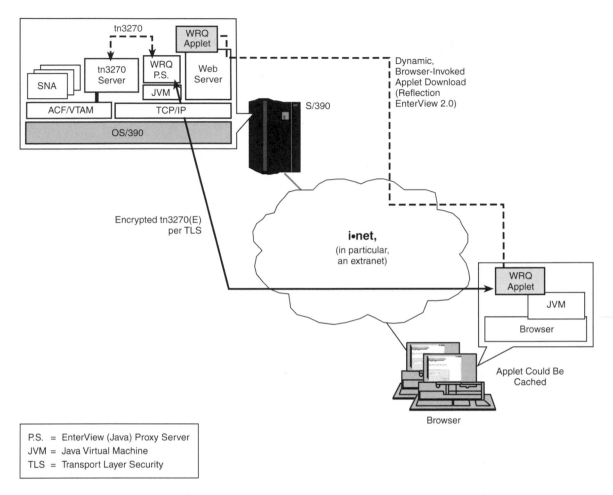

FIGURE 5.3 WRQ's Transport Layer Security scheme for its tn3270(E) Java applet based on a Java Proxy Server, shown here running on a mainframe.

and in Novell's NetWare for SAA 4 now supports SSL-based authentication and encryption. IBM's Java applet Host On-Demand tn3270(E) client already supported SSL, in conjunction with the optional NT Server-based Redirector component of Host On-Demand. Therefore, no changes were required to the Host On-Demand applet per se to ensure that it could interact directly with an IBM or Novell tn3270(E) server that now supports integrated SSL security.

Figure 5.4 shows Host On-Demand with SSL security being used with Communications Server running on a mainframe. Figure 5.5 shows NetWare for SAA 4 supporting SSL in the context of IBM's Host On-Demand along with SSL being used in conventional mode between a Web server and a

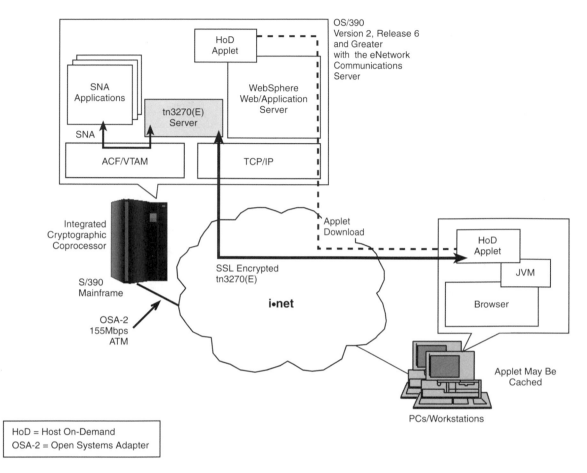

FIGURE 5.4 IBM's Host On-Demand with integrated SSL security being used with IBM's OS/390 Communications Server tn3270(E) server, which supports SSL.

browser to support 3270-to-HTML conversion (à la Novell's HostPublisher solution). The 3270-to-HTML conversion portion of Fig. 5.5 highlights that 3270-to-HTML conversion schemes can always rely on the SSL security available between a Web server and a browser, as all SNA access-related data transfers across an i•net occur directly between these components.

With the exception of Host On-Demand when used with Communications Server or NetWare for SAA 4, all of the other Java applet-based schemes, at present, can provide encryption only through the deployment of an intermediary server component. Hence, if encryption is required, the only option is to adopt a scheme with an intermediary component or to use the Host On-Demand approach.

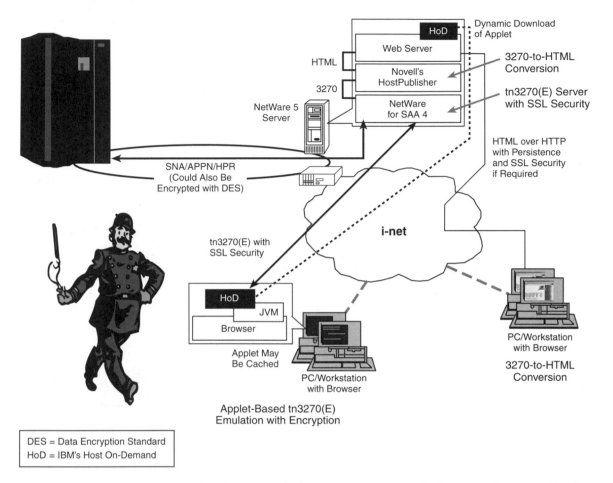

FIGURE 5.5 Secure browser-based SNA access—both 3270-to-HTML or applet-based emulation—with NetWare for SAA 4.

An unsecure applet scheme, without encryption, can obviously be used within the confines of an intranet, provided that an enterprise feels confident that its intranet is adequately secure and safeguarded against external intrusions. An unsecure scheme could also be used across the Internet without undue risk, if it is used in conjunction with a proven auxiliary security mechanism such as VPN. The 3M and State of Idaho Department of Labor case studies cited later in this chapter use this VPN approach to realize industrial-strength security for their applet-based access solutions. When the applet-based access schemes are discussed in more detail in Section 5.6, the role of value-added components such as SNA-Web gateways will be revisited, placing particular emphasis on security.

5.3 ip3270: AN ALTERNATIVE TO tn3270(E)

The terms "ip3270" and its AS/400-specific variant "ip5250" refer to the usage of conventional split-stack SNA-LAN gateways, such as Microsoft's SNA Server and Novell's NetWare for SAA, with TCP/IP being used to interact with a full-function 3270 or 5250 emulator executing on a PC or workstation. Figure 5.6 illustrates the split-stack—with TCP/IP in the middle—configuration used by ip3270, and compares it with a tn3270(E) setup, with the same SNA-LAN gateway supporting both the ip3270 and tn3270(E) modes of operation. All of today's popular full-function 3270/5250 emulators that can work with SNA Server or NetWare for SAA are capable of using TCP/IP as the exclusive transport protocol for all emulator-to-gateway interactions. The 3270 or 5250 data stream becomes embedded within the TCP/IP packets in much the same way as tn3270(E), although the exact encapsulation scheme differs from that employed by tn3270(E) and is specific to each gateway.

Many enterprises and vendors forget that ip3270/ip5250 is an eminently viable and attractive solution for their SNA access for i●net requirements and instead injudiciously opt for tn3270(E)/tn5250 solutions, even when they would have been better off staying with their existing SNA-LAN gateway infrastructure.

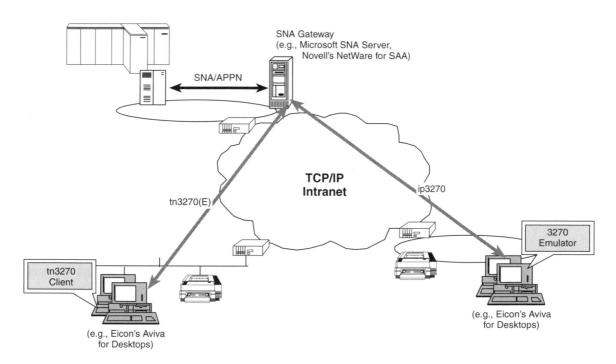

FIGURE 5.6 Often it is difficult to differentiate tn3270(E) from ip3270 since all the components can be the same.

The ip3270 mode of operation is also supported by other, lesser-known SNA-LAN gateways, such as Eicon's SNA Gateway and Attachmate's SNA Gateway. When TCP/IP is not being used, all of these SNA-LAN gateways use a LAN-oriented protocol such as IPX, NetBIOS, or 802.2 for communications between the emulator and the gateway.

The ip3270 mode of operation has been possible since the late 1980s. Split-stack PU Controller SNA-LAN gateways were, and still are, also extensively used to provide PCs and workstations with SNA/APPN access. Nonetheless, as IBM shops started to use TCP/IP within their WAN, the term "tn3270" became the accepted de facto buzzword for describing 3270 mode operation across TCP/IP—irrespective of whether one was dealing with tn3270 or ip3270. Part of the problem was that no accepted term existed for non-tn3270 mode operation; the term "ip3270/ip5250" was coined by the author only in 1998. To exacerbate this problem, most emulators capable of working in ip3270/ip5250 mode also support tn3270(E)/tn5250. The key difference is that an ip3270/ip5250 emulator talks to SNA-LAN gateways, whereas tn3270(E)/tn5250 clients talk to tn3270(E)/tn5250 servers. Some SNA-LAN gateways, such as SNA Server, as shown in Fig. 5.6, can concurrently support both ip3270 and tn3270(E) sessions. The converse is, however, not the case with tn3270(E) servers. Many popular tn3270(E) servers, such as IBM's mainframe tn3270(E) server or Cisco's CIP resident server, support only tn3270(E) sessions.

The indiscriminate use of the term "tn3270" to refer to any 3270-over-TCP/IP scheme disguises and distorts a very important market reality. Enterprises that could expeditiously and gainfully use ip3270 with their *existing* emulator and gateway software instead spend time and money evaluating tn3270(E)-based solutions because of the aura of confusion surrounding tn3270 vis-à-vis ip3270. Ironically, this confusion even extends to vendors that sell ip3270 solutions! Many are so accustomed to talking about "tn3270" as meaning 3270-over-TCP/IP that they actually forget the ip3270 approach— sometimes to their detriment, as other vendors invariably appear on the scene with tn3270(E)-specific solutions.

One can safely assume that at least 60% of the 25 million or so PCs and workstations that were using one of the many popular full-function 3270/5250 emulators in mid-1998 could easily achieve SNA access across i•nets using ip3270/ip5250 rather than undergoing a conversion to a tn3270(E)/tn5250 scheme. The pivotal fact that one does not need tn3270 per se to implement what people think of as "tn3270"—that is, 3270-over-TCP/IP—is currently lost on the market and unfortunately causes many enterprises unnecessary cost, delay, and disruption.

On the other hand, ip3270/ip5250 is *not* the universal panacea for SNA access across i•nets. In fact, tn3270(E) has many tangible advantages. It is standards-based, tn3270(E) server implementations on mainframes are available, and tn3270(E) clients and servers invariably carry lower price tags than their ip3270 equivalents. If an enterprise already has an ip3270-capable SNA access infrastructure however, the most logical and convenient first step in becoming i•net-compatible would be to convert to ip3270, rather than trying to implement an end-to-end tn3270(E) solution.

At this juncture, it is important to note that ip3270 is really an intranet- and extranet-specific solution, with any Internet-based usage limited to telecommuters and mobile users. Moreover, ip3270 should also be applicable only to enterprises that currently have an ip3270-capable infrastructure. Enterprises that use full-stack SNA clients with PU Passthrough or PU Concentrator SNA-LAN gateways may discover that their client software, gateway software, or both may not support ip3270. These organizations should consider browser-based access, tn3270(E), or even DLSw, in preference to ip3270, even though ip3270 has an edge over tn3270(E) and browser-based solutions in that it can support certain LU 6.2 applications. Its support for LU 6.2, however, is restricted to certain specific LU 6.2-related APIs, such as CPI-C. LU 6.2 applications also must be recompiled to work with the relevant 3270 emulator. Resorting to DLSw to accommodate LU 6.2 will therefore be simpler and less disruptive than attempting to migrate a large-scale, full-stack environment into an ip3270 configuration. The bottom line is that it is difficult, and perhaps irrelevant, to justify ip3270/ip5250 as a long-term strategic solution to an enterprise that is not currently using an ip3270/ip5250-capable, split-stack SNA-LAN gateway infrastructure. The real strength and value of ip3270 emerges through its use as a short- to mid-term migration option for enterprises that already have an ip3270-capable infrastructure in place.

If an enterprise already possesses an ip3270-capable infrastructure, moving to ip3270 as the first concrete step in realizing unrestricted SNA access and print services across i•nets offers many irrefutable and immediate advantages. For a start, the client and the SNA-LAN gateway software can stay in situ—the only caveat here being the elimination of any remote SNA-LAN gateways and the consolidation of the gateways at the data center, as described in Chapter 4.* Given that the 3270/5250 emulator on the client system remains unchanged, all of the emulator functions, however esoteric, that were being used prior to the move to ip3270 will

*Remote SNA-LAN gateways, if used, will make a mockery of the rationale behind adopting ip3270, because the output of such a remote gateway is SNA. Thus TCP/IP per ip3270 will be used only locally. A transport scheme such as DLSw must then be harnessed to convey the SNA traffic emanating from the remote gateway across the i•net.

remain available and function as before. The same idea applies to print and file transfer functions.

A move to ip3270, in marked contrast to a move to tn3270, will not impose any limitations on print capability. All print capabilities supported by the gateway and client in non-TCP/IP mode, including 3287 printing, will remain available with ip3270/ip5250. This comprehensive support for printing and file transfer gives ip3270/ip5250 a huge edge over tn3270(E)/tn5250, especially given that the current tn5250 standard does not even address printing. Quite a few enterprises have discovered much to their chagrin that the print options available with most of today's tn3270(E) implementations are not as flexible or extensive as might be desired. One easy way to circumvent the print limitations of tn3270(E)/tn5250 is to use ip3270/ip5250.

The use of ip3270/ip5250 also ensures that an enterprise's emulator-based applications, whether based on LU 6.2, EHLLAPI, LU-LU Session Type 0, or an emulator-specific API, will continue to function following the transition to TCP/IP. This ability to maintain client SNA application continuity and stability for all application classes, despite the move to TCP/IP, is yet another advantage that ip3270 has over tn3270. In essence, the beauty of ip3270/ip5250 is that it seamlessly and effortlessly extends the total functionality and the overall value proposition of feature-rich, full-function 3270/5250 emulators into SNA-capable i•nets.

Despite its inalienable strengths, ip3270/ip5250 does have certain shortcomings. For example, it is the quintessential "fat client" solution. Although tools for centralized distribution, configuration, and maintenance have been developed, 3270/5250 emulators have a justified reputation of being expensive and requiring high maintenance; part of this reputation stems from the fact that emulator vendors relentlessly produce new software releases to add even more features, fix problems, and to justify their annual software maintenance fees. Consequently, one of the prime advantages cited for applet-based emulation solutions, whether dynamically downloaded or cached, is that of automated distribution, version control, and software maintenance, which greatly minimize the cost and effort related to the upkeep of client software. The "fat client" nature of ip3270/ip5250, on the other hand, rules it out as a viable option for casual, public access across the Internet.

Note that tn3270(E) clients and applet-based solutions also tend to be less costly than full-function, feature-rich emulators. IBM is now trying to eliminate this pricing differential by offering its extremely feature-rich PComm emulator at the same price per user as its applet-based Host On-Demand solution. Other vendors will have little choice except to try to match IBM's technique-neutral pricing model. Remember that nearly all full-function emulators that can operate in ip3270/ip5250 mode also support tn3270(E)/tn5250. The pivotal difference is that the standards-based tn3270(E)/tn5250 protocol may not support some of the value-added functions and printing flexibility possible with ip3270/ip5250.

In addition, the tn3270(E)/tn5250 protocol may be more efficient, and hence result in faster data transfers, than the proprietary, SNA-LAN gateway-specific protocol used with ip3270/ip5250. This potential performance differential, if it exists, will be primarily gateway-specific but might also reflect the type of emulator used. It is therefore difficult to characterize or quantify with any precision. The only way to evaluate the likely performance of a given ip3270/ip5250 configuration is to prototype it. Given that the 40-byte TCP/IP headers used with any ip3270/ip5250 solution will likely be longer than the headers employed by the non-TCP/IP, split-stack protocol, ip3270/ip5250 may prove slightly slower given the same amount of WAN bandwidth. Note, however, that tn3270(E)/tn5250 also uses 40-byte TCP/IP headers. Thus any performance comparisons, to be meaningful, must measure ip3270 against tn3270(E). Comparing ip3270 performance with a non-TCP/IP scheme, though an interesting exercise, is not germane because the transition to i•nets dictates the use of TCP/IP-based protocols. As discussed in Chapter 3, additional bandwidth will inevitably be required if one intends to achieve the same levels of SNA performance across an i•net as was possible with an SNA-only network or even a private, multi-protocol network.

Table 5.3 provides a snapshot of the functional capability offered by some popular full-function 3270/5250 emulators that can work in ip3270/ip5250 mode.

The bottom line when it comes to ip3270/ip5250 is very simple and straightforward. This protocol is a very attractive short- to mid-term SNA access over i•net solution for enterprises that already have an SNA-LAN gateway-centric infrastructure that is capable of operating in this mode. It has limited, if any, appeal for enterprises that have not used 3270/5250 clients previously. In addition, the ip3270/ip5250 solution is suited for "employees-only" use and as such is oriented toward intranet and extranet applications. Much like tn3270/tn5250, ip3270/ip5250 is not suited for casual, public access to SNA applications over the Internet, because these "fat client" schemes rely on preinstalled client software. Enterprises that have a split-stack SNA-LAN gateway infrastructure should evaluate ip3270/ip5250 as their first and most effective option for achieving SNA access across i•nets, before they consider any other options. Once an SNA-capable i•net has been successfully realized via ip3270/ip5250 and DLSw, an enterprise should look at newer access solutions, such as browser-based access, to minimize the software maintenance burden and to force the issue of user interface rejuvenation. Table 5.4 summarizes the pros and cons of ip3270/ip5250.

TABLE 5.3 Functional capability of 3270/5250 emulators.

	Attachmate EXTRA! Family	CNT 3270 Open Client	Eicon Aviva for Desktops	FTP OnNet Host	IBM Personal Communications Family	Netscape/Portfolio, Chameleon	OpenConnect OpenUp	WRQ Reflection Family	Wall Data RUMBA Family
Client Operating System	DOS, Win 3.x, Win 95/NT	UNIX, Win 3.x, Win 95	Win 95/NT	Win 95/NT	DOS, Win 3.x, Win 95/NT, OS/2	Win 3.x, Win 95/NT	Win95/NT, OS/2, UNIX, Alpha, Mac	DOS, Win 3.x, Win 95/NT, Mac	Win 3.x, Win 95/NT
Hosts									
Mainframe	✓	✓	✓	✓	✓	✓	✓	✓	✓
AS/400	✓		✓	✓	✓	✓	✓	✓	✓
DEC VAX	✓				✓	✓		✓	✓
Hewlett-Packard	✓							✓	✓
Unisys	✓								
UNIX	✓			✓	✓	✓		✓	✓
Upstream Protocols									
NetWare for SAA	✓	✓	✓		✓	✓	✓	✓	✓
MS SNA Server	✓	✓	✓		✓	✓	✓	✓	✓
TN3270/TN3270E	✓	✓	✓	✓	✓	✓	✓	✓	✓
TN5250	✓		✓	✓	✓	✓	✓	✓	✓
SNA direct (e.g., LLC,SDLC)	✓		✓		✓	✓		✓	✓
MPTN/AnyNet	✓		✓		✓			✓	✓
Cisco NCIA	✓								✓
Desktop DLSw			✓						✓
HPR						✓			
DLUR						✓			✓
VT, Telnet, LAT, Async	✓			✓	✓	✓		✓	✓
API									
HLLAPI/EHLLAPI	✓	✓	✓	✓	✓	✓	✓	✓	✓
APPC/CPI-C	✓				✓	✓			✓
TCP/IP									
Stack included	✓					✓		✓	✓
FTP client/server	✓		✓	✓		✓	✓	✓	✓
NFS client/server	✓			✓				✓	✓
LPR/LPD support	✓			✓		✓		✓	✓
Internet access	✓					✓		✓	✓
Number of packages currently sold	29	1	2	2	2	9	1	15	15
Centralized management	✓		✓	✓	✓	✓		✓	
Centralized software distribution and update	✓		✓	✓	✓	✓		✓	
Other features	Database access, EXTRA! Objects, OLE	DDE/OLE	File transfer compression SNA-to-HTML conversion	OLE, ActiveX	DES security, compression, database access	OLE, NS/Rtr, AS/400 folders, ODBC, . . .	FTP compression, encryption	TCP utilities, Citrix support, Active Document	RUMBA Notebook ActiveX, ARPEGGIO, APPN

TABLE 5.4   Pros and cons of ip3270/ip5250.

Salient Characteristics

- Conventional split-stack operation with TCP/IP being used between standard, full-function 3270/5250 emulators and popular SNA-LAN gateways

- Seamless, zero-disruption i•net migration path for many enterprises

- Supported by Microsoft SNA Server, Novell NetWare for SAA, Attachmate SNA Gateway, and Eicon SNA Gateway, among others

- Ideal i•net migration path for enterprises that have existing ip3270/ip5250-capable SNA-LAN gateway infrastructures

- Geared for intranet and extranet usage, rather than casual, public access over the Internet

- Direct alternative to tn3270(E)/tn5250

Pros	Cons
✓ In most cases, works with existing 3270 emulators and SNA-LAN gateway configuration, in which case it is a good tactical solution	✗ Proprietary protocol
✓ Total support, without exception, for all terminal emulation and PC/workstation customization features	✗ No mainframe-resident gateways
✓ Extensive and flexible support for printing	✗ Software distribution, version control, and maintenance issues associated with "fat clients"
✓ Support for LU 6.2 and, in some cases, LU-LU Session Type 0	✗ Not promoted by any vendors—even though this omission is probably an oversight because many forget the distinction between tn3270 and ip3270
✓ Support for other non-LU 6.2, emulator-provided APIs	✗ Client emulator may be more expensive than a tn3270 client, although IBM has taken steps to price emulation software on a per-user basis, irrespective of whether it is a full-function emulator or an applet that supports tn3270(E)
✓ End-to-end persistent connections between the client and the SNA application	✗ No standard encryption scheme, in common with tn3270(E)
✓ Supported by certain channel-attached SNA-LAN gateways (e.g., Bus-Tech NetShuttle)	✗ Enterprises may wish to upgrade their existing 3270/5250 emulators to the higher-performance 32-bit versions as a part of the transition to i•nets
✓ Extends and protects the current investment in SNA-LAN gateways and 3270/5250 emulators	✗ Most enterprises do not understand that this protocol is a viable option for SNA-capable i•nets
✓ Greatly minimizes, if not eliminates, additional retraining, support, and Help desk-related costs, as the pre-i•net infrastructure and procedures remain unchanged	
✓ Wall Data plans to have an applet that could talk ip3270	

5.4   tn3270(E) AND tn5250—THE "OLD FAITHFUL" OF ACCESS SCHEMES

Standards-based tn3270(E)/tn5250 is the strategic, ubiquitous, and widely endorsed "fat client" solution for SNA access over i•nets. Nearly all applet-based emulation solutions use tn3270(E)/tn5250 as their underlying protocol. Highly scalable mainframe-resident and channel-attached off-load servers enhance its appeal.

The tn3270 protocol has the distinction of being the first technology that permitted SNA interworking across TCP/IP. At present, with an estimated 10 million users relying on it for their SNA access, tn3270 (along with DLSw) is by far the most prevalent and significant SNA-to-TCP/IP integration methodology. Indeed, nearly all of the applet-based terminal schemes use tn3270(E) as their underlying access protocol. The first tn3270 implementations, with the server invariably located on a mainframe running VM, appeared in the mid-1980s with academic institutes doing much of the pioneering work. IBM's first tn3270 server made its debut in 1987 hand-in-hand with IBM's first major foray into Ethernet, when the company unveiled the then-revolutionary ES/9370 family of S/370 mainframes that were packaged and priced to compete with mid-range minicomputers.

Today, tn3270 servers are available on all of IBM's mainframe operating systems. The tn3270(E) server for OS/390, which is available with the Communications Server version 2, release 5 (and greater), is able to sustain more than 60,000 concurrent sessions. Figures 5.3 and 5.4 show mainframe-based tn3270(E) server configurations. IBM tn3270(E) servers are also available on the channel-attachable 2216 bridge/router, the AS/400, and the Communications Server offerings for various platforms, including NT, AIX, and OS/2. All of the major SNA-LAN gateway vendors offer tn3270(E) servers, as do vendors such as Cisco, CNT, Bus-Tech, and Attachmate. All of the popular 3270/5250 emulator offerings either support tn3270(E)/tn5250 along with ip3270/ip5250 or have lower-priced tn3270(E)/tn5250-specific variants.

The tn3270(E)/tn5250 protocol is a PU Controller SNA-LAN gateway scheme that uses TCP/IP for all communications between the client and the gateway. The primary distinction between tn3270(E)/tn5250 and ip3270/ip5250 is that tn3270(E)/tn5250 relies on a set of IETF adjudicated industry standards, whereas ip3270/ip5250 implementations are proprietary and gateway vendor-specific. Being based on industry standards gives tn3270(E)/tn5250 the huge advantage of multivendor interoperability. This factor, along with the typically lower prices of tn3270(E)/tn5250 clients, makes tn3270(E)/tn5250 extremely attractive. Unlike with ip3270/ip5250, an enterprise is not locked into a specific SNA-LAN gateway and the clients that support it.

Moreover, with implementations for mainframes, potent channel-attached bridge/routers, and beefy UNIX systems, tn3270(E) can offer a considerably more scalable solution in terms of simultaneously active sessions than is possible with PC server-based SNA-LAN gateways. In early 1998 some OS/390 implementations supported more than 22,000 concurrent sessions. The server implementation on a Cisco CIP can support in excess of 16,000 sessions, with a Cisco 7500 being able to accommodate as many as 10 CIPs, giving it a theoretical tn3270(E) session capacity in excess of 160,000.

In common with other PU Controller SNA-LAN gateways, tn3270(E) and tn5250 employ a standard client/server paradigm; multiple clients, each with one or more sessions, are serviced by a single server. To cope with large numbers of concurrent sessions and to protect against server failures, it is possible to have multiple tn3270(E)/tn5250 servers handling the same pool of clients. An IP address or domain name-based "server switching" component such as Cisco's Local Director or IBM's Interactive Network Dispatcher is required as an adjunct to the tn3270(E)/tn5250 servers for this type of load-balancing and redundant mode operation.

5.4.1 Overview of the tn3270(E)/tn5250 Functional Model

A tn3270(E) or tn5250 server performs two distinct tasks. First, it provides ongoing protocol conversion between the SNA/APPN used in the upstream data-center end and the TCP/IP used downstream with the clients. In common with other PU Controller schemes, a tn3270(E)/tn5250 server implementation emulates a downstream SNA network relative to the upstream SNA hosts. To perform this task, a tn server will contain the implementation for one or more SNA type 2 nodes within it, each with a **PU** and a maximum of 254 **LUs**. Support for more than 254 LUs, and thus for more than 254 concurrent LU-LU sessions, is realized by implementing multiple PUs—in some cases, as many as 64. Consequently, a tn3270/5250 server interacts with and appears to a mainframe or AS/400 as a collection of real SNA devices, à la 3174. Thus the SNA access is realized with the mainframe or AS/400 via standard SNA LU-LU sessions using these LUs located within the tn server. Figure 5.7 illustrates the general architecture of a tn3270(E) server and shows its relationship to a tn3270(E) client.

The tn3270(E)/tn5250 clients identify and make contact with a designated tn server by using an IP address or a host name assigned to that server. (The host name will be associated with an IP address by a DOMAIN Name Server (DNS).) All of the client/server communications occur across the standard TCP port designated for Telnet applications—that is, port number 23. The tn3270/tn5250 clients running on downstream PCs and workstations are mapped to individual LUs within the server once they establish a bilaterally negotiated connection with the server. With the new, enhanced versions of the servers that support printing, a client can request a connection to a specific LU name. This capability, called LU naming within the context of tn3270(E), is particularly significant for printing because it enables a terminal session to be associated with a specific print session. LU naming is also used as a first-level security measure in that it permits a given IP address to be mapped to a specific LU name. Network administrators can therefore mimic the LU name-to-controller port correlation possible with an actual 3x74 control unit.

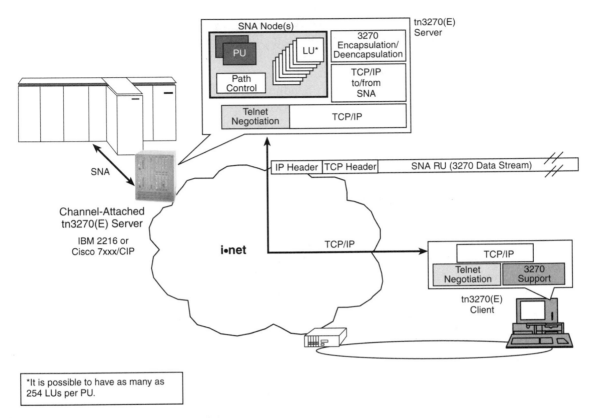

FIGURE 5.7   A high-level view of the tn3270 client/server architecture.

The Telnet protocol used between the server and client, as with other TCP-based schemes, is connection-oriented. Thus, with tn3270(E)/tn5250, one can have end-to-end persistent connections from the client to the SNA application, much like the end-to-end LU-LU sessions that will be used in a true SNA network between the application and the LU sustaining the end user. The difference in this case is that the persistent, end-to-end connection involves two steps: a TCP connection between the client and the server, and then an LU-LU session between the server and the application. These end-to-end, persistent connections inherent with tn3270(E)/tn5250 are also used by applet-based terminal emulation schemes that use tn3270(E)/tn5250 as their host access protocol.

Second, a tn3270(E)/tn5250 server provides for the encapsulation of the entire 3270 or 5250 data stream—that is, the entire contents of an SNA Request/Response Unit (RU)—untouched, into a TCP/IP packet for transmission to the appropriate client, across the Telnet connection. With enhanced

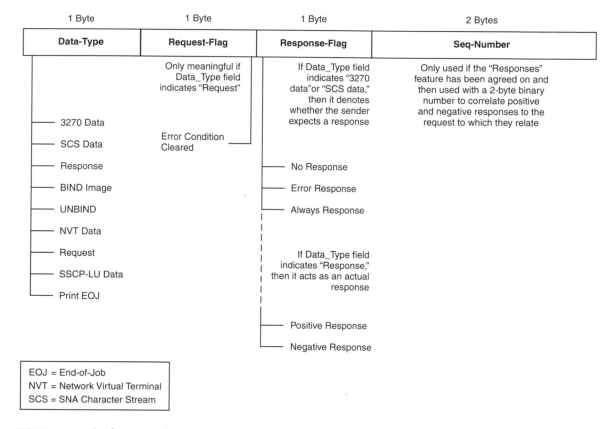

FIGURE 5.8 The format and information conveyed by the tn3270(E) header.

tn3270, or tn3270(E), the SNA RU is prefixed by a 5-byte tn3270E header that contains information about data and request/response type, as well as a 2-byte sequence number field that correlates requests and responses. Figure 5.8 depicts the format and contents of the 5-byte tn3270E header. This header is not present in traditional tn3270 or tn5250. A tn3270E header can, in certain circumstances, be sent by itself without an RU. For example, a server indicates the completion of a print job by sending "PRINTER-EOJ" within the tn3270E header.

The forwarding of the complete 3270 data stream corresponding to a given screen image to the client, without any modifications whatsoever, is an important and often overlooked principle of operation of tn servers. Consequently, the availability or the exact behavior of a given 3270 data stream capability is a function of the tn client, as opposed to the server. Note, however, that the SNA TH and RH are not included as part of the encapsulated data; the recipient therefore does not see them. The encapsulation scheme

used by tn3270(E) stakes out a middle ground between the schemes used
by DLSw and AnyNet. DLSw includes the TH, RH, and a DLSw-specific
16-byte header. AnyNet does not include the TH, but does include the RH
along with a 7-byte AnyNet-specific header.

The omission of the 3-byte Request/Response Header (RH) is unfortunate, because this header embodies all of the information pertaining to the
SNA response type, message chaining, transaction bracketing for grouping a
set of bidirectional messages, and the presence of status information within
the RU. Given the absence of this header, tn3270(E)/tn5250 has had to resort
to other Telnet-specific extensions, such as the 5-byte tn3270E header, to
convey some of the information that would normally have appeared in the
RH. (In SNA, the SNA sequence number field used to correlate responses
with requests is contained in the Transmission Header.)

Each SNA RU sent in either direction is delimited by a Telnet End
of Record (EOR) command, which is a 2-byte sequence corresponding to
x"FF FE," where the x"FF" is the designation of the Telnet command "Inter-
pret next octet As Command" (IAC). This EOR is required because SNA—
which sought to be highly parsimonious with header lengths so as to be
ultra-efficient—does not include a data length field with the messages sent to
peripheral, Type 2 nodes. Instead, peripheral nodes rely on the Layer 2 Data
Link Control protocol to provide message delimitation. The EOR inclusion
does not take into account SNA chaining, because an EOR is automatically
placed at the end of each SNA RU, irrespective of that RU's position within
a chain. The tn3270(E)/tn5250 scheme does, however, provide the capability whereby multiple RUs delimited by EORs to or from the same client can
be included within a single TCP/IP frame, or where a single RU may span
multiple TCP/IP frames.

5.4.2   RFCs Included in the Standard

A series of IETF RFCs pertain to tn3270 and together make up the tn3270
standard. The tn3270 family of RFCs can be categorized and described as
follows:

RFC 1576

This "tn3270 Current Practices" document, produced in January 1994, set out
to formalize the procedures hitherto used to implement tn3270. The class of
tn3270 functions described in this seminal document, which did not embrace
printing, is now referred to as "traditional tn3270." **RFC 1041**, "Telnet 3270
Regime Option," had attempted to standardize the method for negotiating
3270 support within the context of TCP/IP Telnet operation in 1988. RFC
1041, however, was not widely embraced. Hence RFC 1576, which established a baseline for tn3270, became the first standard. The Telnet negotiation

process required for 3270 support, as specified in this RFC, is described later in this chapter. The underlying Telnet protocol upon which tn3270 is built is described by the 1983 **RFC 854**, "Telnet Protocol Specification." Many, but not all, of the 3270 terminal types values used by tn3270 during the client/server negotiation process are included in RFC 1340, "Assigned Numbers."

RFC 1646

This document, submitted in July 1994 by OpenConnect Systems, has the title "tn3270 Extensions for Luname and Printer Selection" and is colloquially known as the specification for **tn3287**—3287 is the model number of a highly popular IBM desktop printer introduced in 1976 along with the original 3274 control unit. RFC 1646 describes how printer sessions that supported both SNA LU-LU Session Type 1 (3270 data stream) and LU-LU Session Type 3 [SNA Character String (SCS)] can be set up—where necessary using a specific LU name—and how a printer client can send characteristic 3270 status information such as "intervention required" and "data check." As specified by this RFC, tn3287 was implemented within some gateways as well as quite a few clients. In 1994, the OpenConnect implementation of this RFC on the OCS II Gateway heralded the availability of printing via tn3270. It provided the impetus for the adoption of this RFC by many clients.

Printing based on RFC 1646 was available prior to printing based on RFC 1647 (described below). RFC 1647 required fundamental changes to the option negotiation process and to the overall data transfer process, with a 5-byte header having to be added to each RU exchanged in either direction. RFC 1646, on the other hand, worked within the content of traditional tn3270 as described in RFC 1576. Thus implementing RFC 1646 as a means of offering printing was more expeditious than trying to conform to RFC 1647. Today, some servers (such as the Cisco CIP) and clients still support both RFC 1646 and 1647. Eventually, RFC 1647 and its follow-on RFC 2355 will prevail at the expense of 1646.

RFC 1647

This **tn3270 enhancements** document describes the tn3270(E) mode of operation. It was submitted in July 1994, around the same time as RFC 1646, and goes beyond the printer, status notification, and LU naming extension proposed by RFC 1646. RFC 1647 is a superset of RFC 1646. RFC 1647 and RFC 1646 have now been superseded by **RFC 2355**, also referred to as tn3270 enhancements, which was submitted in June 1998.

The SNA RU encapsulation scheme used by this enhanced mode of operation always prefixes the RU with a 5-byte tn3270E header. It also introduces a new Telnet negotiation option, known as tn3270E, which fundamentally alters the negotiation process used by traditional tn3270 (as described in RFC 1576).

In addition to providing for printing and the requesting of specific LU names per RFC 1646, RFC 1647/2355 formalizes support for the following features:

- 3270 extended data stream and the structured field processing required to specify seven-color operation, blinking, underscore, reverse-video, screen partitioning, programmed symbols, and so on.
- SNA's positive/negative response mechanism
- The SYSREQ key, to toggle between the data-carrying SNA LU-LU session and the SSCP-LU session used for logon/logoff processing as well as status notification
- The ATTN key used to interrupt data flow on the LU-LU session
- The SNA BIND request—used to establish a given LU-LU session— which contains the exact session characteristics envisaged for that session by its initiator

A growing collection of draft documents also proposes future extensions to tn3270(E). Key among these are documents dealing with LU 6.2 over TCP/IP (which is based on IBM's AnyNet protocol conversion), tn3270E Service Location and Session Balancing, Transport Layer Security (TLS)-based Telnet Security, and Telnet Authentication Using the Digital Signature Algorithm (DSA).

Basic tn5250 operation, sans printing, is specified in the 1991 **RFC 1205**, "5250 Telnet Interface." This RFC was updated in February 1998 and renamed "5250 Telnet Enhancements." The updated RFC supports printing, replete with the capability whereby a tn5250 client can request a specific terminal or printer session using a device name (that is, an LU name).

5.4.3 The Telnet Connection

Telnet is TCP's standard, device-independent application for bidirectional, terminal-oriented interactions, whether they be terminal-to-application, terminal-to-terminal, or process-to-process (that is, application-to-application). The basic Telnet specification, formalized in 1983, is documented in RFC 854. The term "Telnet," though not defined in the RFC, is most likely an allusion to "networked teletype," given that TTY teletypewriters in the 1980s were the most widely used terminal class in the non-IBM world.

Telnet uses a symmetrical, peer-to-peer protocol, where all the communications are achieved using 8-bit bytes, even when transmitting 7-bit ASCII characters. Telnet realizes its device-independence by basing its interactions on a generic and imaginary, lowest-common-denominator device known as the **Network Virtual Terminal (NVT)**. The Telnet specification defines a set of basic NVT commands. These NVT commands are sent in-band, and as such are demarcated from ordinary data by having an x"FF" IAC preceding them. They include commands for functions such as EOR, erase line, end-of-file, abort, output, abort process, and interrupt process, as well as for bilateral negotiation of options (or capabilities). This negotiation process revolves around a set of four commands: WILL, WONT, DO, and DONT. A transmitter uses WILL to request permission from the receiver to use a certain capability. A receiver grants permission for the capability indicated in a WILL with a DO command or denies that request with a DONT. WONT denotes that the receiver wishes to disable a capability.

Telnet servers and clients support specific real-world terminal types, such as 3270s, by mapping and extrapolating the NVT commands, options, and protocol to the actual terminal. Both tn3270 and tn5250 use the Telnet NVT-based protocols to realize two key functions:

- Negotiation of a set of options that will make a Telnet session tn3270(E)- or tn5250-specific
- Transfer of SNA RUs containing a 3270 or 5250 data stream between the server and a client

In addition, a client has the optional capability to interact with the server, outside the scope of SNA and 3270/5250, to ascertain implementation-specific, server-related information such as a list of SNA applications that may be accessed via that server.

The tn3270 and tn5250 schemes are contingent on the client and server successfully negotiating three basic options. These three prerequisite options, which effectively define tn3270 or tn5250 within the content of general Telnet NVT operation, are as follows:

1. TERMINAL-TYPE: 3270 or 5250 mode of operation is agreed upon as a part of this option negotiation through the specification of a valid 3270/5250 terminal or printer type. The terminal types that may now be specified with tn3270(E) include IBM-3278-2, IBM-3287-1, IBM-DYNAMIC, and IBM-3278-4-E, where the "-E" designates support for some level of extended data stream capability. The "3278" designation is essentially generic—that is, extended data stream mode of operation akin to an IBM 3279 is indicated using the "3278" label, albeit with the "-E" suffix. The "-2" to "-5" numerals that come after the 3278 are significant, however, and specify maximum screen size per the original 3278 models, with "3278-2" indicating 24 rows of 80 columns, "-3" indicating 32×80, "-4" indicating 43×80, and "-5" indicating 27×132. "IBM DYNAMIC" is used when the exact size of the presentation space will be specified within the SNA BIND command issued by the SNA application. Note that the terminal-type negotiation process used by tn3270(E), which is described below, differs somewhat from the terminal-type negotiation performed by traditional tn3270, even though the purpose and the end result are the same in both instances.

2. TRANSMIT BINARY: Agreeing on this option ensures that 8-bit EBCDIC characters, as used in standard 3270 or 5250 data stream, are employed in all of the tn32370(E)/tn5250 sessions, rather than the 7-bit ASCII character set defined for basic NVT. x"FF", which corresponds to the NVT IAC command, can occur as a data byte within the 3270 data stream, especially if programmed symbol sets are being used. An additional x"FF" is therefore inserted in front of each x"FF" data byte. Checking all RUs received from clients for x"FF" on a character-by-character basis, prior to transmitting the RUs to the SNA application, increases the processing load of tn servers compared with other SNA-LAN gateways or a 3174 type controller.

3. END OF RECORD (EOR): An EOR character will be used to delimit each RU exchanged in either direction, as discussed earlier.

The tn3270(E) protocol differs markedly from tn3270 in that it introduces a specific Telnet option—TN3270E. Clients and servers capable of extended-mode operation agree on support for this TN3270E option using the standard NVT WILL and DO processes. If they cannot agree on this option, they must use traditional tn3270 mode. If the TN3270E option is agreed upon, there is no need for the Transmit Binary and EOR options to be negotiated because they are implied within the tn3270(E) mode of operation.

Once the tn3270(E) mode has been agreed upon, the server and client determine the exact set of 3270 functions that they can support by using a suboption negotiation process, based on the NVT "Sub Option" (SB) command. What was negotiated as the "terminal type" in traditional tn3270 is now carried out as a "device type" suboption negotiation. The terminal and printer types described above can be specified and agreed upon as a part of this process.

The tn3270(E) protocol provides a capability whereby a client can request to be explicitly connected to a specific LU, which is identified by the name given to it within the ACF/VTAM or ACF/NCP definitions. Another option allows a terminal session to be associated with a specific printer session so that print output requested on the terminal session will appear at the appropriate printer.

Figure 5.9 illustrates the flow of a negotiation process for a tn3270(E) session along with annotations of some of the key suboptions. The tn3270(E) scheme supports both LU-LU Session Type 1 for SCS-based printing and Type 3 for 3270 data stream-based printing, positive and negative SNA responses, the SYSREQ key, and the ability to examine the SNA BIND command issued to establish the LU-LU session involving a given client. The support of these functions is contingent on the presence of the 5-byte tn3270E header, which was discussed earlier.

At present, no tn3270(E) clients have been specifically designed for printers. Instead, tn3270(E) and the nascent tn5250 printing are supported by clients

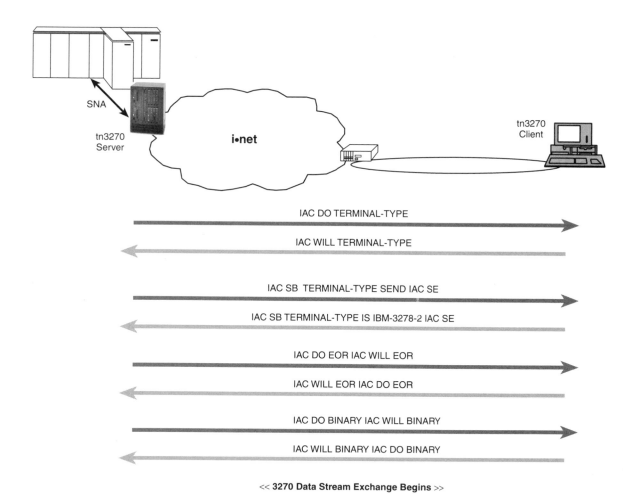

FIGURE 5.9   The overall flow of the tn3270 negotiation process.

running on PCs or workstations. Thus tn3270(E)/tn5250 printing is a two-stage process. The printer data stream is first sent to a PC or workstation by the server. The client on the PC/workstation then spools the data to the appropriate printer using an implementation-specific printing scheme. Consequently, the exact printing capabilities available with tn3270(E) or the new tn5250 are implementation-dependent, as opposed to being dictated by the standard.

TABLE 5.5   Pros and cons of tn3270(E)/tn5250.

Salient Characteristics

- Standards-based, split-stack PU concentrator-type SNA-LAN gateway, with TCP/IP communications occurring between a client and a server through a Telnet port.
- Scalable tn3270(E) servers available on mainframes and channel-attached off-load servers
- tn3270(E)/tn5250 clients available from all major 3270/5250 emulator vendors
- As with ip3270/ip5250, primarily geared for intranet and extranet usage, rather than casual, public access over the Internet—unless emulation is realized via a dynamically downloaded applet
- Continual updating of the relevant RFCs to accommodate new functionality and emerging i•net technologies, such as digital certificate-based authentication

Pros	*Cons*
✓ Standards-based	✗ No built-in encryption—any encryption schemes are vendor-specific
✓ Proven and cost-effective	
✓ Servers and clients readily available from a wide range of vendors	✗ The exact scope and capabilities of printing are not addressed by the standards—thus implementations may differ in terms of flexibility and functionality
✓ Highly scalable servers, including mainframe implementations	
✓ Fairly comprehensive support for terminal functions, including extended data stream capability	✗ No support for applications that use LU 6.2 or LU-LU Session Type 0
	✗ Limited possibilities for user interface rejuvenation
✓ Well-suited and cost-compelling solution for heads-down, 3270 data entry applications	✗ A "fat client" scheme, much like ip3270, that requires the client to be installed on the hard disk of a PC/workstation—even though downloadable, applet-based schemes are now available within the context of browser-based access
✓ Widely supported and endorsed by the industry and universally deemed to be strategic	
✓ Servers available on many disparate platforms, including channel-attached or stand-alone bridge/routers	✗ Some enterprises prematurely opt for tn3270(E)/tn5250 without realizing that they could use ip3270/ip5250 instead
	✗ The status and viability of RFC 1646, now that RFC 1647 and 2533 are gaining favor, could cause confusion because some servers and many clients support both 1646 and 1647

5.4.4 The Pros and Cons of tn3270(E)/tn5250

Both tn3270(E) and tn5250 will play a pivotal role in SNA-capable i•nets for many years. The use of tn3270(E)/tn5250 has been growing more or less exponentially since 1994. Much of this growth has been insidious, with many users remaining unaware that they are using tn3270(E)/tn5250 for their green-on-black SNA application access, rather than a conventional 3270/5250 emulator. In some cases, the move to tn3270(E)/tn5250 may have been unnecessary and ip3270/ip5250 may have sufficed. Nonetheless, with applet-based solutions using tn3270(E)/tn5250 as their underlying protocol, and with highly scalable servers emerging, especially on mainframes, tn3270(E)/tn5250 appears to be the long-term, strategic option—with ip3270/ip5250 being a tactical solution for enterprises that already had the appropriate infrastructure. Table 5.5 on the previous page outlines the pros and cons of tn3270(E)/tn5250.

TABLE 5.6 Comparison of ip3270/ip5250 with tn3270(E)/tn5250.

ip3270/ip5250	*tn3270(E)/tn5250*
Pros	**Pros**
✓ In most cases, works with existing 3270 emulators and SNA-LAN gateway configurations, in which case it is a good tactical solution	✓ Widely adopted industry standard
	✓ Highly scalable tn3270(E) servers available on mainframes and channel-attached routers (e.g., Cisco 7xxx/CIP)
✓ Total support for all terminal emulation and workstation customization features	✓ The underlying applet-to-gateway protocol used by many browser-based access solutions, including IBM's **Host On-Demand** and **WRQ's Reflection EnterView**
✓ Extensive support for printing	
✓ Support for LU 6.2	✓ Efficient, nonverbose protocol
✓ Support for other emulator-provided APIs	✓ Deemed by all to be a strategic technology for building SNA-capable i•nets
✓ Availability of channel-attached SNA-LAN gateways (e.g., **BusTech NetShuttle**)	
✓ Wall Data plans to have an applet that could talk ip3270	✓ Enjoys both vendor and customer mindshare
Cons	**Cons**
✗ Proprietary protocol	✗ No support for LU 6.2
✗ No mainframe-resident gateways	✗ Printing options not as extensive or flexible as those potentially possible with ip3270/ip5250
✗ Not promoted by any vendors—even though this is probably an oversight because many forget the distinction between tn3270 and ip3270	✗ Cannot match ip3270 when it comes to the esoteric, power-user-oriented terminal emulation and customization features
✗ Client emulator may be more expensive than a tn3270 client	✗ Unlikely to support the same APIs supported by ip3270 emulators
✗ Most customers do not understand that this option is open to them	✗ Any end-to-end encryption available is vendor-specific or realized through the use of virtual private networks (VPNs)
✗ No standard encryption schemes	

Given their similarities and the possibility of using these protocols more or less interchangeably in some scenarios, Table 5.6 on the previous page provides a side-by-side, pros-and-cons comparison of ip320/ip5250 with tn3270(E)/ tn5250, looking at some of the issues with a slightly different perspective.

5.5   3270-TO-HTML CONVERSION: THE PANACEA FOR INTERNET ACCESS

3270/5250-to-HTML conversion, with its inherent user interface rejuvenation capability, is the ultimate "thin client" solution when it comes to SNA access across i•nets. As such, it is the optimal approach for enabling the general public to gain casual and totally transparent access to SNA applications over the Internet.

Browser-based access to SNA applications was initially made possible, in late 1995, by 3270-to-HTML conversion. With HTML emerging as the native language for creating Web pages, converting the 3270 data stream to HTML (and vice versa), was the obvious, logical, and most straightforward way to Web-enable SNA applications. Alluding to the fact that Web site and Web page creation is often referred to as Web publishing, 3270-to-HTML conversion became known as host publishing. Many product names, such as Attachmate's HostPublishing System, Farabi's HostFront Publishing, Novell's HostPublisher, and IBM's Host Publisher feature in version 6.0 of CS/NT reflect this theme of having host data readily published on the Web.

3270-to-HTML conversion and its AS/400-specific counterpart 5250-to-HTML conversion offer three incontrovertible advantages over the other green-on-black emulation-oriented approaches, whether they be ip3270, tn3270(E), or applet-based terminal emulation:

1. 3270/5250-to-HTML conversion is truly a "thin client" scheme that does not require any other software at a PC or workstation than a standard browser. This setup obviates any issues related to applet downloading times and the time taken to establish a persistent end-to-end connection between the client software and the pertinent data center component, especially if the SNA access occurs across the Internet. Eliminating the need for an applet also makes 3270-to-HTML conversion essentially browser-agnostic. Consequently, 3270-to-HTML conversion can, theoretically, work with Mosaic and other niche browsers, in addition to Netscape and Internet Explorer. Its independence from applets also ensures that this scheme is not held hostage to the exact level of applet support available within a given version of a browser, especially when it comes to the variances regarding whether the applet is written in ActiveX or Java. It is therefore a truly platform-independent solution that will work with any platform that has a browser on it.

2. 3270-to-HTML conversion always delivers at least a default amount of user interface rejuvenation, such as the automatic inclusion of a background and Web page-like clearly defined "trenches" to denote input fields. Extensive rejuvenation is possible, usually with the aid of visual programming tools such as JavaScript or JScript. Figure 5.10 shows six examples of 3270 screens that have been rejuvenated using 3270-to-HTML conversion. The 3270 user interface rejuvenation options and processes are discussed in Chapter 6.

3. SSL-based authentication and security can be effortlessly invoked for security through the standard SSL support, now built into major Web servers and browsers.

Thus 3270-to-HTML conversion is ideally suited for Internet-based SNA access—in particular, to give the public casual and transparent access to mainframe or AS/400 applications for functions such as the querying of the

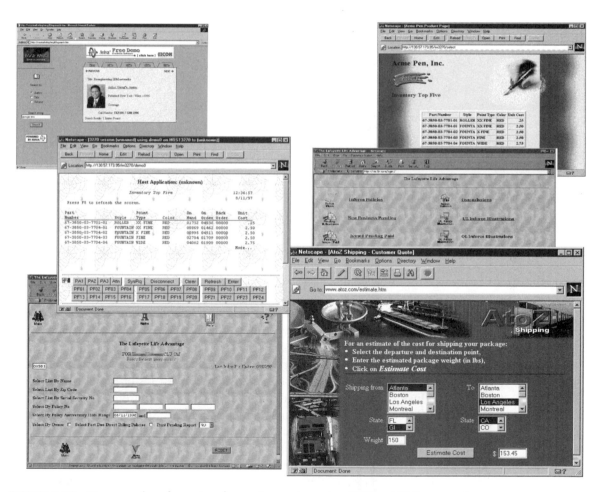

FIGURE 5.10   Six examples of user interface rejuvenation using 3270-to-HTML conversion.

status of a parcel delivery or checking the availability of airline flights to a certain destination. Not having to download an applet will expedite the access process, while the rejuvenation capabilities will protect the innocent from the inherent hostility of the green-on-black 3270 interface.

Despite being compelling and easy to implement, 3270-to-HTML conversion was not an instant success. Ironically, it was ahead of the times. During the 1995 to 1998 time period, most IBM shops were primarily interested in browser-based access to SNA within the context of their emerging intranets, as opposed to public access over the Internet. They sought a browser-based equivalent to ip3270 or tn3270(E). 3270-to-HTML conversion did not exactly fit this bill, in that it had too many small but frustrating anomalies to make it a truly turnkey replacement for ip3270 or tn3270(E).

For example, 3270-to-HTML solutions do not respond to the function keys found on PC/workstation keyboards that are normally used to emulate 3270 program function (PF) keys. This anomaly is not due to any shortcoming on the part of the 3270-to-HTML conversion software, but rather to the fact that today's browsers to not recognize these function keys. Novell's HostPublisher, which unfortunately works only in Novell NetWare environments, circumvents this problem by downloading a small, 5KB applet to detect and intercept function key invocation, independent of the browser, and pass the keystrokes back to the conversion program. Eicon's Aviva Web-to-Host Server also supports PF keys using an analogous applet approach. The printing capabilities of 3270-to-HTML solutions also tend to be usually restricted to the "screen print" function provided by the browser.

Response times could also sometimes be an issue. The byte count of an HTML page representing a 3270 screen, even with just default transformations could be considerably larger than that corresponding to the original 3270 screen because HTML is more verbose than a 3270 data stream. With 3270-to-HTML conversion, the Web pages representing 3270 screens must be downloaded to the intended browser user by a standard Web server. Consequently, response times can fluctuate based on the demands made on the Web server by non-3270 users.

To compound these irritations, many of the original schemes did not have credible work-around solutions to compensate for the fact that browsers do not maintain a persistent end-to-end connection with a given server. The lack of a persistent end-to-end connection could result in out-of-sequence delivery of Web pages, in addition to potentially compromising access security—both of which are heinous shortcomings for SNA. The bottom line was that 3270-to-HTML was, and to an extent still is, not the optimal browser-based solution for heads-down 3270 users (as highlighted in Table 5.1).

The applet-based solutions that started to appear in 1996 addressed all of these limitations of the initial 3270-to-HTML conversion schemes—albeit usually without the powerful user interface rejuvenation capabilities possible with a 3270-to-HTML approach. The applet solutions, with their green-on-black tn3270(E)/tn5250 emulation, offered an ideal, browser-based, "thin client" alternative to ip3270/ip5250 as well as conventional "fat client" tn3270(E)/tn5250. During the 1996 to 1998 period, applet-based solutions garnered the most amount of corporate attention, with 3270-to-HTML conversion taking a back seat to these schemes. The fact that IBM's initial venture into browser-based access was applet-based added credibility and momentum to this trend.

Fortunately, 3270-to-HTML conversion is now on the ascent. Many vendors, including market heavyweights IBM, Attachmate, Wall Data, and Eicon, which collectively owned 75% of the 3270/5250 emulators that were in use in 1996, now offer 3270-to-HTML conversion alongside applet-based emulation. 3270-to-HTML conversion, quite rightly, is positioned for casual access to SNA and the applet schemes are geared toward dedicated 3270 users.

One way to characterize the role of 3270-to-HTML conversion is to note that it is best suited as the access mechanism for people who have never seen a green-on-black 3270 screen and would be totally bemused by the terms "mainframe," "SNA," or even "3270." In other words, 3270-to-HTML is the optimal solution for providing the general public with casual and totally transparent access to mainframe- or AS/400-resident applications. In the future, 3270-to-HTML conversion is likely to be increasingly realized as a by-product of application servers rather than through today's 3270-to-HTML-specific products.

Table 5.7 on the next page lists the salient properties of some popular 3270-to-HTML conversion solutions on the market today.

5.5.1   The Operational Concepts of 3270-to-HTML Conversion

3270-to-HTML conversion is invariably performed by a software gateway component that runs on an NT, UNIX, or NetWare server. The Sterling VM:Webgateway, which runs on a VM-based mainframe, is a notable exception. The 3270-to-HTML conversion gateway always sits between a Web server and an SNA gateway, with the Web server being on the i•net side and the SNA gateway being on the data-center side. In some instances, the 3270-to-HTML component, the Web server, and the SNA gateway must be co-resident on the same server. Other implementations permit these three components to be dispersed across multiple, but adjacent, servers. Figure 5.11 shows the typical architecture of a 3270-to-HTML conversion process.

Figures 5.12 to 5.14 expand upon this architecture to show the specific approaches used by Novell's HostPublisher, Sterling's VM:Webgateway, and Eicon's Aviva Web-to-Host Server. Note that HostPublisher is a classic five-component solution per the component matrix shown in Table 5.2,

TABLE 5.7   Properties of 3270-to-HTML conversion solutions.

			Server Platform Integration				Rejuvenation		Security		Terminal Input	
	Upstream Protocols	Maximum Concurrent Sessions/ Users	Server Operating System	Coresident Web Server	Coresident Gateway	Application Programming	Default	Complex Rejuvenation	Supports SSL	Support for Session	PF Key Support	Light Pen Support
Attachmate HostPublishing System	3270,* 5250,* TN3270, TN5250	250	NT 4.0	Any	Attachmate SNA Gateway (optional)	CGI, ISAPI, NSAPI, ASP	✓	QuickApp, QuickDB, ASP Design Time Control	✓	✓		
Eicon Aviva Web-to-Host Server	3270, 5250, TN3270, TN5250	256	NT	MS IIS		ASP	✓	JScript, VBScript	✓	✓	✓	
Farabi HostFront Publishing	3270,* 5250*	128	NT	Any	MS SNA Server (required)	CGI, ISAPI, NSAPI		HostFront Publishing scripts	✓	✓		
Information Builders Web390	N/A	**	MVS	Integrated		CGI, REXX, others	✓	Program APIs	✓	✓		
Intelligent Environments ScreenSurfer	3270, TN3270	**	NT	Integrated			✓	HTML templates, DevCenter		✓		
Mozart Systems MozNet, MozNet3270	TN3270, TN5250	**	NT	Any		CGI, NSAPI, ISAPI	✓	Standard Web authoring tools	✓	✓		
Novell HostPublisher	3270*	~4000	NetWare	Novell or Netscape	NetWare for SAA (required)	HLLAPI	✓	JavaScript, HTML templates	✓	✓	✓	✓
Simware Salvo Server	TN3270E TN5250, VTxxx	**	NT	Integrated or any external		NSAPI, ISAPI	✓	Salvo Impact, Screen Insight	✓			
Sterling VM:Webgateway	N/A	**	VM	Integrated	N/A	CGI	✓	CGI Scripts	✓	✓		
Teubner Corridor	3270* or TN3270	1000s	OS/2, NT, UNIX	Any	MS SNA Server, IBM Communications Server (optional)	CGI, NSAPI, ISAPI	✓	AppTag facility	✓	✓		
Wall Data Cyberprise Host HTML	3270,* TN3270, TN5250	1000	NT, UNIX (future)	Any	MS SNA Server (optional)	ISAPI, CGI, NSAPI	✓		✓	✓		✓

N/A = Not applicable to this approach.

*Requires coresident gateway.

**No session or user limit provided; limit based on processing ability of server.

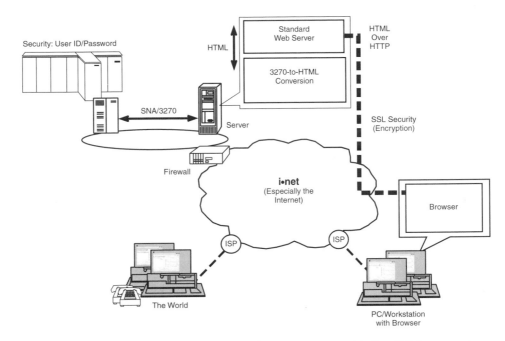

FIGURE 5.11 The typical architecture of browser-based SNA access via 3270-to-HTML conversion.

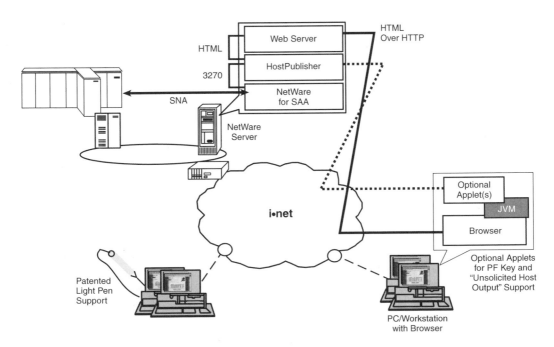

FIGURE 5.12 Novell's feature-rich HostPublisher for 3270-to-HTML conversion.

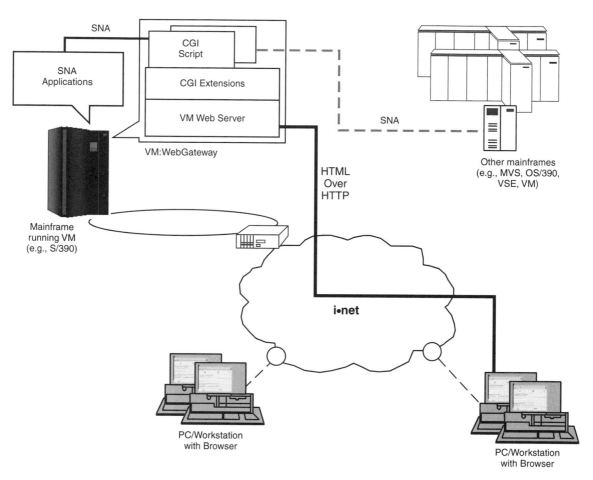

FIGURE 5.13   Sterling's highly scalable VM-based VM:Webgateway 3270-to-HTML solution.

whereas Aviva Web-to-Host Server is a four-component solution. In a few instances, such as with Farabi's HostFront Publishing, the 3270-to-HTML conversion functionality is split across two components: an SNA-Web gateway component that interfaces with Microsoft's SNA server, and a separate component that performs the data stream conversions. The same SNA-Web gateway component is used by Farabi's applet-based emulation scheme. With this additional component, the Farabi approach is a six-component architecture, as described in the Al Rajhi Banking case study later in this chapter.

The SNA gateway that provides the 3270-to-HTML conversion component with access to mainframe- or AS/400-resident applications can be a tn3270(E)/tn5250 server or an SNA-LAN gateway, such as NetWare for

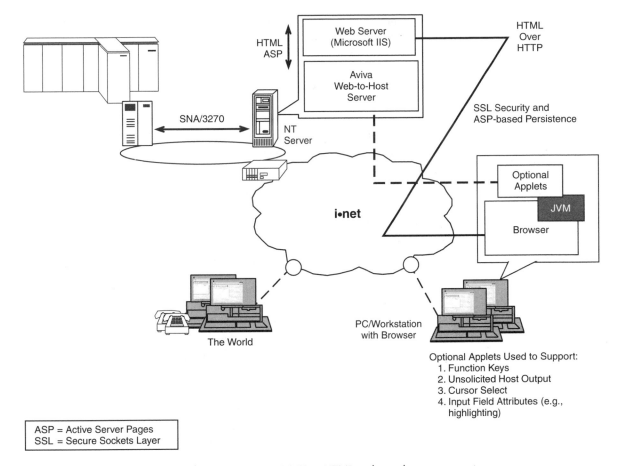

FIGURE 5.14 Eicon's Aviva Web-to-Host Server 3270-to-HTML with applet augmentation.

SAA. Depending on the type of SNA gateway employed, the 3270-to-HTML component would have an embedded client subcomponent that acted as either a tn3270(E)/tn5250 client or a conventional 3270/5250 emulator. In some instances, as with Eicon's Aviva Web-to-Host Server, the SNA gateway may be tightly integrated within the 3270-to-HTML component, as shown in Fig. 5.14.

A user wishing to gain access to an SNA application via 3270-to-HTML conversion would kick off the process by selecting a predesignated button on a specific Web page. Because 3270-to-HTML conversion is totally browser-based, this button represents the only avenue through which SNA access can be initiated. In many instances, and especially in the case of public access over the Internet, a user invoking a button to initiate the 3270-to-HTML process may remain totally oblivious to the fact that he or she is accessing an SNA application running on a cosseted mainframe in a distant data center. The link to the 3270-to-HTML process, and via it to an SNA application, will neither look nor act any differently than any other HTML-based link, as it is actually a standard HTML link.

Invoking the link to the 3270-to-HTML process will cause a *script* to be activated at the Web server, which is responsible for handling the Web page that contained the SNA access button. A script is a program that is executed by a Web server. Scripts are the standard mechanism through which Web servers communicate with other servers or programs. In Web jargon, a Web script that enables a Web server to interact with another server or an online service is known as a gateway script. A widely used standard, called the **Common Gateway Interface (CGI)**, defines how a Web server invokes a script and how data are passed between the script and the Web server. 3270-to-HTML conversion components get invoked from, and subsequently inter-act with, a Web server using one or more scripts. In most cases, CGI is used to ensure Web server compatibility.

Upon receipt of an invocation request from a browser user, the 3270-to-HTML component has the option of performing a user ID and password-based authentication to confirm that the user is authorized to access the requested SNA application. This step is optional and would not be applica-ble for many Internet-based, casual access applications. The application that the user wishes to access would typically be implied either by the Web page itself or by the user's use of a pertinent button within the Web page. The 3270-to-HTML component will then attempt to log on to the requisite appli-cation by initiating a logon process with the SNA gateway, using its SNA client subcomponent. The SNA gateway eventually establishes an LU-LU session with the SNA application, and the first 3270 screen is sent out from the application. This screen is forwarded to the 3270-to-HTML component by the SNA gateway.

The 3270-to-HTML conversion component applies a series of prede-fined transformations to the 3270 screens it receives so as to convert the 3270 data stream representing the screen image to a corresponding Web page defined in terms of HTML. The transformations applied could comprise a set of default transformations that apply to all screens irrespective of the appli-cation; alternatively, they might be highly customized transformations, re-plete with auxiliary graphics elements intended to be embedded within the Web page. In the case of highly customized user interface rejuvenation scenarios, the 3270-to-HTML component might take advantage of applica-tion-specific scripts. If customized transformations are performed, the 3270-to-HTML component will typically identify the various output screens sent out by the application and correlate them with the necessary transformations for that page by searching for specific, predefined character strings appear-ing within the 3270 screen at predesignated locations.

Once a Web page representing the 3270 output from the application has been created, the 3270-to-HTML component passes this page to the Web server through the script. The Web server then ensures that this page reaches the browser. The user types the relevant data into the input fields that appear on this page. The page might also include the option to modify certain other fields or to select follow-on action by clicking an appropriate button or link.

When the user has made the necessary updates, the Web page is read by the Web server. As this page is associated with a particular script, the Web server forwards it on to the 3270-to-HTML conversion component. It then reads the page, extracts the input data, and creates the appropriate 3270 data stream to send back to the SNA application. The 3270 input is then passed to the SNA gateway for forwarding to the application via the LU-LU session. This bidirectional 3270-to-HTML transformation continues for the duration of the SNA session.

Standard, Web server-to-Web browser authentication and encryption schemes, such as SSL version 3.0, can be used to add security to 3270-to-HTML conversion—all SNA-related data that traverse the i•net will always flow only between a Web server and a Web browser in the form of Web pages. Unlike with applet-based schemes, an intermediary component, such as an SNA-Web gateway, is not required to realize end-to-end encryption across the i•net.

All 3270-to-HTML products overcome the fact that today's browsers do not support the function keys available on PC/workstation keyboards by providing on-screen buttons to simulate the 3270 keystrokes required by the application. Novell's HostPublisher, however, goes further. It provides an optional 5KB Java applet that can be downloaded to gain full keyboard support, plus the ability to use overtype-mode text entry and the insert mode; the latter is all that a browser permits when it comes to text entry. This optional applet transforms HostPublisher into a unique, hybrid solution. To be fair, a 5KB applet is a very far cry in terms of size from the applets used for tn3270(E)-based terminal emulation such as IBM's Host On-Demand. Other solutions might eventually opt for such an applet-based solution, because it persuasively overcomes one of the most glaring shortcomings of 3270-to-HTML conversion, particularly in the context of any intranet or extranet applications.

Some 3270-to-HTML products, including HostPublisher, support 3270 light pen applications—as well as any specific "inbound" cursor positioning required by an application—without resorting to an applet. They usually accomplish this task by generating an active bitmap screen image using the Graphics Interchange Format (GIF) standard for image rendering. The user can click on any character in this bitmap to simulate a light pen "pick" or any other cursor select action.

The lack of persistent end-to-end connections, and the data integrity and session security pitfalls that could arise as a result, once constituted another shortcoming often cited as an argument against 3270-to-HTML conversion (especially by vendors promoting applet solutions). The good news is that many of today's 3270-to-HTML solutions have implemented innovative techniques to cogently and reliably overcome the potential problems inherent in not having persistent end-to-end connections. Most use hidden HTML fields within each page to store unique session IDs relative to an SNA application as well as screen sequence numbers. Thanks to such techniques, these solutions can ensure in-sequence delivery of screens to the SNA application and detect any screens lost in transit.

HTTP, in marked contrast to SNA and TCP, is a connectionless and stateless protocol. ("Stateless" in this context means that the outcome of a particular action item is not necessarily contingent on previous actions and the outcome of those actions.) Once a Web server has downloaded a requested Web page to a browser, no ongoing connection, or even awareness, exists between that browser and the Web server. Under this scenario, one can envision many plausible situations in which a 3270-to-HTML approach might severely compromise session security.

For example, imagine that a browser user invokes an SNA session by selecting the appropriate button on a Web page. The 3270-to-HTML component eventually sees this request and contacts the SNA gateway to obtain an LU for the resultant LU-LU session. This LU is correlated with the IP address of the browser user. The SNA application is contacted; it sends forth the "Welcome" screen for that application, requesting that the user enter a user ID and password. This screen is converted to a Web page and sent out to the browser. The browser user enters his or her user ID and password. Before the logon is complete, however, the user decides to turn off the PC and go home. Although not a normal occurrence, such things do happen and allowances must therefore be made for them. Given that HTTP is connectionless, the Web server, the 3270-to-HTML component, and the SNA gateway remain unaware that the user who was in the process of logging on to the application has terminated the logon process. The logon proceeds successfully at the mainframe end and the first data screen from the application is transmitted via the SNA gateway to the 3270-to-HTML component.

In the meantime, another user decides to get through to the Web server—and then via it to the mainframe. To exacerbate this scenario, assume that the company in question uses dynamic IP address allocation with **Dynamic Host Configuration Protocol (DHCP)**, to preclude having to manually assign IP addresses to all users. Because the previous user's PC is no longer active, DHCP could allocate to the new user the same IP address that was given to the previous user. An LU name-to-IP address correlation remains in force at the data center side because none of the components there knows that the previous user has gone home without waiting for the arrival of the first screen from the application.

In this scenario, the new user now gets through to the Web server, with the DHCP reallocated IP address, just as the 3270-to-HTML component is ready to send out the first data screen, suitably rejuvenated, to the original user. A valid concern for network professionals is whether the new user will receive that screen, perhaps gaining unauthorized access to a mission-critical SNA application. Fortunately, this situation cannot occur. The HTML page will go the new user, but it will be discarded by the browser because it is "unsolicited" within the context of the current HTTP interchange, which involved a different page. The relevant security in this case was provided by the browser rather than the 3270-to-HTML component or the Web server.

In other scenarios, however, it is theoretically possible for the new user to "barge in" to a previously established—but later abandoned—session. All of these scenarios, however, all revolve around the reallocation of IP addresses to users who just happen to have the same user name or SNA session name. Some 3270-to-HTML offerings, such as Novell's HostPublisher, handle such situations by enforcing explicit user authentication and randomly generating the session names used to identify SNA sessions within the context of 3270-to-HTML conversion.

Most of the potential security pitfalls can be circumvented by controlling the method for reallocating IP addresses. One obvious approach that would work with all 3270-to-HTML solutions is to set the DHCP "address reallocation delay" to exceed the period established for the SNA session to timeout at the 3270-to-HTML component, because of inactivity on the SNA session. This approach would prevent the IP address from being reused while the SNA session remains active.

The good news is that more 3270-to-HTML products are beginning to implement some form of end-to-end persistence emulation. Eicon's Aviva Web-to-Host Server, for instance, uses a built-in integrity feature of Microsoft's Internet Information Server (IIS) to realize end-to-end, browser-to-server persistence. Other solutions emulate persistence using hidden fields representing session identifiers and sequence numbers. As yet, however, end-to-end persistence is not available on all 3270-to-HTML products.

The lack of an end-to-end persistent connection makes it difficult for 3270-to-HTML solutions to deal cogently with any unsolicited screens transmitted by the SNA applications. Fortunately, most SNA applications do not transmit unsolicited screens. In situations where unsolicited screens could occur, the 3270-to-HTML component will automatically buffer them on the server. A refresh button is provided on each page that can be invoked to receive any such buffered screens. Eicon's Aviva Web-to-Host Server and Novell HostPublisher both support unsolicited host output, without the need for the user to invoke a refresh button—albeit by resorting to a small applet. This applet establishes a persistent connection with the 3270-to-

HTML gateway that then conveys unsolicited host updates. Note that Novell and Eicon also use applets to provide support for PF keys.

5.5.2   Case Studies: 3270-to-HTML Conversion in Practice

Ohio State University (OSU) and Al Rajhi Banking and Investment Corporation of Saudi Arabia provide two examples of how 3270-to-HTML conversion can be gainfully leveraged to provide convenient SNA access across the Internet, replete with extensively rejuvenated user interfaces. OSU uses 3270-to-HTML conversion to provide online, real-time student services; Al Rajhi, Saudi Arabia's largest bank, relies on it to provide home banking services.

At OSU, most of the information related to courses, syllabuses, students, and event calendars is stored on an IBM mainframe. Students did not have direct access to this information, including details of their grades or course requirements. The same applied to prospective students, who might want details on courses and syllabuses. The mainframe-resident information was available only through the Administrative Center, where OSU employees pulled down the relevant information using 3270 emulation on PCs. As a result, students had to visit the Administrative Center or contact it by telephone to obtain relatively routine information. Managers noted that direct, but authorized, access to some of the mainframe data would make life much more convenient for all parties and dramatically reduce the workload of the administrative staff—not to mention the number of interruptions to their work.

Given that all students had ready access to the Internet, OSU decided to pursue a simple, browser-based access scheme. Providing some of this information over the Internet would also allow OSU to showcase its offerings, including photographs of the campus facilities, to prospective students over the Net.

OSU, which already used Attachmate emulators, opted for Attachmate's HostPublishing System (HPS) as its means of delivering browser-based access to the mainframe-resident SNA applications. Figure 5.15 shows the architecture of the HPS-based 3270-to-HTML conversion scheme used by OSU. Like many academic institutions that operate mainframes, OSU already had a tn3270 server on its mainframe. HPS used this mainframe-resident tn3270 server as its SNA gateway. HPS can also work with non-mainframe-resident tn3270(E) servers and some SNA-LAN gateways, including Attachmate's own SNA gateway. Microsoft's IIS is used as the Web server in this instance. HPS, like most of the other 3270-to-HTML conversion solutions, will work with most Web servers. (A few offerings, such as Sterling's VM:Webgateway and Novell's HostPublisher, work only with specific Web servers.)

Home banking across the Internet is a compelling application. Internet access offers an added bonus; the bank no longer has to deal with the cost

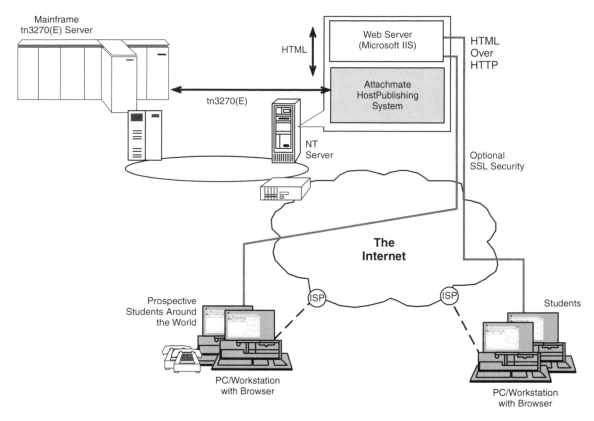

FIGURE 5.15   The architecture of the Attachmate HostPublishing System-based, 3270-to-HTML solution used by Ohio State University.

and upkeep of a large pool of dial-up access equipment. That is, a bank essentially outsources, with impunity, all of the headaches related to dial-up access. With Internet-based home banking, customers dial up a local ISP rather than the bank itself. The ISP, as opposed to the bank, now has the responsibility of providing a reliable dial-up access system. ISPs, however, are committed and well equipped to do so—providing such access is the basis of their business. Internet-based home banking is thus a no-lose proposition to a bank. The bank can provide more value-added service and garner additional customer satisfaction, without incurring the relatively high and ongoing costs of providing remote access.

Before offering its Internet-based system in 1997, Al Rajhi, although the largest bank in Saudi Arabia, did not have a home banking system. The growing popularity of the Internet in Saudi Arabia gave the bank the impetus to bypass a dial-up system altogether and go directly with an Internet-based scheme. It had one special requirement, however; it needed support for both Arabic and English, despite Arabic being a "right-to-left" language. Farabi Technology, which has had extensive experience with Middle Eastern languages, was able to satisfy all of Al Rajhi's needs, including support for Arabic within the context of extensive user interface rejuvenation, with its HostFront Publishing 3270-to-HTML conversion product.

Figure 5.16 shows the overall architecture of the home banking scheme selected by Al Rajhi. Security in this system is provided by standard SSL version 3 between the IIS server and the individual browsers. HostFront

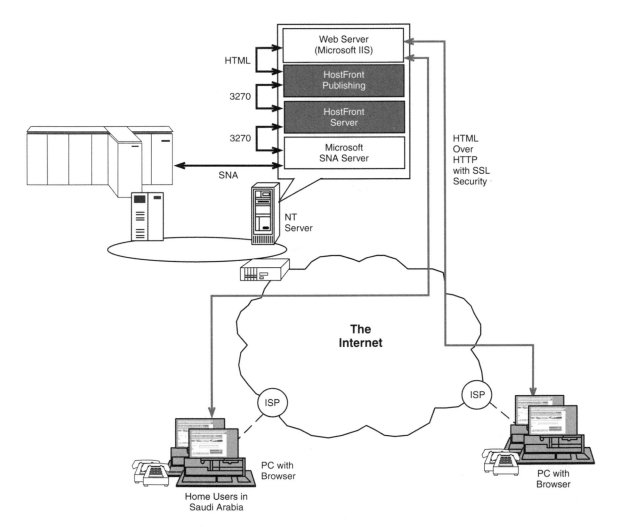

FIGURE 5.16   Architecture of the Farabi-centric home banking system used by Al Rajhi Banking and Investment Corporation in Saudi Arabia.

TABLE 5.8   Pros and cons of 3270/5250-to-HTML conversion.

Salient Characteristics

- Epitome of a "thin client" scheme in that the only software required at the client is a Web browser
- Data stream conversion technique that continually translates 3270 to HTML, and vice versa, using a set of extensively customizable transformations
- Ideally suited for casual, Internet-based access to SNA applications
- Can rely on standard, Web server-to-Web browser encryption schemes, such as SSL version 3.0
- Value-added features, such as support for PF keys, unsolicited host output, cursor select, and input field highlighting handled by small, optional applets from vendors such as Novell and Eicon
- Always provides some level of user interface rejuvenation, even when just the default transformations are in play
- End-to-end persistence emulation now being offered by some vendors
- Most of the major emulation vendors, including IBM, now offer 3270-to-HTML solutions along with their applet-based access solutions
- Can be used in conjunction with applet-based emulation schemes, as shown in the Nestle case study in Section 8.1

Pros	*Cons*
✓ Requires a browser only at the client side	✗ Most solutions do not support function keys and light pens because browsers do not currently recognize these items
✓ Works with any browser as no applets or JVMs are involved	✗ No SNA-specific printing or file transfer, with printing typically limited to the screen printing functions provided by a browser
✓ A client platform-agnostic solution, in that this access scheme will work on any platform that can run a Web browser	✗ Only a few solutions can deal with unsolicited screens from an application
✓ Facilitates and forces user interface rejuvenation	✗ Schemes to ensure data integrity and session security in the absence of end-to-end persistent connections are implementation-specific, with some implementations being significantly better than others
✓ Able to automatically exploit any standard, server-to-browser security schemes, including end-to-end encryption as in SSL version 3.0	
✓ Relatively simple, cost-effective solution that can be easily implemented on a PC server	✗ Rejuvenation schemes, although typically using off-the-shelf products such as JavaScript, are implementation-specific with no real commonality between the various products
✓ Ideal for enabling Internet users to gain casual access to SNA applications	✗ Corporate users who require access to SNA applications and other Web information concurrently will need to open multiple browser windows
	✗ Some solutions may support only a few hundred concurrent SNA sessions per server

Publishing, as mentioned earlier, is somewhat unique in that it uses an SNA-Web gateway component (HostFront Server) between the 3270-to-HTML conversion component and the SNA gateway. In this case, HostFront Server is common to Farabi's applet-based access scheme as well as the HostFront Publishing 3270-to-HTML conversion. Consequently, the enterprise can use both applet-based emulation and 3270-to-HTML side-by-side. The Farabi approach also differs from most other solutions in that Hostfront Server currently works with only Microsoft's SNA Server. Novell's HostPublisher is similar in that it works with only NetWare for SAA. Most other 3270-to-HTML products accommodate a variety of SNA gateways.

HostFront Publishing, at present, supports only 128 concurrent SNA sessions per server. Although low, this limit is not particularly unusual. Most products address the higher densities of concurrent sessions by recommending the use of multiple, stacked servers. This scalability problem will improve over time as the 3270-to-HTML conversion software is optimized and as the costs of multiprocessor servers continue to decrease.

5.5.3   The Pros and Cons of 3270/5250-to-HTML Conversion

3270/5250-to-HTML conversion was never geared toward or intended for heads-down, high-volume data entry. For that application, you cannot beat green-on-black emulation, irrespective of whether the emulation is provided by an applet, a tn3270(E)/tn5250 client, or a 3270/5250 emulator. When it comes to SNA access across the Internet, however, 3270-to-HTML conversion is hard to beat, as demonstrated by the preceding case studies. Thus one can think of applet-based schemes as being optimal for most intranet and extranet applications, and 3270-to-HTML conversion as being the first choice for Internet applications. 3270/5250-to-HTML conversion's applicability for Internet access becomes even greater when the access is of a casual nature, where the users should have no idea that they are interacting with a mainframe or AS/400 application. Table 5.8 on the previous page outlines the pros and cons of 3270/5250-to-HTML conversion.

5.6   BROWSER-BASED SNA ACCESS USING APPLETS FOR 3270/5250 EMULATION

Applet-based emulation with TCP-based, end-to-end, persistent connections provide enterprises with the best of all worlds—powerful, browser-invoked tn3270(E)/tn5250 emulation, across i•nets, using cachable "thin clients," with data encryption.

Browser-based access to SNA, after a faltering start in 1996, finally captured corporate attention in 1997, with research institutes estimating that North American corporations spent approximately $25 million on SNA-specific browser-based software. At least five times this amount of software was installed for evaluation and prototyping purposes. Nearly 80% of the revenues related to applet-based access solutions, although browser-based access to SNA was pioneered by 3270-to-HTML conversion software.

Applet-based access schemes have a clear advantage in that they provide a nearly complete green-on-black, tn3270(E)/tn5250-centric emulation scheme, replete with TCP-based, end-to-end persistent connections in the form of a dynamically downloadable "thin client."

Distributing and maintaining 3270/5250 emulation and tn3270(E)/tn5250 clients, especially given the incessant barrage of updates for such software, had become a costly and time-sapping endeavor for most SNA shops. Applet-based emulation, once host printing, IND$FILE-based file transfer, and cut-and-paste between windows became available, emerged as a tempting proposition. It delivered tn3270(E)/tn5250 functionality, except for some esoteric and little-used 3270 graphical capabilities, in the form of a browser-invoked thin client. In addition, applet-based emulation made SNA applications i•net-ready and promised to deliver user interface rejuvenation.

Versions 4 and greater of both Netscape and Internet Explorer, which now support version 1.1 of the Java Virtual Machine, permit both Java and ActiveX applets to be cached on the hard disk of a PC or workstation. Caching eliminates the need for an applet to be downloaded from a Web server for each invocation. Caching, however, does not compromise the version control and automatic software updating advantages of downloaded applets. With cached applets, a Web server is still automatically queried upon each invocation of the applet to determine whether a newer version of the applet exists. If so, the user has the option of dynamically downloading it from the Web server. In this way, cached applets provide both users and network administrators with the best of all worlds—automatic version control, without the continual wait for an applet to be downloaded.

To be fair, it is possible to envisage plausible network meltdown scenarios, akin to what happened in Token Ring networks with broadcast storms, with both downloaded and cached applets. If users turn off their machines each night or on weekends, a spate of simultaneous applet download requests will occur when users restart their browsers and set about accessing SNA applications. Although cached applets will eliminate the "first-thing-in-the-morning" crunch for applet downloads every day, the danger remains that a flurry of downloads will ensue with the installation of a new version of the applet.

So far, the thousand or so enterprises that have adopted applet-based SNA access have not experienced undue problems dealing with such applet download storms. Much of this smooth sailing can be attributed to the relatively small size of many of the applets, which tend to be in the 500KB range, although a few are 2MB or larger. Most vendors permit the enterprises to control the size of the applet, within reason, by permitting customization of the emulation functions to suit the customer's exact requirements. Bare-bones emulation for data entry applications, without printing or file transfer, can sometimes be realized with applets that are in the 20KB to 70KB range.

In nearly all cases, the applet is transmitted across the i•net in compressed form to expedite download times.

Some vendors—most notably, the 1997 market leader OpenConnect Systems—further minimize the size of their applets by splitting the emulation and tn3270(E) client functionality between the applet and an SNA-Web gateway component. This split-functionality paradigm enables these vendors to offer more functionality without incurring applet bloat. Such an intermediary SNA-Web gateway also enables vendors to provide end-to-end encryption across an i•net, given that tn3270(E)/tn5250 does not, as yet, provide built-in encryption between the client and server.

5.6.1 The Operational Model for Applet-Based Emulation (with Case Study)

A browser user invokes a terminal emulation applet by clicking on a button on a predesignated Web page in much the same way that the user invokes 3270-to-HTML conversion. A key difference, however, is that no script is involved, as is the case with 3270-to-HTML conversion. Instead, the need for the applet download and activation is embedded within the Web page. Invoking the applet causes its activation. The applet may either be downloaded from the Web server hosting the "mother" page that incorporates the applet or be started up from a cached version following a quick version validation. Today, most applets perform a tn3270(E) or tn5250 client emulation. Exceptions include Wall Data's Cyberprise Host Pro and Farabi, both of which work with SNA-LAN gateways rather than tn3270(E) servers.

At first, nearly all SNA access applets were based on Java. Now, however, vendors such as Attachmate, Wall Data, and Farabi offer both ActiveX and Java applets. Many other vendors will likely follow suit to avoid having to argue the merits of Java relative to ActiveX, especially given that ActiveX continues to garner mindshare thanks to its association with Microsoft and Windows. Some politically motivated exceptions to this trend will undoubtedly arise; IBM, for example, appears somewhat loath to endorse ActiveX. Java, of course, continues to have the advantage because it is platform-neutral and widely supported across diverse operating systems and hardware platforms. Consequently, Java-based access solutions can run on a much wider range of end-user equipment.

Most of the applet solutions open up a separate emulation window alongside the browser window, rather than having the emulation screen appear as a pane inside the browser window. The advantage of keeping the applet emulation window separate is that this window does not block the browser from accomplishing other tasks. That is, the browser is not locked into an SNA session, as is the case with 3270-to-HTML conversion. A user can interact with an SNA application through the applet window while simultaneously accessing other information through the browser. Most implementations now permit data to be cut and pasted between the browser and the applet window. Multiple applet emulation windows may be open and active at the same time if a user needs to engage in concurrent sessions with multiple SNA applications. Some vendors, such as WRQ, provide the option of embedding the applet emulation window inside the browser window.

Regardless of whether the applet window runs alongside or within the browser, today's SNA access solutions invariably rely on a virtual machine provided by the browser, as opposed to the operating system, on which to run the applet. As a result, the applet window will be abruptly and unceremoniously terminated if the browser hosting that applet is closed. In theory, an SNA access applet could be converted and run as an application on a virtual machine provided by the operating system, if one really wanted to eliminate this dependence on the browser.

A standard applet emulation window, without any user interface rejuvenation, really looks no different than the traditional green-on-black 3270/5250 emulator appearing on a tn3270(E)/tn5250 client window. This similarity is the basic premise and the innate beauty of applet-based emulation—it is merely a browser-invoked tn3270(E)/tn5250 emulation in the form of a thin client. Applet-based solutions, just like tn3270(E)/tn5250 clients, support PC/workstation function keys. In tn3270E extended mode, they recognize SYSREQ and ATTN keys.

Figure 5.17 shows a typical applet-based tn3270(E) emulation configuration. The screen rendering within the applet window is not performed using HTML because the applet window, once activated, runs totally independently of Web pages and the Web server. Instead, the applet uses a platform-specific display methodology to paint the emulation window, just as a tn3270(E) client or a 3270 emulator might create this window. The applet also does not use HTTP as its underlying data transfer protocol, given that its data interchanges never involve a Web server.

Contrary to a common misconception, not using HTML and HTTP does not preclude applet-based schemes from offering extensive rejuvenation capability. OpenConnect has always offered a rejuvenation capability for its applet-based solution with its OpenVista product; IBM formally added rejuvenation to its Host On-Demand offering with version 3. Both companies, however, employ vastly different rejuvenation approaches. With OpenVista, one creates an application-specific applet that displays the rejuvenated interface, using a Visual Basic-like drag-and-drop programming methodology. With the IBM approach, a component called ResQ!Net is loaded into each PC or workstation to work alongside the standard Host On-Demand applet. ResQ!Net intercepts the 3270 data stream from the emulation applet and then applies a set of predefined transformations to obtain the new look and feel.

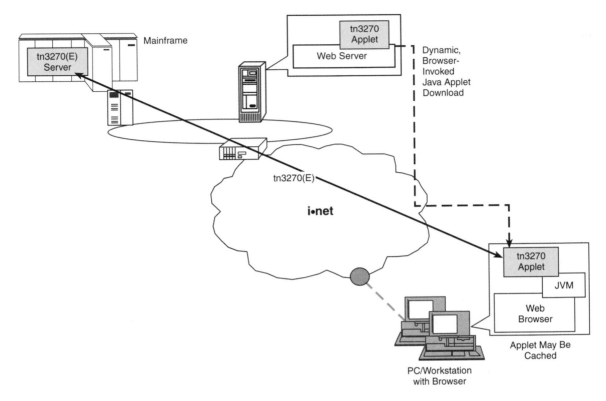

FIGURE 5.17 A "home-run" configuration where a tn3270(E) applet talks directly to a tn3270(E) server on a mainframe.

An applet-based emulator, in addition to presenting the same façade as that of a tn3270(E)/tn5250 client, acts much like one for SNA access and data transfer purposes. In the case of the solutions that can work without an intermediary SNA-Web gateway function (such as IBM's Host On-Demand, WRQ's Reflection EnterView, and Eicon's Aviva for Java), the applet is a true tn3270(E) client. Such applets establish a persistent, end-to-end TCP connection directly with a tn3270(E) server. The location of the tn3270(E) server is immaterial; it could reside on a PC server, a channel-attached off-load server, or the mainframe.

These days no limitations exist on the destination location of a connection established from an applet. JVMs developed prior to JDK 1.1 insisted that an applet could establish a connection only back to the server from which it was downloaded. Today's browsers have JDK 1.1-based JVMs, and most solutions require such JVMs at a minimum. The scalability of applet-based emulation schemes is typically gated by the capacity of the tn3270(E) server employed. At the start of 1998, some corporations were already using nearly 10,000 concurrent applet-based SNA sessions, albeit with multiple tn3270(E) servers running on UNIX servers. One example of this setup is depicted in the General Motors Acceptance Corporation (GMAC) case study in Chapter 6.

Figure 5.17 shows the architecture of an applet-based SNA access scheme, where the applet talks directly to a mainframe-resident tn3270(E) server, with no intermediary SNA-Web gateway between the two. Figure 5.18 shows a system with the same architecture as that depicted in Fig. 5.17, but with the tn3270(E) server on a LAN-attached PC server. Despite their different appearances, both architectures are 4.5-component schemes (see Table 5.2). Note that both show the applet as being downloaded from a PC- or UNIX-based Web server external to the mainframe. In the case of IBM's Host On-Demand for OS/390, the applet could be downloaded from a main-frame-based Web server. The 4.5-component scheme shown in Fig. 5.18 does not explicitly provide end-to-end encryption, as the tn3270(E) standard does not include encryption as yet. Such architectures, sans security, are thus best used within the confines of a secure intranet or across the Internet with VPN-based security.

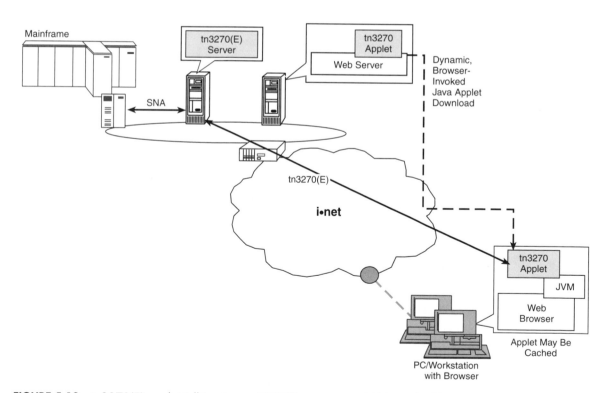

FIGURE 5.18   tn3270(E) applet talking to a tn3270(E) server on a LAN-attached box.

The industrial conglomerate 3M, which is best known for its ubiquitous yellow 'Post-It' notes, provides a good case study of how a 4.5-component, applet-based, SNA access scheme can be gainfully used across the Internet. 3M operates research and development facilities scattered across the globe. Ready information sharing between these locations occurs through a mainframe-centric, SNA-based network known as the "Innovation Network." In the past, users accessed the network using 3270 emulation. Telecommuters and mobile users also used 3270 emulation across dial-up connections. To reduce the costs associated with maintaining and managing the thousands of 3270 emulators installed on PCs across the world, and to standardize the remote-access scheme, 3M elected a scheme providing SNA access over the Internet with thin clients. Given that the company was already using WRQ emulators, 3M decided to be a beta-test customer for WRQ's Reflection EnterView solution. Figure 5.19 illustrates the architecture selected by 3M. This pure, 4.5-component solution relies on a mainframe-resident tn3270(E) server. In its beta-test configuration, 3M is using green-on-black terminal emulation without any user interface rejuvenation. Security in this instance is realized using VPNs.

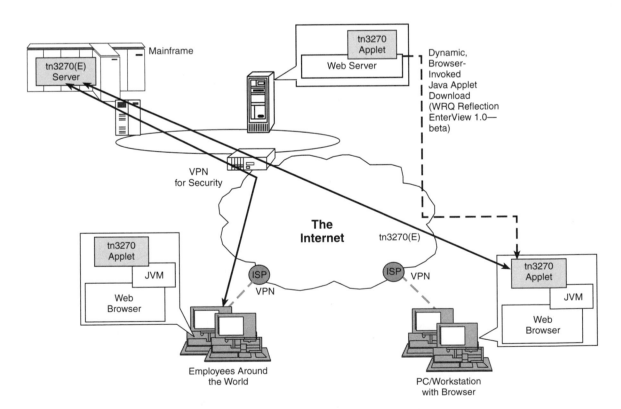

FIGURE 5.19   The architecture used by 3M to beta-test WRQ's Reflection EnterView Java tn3270 applet.

5.6.2   The Possible Need for an SNA-Web Gateway (with Case Study)

Quite a few of the applet-based emulation schemes require an intermediate SNA-Web gateway between the applet and the tn3270(E)/tn5250 server. Attachmate's HostView Server, IBM's secure-mode Host On-Demand with the Redirector component, OpenConnect's OC://WebConnect Pro, and Farabi's HostFront are all examples of such 5.5-component access schemes. Providing security, both in terms of authentication and encryption, is the overriding rationale for these intermediary SNA-Web gateways. In fact, if an applet-based access scheme does not use an intermediary server component, one needs to immediately consider auxiliary security measures such as a VPN. This situation will change in the future when the tn3270(E) standard incorporates native end-to-end encryption. It is unlikely that solutions implementing standards-based tn3270(E) encryption will become available much before the end of 1999, if then.

Applet solutions that rely on the intermediary server component for encryption purposes will continue to run the standard tn3270(E)/tn5250 protocol between the applet and the intermediary component—albeit with the data and the tn3270(E) header encrypted. The data will be deencrypted at the intermediary component, resulting in plain-text tn3270(E)/tn5250. The unencrypted tn3270(E)/tn5250 packets will then be forwarded to the tn3270(E)/tn5250 server.

Figure 5.20 shows the architecture of a 5.5-component access solution, where the intermediary component is used only to realize authentication and encryption. In all cases, the end-to-end persistent connections, authentication, and encryption take place at the Session and Transport layers of the TCP-based connection across the i•net. This i•net-specific security is always an adjunct, and never an alternative, to traditional data-center-oriented security measures. Thus conventional mainframe security packages such as RACF, ACF2, and TopSecret will be employed to police mainframe access, just as they have been used in the past with SNA-only or multiprotocol networks. The application-specific user ID and password protection that represents a hallmark of mainframe and AS/400 applications will, obviously, continue to be rigorously enforced. Consequently, security with applet-based access solutions should be viewed as a multitier approach with persistent end-to-end connections, SNA-Web gateway-based authentication, and encryption across the i•net augmenting the traditional data-center and application-level security.

Some implementations, such as OpenConnect's OC://WebConnect Pro, use the intermediary SNA-Web gateway not only to provide security, but also to augment the functionality of the applet. With such implementation, the terminal emulation and tn3270(E)-based access functions are split between the applet and the SNA-Web gateway. The applet typically concentrates on

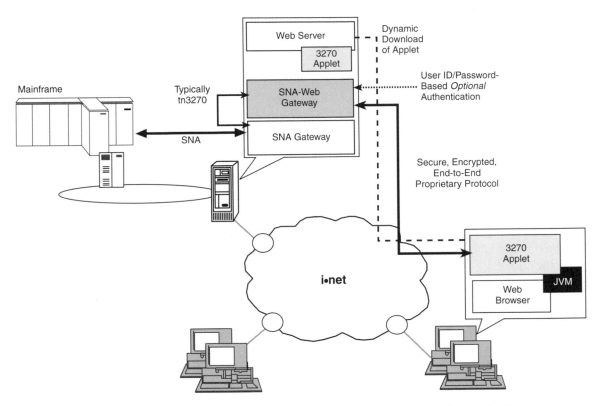

FIGURE 5.20   Using an intermediary SNA-Web gateway to realize encryption and server-level user authentication.

the actual terminal emulation and display management functions; the bulk of the interactions related to negotiating a specific tn3270(E) session with the tn3270(E) server and the sustenance of that session are, in turn, handled by the gateway component. Hence the protocol that flows between the applet and the SNA-Web gateway is not really based on tn3270(E). Instead, tn3270(E)-based interactions occur only between the tn3270(E) server and the SNA-Web gateway. A proprietary protocol (such as OpenConnect's Java Control Protocol) is used between the SNA-Web gateway and the applet. Two case studies involving OC://WebConnect Pro and extensive user interface rejuvenation (GMAC and FedEx) are described in Chapter 6.

OpenConnect offers an entry-level tn3270 applet in OC://WebConnect Pro 4.0 that can talk directly to a tn3270 server without requiring the hitherto obligatory intermediary component. This entry-level applet does not support encryption or printing. Figure 5.21 illustrates the applet interacting with a tn3270(E) server running on a channel-attached IBM 2216.

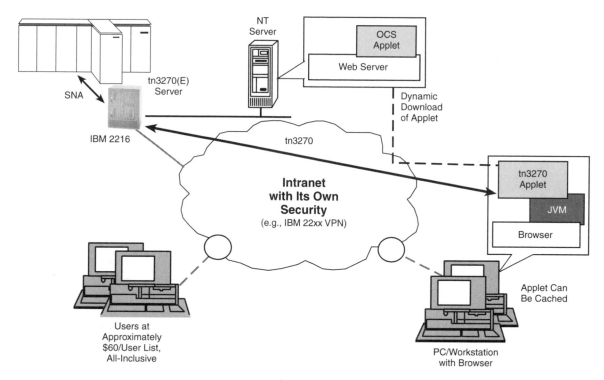

FIGURE 5.21 OpenConnect's entry-level tn3270 applet being used with a tn3270(E) server on a channel-attached IBM 2216-400 bridge/router.

The use of a proprietary protocol does not detract from these solutions providing end-to-end, persistent connections between the applet and the tn3270(E) server and between that server and the SNA application. Instead, the persistent connection is achieved in terms of a series of separate hops: one connection from the applet to the gateway, another from the gateway to the tn3270(E) server, and finally a bona fide LU-LU session, from the server to the SNA application. OpenConnect holds a patent covering such end-to-end connections from a downloaded applet all the way to a mainframe- or AS/400-resident SNA application.

Figure 5.22 shows the generic architecture of applet-based access schemes that rely on an intermediary SNA-Web gateway to provide security and to augment the functionality of the applet. Figure 5.23 shows another implementation of this architecture, where the SNA-Web gateway resides on the mainframe. In this instance, the SNA-Web gateway includes SNA gateway functionality, obviating the need for a separate tn3270(E) server. It therefore

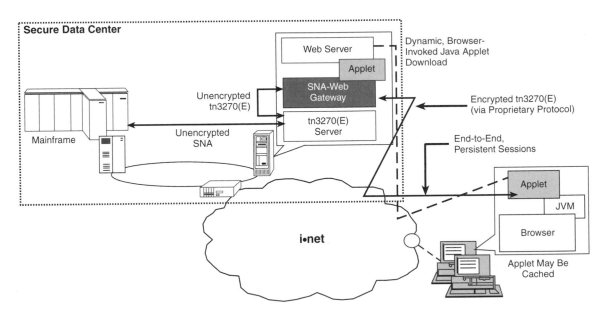

FIGURE 5.22   The general architecture of an applet-based SNA access scheme that relies on an intermediary SNA-Web gateway.

represents a 4.5-component solution, despite the presence of the SNA-Web gateway. The presence of the SNA-Web gateway ensures that encryption remains available from the applet to the mainframe. This mainframe-centric approach thus comprises a 4.5-component based applet solution that includes encryption.

The bottom line for intermediary SNA-Web gateways is that they provide a valuable service—whether it be security enhancement or applet function augmentation. It would be wrong to dismiss 5.5-component solutions as being less streamlined or efficient than a 4.5-component solution. Think of the additional component, at least for now, as a prerequisite for encryption across the i•net.

The Chickering Group, based in Cambridge, Massachusetts, provides a good example of a fast-striding corporation that is gainfully exploiting a highly secure, 5.5-component scheme to provide AS/400 access over the Internet and rapidly grow its customer base. The Chickering Group is a leading provider of health insurance products and services to students pursuing higher education. It currently insures roughly 200,000 students who study at more than 100 college and university campuses around the United States. Providing health insurance in general, and student health insurance in particular, is a highly competitive and price-sensitive endeavor. Health insurance providers such as The Chickering Group therefore aggressively seek means to reduce

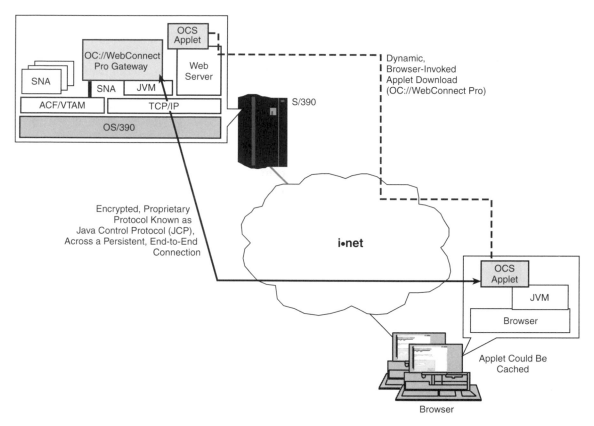

FIGURE 5.23   Mainframe-resident SNA-Web gateway as implemented by OpenConnect Systems.

costs, improve their efficiency, provide more services, and respond more effectively to the changing needs of their clients. Consequently, they are highly motivated and unhesitant about reengineering their business processes to garner all possible benefits from promising new technology.

The spread of the Internet and the availability of technology to enable browser-based access to SNA applications running on AS/400s provided The Chickering Group with a wonderful opportunity to reduce its operational costs while simultaneously increasing their reach into the student population. Whenever possible, The Chickering Group has tried to provide universities and colleges with the ability to remotely access the company's AS/400-centric computing system to obtain real-time information on its insurance plans, insurance coverage, and insurance participant data. Such remote access was originally provided via either dial-up systems or leased point-to-point connections, in the case of the larger institutions. Offering this type of remote access is a relatively expensive proposition, particularly as the number of remote sites that must be supported increases at a rapid clip. The cost issues become even more exacerbated if the client base at some remote sites is relatively small.

The Chickering Group desperately needed an alternative means of providing remote access that was flexible, scalable, cost-effective, and secure. The Internet proved to be the ideal solution, particularly since all of the company's clients (academic institutions) already had excellent access to the Internet. Using browser-based access over the Internet, The Chickering Group could cost-effectively and securely connect its branch office employees and its scholastic clients to the firm's AS/400-centric health care insurance system. It opted for the 5.5-component Farabi HostFront solution—Farabi, in addition to its prowess with Middle Eastern languages, is a major provider of AS/400 solutions. Figure 5.24 depicts the architecture of the

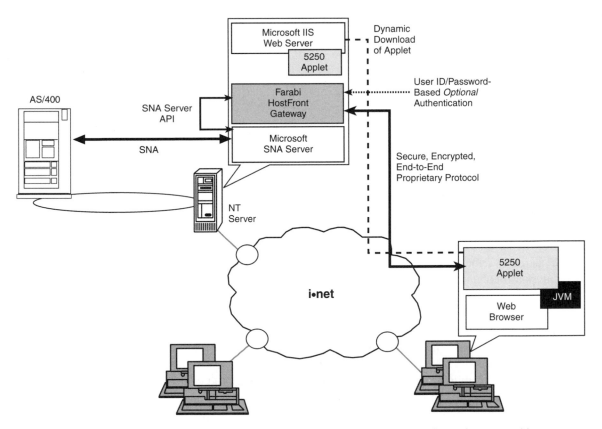

FIGURE 5.24   The architecture of the Farabi HostFront-centric AS/400 access solution being used by The Chickering Group.

TABLE 5.9　Pros and cons of applet-based 3270/5250 emulation.

Salient Characteristics

- Browser-invoked, tn3270(E)/tn5250, thin client scheme, where the applet can be routinely downloaded or cached

- Uses TCP connections to realize persistent, end-to-end connections

- Authentication and encryption provided by intermediary SNA-Web gateways

- Will work with PC server, bridge/router, channel-attached off-load server, or mainframe-resident tn3270(E) servers

- Scalability is invariably dictated by the capacity of the tn3270(E)/tn5250 server being used, with 10,000 to 20,000 concurrent sessions not being a problem with mainframe or channel-attached off-load servers

- Although they do not use HTML for screen rendering, extensive user interface rejuvenation is possible with some solutions

- Best suited for intranet and extranet applications

Pros	*Cons*
✓ Powerful terminal emulation comparable to that offered by tn3270(E)/tn5250 clients	✗ Rejuvenation possible only with certain solutions
✓ Thin client solution that minimizes software distribution and maintenance cost and effort, with the added attraction of cachable applets	✗ Encryption contingent on the presence of an SNA-Web gateway or the use of IBM's or Novell's tn3270(E) servers with SSL support
✓ Support for host printing as with tn3270(E), IND$FILE file transfer, and cut-and-paste operations between windows	✗ Potential delays when the applet is being downloaded, if caching is not used
✓ Applet window can run alongside browser, leaving the browser window free for other interactions	✗ Most solutions currently support only Java applets
✓ End-to-end persistent connections ensure data integrity and session security	✗ May not work with older (e.g., version 3) browsers
✓ Encryption supported by most implementations	✗ A patent covering many of the facets of applet-based emulation, held by OpenConnect Systems, may distract and constrain the industry, in much the same way that IBM's patents related to APPN worked against APPN's popularity
✓ AutoGUI rejuvenation now being supported by some solutions, such as IBM's Host On-Demand, OpenConnect's AutoVista, and WRQ's Reflection EnterView 2.0	
✓ Tools or an API for extensive rejuvenation available with nearly all solutions	
✓ Java applets facilitate cross-platform portability	

AS/400 access scheme used by The Chickering Group. This configuration is currently constrained to 128 concurrent sessions. As its client base grows, The Chickering Group anticipates installing another server to double this capacity. Farabi will use a Microsoft-supplied Windows NT utility to load-balance the applet TCP connections between the two servers.

When clients or remote-site employees connect to The Chickering Group's home page, they see a user-friendly menu that provides an option to access either public domain information or the company's internal secure site. If the user chooses the latter option, HostFront authenticates the user, downloads a Web-based thin client interface in the form of a Java applet or ActiveX control, and then establishes a secure end-to-end connection. The remote Web browser users can then initiate secure AS/400 host sessions over the Internet.

5.6.3 The Pros and Cons of Applet-Based 3270/5250 Emulation

Applet-based emulation provides SNA shops with the best of all worlds when it comes to reliable, highly secure, high-volume, green-on-black SNA access across intranets and extranets. The applet-based solutions are, in effect, browser-invoked tn3270(E)/tn5250 thin clients, replete with built-in end-to-end encryption (in the case of the solutions involving an intermediary SNA-Web gateway). The ability to cache applets eliminates the need for continual downloading of applets while simultaneously providing automatic version control. Although they do not use HTML for their screen rendering, some applet-based schemes can deliver extensive user interface rejuvenation capabilities. In most instances, such solutions are likely to be overkill when it comes to providing the general public with casual access to SNA applications over the Internet. 3270-to-HTML conversion will invariably be a better approach for casual access.

Table 5.9 on the previous page outlines the pros and cons of applet-based 3270/5250 emulation.

5.7 THE LAST WORD

Ironically, too much choice is a major distraction when selecting an effective terminal-oriented access scheme to use across i•nets. Four viable options exist: ip3270/ip5250, tn3270(E)/tn5250, 3270/5250-to-HTML conversion, and applet-based emulation. That list does not include the versatile programmatic or user interface rejuvenation-oriented solutions discussed in Chapter 6.

The ip3270/ip5250 protocol is a sound interim solution and a direct alternative to tn3270(E)/tn5250 for enterprises that already have an SNA-LAN gateway infrastructure that permits the use of TCP/IP between the 3270/5250 emulators and the gateway. Standards-based tn3270(E)/tn5250, with its highly scalable servers, is a strategic, popular, fat client option for intranet/extranet applications, even though it currently lacks built-in support for encryption. The 5.5-component applet emulations, in effect, provide thin client tn3270(E)/tn5250 solutions, replete with authentication and encryption. Applet-based emulation is the ideal mid- to long-term solution for intranet/extranet applications, especially if no user interface rejuvenation is required. 3270/5250-to-HTML conversion, the ultimate thin client SNA access solution, should always be viewed as the first choice for providing casual access to SNA applications across the Internet. In most cases, enterprises should think about using multiple SNA access schemes to best fit the needs of specific users and applications, rather than trying to select one global approach that may require compromises in terms of flexibility and functionality.

User Interface Rejuvenation, Application-Specific Gateways, and Programmatic Access

Browser-based access to SNA, even in plain green-on-black tn3270(E) emulation mode, offers considerable tangible advantages over all previous terminal-oriented SNA access schemes. At a single stroke, it Web-enables mission-critical SNA applications. It is the obvious and optimal answer, especially with 3270-to-HTML conversion, regarding how SNA applications can be easily accessed across the Internet. Moreover, it minimizes overall software costs while obviating the software installation and maintenance issues associated with "fat client" SNA/3270 emulators. In addition, the SNA access capability elevates the browser to become the *universal user interface* or the *universal client*, through which PC and workstation users can gain unfettered access to all applications and data, whether they are based on the Internet, SNA, UNIX, Windows NT, intranets, or minicomputers. The SNA-savvy browser at last brings to fruition what IBM has, since 1987, been wistfully referring to as the platform-independent, **Common User Access (CUA)** for all application types.

With the browser acting as the universal client, users will not have to continually shuffle between, and become reacclimatized to, vastly disparate user interfaces—some of which do not even support mouse-driven, point-and-click navigation—depending on which applications or data must be accessed. The standardization on the browser as the universal user interface, coupled with users' growing familiarity with its intuitive and inviting persona, will eventually improve user productivity and user satisfaction. In conjunction, it will markedly reduce user training costs, calls to the help desk, and data entry errors. Browser-based access also ensures that corporations around the world can readily tap into a huge and growing pool of trained and Web-literate terminal users, now that most teenagers are prolific and seasoned Internet surfers. Thus browser-based access is the most significant

Using the dated green-on-black, alphanumeric, mouse-averse, 3270 user interface on a multimedia-capable PC with a 17-inch color monitor is akin to purchasing a 52-inch color TV with built-in surround sound and then using it exclusively to watch black-and-white silent movies. Today, no valid excuses remain for persevering with this anachronistic user interface. Innovative solutions abound for reengineering the user interface without changing applications or for accessing the existing SNA applications through Web-oriented applications. The time is now ripe to smell the Java of what is to come.

development for corporate data access in general, and for SNA access in particular, since the advent of the PC in 1981.

The incontrovertible advantages of browser-based access, especially when it includes SNA application access, can be summarized as follows:

- A consistent and standardized universal user interface for accessing all applications and data irrespective of their type, location, or origins
- A thin client solution that is cost-effective and simplifies software distribution and installation, along with minimizing software maintenance costs and effort
- A large pool of users who are very comfortable with the interface and its operation
- A reduction in training, help desk, and support costs
- Enhanced user productivity and satisfaction
- Fewer navigation and data entry errors, which promotes higher transaction processing rates

On top of all of these other inducements, browser-based access to SNA provides one more serendipitous and far-reaching advantage. That is, it offers the means and the motivation for painlessly and economically rejuvenating the grossly dated and visually jarring green-on-black, text-only, 3270 user interface of most SNA applications. The 3270 user interface was developed in the early 1970s for nonintelligent terminals. Using it on powerful, multimedia-capable PCs and workstations and thus depriving users of point-and-click navigation, as well as the visual gratification of contemporary screen design, is really a crime; in most instances, it saps user productivity and stymies user satisfaction. Although some will argue that the spartan green-on-black 3270 interface is optimal for heads-down data entry, one must wonder whether even the most single-minded data entry operator would not become more efficient if presented with even a slightly more visually stimulating view.

The beauty of facelifting the user interface of SNA applications, within the context of browser-based access, is that it can be realized without any changes to mainframe- or AS/400-resident SNA applications. Unlike previous middleware-oriented client/server approaches or new client GUIs built upon APIs such as HLLAPI, browser-based user interface rejuvenation can typically be achieved without any heavy-duty programming. Some "straight-out-of-the-box" AutoGUI schemes actually require no work on the part of the customer, such as IBM's ResQ!Net, OpenConnect's AutoVista, Eicon's Aviva Web-to-Host Server, and J&BCS's J42 (available with WRQ's Reflection EnterView 2.0). Most non-AutoGUI solutions facilitate rejuvenation either via a Visual Basic-like, drag-and-drop interface development environment or through the use of an easy-to-follow contemporary scripting scheme such as **JavaScript**.

Figure 6.1 shows actual screen images from four production-use SNA applications whose previous 3270 user interfaces were dramatically rejuvenated via browser-based access-related solutions. The "GM Truck" logon screen, for example, plays the "Like a Rock" soundtrack used by GM in some of its truck commercials as users (mainly truck salespeople) log on to the system. Some may deride such user interface extensions, which are achieved by inserting multimedia elements within the applet or HTML page invoked by the browser, as being merely facile, bandwidth-sapping gimmicks. On the other hand, however, music, graphics, or even video clips might be judiciously used within rejuvenated user interfaces, as in the case with the GM example, to motivate users throughout the workday.

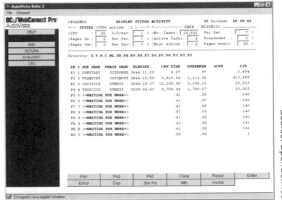

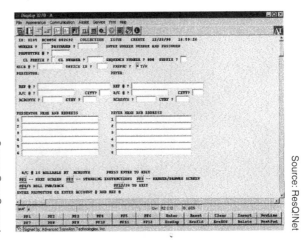

FIGURE 6.1 Rejuvenated 3270 screens. (*Source:* © Copyright Sterling Software, Inc. All rights reserved. VM:Webgateway is a trademark of Sterling Software, Inc. All other trademarks are the property of their respective owners.)

Given the relative ease with which anachronistic 3270 user interfaces can be rejuvenated with today's tools, no rational or fiscal justification remains for persevering with green-on-black screens for any SNA application outside that of heads-down, high-volume data entry. A rejuvenated user interface is more or less a prerequisite if the general public will be granted access to certain SNA applications across the Internet so as to perform functions such as home banking, investment management, travel reservations, or package tracking. Rejuvenated user interfaces will also provide corporate users with an easier and logical transition from the browser to the browser-invoked SNA/3270 windows. Without some level of rejuvenation, browser-based access to SNA will indubitably be somewhat awkward and incongruous, with old-style windows being juxtapositioned alongside or perhaps within contemporary Web pages.

Most of today's browser-based access-related rejuvenation tools do not confine the facelifting function to just "one-for-one" screen rejuvenation, with each rejuvenated screen corresponding to a single old 3270 screen. Instead, the rejuvenation schemes permit the consolidation of input and output operations of multiple 3270 screens within one rejuvenated screen. The up-and-down scrollable, point-and-click selectable, multiple-item option fields widely used in contemporary screen dialogs facilitate this type of consolidation by permitting the output and input fields hitherto displayed on separate 3270 screens to be grouped together within one screen.

Figure 6.2 depicts the rejuvenated screen image of an in-house FedEx SNA application known as Free Bird. This screen was produced with OpenConnect Systems' OpenVista tool, which produces Java applets that perform the user interface rejuvenation; it corresponds to what had been more than 20 separate 3270 screens. The details of this application and the rejuvenation of its user interface so as to streamline and greatly expedite user interactions are described in Section 6.1.

This ability to combine the information content of several different 3270 screens when constructing a new user interface can typically be extended to embrace screens from multiple SNA applications, instead of all screens having to be derived from the same SNA application. As a result, information that was previously confined to separate emulation windows can be logically synthesized into a single integrated user interface. Rather than shifting between different emulation windows to obtain and enter various data elements required to complete a specific task, a user can now execute that task much more easily from within one new-look interface. Some rejuvenation tools permit this screen consolidation notion to be extrapolated even further to include data access and update involving non-SNA- or non-3270-based applications. Thus a rejuvenated user interface can now display and deal with data that are not directly available to an SNA application.

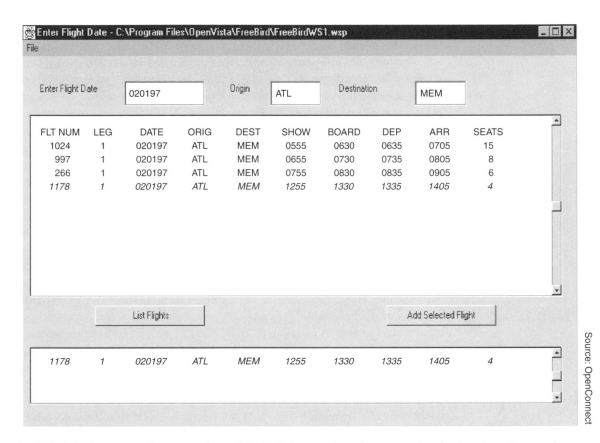

FIGURE 6.2   Rejuvenated user interface of FedEx's Free Bird application realized using OpenConnect's OpenVista product.

For example, the rejuvenated user interface for a mainframe-based investment management application might include certain stock market indices and business news items obtained from a non-mainframe-based financial data feed. Another example could be a situation where the processing of a transaction might require reference to some data from a non-SNA application source such as a minicomputer, followed by the updating of multiple databases resident on different hosts. All of the user interactions required to successfully perform such a transaction can now be combined into a single user dialog—without any modification of the original SNA and non-SNA applications. The new user interface, in essence, sits in front of the original disjointed user interfaces and interacts with them behind the scenes, through the exchange of data records based on the commands and data entered at the new user interface.

Programmatic solutions, centered on applications servers, are also gaining popularity as a means for synthesizing disparate data input streams into a contemporary user interface. This type of programmatic solution is described later in this chapter.

The term *data normalization* is sometimes used to refer to the process whereby multiple disparate data sources are integrated and manipulated from within a single browser-invoked, new-look application window. This capability to synergistically weave together diverse data sources within a rejuvenated user interface permits enterprises to rapidly develop and deploy highly customized, problem-solving and productivity-enhancing applications. The real beauty is that these new applications are developed bottom-up, starting from the perspective of the user interface and relying exclusively on relatively simple user interface rejuvenation tools, without resorting to complex middleware or multitier, client/server methodologies.

Creating completely new applications using user interface rejuvenation and possibly data normalization is merely the first step toward transforming today's mission-critical SNA applications into background tasks that provide mainframe- or AS/400-based data feeds to other emerging next-generation applications. This moves SNA interactions into the realm of programmatic access. Today, the bulk of SNA applications are accessed in real time, through an interactive mode via some type of 3270/5250 terminal interface, whether the access takes place on an actual 3270 terminal or emulated on a PC or workstation via ip3270/ip5250, tn3270(E)/tn5250, or browser-based access. This situation will change after 2001, once most enterprises have regrouped after the trials and tribulations of coping with the Year 2000 issues. The long-in-the-tooth SNA mission-critical applications that still rule the data center roost, despite mostly being developed more than 15 years ago, will finally begin to be replaced by a new genre of twenty-first-century applications.

The highly popular, client/server-based, industry-specific, integrated enterprise information systems will represent one class of such new applications. In particular, SAP R/3 has already made huge inroads into the SNA base with more than 5000 installations on large IBM servers. In enterprises that have mainframes, SAP R/3 software (which runs on myriad operating systems, including MVS and OS/390) will typically be deployed in a three-tier, client/server architecture, where the mainframe will act as a data server to an NT- or UNIX-based application server running the actual business and problem-solving logic. Figure 6.3 depicts the popular three-tier architecture for SAP R/3 in mainframe environments. This architecture will be used for other client/server solutions for total business systems, **Enterprise Resource Planning (ERP)**, **Online Transaction Analysis (OLTA)**, and other products from companies such Oracle, Peoplesoft, and BANN.

Mid-size to large enterprises are also likely to develop their own, enterprise-specific applications using today's highly visual, object-oriented,

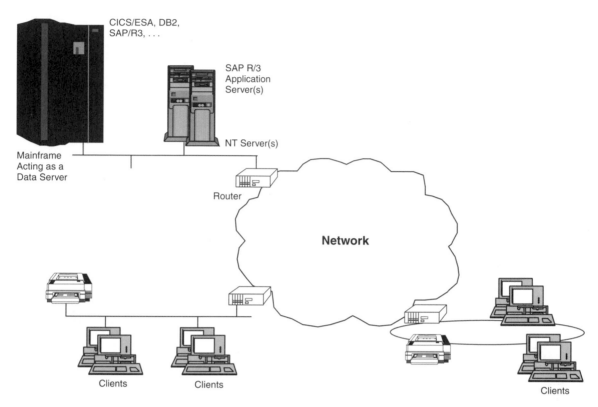

FIGURE 6.3 Three-tier, client/server architecture for modern enterprise applications, where the mainframe acts as a data server.

and platform-independent application development methodologies, such as Java-based application servers. Many of these new applications will not be deployed on mainframes running SNA/APPN—even though mainframes and AS/400s are indeed viable and very scalable Java platforms. Instead, Windows NT, Web servers, UNIX, or AS/400s running TCP/IP will be the preferred platforms. Much like SAP R/3-type solutions, these new applications will require access to files and databases only reachable through a mainframe or perhaps an AS/400. Hence, they will also rely on a three-tier, client/server architecture no different to that shown in Fig. 6.3.

Most IBM shops that currently have much of their operational data on mainframe databases have no immediate plans to move this information to any other platform, despite the fact that nearly all of their new applications are targeted at nonmainframe platforms. They intend to continue to use mainframes as relatively cost-effective, eminently scalable, and thoroughly

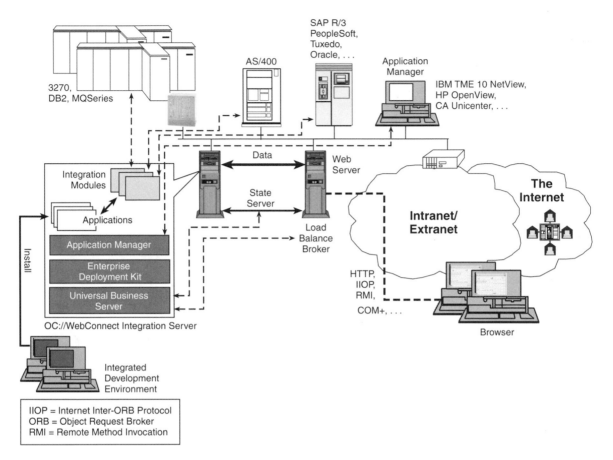

FIGURE 6.4 The architecture of OpenConnect's Integration Server.

proven enterprise data repositories. This tendency will be reinforced as IBM continues to drive the cost of mainframe down on a yearly basis with the new **CMOS**-based S/390 Parallel Enterprise Servers and the Parallel Sysplex mainframe clustering technology

Middleware software, such as IBM's MQSeries product set and CNT/Apertus's Enterprise/Access, have been around for many years to facilitate three-tier, client/server solutions where a mainframe acts as a data server. Directly accessing mainframe or AS/400 DB2 databases, where possible and applicable, using a solution based on **Open Database Connectivity (ODBC)** and the **Distributed Relational Database Architecture (DRDA)**, is another increasingly popular alternative for integrating mainframe databases with nonmainframe applications. Such solutions are available with

Microsoft's SNA Server, StarQuest Software's StarSQL, Informix's Enterprise Gateway, and Sterling Software's VISION:Webaccess.

With the ongoing proliferation of Java, ActiveX, and JavaBeans software, enterprises now have even more alluring programmatic options for realizing their data center access needs. Many vendors that provide applet-based tn3270(E)/tn5250 emulation are extending their product sets to embrace this type of highly object-oriented, programmatic access to data center resources. Early examples of such solutions include OpenConnect Systems' Integration Server and Wall Data's Cyberprise. Figure 6.4 depicts the high-level architecture of OpenConnect's Integration Server.

The remainder of this chapter will elaborate on the technology, options, and issues pertaining to user interface rejuvenation, applet-oriented programmatic access, and application-specific data center access solutions. It reinforces the theme that browser-based access-related user interface rejuvenation of SNA applications is merely a precursor to full-blown, programmatic access, where SNA applications become background data feeds to next-generation applications. Figure 6.5 depicts, in terms of a timeline-oriented spectrum, how the green-on-black terminal emulation that characterized SNA access will evolve over the next few years.

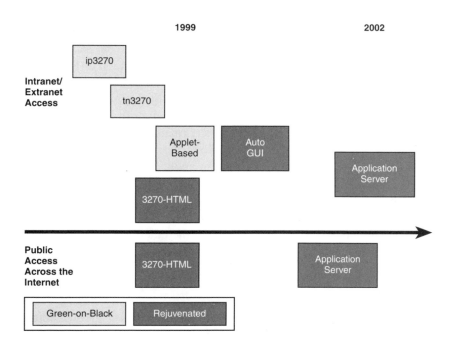

FIGURE 6.5   The gradual move away from the green-on-black 3270 user interface through the use of contemporary technologies.

6.1   REJUVENATING THE DATED 3270/5250 USER INTERFACE

Two very different levels and means of user interface rejuvenation exist. Default, or AutoGUI schemes are essentially application-independent. Highly customized, application-specific approaches are the second. 3270/5250-to-HTML conversion and applet-based emulation solutions typically cater to both types of rejuvenation.

User interface rejuvenation for browser-based access purposes is possible with both 3270/5250-to-HTML conversion and applet-based terminal emulation—not to mention programmatic application server solutions. The "GM Trucks" screen (shown in Fig. 6.1) and the FedEx "Free Bird" screen (shown in Fig. 6.2) are both examples of applet-based rejuvenation; the top left screen shown in Fig. 6.1 reflects 3270/5250-to-HTML conversion. The rejuvenated screens from 3270/5250-to-HTML conversion appear within a browser frame, whereas the applet-based screens appear in their own windows.

At present, 3270/5250-to-HTML is used more often for rejuvenation than applet schemes are, for two interrelated reasons. The first reason has to do with its popularity as a thin client solution for easily and quickly Internet-enabling an SNA application, such as a travel reservation query or package tracking system, so as to open it up to the public. The other reason has to do with the fact that most HTML conversion solutions offer some type of easy-to-grasp, straightforward scripting mechanism to facilitate rejuvenation; a few, such as Eicon's Aviva Web-to-Host Server, offer a built-in AutoGUI feature. Given that a rejuvenated interface is essential for most Internet-based applications intended for public access, most enterprises end up squeezing "double-duty" out of 3270/ 5250-to-HTML conversion by using it to provide relatively easy interface rejuvenation as well as quick and painless Internet enablement. In reality, some symbiosis occurs, as the popularity of 3270/5250-to-HTML as a means of Internet enablement is highly dependent on its prowess for expeditious interface recrafting. Application servers are now beginning to gain popularity as general-purpose, yet very powerful and flexible way to realize 3270-to-HTML conversion along with data normalization.

With 3270/5250-to-HTML conversion, one always encounters some amount of automatic rejuvenation brought about by the mere fact that the screens are rendered in HTML, and displayed within a browser window as true Web pages. For a start, the HTML-converted output, even if devoid of graphical elements and mainly textual, is unlikely to have the trademark black background of 3270/5250 screens. On the other hand, automatic rejuvenation rarely arises with applet-based emulation schemes. True to their claim of being merely tn3270(E)/tn5250 emulations, most such solutions opt for a green-on-black emulation window, unless explicit steps have been taken to update the screen image displayed by the applet.

This situation, however, is beginning to change with the AutoGUI options from IBM, OpenConnect, and WRQ as well as Client/Server Technology's Jacada offering. Such AutoGUI capability ensures that applets can perform some level of automatic rejuvenation similar to what was previously available only with 3270/5250-to-HTML conversion. This feature is bound to evolve over time, as more sophisticated automatic conversion becomes possible because of rules-based algorithms. For example, the AutoGUI feature of an applet might be able to automatically detect traditional ACF/VTAM "welcome banners" that customarily appear on application logon screens and either replace or augment them with company-specific greetings complete with the actual company logo. Figure 6.6 illustrates the potential of applet-based AutoGUI schemes.

Both 3270/5250-to-HTML and applet-based schemes consequently cater to two different levels of rejuvenation:

- Simple default transformations, such as the inclusion of a colored background, substitution of Web page-like input trenches, and some screen-color remapping, that are, in effect, screen-neutral and apply to all 3270 screens of a given application that use the rejuvenation process

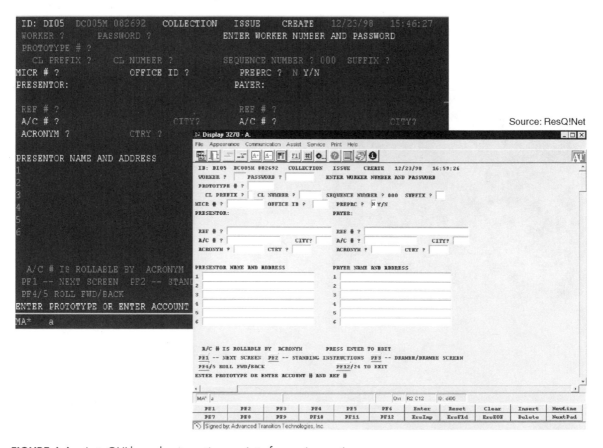

Source: ResQ!Net

FIGURE 6.6 AutoGUI-based automatic user interface rejuvenation.

- Application-specific, highly customized facelifts, replete with many graphical and possibly even multimedia elements, akin to the GM Trucks screen shown in Fig. 6.1

The two side-by-side screens on Fig. 6.7 illustrate the notion of default transformations that are independent of screen content. The screen on the left side represents a quintessential green-on-black SNA logon screen as it appears within an Attachmate EXTRA! Personal Client emulation window. The screen on the right is the same logon screen somewhat "Webified" through the application of noncustomized transformations via Attachmate's HostPublishing System (HPS) 3270-to-HTML conversion product. Note that the content and overall appearance of the rejuvenated HTML-based screen are much the same as those of the original screen. This type of minimal intervention and marginal reconstitution is the hallmark of default-transformation-based rejuvenation. Nonetheless, even with this modicum of

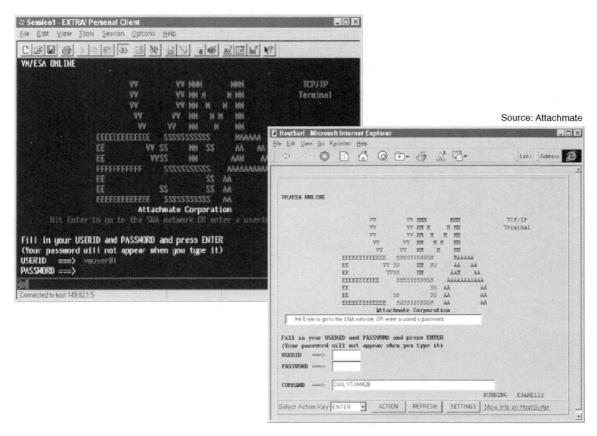

Source: Attachmate

FIGURE 6.7 Default transformation of a 3270 user screen using Attachmate's 'HostSurfer'.

modernization, the rejuvenated screen is considerably more appealing to the eye and contemporary-looking than the original. The bottom of the rejuvenated screen includes a command field to compensate for the absence of the toolbar found in the emulator window, as well as a set of buttons and an action key input box to emulate 3270 program function (PF) key actions given that browsers currently do not support the function keys found on PC/ workstation keyboards. With this example of 3270-to-HTML conversion, observe the presence of a Refresh button on the bottom row of buttons to cater for the eventuality of unsolicited output from the mainframe, as was discussed in Section 5.5.1. The overall architecture of an Attachmate HPS solution is shown in Fig. 5.15.

Unfortunately, as with all things related to browser-based rejuvenation, no standard conventions apply across the 30 or more various solutions regarding how default transformation is invoked and made to apply to the screen output of different applications. The applet-based schemes obviously use different paradigms than those preferred by the 3270/5250-to-HTML solutions, given the overall differences in how these two techniques handle SNA/3270 access and screen rendering. At present, having an AutoGUI option of some sort for invoking default transformations appears to be the favored approach for the applet solutions.

The process for realizing default transformation with 3270/5250-to-HTML solutions varies from product to product. Attachmate's HostPublishing System and Farabi's HostFront, for example, have built-in, on-the-fly 3270-to-HTML AutoGUI-type features. Attachmate refers to its feature as Host-Surfer; Farabi calls its HTML Emulator. The rejuvenated screen shown in Fig. 6.7 is actually the handiwork of HostSurfer. HostSurfer comes with a set of Attachmate-specified defaults that an enterprise can quickly override if it chooses by using a point-and-choose color selection palate that controls the colors of the background and the various different type of fields (that is, protected in one color, unprotected in another). Novell's HostPublisher, on the other hand, allocates three HTML templates to each application: one template for the data-transporting LU-LU session, another for the SSCP-LU control session, and the third for the bitmap Web page that supports light pen and cursor positioning operations as described in Section 5.5.1. The template associated with the LU-LU session can be customized, typically with a JavaScript, to provide a set of conversions that apply to all 3270 screens displayed by an application.

Figure 6.8 contrasts default-transformation-based rejuvenation with highly customized, application-specific rejuvenation by showing another set of "before and after" screens. The rejuvenation in this instance was achieved via 5250-to-HTML conversion, this time using Farabi technology's HostFront Publishing. Unlike with a default-transformation-based rejuvenation, the screen images of a custom rejuvenated user interface will bear

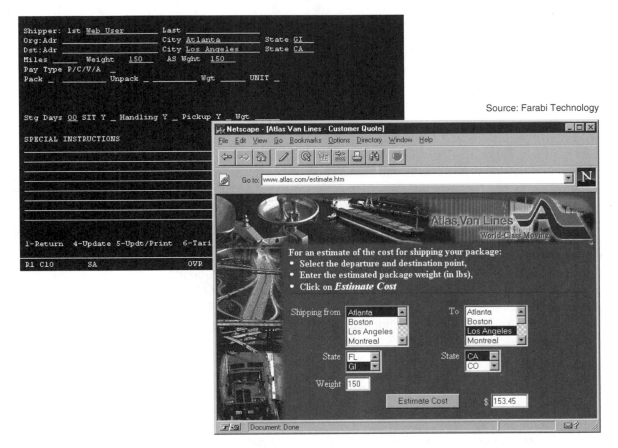

Source: Farabi Technology

FIGURE 6.8   Highly customized, rejuvenated 5250 user screen using 5250-to-HTML conversion.

little, if any, resemblance to the original 3270/5250 screen. This difference arises even when the rejuvenation takes place on a screen-by-screen basis, as is the case with the example shown in Fig. 6.8; it also occurs when the rejuvenation consolidates multiple screens, as is the case with the FedEx Free Bird example shown in Fig. 6.2. The extensive new façade created with this type of custom rejuvenation allows the SNA/3270 basis of an application to remain totally hidden from its users, without the developer having to modify the underlying application. The power of this type of rejuvenation is such that one can create essentially a brand new application with a very modern, point-and-click GUI—and do so without resorting to any middleware or three-tier client/server schemes involving intermediary, server-resident software.

The Free Bird example demonstrates the next level of user interface rejuvenation—that of combining, consolidating, and rationalizing the input/output functions of multiple 3270 screens into a single, multifunction, point-

and-click interface. The Free Bird application enables FedEx employees to check for the availability of unallocated seats on the company's large fleet of planes flying between various source and destination cities and reserve any free seats for their personal use, subject to certain rules and guidelines. This mainframe-resident SNA application is understandably highly popular and heavily used. Before the interface was rejuvenated, users would typically have to laboriously navigate through more than thirty 3270 screens to obtain the necessary list of potential flights, check for seat availability, and then book a seat. Given that this application represents an employee benefit, rather than a true work-related function, minimizing the time and effort required to make a Free Bird seat reservation was obviously advantageous to FedEx.

Rather than pursuing a costly and time-consuming rewrite of the mainframe application, FedEx opted to streamline and condense the user interface using browser-based rejuvenation. This approach had the added benefit that the application could be easily accessed by authorized employees across the Internet, from anywhere around the world. The rejuvenated user interface is displayed by a browser-invoked Java applet that runs on the user's PC or workstation. This applet, which contains the pages representing the rejuvenated user interface, was produced using OpenVista's drag-and-drop methodology. The back end of this applet interacts with the unmodified 3270 interface of the original Free Bird application using tn3270(E) emulation through OpenConnect's OC://WebConnect Pro SNA-Web gateway; among other things, this setup ensures that a persistent end-to-end connection links the applet and the mainframe application. Authorized users gain access to the application via a revamped user authentication screen (shown in Fig. 6.9), which solicits the user's user ID, password, date of birth, and Social Security number to validate their identity. The Java applet accepts these four input items from the new interface and creates a 3270 data stream containing a function key (such as the Enter key) Attention Identification (AID) code, the current cursor position coordinates, and the relevant Set Buffer Address (SBA) orders to denote the screen locations of the four embedded input items on the original 3270 screen. This 3270 data stream is then sent to the application as the input expected from the 3270 logon screen.

The applet displays the primary screen of the new Free Bird user interface (shown in Fig. 6.2) when it receives the data stream corresponding to the next 3270 screen from the application; the receipt of this information signals that the user has been authenticated and is being permitted to enter the main body of the application. The application's logic uses multiple 3270 screens to determine the source and destination cities and the preferred dates and to subsequently display the possible flights. The user selects his or her flight of choice using another set of screens. With the new interface, all of these query, display, and flight selection functions occur within the context of the main screen shown in Fig 6.2. The start city, destination city, and preferred

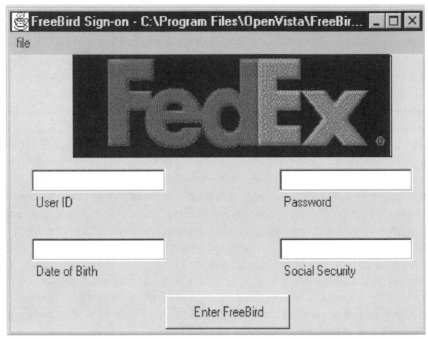

Source: OpenConnect

FIGURE 6.9   The rejuvenated logon screen used by FedEx for its Free Bird application.

date are entered into the input fields that appear at the top. The applet takes the input from these three fields, constructs the appropriate 3270 data streams, and sends them to the application as the input sought by the various 3270 screens associated with the application. The application then collects the flight data sent out by the application in response to the previous input, by reading 3270 data streams representing the output screens transmitted by the application. The flight data appear within the main display area in the middle of the screen. The user can select a flight by simply pointing and clicking on its entry within the display area. This "all-in-one" screen obviously eliminates much keystroking and dead time spent waiting for new screens to be displayed, consequently making the process of using this application much easier and faster.

The mechanics of intercepting and dealing with the original Free Bird screens, as well as the process of transferring data to and from the old screen and the new interface, happen in the background in real time, unbeknownst to the user. Although the applet works at the 3270 data stream level, interpreting the screen content of the output screens and constructing input data flows, the developer who produced the applet using OpenVista did not have to know anything about 3270 data stream. Instead, the developer relied on a visual paradigm that enables the creation of the rejuvenated interface by selecting and moving, within OpenVista's Integrated Development Environment (IDE) screen, the various output and input fields in the 3270 screens that correspond to the equivalent structures in the rejuvenated interface. Figure 6.13 shows a representative screen image of the OpenVista IDE that highlights its 3270 field-oriented development methodology. Figure 6.10 shows the i•net-specific architecture now in use by this application. Note that OpenVista, which is merely an applet development environment, does not appear as a part of the final, deployed production system. Also note that, as with most OC://WebConnect-based solutions irrespective of whether the applet displays a green-on-black emulation or a multimedia rejuvenated interface, this FedEx system relies on an intermediate SNA-Web gateway component that provides a front end to the applet.

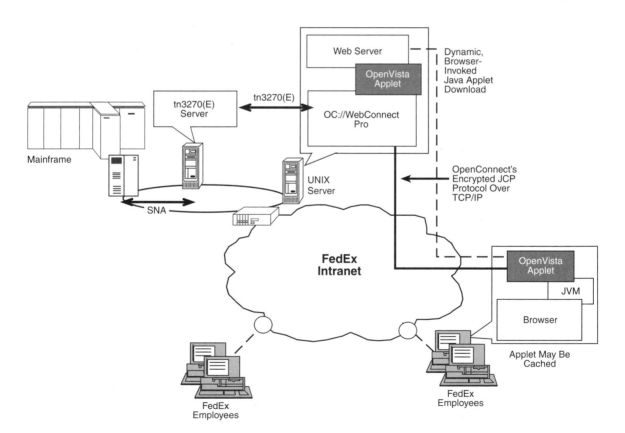

FIGURE 6.10   The architecture of FedEx's Free Bird access scheme, which relies on OpenConnect's OpenVista for its user interface rejuvenation.

6.1.1   The Rejuvenation Process for 3270/5250-to-HTML Solutions

At present, no market-leading approach or even any standards have emerged for browser-oriented user interface rejuvenation. This situation is unlikely to change in the short to mid-term. All of the current rejuvenation techniques are vendor- and product-specific, each with its own foibles and nuances. Obviously, all must provide mechanisms for realizing basic operations such as session establishment, screen identification, screen-to-screen and intra-screen navigation, input and output field selection via either a row-and-column position designation or an indexing (for example, third field on the screen) scheme, and function key management. Most provide a screen action record and playback mechanism that can capture and automate the key-strokes and data entry necessary to navigate through certain portions of the application's dialog, such as the initial application logon.

The diverse schemes available for customized (as opposed to default) interface rejuvenation with the leading 3270/5250-to-HTML conversion products are described in Table 5.7 on page 202. Table 5.7 also lists the various APIs supported by these products. As can be seen, 3270/5250-to-HTML products typically offer two techniques for facilitating user interface rejuvenation:

- A script-based mechanism that either leverages a popular scripting scheme such as JavaScript or is vendor-specific and proprietary, such as Farabi's Farabi Script Language.
- One or more APIs that can be accessed from a programming language such as C, C++, Visual Basic, Visual J++, or Microsoft's new Visual InterDev.

Scripting typically is the easiest, most expeditious, and consequently most popular way to realize interface reengineering with 3270/5250-to-HTML conversion. Scripts enable dynamic content to be added to Web pages. The scripting scheme may be client-centric or server-centric. Both schemes enable the browser image seen by the user to be created from intermingled HTML code, scripting code, Java applet code, and objects such as Enterprise JavaBeans. With the client-centric approach, the script code (for example, JavaScript code) necessary to handle the new presentation elements is embedded within the HTML page representing one or more 3270 screens. This code is downloaded to the client PC or workstation along with the rest of the Web page. It will execute on the client, typically within the Java Virtual Machine within the browser, to handle various components of the new interface. Most server-centric approaches revolve around Microsoft's **Active Server Page (ASP)** methodology for browser-neutral, server-based scripting.

Extensive rejuvenation with 3270/5250-to-HTML conversion is realized via either a script-based mechanism or the use of an API. Active Server Page (ASP) methodology is beginning to play an increasingly important role in script-oriented rejuvenation.

Support for ASP-based scripting emerged with Microsoft's Windows NT-based **Internet Information Server (IIS) 3.0** Web server. ASP is now supported by Microsoft Peer Web Services Version 3.0 on Windows NT Workstation and Microsoft Personal Web Server on Windows 95/98.

ASP permits the creation of dynamic, highly interactive, high-performance Web server applications. It works with any ActiveX scripting language and has integrated support for VBScript, JScript, and InterDev. Support for other popular scripting languages, such as IBM's REXX and Perl (Practical Extraction and Report Language), is available via plug-ins from third parties. ASP also permits multiple scripting languages to be used interchangeably to create a single Web server application. It relies on scripting engines developed using Microsoft's **Component Object Model (COM)** architecture to process scripts.

Irrespective of the scripting scheme used, the output of an ASP application is always HTML. It is therefore ideally suited for creating and manipulating HTML within the context of interface reengineering based on 3270/5250-to-HTML conversion. Figure 6.11 contains a sample of the VBScript used by Farabi Technology, in conjunction with ASP, to create the highly graphical, rejuvenated screen shown in Fig. 6.8.

At present, ASP can be used only with Microsoft Web servers. To accommodate other servers, most vendors that offer ASP based interface rejuvenation also provide a non-ASP based scheme. For example, Attachmate provides a Visual Basic-to-HTML capability in addition to its ASP support, while Farabi offers its Farabi Script Language (FSL) to developers who want a non-ASP scheme. Figure 6.12 shows a Farabi-supplied sample of FSL code that could be used to render the screen shown in Fig. 6.8, instead of the VBScript sample shown in Fig. 6.11.

Interface rejuvenation via an API as provided by many of the 3270/5250-to-HTML products is, in essence, a logical equivalent of the HLLAPI and EHLLAPI interfaces available with all major 3270/5250 fat client emulators and tn3270(E) clients for the development of screen-scraping-based client applications. **Screen scraping** refers to the notion of dynamically capturing, via the API, what would be the 3270/5250 screen images displayed by an SNA application by intercepting and interpreting the data streams transmitted by that application. Screen scraping, which is performed at the client, permits the content of the 3270/5250 data stream to serve as input to a client-resident application driving a GUI or performing a different business task than the SNA application whose screens are being scraped. In reality, 3270/5250-to-HTML is also a screen-scraping technique—albeit one based on the server and HTML-centric.

The APIs, which can typically be invoked from any contemporary programming language, permit the development of a server component that talks 3270/5250 on the host side and generates HTML on the Web server

```
<%@ LANGUAGE="VBSCRIPT" %>

<%
'Edited by: Ana Paula Varanda
'Date: Mars 1998
%>

<%      Set oHostLink = Server.CreateObject("Hfp.HostLink.1")        %>

<!--#include FILE="keys.inc"-->

<SCRIPT LANGUAGE=VBScript RUNAT=Server>
        Sub LogOn
                oHostLink.Connect

                oHostLink.PutField "ATLAS", 6, 53
                oHostLink.PutField "VANLINES", 7, 53
                oHostLink.PushKey ENTER
        End Sub

        Sub LogOff
                oHostLink.PushKey PA1
                oHostLink.PushKey PF1
                oHostLink.PushKey PA1
                oHostLink.PushKey PF7
                oHostLink.PutField "80", 19, 53
                oHostLink.PushKey ENTER
                oHostLink.PutField "90", 4, 31
                oHostLink.PushKey ENTER

                sScreenTitle = oHostLink.GetField(1, 28, 34)
                If sScreenTitle = "Display Program Messages" Then
                        sData = oHostLink.GetField(20, 4, 8)

                        If sData = "Reply" Then
                                oHostLink.PutField "c", 20, 18
                                oHostLink.PushKey ENTER
                        End If
                        oHostLink.PushKey ENTER
                End If

                oHostLink.Disconnect
        End Sub

        Sub ProcessRequest

                LogOn

                Session("bExceptionalError") = FALSE
                Session("bSignOnFailed") = FALSE
                Session("bErrMsg") = FALSE
                bContinue = TRUE

                While bContinue

                        bKnownScreen = FALSE

                        sScreenTitle = oHostLink.GetField(1, 36, 42)
                        If sScreenTitle = "Sign On" Then
                                oHostLink.Disconnect
                                Session("bSignOnFailed") = TRUE
                                bKnownScreen = TRUE
                                bContinue = FALSE
                        End If# Edited by: Ana Paula Varanda
```

FIGURE 6.11 A sample of the VBScript used with Farabi's HostFront Publishing to produce the highly customized 5250 screen shown in Fig. 6.8. (*Source:* Farabi Technology)

```
# Date:        Feb 1998
#
#
#Set the default HTX file name
SETHTX "AtlasResults"
#
#
#Log on to the host application
LogOn:
# PUT 6 53 UserName
# PUT 7 53 Password
PUT 6 53 "ATLAS"
PUT 7 53 "VANLINES"
PUSH ENTER
GOTO TestScreens
#
#
#Current screen is "Display Program Messages"
#Check if the current screen has the "Reply" line
DisplayProgramMessages1:
GET 20 4 8 Validate
IF Validate EQ "Reply"    GOTO DisplayProgramMessages2
GOTO DisplayProgramMessages3
#
#
#Current screen is "Display Program Messages"
#Put "C" and push ENTER on the "Reply" line
DisplayProgramMessages2:
PUT 20 18 "c"
PUSH ENTER
GOTO DisplayProgram Messages3
#
#
#Current screen is "Display Program Messages"
#"push ENTER" to exit the current screen
#if the next screen is "Sign On" disconnect the host session
DisplayProgramMessages3:
PUSH ENTER
GET 1 36 42 Validate
IF Validate EQ "Sign On" GOTO Disconnect
GOTO TestScreens
#
#
#Current screen is "Attempt to Recover Interactive Job"
#Put "1" and push ENTER to exit this screen
AttemptToRecoverInteractiveJob:
PUT 22 7 "1"
PUSH ENTER
GOTO TestScreens
#
#
#Check if the current screen title is: "Sign On"
#or "Sales Registration" or "Agent Communication Menu"
#or "Display Program Messages" or "Attempt To Recover Interactive Job"
TestScreens:
GET 1 36 42 Validate
IF Validate EQ "Sign On" GOTO SignOnFailed
GET 5 38 42 Validate
IF Validate EQ "Sales"    GOTO SalesRegistration
GET 1 25 29 Validate
IF Validate EQ "Agent"    GOTO AgentCommunicationsMenu
GET 1 28 34 Validate
IF Validate EQ "Display" GOTO DisplayProgramMessages1
GET 1 24 30 Validate
IF Validate EQ "Attempt" GOTO AtemptToRecoverInteractiveJob
GOTO ExceptionalError
#
```

FIGURE 6.12 A sample of the Farabi Script Language (FSL) that could have been used to create the image in Fig. 6.8. (*Source:* Farabi Technology)

side. This API approach, which is obviously highly flexible and extensible but significantly more complicated than scripting, is best suited for developing sophisticated new applications that extract data from SNA applications, rather than for just realizing user interface rejuvenation. The exact machinations involved in reengineering a user interface via an API-based scheme, as might be expected, are both product- and application-language-specific. To review the options available, readers are urged to refer to the product literature for products such as Attachmate's QuickApp, Novell's server-side HLLAPI equivalent within HostPublisher, and Simware's Salvo Screen Insight.

6.1.2 The Rejuvenation Process for Applet-Based Solutions

Whereas 3270/5250-to-HTML conversion offers two separate techniques for rejuvenation, at least four disparate rejuvenation schemes are available with applet-based emulation schemes that encompass drag-and-drop development environments, rules-based systems, and programmatic approaches.

Essentially four very different ways exist to realize complex user interface rejuvenation with applet-based schemes:

1. Use a visual, drag-and-drop programming environment to extend a standard SNA access applet, on an application-specific basis, so that it displays a rejuvenated user interface per the methodology pioneered and popularized by OpenConnect's OpenVista. With this approach, all of the rejuvenated screen images that will likely be used by the application are appended to the applet and downloaded "in-bloc" each time the applet is downloaded.

2. Have an intelligent, customizable, applet-based, front-end client that executes on a PC or workstation and performs the transformations necessary to convert the 3270/5250 data stream into a rejuvenated interface, on the fly, without any assistance or intervention of an intermediary server-based component. This approach is exemplified by IBM's ResQ!Net and its Customization Studio component.

3. Create an applet using a heuristic, rules-based scheme to automatically convert much of the 3270/5250 structure to GUI elements. This applet, which will contain screen images that are roughly 3KB in size for each screen required, is executed on a client PC or workstation in conjunction with a server component that intercepts and preprocesses both the outbound and inbound data streams. Client/Server Technology's (CST) Jacada for Java is the quintessential example of this approach.

4. Take a standard, green-on-black tn3270(E) emulation access applet, such as Eicon's Aviva for Java, and use one of the popular Java development tools such as Visual Café, Visual Age for Java, or Visual J++ to augment it at the Java source code level to realize the requisite user interface reengineering. In some cases, this process may involve exploiting a built-in JavaBeans API as provided in Aviva for Java or the

Host Access Class Library API in IBM's Host On-Demand. This approach is the applet equivalent of the API schemes offered by the 3270/5250-to-HTML conversion products.

The GM Truck screen shown in Fig. 6.1 and the FedEx Free Bird screens shown in Figs. 6.2 and 6.9 are rendered by applets that were developed using OpenVista's Visual Basic-like drag-and-drop paradigm. Figure 6.13 shows an example of OpenVista's development environment. Like many of the other rejuvenation schemes, whether 3270/5250-to-HTML conversion or applet-based, OpenVista provides a mechanism through which the developer can capture the screen-by-screen dialog associated with a given application, along with the data entry and the navigation through the various screens required to complete a dialog or intercept error conditions. With OpenVista, the developer would typically have an open and active window (a "frame") that displays online the green-on-black 3270 screens being rejuvenated. The rejuvenated interface, along with any required graphical and multimedia components such as sound or animation, is formulated within another window (or "frame"). Using the Visual Basic-type tool set, displayed in the form of floating palettes, the developer can select fields within the 3270 screen, drag them across to the window displaying the emerging rejuvenated interface, and then

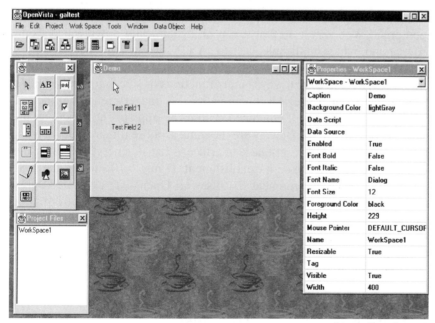

Source: OpenConnect

FIGURE 6.13   Example of OpenConnect's OpenVista development environment.

imbue them with the desired visual attributes. In this manner, the developer can add features such as scroll bars, labels, list boxes, and text boxes.

OpenVista, without any help, intervention, or even encouragement from the developer, generates the Java code needed to create a single applet that will display and handle the new rejuvenated interface, along with all of the underlying tn3270(E)-oriented interactions necessary to communicate with the SNA application. Thus the applet has at its core the standard code used by OC://WebConnect to establish and maintain a green-on-black emulation window. At present, the applet always needs to be front-ended by an SNA-Web gateway component, irrespective of whether it performs green-on-black emulation or handles a rejuvenated interface. This SNA-Web gateway provides for encryption and handles some of the tn3270(E) session establishment chores. The Java code to display and handle the entire rejuvenated interface for all interactions anticipated with the subject application, as well as all necessary screen images, graphical elements, and possible multimedia clips, is then built around the basic core.

With the OpenVista approach, rejuvenation-related transformations are not done "on-the-fly" by the applet at the client as it receives 3270/5250 data stream from the application. Instead, the required transformations are designed into the applet. If desired, a Java applet produced by OpenVista can be modified, augmented, or refined using any of the popular Java development tools. For example, an OpenVista-provided API facilitates quick access into the Java classes that appear in the applet. The finished applet is then stored at the appropriate Web server so that it can be dynamically downloaded from a browser and, where applicable, cached on a PC/workstation hard drive.

When executing, an OpenVista-generated applet does not rely on the intermediary SNA-Web gateway for any functions or screen images related to the rejuvenated interface. All functionality and imagery related to the rejuvenated interface are self-contained within the applet. The functions provided by the SNA-Web gateway are the same as those for an applet that uses a nonrejuvenated, green-on-black interface—that is, encryption and some support for tn3270(E) session establishment. Figure 6.10 showed the architecture of an i•net environment that uses an OpenVista generated applet, demonstrating that OpenVista, which is just a development platform, does not play any role in the production environment. A pivotal difference between the OpenVista approach and the CST Jacada approach is that the former does not rely on a server component for rejuvenation-related functions, whereas intervention and augmentation by the Jacada Server are features of the latter approach.

The total, self-contained nature of the rejuvenation provided by an Open-Vista applet is both a strength and a drawback of this approach. The Open-Vista approach is very powerful and compelling for SNA applications whose entire 3270/5250 user interface, including the exception scenarios, is limited to approximately 30 to 40 individual screens. In reality, quite a few SNA applications fall into this category. With such applications, OpenVista can create a very compact applet, most likely in the 1MB to 2MB range, that displays and manages a highly attractive, fully featured, contemporary user interface. In many instances, as with FedEx's Free Bird application, interactions that required 20 or more 3270 screens can be achieved within a single new screen. For applications with 50 or more separate 3270 screens, however, the OpenVista approach may prove too cumbersome—especially if the underlying logic of the application thwarts the possibility of combining multiple 3270 screens to reduce the overall depth and breadth of the user dialog. Consequently, OpenConnect now offers its totally automatic AutoGUI Auto-Vista solution as a complement to the OpenVista approach.

IBM's tn3270(E) applet-based Host On-Demand provides two means for realizing user interface reengineering, as well as a complete set of JavaBeans, with version 3.0 onward, to facilitate programmatic access. The first method is the provision of a **Host Access Class Library (HACL) API** that can be used with any Java development tool (as well as with C/C++, Visual Basic, PowerBuilder, and LotusScript) to create a reengineered user interface or to realize programmatic access. The second option is the use of Advanced Transition Technologies' (AT^2) ResQ!Net product, which is also marketed by IBM. ResQ!Net realizes its integration with Host On-Demand by using the HACL API.

The HACL includes a set of classes and methods that provide object-oriented abstractions to perform the following tasks on a tn3270(E) or tn5250 connection with an SNA application:

- Read a screen image in terms of its 3270/5250 data stream
- Send input to the application, in 3270/5250 data stream, as if it were coming from a 3270/5250 screen
- Specify a field relative to a display image through a numerical indexing scheme (for example, the third unprotected field on this screen)
- Read and update the 3270/5250 status line that appears at the bottom of 3270/5250 screens in an area designated as the Operator Information Area (OIA)
- Transfer files
- Receive and post notifications asynchronously (that is, not in real time) of designated events, such as the arrival of a new screen

ResQ!Net, somewhat like Jacada, relies on the premise of dynamic pattern recognition and substitution as the basis of its rejuvenation process. With ResQ!Net, however, all processing takes place at the client without any dependence on an intermediate server. ResQ!Net is typically a 300KB to

500KB "intelligent client" Java applet. In the context of IBM, this applet relies on Host On-Demand functionality, accessed via the HACL API, to establish communications with an SNA application and to interchange data with it. (AT^2 offers other versions of ResQ!Net that work outside the framework of Host On-Demand.) ResQ!Net has a standard, built-in AutoGUI capability. Thus, without any customization, it will "Webify" a 3270/5250 screen-based dialog, including the background, menu buttons, color remappings and any "hot spots."

Additional customization can be achieved using the separately priced Customization Studio and Administrator options of the product. The Administrator capability permits the capture of the screens that can then be further customized by the Customization Studio. Through the Customization Studio, one can rearrange fields, insert graphical images, include check boxes, add new fonts, and perform any kind of text string translation, including translation from one language or character set to another. The output of the ResQ!Net Customization Studio is not an applet, but rather a compressed **Extensible Markup Language (XML)** file that contains descriptions of the changes (above those normally performed by the ResQ!Net AutoGUI function). This compressed XML file is downloaded to PCs or workstations that require new, highly customized user interfaces. The standard ResQ!Net applet uses the changes described in the XML file to create the requisite user interface.

ResQ!Net differs markedly from OpenVista in that all rejuvenation-related transformations, even in the case of customized transformations, are done on the fly. This strategy certainly makes the ResQ!Net approach very nimble and minimizes the size of the applet produced. On the other hand, it is not suitable for realizing very high customization that requires the consolidation of multiple source screens (such as in FedEx's Free Bird application) and sets out to change the overall flow of the application's user dialog. ResQ!Net's Customization Studio and Administrator functions can be run on a Java Virtual Machine to achieve platform independence. Figure 6.6 shows the "before and after" images, supplied by AT^2, of a screen rejuvenated using ResQ!Net.

CST's Jacada for Java is another popular and powerful applet-based means for realizing user interface reengineering. Figure 6.14 shows "before and after" images, supplied in this case by CST, of the dramatic rejuvenation possibilities of Jacada for Java. Much of the user interface conversions performed by Jacada rely on a potent, rules-based system known as CST KnowledgeBase. CST claims that the KnowledgeBase contains more than 700 3270/5250-centric pattern definitions that permit the dynamic recognition of frequently encountered 3270/5250 screen elements—for example, the F8-Forward, F7-Backward, F3-Exit, and other PF key definition designations that invariably litter the bottom of most 3270/5250 applications.

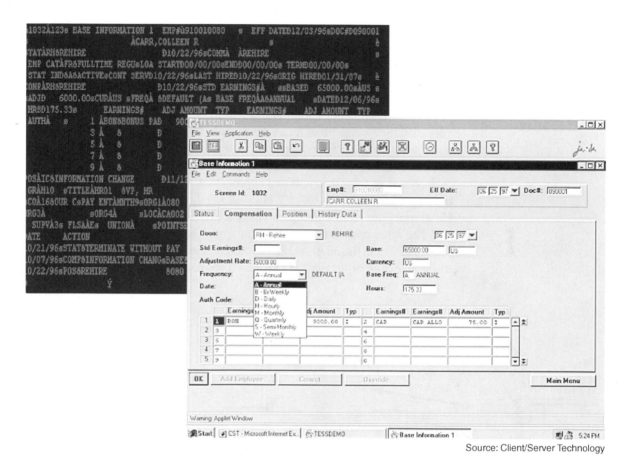

Source: Client/Server Technology

FIGURE 6.14   Rejuvenation through Client/Server Technology's Jacada.

Each pattern definition included in the KnowledgeBase is associated with a substitution string, which may involve graphical elements.

The conversions specified in the KnowledgeBase can be automatically applied in offline mode to an application's screens through CST's Jacada Automated Conversion Environment (ACE). The Java applet that will render and manage the rejuvenated interface and provide host communications, albeit with ongoing support from a Jacada server, will be generated by ACE without any developer intervention. The conversions specified within the KnowledgeBase can also be overridden for a particular rejuvenation process by ACE. Extensive customization is possible using ACE: a developer, aided by easy-to-follow wizards, can capture online the screens to be reengineered and perform the necessary conversions using a combination of the transformations included in the KnowledgeBase and the required alterations. The average size of a Jacada Java applet required to render a typical rejuvenated screen is approximately 3KB. Often-used Java classes and screen layouts can be cached on a PC's hard drive or RAM memory to minimize the amount of data downloaded from the Jacada server.

A Jacada applet can communicate with the host SNA application in two very different ways. First, it can use a **sockets**-based, dedicated, and persistent end-to-end TCP/IP connection with a Jacada server, which in turn will have an SNA session with the appropriate application. Figure 6.15 shows the architecture of this sockets-based approach. This architecture resembles that used by OpenConnect's OC://WebConnect (shown in Fig. 6.10) and Farabi's HostFront (shown in Fig. 5.24 on page 226).

The other approach, unique to an applet-based emulation scheme, is to use HTTP (as in the 3270-to-HTML conversion schemes). Figure 6.16 shows the architecture of Jacada's HTTP-based connectivity scheme. The applet, as

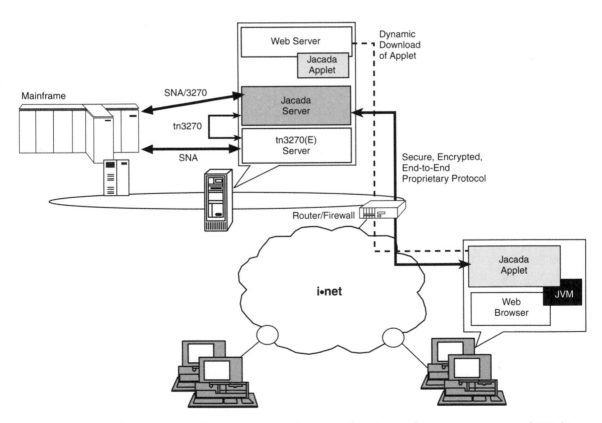

FIGURE 6.15 Client/Server Technology's Jacada architecture when the applet uses a conventional TCP/IP socket connection back to the Jacada server.

can be clearly seen in Fig. 6.16, talks via HTTP to a CST-supplied servlet through a Web server; a *servlet* is an applet running on a server. The servlet then has a connection with the Jacada server that, as in the case of the sockets-based connectivity option, has an SNA session with the necessary application. The advantage of using HTTP is that it provides immediate and automatic access to Web server-centric security measures such as SSL and Secure-HTTP (HTTPS). It also ensures that existing firewall configurations and access definitions between the Web server and the i•net do not have to be changed because authorized users will continue to access only the Web server, rather than any new components.

With Jacada, irrespective of whether the sockets-based or HTTP approach is employed, all the host traffic, in both directions, flows through the Jacada server component. This server component preprocesses the traffic, eliminating data stream components prior to the data being sent to the applet and adding necessary data stream structures to the data received from the applet before

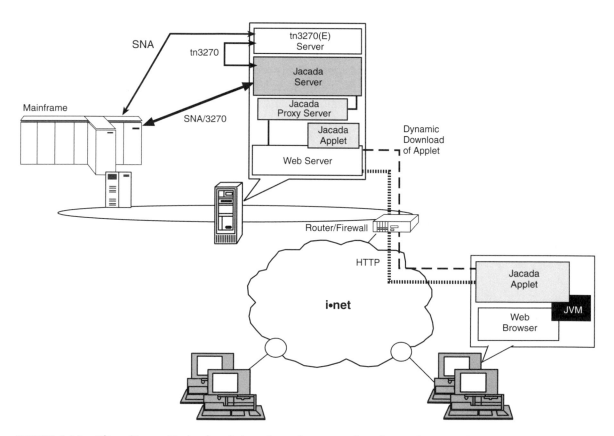

FIGURE 6.16 Client/Server Technology's Jacada architecture when the applet uses HTTP to communicate with the Jacada Server via a Web server and a proxy component.

sending it to the host. This involvement of the Jacada server is clearly evident in Figs. 6.15 and 6.16. When using the sockets-based approach, Jacada represents a 4.5- or 5.5-tier scheme, depending on whether a tn3270(E)/tn5250 server is being used; it is a 6- or 7-tier scheme when HTTP is used, with the seventh component being a tn3270(E)/tn5250 server. The Jacada sockets-based approach is analogous, at least in terms of the components involved, to the schemes used by OpenConnect's OC://WebConnect Pro, Attachmate's HostView Server, and Farabi's HostFront.

The preprocessing performed by the Jacada server on traffic received from the host involves stripping off all 3270/5250 data stream-specific commands, orders, and field attributes, as well as any fields or field headers that do not appear in the rejuvenated user interface. The data stream elements are not sent to the applet, as the user interface rendering performed by a Jacada applet does not rely on the formatting specified by the data stream. This approach minimizes the amount of data sent to the applet, thereby conserving bandwidth and enhancing throughput. The applet receives only the actual data fields, appropriately delimited and enumerated (that is, indexed) relative to the layout of the new interface. The same concept, albeit in reverse, applies to the data sent up by the applet. The Jacada server component receives only the delimited and appropriately sequenced data fields. The server adds the necessary 3270 or 5250 data stream elements around these data fields to ensure that the host application properly interprets and processes them.

The bottom line for user interface rejuvenation is that many choices exist, whether it be for 3270-to-HTML conversion solutions or applet-based emulation approaches. The spectrum of possibilities ranges from "out-of-the-box" AutoGUI schemes to those involving Java applet programming with a tool such as Visual Café or Microsoft's InterDev. The key drawback is the lack of any commonality among the approaches advocated by the market-leading vendors. With luck and in time, at least some of the more prevalent techniques—such as scripting—may become standardized. Eventually, a baseline, vendor-independent, script-based language for 3270/5250 rejuvenation could emerge along the same lines as the HLLAPI API scheme, which has been ubiquitously available on 3270 emulators for many years to facilitate the development of portable, emulator-neutral client applications.

6.1.3 Two More Case Studies that Highlight User Interface Rejuvenation

Lafayette Life Insurance

Lafayette Life Insurance (Lafayette, Indiana) was founded in 1905. It is now a $9.5 billion super heavyweight operating in 48 states and the District of Columbia. In addition to traditional life insurance products, it offers a broad range of insurance and financial planning services, including estate planning, trusts, annuities, pension plans, profit-sharing plans, and retirement income plans. Lafayette's growing business is sustained by a large corporate staff in Indiana, augmented by approximately 1000 field agents across the country.

All of the company's field agents and corporate staff members have real-time, online access to policy information, customer records, beneficiary status, marketing material, and forms and documentation. High-quality, responsive customer service, instantaneous quotes on policies, and on-the-spot information provision are imperative to success in today's competitive insurance and financial planning market. Lafayette excels in ensuring that its agents have access to all of the information they need, around the clock, to help them be successful. To this end, Lafayette developed a Policy Information System in-house. This system was written in S/370 Assembler to maximize performance and efficiency. Known as the New On Line Administration System (NOLAS), it provides online access to all of the requisite information, forms, and documentation. Lafayette is a VM/SP shop that currently has a two-processor unit, IBM 9672-R24, third-generation CMOS (circa 1996), S/390 Parallel Enterprise Server.

Field agents initially gained access to NOLAS via IBM's Advantis Global Network. This network, however, became an expensive proposition that cost Lafayette $6.50 per hour for every agent logged on. Agents who were not served by a local access number for Advantis were forced to use a toll-free number that cost Lafayette $6.00 per hour per user. Proactively containing costs is vitally important in today's competitive insurance market, with any measures that reduce costs typically being reflected in a positive way on the bottom line. To dramatically slash these access costs, Lafayette decided to pursue an Internet-based access solution.

Lafayette chose Sterling's VM:Webgateway 3270-to-HTML conversion offering as the means to provide browser-based access, replete with user interface rejuvenation, to its SNA/3270-based Policy Information System. VM:Webgateway is a highly scalable, secure, VM-based, 3270-to-HTML conversion product. Contrary to what its name might imply, VM:Webgateway is not a VM-only solution. Instead, think of it as a very-high-capacity 3270-to-HTML offering that happens to run on a VM server rather than an NT or Novell server. It can be profitably used to Web-enable any SNA/3270 application running on an MVS, OS/390, VM, VSE, or TPF system. It requires only standard SNA connections between the VM system running VM:Webgateway and the other mainframes containing the SNA/3270 applications. Figure 5.13 depicts the operational model of VM:Webgateway and shows how it can be used by SNA applications running on other mainframes. VM:Webgateway is an excellent Web-enablement solution for enterprises that are VM-based, such as Lafayette, or for those that use a small VM machine

A rejuvenated user interface can alter the complexion and persona of an SNA application and make it amenable to use by casual, untrained users across the Internet. Royal Jordanian Airlines' freight-tracking system demonstrates this possibility, whereas Lafayette Life affirms that significant cost savings can be achieved with SNA remote access over the Internet.

as a test bed for their production systems. VM:Webgateway includes a built-in, full-function Web server that supports SSL-based security as well as Java applets.

On a medium-size, second-generation CMOS machine, VM:Webgateway can support several thousand concurrent sessions, including screen rejuvenation, without any problem. This number obviously becomes higher on the newer and more powerful fourth- and fifth-generation CMOS machines. A scalability number that is in the thousands, as opposed to tens of thousands, might appear to be incongruous with SNA access. In the case of 3270-to-HTML conversion, however, one must factor in the processing associated with bidirectional conversions and the overhead of performing the rejuvenation-specific functions, such as executing the scripts that do the actual user interface customization. Consequently, many 3270-to-HTML offerings that run on NT-based PCs do not typically advertise concurrent session counts that are in excess of 1000. Hence the mainframe-based VM: Webgateway approach is definitely more scalable than most other 3270-to-HTML solutions.

With VM:Webgateway, the 3270-to-HTML conversion occurs via individually created Common Gateway Interface (CGI) scripts that are written using IBM's REXX (Restructured Extended Executor Language) job scripting language. The CGI scripts gain access to the mainframe applications that are to be Web-enabled by logging on to them using standard, mainframe user ID/password-based logon conventions. Sterling provides an automatic tracing facility that records—in terms of a CGI script—the navigation process employed by a user to access and interact with 3270 screens. A skeleton CGI script obtained via this tracing scheme can then be fleshed out to provide the complete rejuvenated user interface. In addition, Sterling provides CGI scripts that automatically apply a set of default transformations, such as background and buttons, to any green-on-black 3270 screens. To ensure session integrity and security, VM:Webgateway uses hidden HTML Form fields to store session ID numbers in much the same way as Novell's HostPublisher, as discussed in Chapter 5.

Given that the company was a long-standing, dedicated VM shop, Lafayette did not hesitate in opting for a VM-based mainframe solution for its Web server and its Web-to-SNA gateway. Implementing NT- or UNIX-based servers to realize Web enablement was viewed as an unnecessary distraction and overhead, especially given that Sterling could provide a highly integrated, VM-resident solution. The conversion to Internet-based access was expedited by Lafayette's use of VM Assist, Sterling's professional services partnership program. Figure 6.17 shows screen shots of the same NOLAS screen before and after rejuvenation, while Fig. 1.5 shows the general architecture of the VM:Webgateway solution as deployed at Lafayette. This Web enablement scheme has been a huge success, and Lafayette now readily endorses the advantages of Internet-based mainframe access at every opportunity.

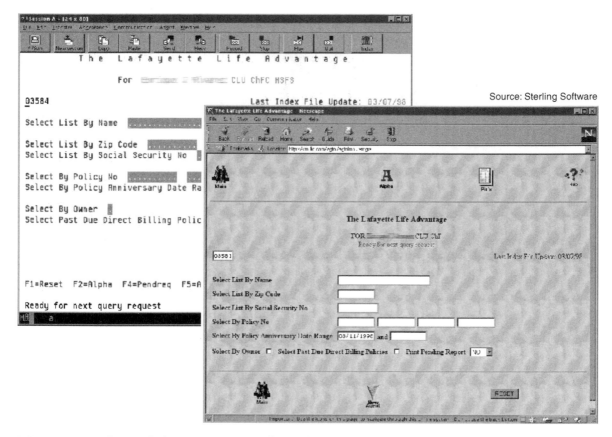

Source: Sterling Software

FIGURE 6.17   Before and after screen images of the Lafayette Life application where the HTML conversion and rejuvenation is being done by Sterling's VM:Webgateway.   (*Source:* © Copyright Sterling Software, Inc. All rights reserved. VM:Webgateway is a trademark of Sterling Software, Inc. All other trademarks are the property of their respective owners.)

VM:Webgateway has an optional, customized solution for the still relatively large and loyal user base of IBM's OfficeVision/VM, e-mail, calendaring, and personal productivity system known as the Office Vision Interface. Figure 6.18 shows the "before and after" screen shots of the OfficeVision main menu screen, which clearly demonstrate the power and flexibility of HTML-based rejuvenation. The facelift provided to OfficeVision, as shown in Fig. 6.18, is extremely dramatic and gives OfficeVision the type of GUI it should have had 10 years ago. This new interface makes a huge difference in OfficeVision's e-mail capability. With Sterling, the e-mail window looks contemporary and inviting. Ideally, IBM should license VM:Webgateway with the Office Vision Interface from Sterling and bundle it in with Office-Vision. The OfficeVision Interface requires Netscape Navigator 3.0 or Internet

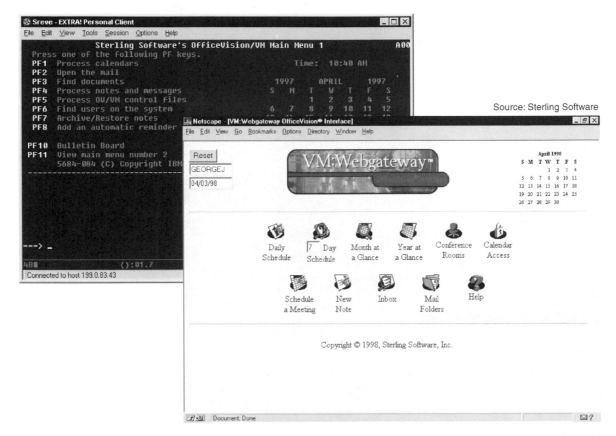

Source: Sterling Software

FIGURE 6.18   Before and after screen images of IBM's OfficeVision/VM where the rejuvenated, HTML-based image is created via Sterling's VM:Webgateway.   (*Source:* © Copyright Sterling Software, Inc. All rights reserved. VM:Webgateway is a trademark of Sterling Software, Inc. All other trademarks are the property of their respective owners.)

Explorer 4.0 at a minimum, because it relies on both Web page tables and JavaScript 1.1.

Royal Jordanian Airlines

Royal Jordanian Airlines, Jordan's national airline, provides another real-life case study in how enterprises are now using Web-to-SNA solutions, augmented with user interface reengineering, to enable the public to gain easy access to mainframe- or AS/400-resident SNA applications through the Internet. Royal Jordanian Airlines is one of the largest Middle East-based passenger carriers, offering daily service to the United States, Europe, the Middle East, and the Far East. It was established in late 1963, based on a Royal

Decree from the late King Hussein of Jordan. At present, it has a fleet of 17 jetliners, including TriStar L-1011s, Airbus 310 and 320s, and three venerable 707s used for cargo.

Royal Jordanian is initially using Farabi's HostFront Publishing's browser-based access to SNA capability to provide Internet access to its cargo shipment tracking system. This architecture, another 3270-to-HTML conversion solution, is shown in Fig. 6.19. Prior to the implementation of this system, cargo customers could obtain information about the status and progress of their shipments only by calling their nearest Royal Jordanian office. Cargo tracking in this manner was possible only during local office hours, and callers invariably were put on hold while queries from prior callers were handled. This situation obviously was not ideal for a global cargo shipment operation with flights arriving and leaving various cities around the world at all times of the day and night.

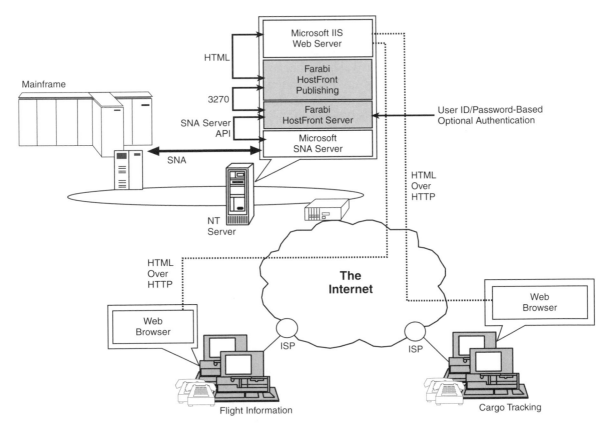

FIGURE 6.19 The architecture of the Farabi Technology-centric, browser-based SNA access solution, based on 3270-to-HTML conversion, implemented at Royal Jordanian Airlines.

With the browser-accessible system, authorized customers from around the world can have 24-hour access to the cargo-tracking system, much like what has been available from FedEx since 1997. Providing authorized access is one of the most desirable features of HostFront-centric solutions. The HostFront server, which is a prerequisite for all Farabi Web-to-SNA solutions, provides a built-in capability for extensive access control based on user IDs and passwords. This HostFront-specific access control augments other security measures, such as firewalls, and mainframe tools, such as RACF and ACF/2.

With the cargo-tracking system now in production, Royal Jordanian is working on providing browser-based real-time access to its flight information system, again using 3270-to-HTML conversion via Farabi's HostFront Publishing. Its flight information system, like those of most other airlines, includes up-to-the-second information on flight schedules, flight arrival times, and terminal and gate information. Thanks to browser-based access, the public will be able to get instantaneous information about Royal Jordanian's flights without having to call one of its offices or a travel agent. This flexibility will help the company's bottom line in multiple ways: it greatly increases Royal Jordanian's ability to reach prospective passengers around the world; it minimizes flight arrival query phone calls to local airline offices; and it will reduce the call center resources required to field flight option queries from travelers planning an itinerary. As the total Farabi HostPublishing system is relatively inexpensive, and prospective users need only a standard browser on their PCs to access the Royal Jordanian systems with this thin client 3270-to-HTML solution, these browser-based solutions are truly win-win propositions benefiting both Royal Jordanian and its clientele.

Other airlines are rushing to Web-enable their information systems as well. American Airlines/Sabre now provides quite extensive Web-based access using a variety of solutions from Novell, Eicon, and other vendors. SwissAir, on the other hand, has used in-house development to create a system and some applications that use OpenConnect.

HostFront Publishing permits extensive user interface rejuvenation through the 3270/5250-to-HTML conversion process via ASP and FSL, which is a very straightforward and rather intuitive scheme. Ease of implementation, ease of use, and user interface customization were major factors in Royal Jordanian's selection of the Farabi solution. Ease of deployment is a hallmark of HostFront, as other case studies in this book have demonstrated.

HostFront Publishing, although typically deployed with IIS, is also compatible with Netscape's FastTrack and O'Reilly's WebSite. For the time being, HostFront Publishing, through its Web-to-SNA gateway, is inextricably tied to Microsoft's SNA Server as the only means of realizing its mainframe or AS/400 connectivity. In this respect, it is analogous to Novell's HostPublisher, which works with only NetWare for SAA.

Given the incontrovertible advantages it brings, Royal Jordanian is understandably very happy with its Web-to-host solution. Its IT management is on record as saying: "The benefits to us are enormous. . . . Thanks to the solution, [the] business is now open 24 hours a day, 365 days a year. . . ." That endorsement typifies what i•net-to-data center integration is all about and confirms the tangible cost, customer reach, and customer satisfaction advantages that enterprises can easily leverage from the large spectrum of proven solutions now on the market.

6.2   APPLICATION-SPECIFIC WEB-TO-SNA GATEWAYS AND CLIENTS

All of the browser-based access to SNA schemes discussed to this point, as well as those mentioned in Chapters 4 and 5, are application-agnostic approaches—that is, they will work with any SNA application. Of course, their terminal-oriented interactions use 3270 or 5250 data streams. The beauty and power of such an approach is that a single solution, whether it be 3270-to-HTML or applet-based emulation, can provide universal interactive access to all SNA/3270 applications being used by an enterprise, without exception or compromise. Despite the obvious advantages of this type of universal access solution, there now exists a large and growing family of application-specific Web-to-SNA solutions. These application-specific solutions, which are available for only the most widely deployed IBM applications, are intended to expedite the "Webification" of those select applications.

Only a very few of these solutions, such as CICS Web Interface and IMS Web, are tightly integrated into the application they serve. Others essentially function as adjuncts, in the form of gateways; these gateways may run on an intermediate server relying on NT, UNIX, or OS/2, rather than alongside their target application on the mainframe or AS/400. Irrespective of the level of integration, none of these solutions claims to offer any functionality or customization features not readily available from a good, general-purpose solution. With the few tightly integrated solutions, Web enablement may be marginally easier to implement than with a general-purpose solution. The difference in the effort involved in implementing the application-specific approach rather than a general-purpose solution is likely to be a matter of days at best, rather than weeks or months.

Any additional effort involved in implementing a general-purpose solution would be more than recompensed if multiple applications (such as CICS, DB2, IMS, and TSO) need to be Web-enabled, rather than just a solitary application. Extending the scope of a general-purpose Web-to-SNA solution to embrace a new application, replete with AutoGUI-based rejuvenation, is a rather easy task that typically involves setting up a Web page that has the

A tightly integrated application-specific solution, such as the CICS Web Interface is an expedient way to Web-enable an application such as CICS or IMS—but only if just one data center application needs Web enablement.

necessary links to the Web-to-SNA product and creating a URL for that page. In some instances, even this effort might not be necessary—especially if the enterprise uses an SNA Session Manager system, such as NetView Access Services, to enable users to switch between different SNA applications from a menu page that lists all applications.

This highly focused, "silver-bullet" approach could be justified to some extent around early 1996, when few general-purpose solutions were available. The merits of opting for an application-specific solution in the current market, when more than 40 vendors offer proven and compelling general-purpose solutions, is highly debatable, however—particularly if the scheme is not tightly integrated or if multiple applications need to be Web-enabled. In general, an application-specific solution should be considered only in the rare occasions when an enterprise wishes to Web-enable just one application and when a viable and proven application-specific Web-to-SNA solution exists for that application. In all other situations, one should at least carefully evaluate widely deployed general-purpose solutions.

Table 6.1 lists most of the major application-specific Web-to-SNA solutions that were available around mid-1998. CICS and IMS—the doyens of mainframe-based transaction processing and database management, respectively—have the lion's share of the solutions available; IBM is, by far, the leading purveyor of these solutions.

6.2.1   Examples of CICS-Specific Web-to-SNA Solutions

Application-specific Web-to-data center solutions concentrate quite heavily on CICS, IMS, and DB2. CICS, by far, enjoys the lion's share of IBM and third-party solutions.

CICS is the major benefactor of the largest number of application-specific Web-to-SNA solutions, including solutions from both IBM and third parties. Given the range of solutions available, one can get a good appreciation of the possibilities of application-specific solutions by studying a cross section of the available products. To that end, this section will examine the structure of the following CICS solutions:

- IBM's CICS Web Interface
- IBM's CICS Internet Gateway
- IBM's CICS Gateway for Java
- Blue Lobster's Mako Server
- Interlink's ActiveCICX

First, however, the section reviews the client/server options now available with CICS; some of these solutions rely on using some of the APIs in place to facilitate client/server mode operation. CICS is no longer the mainframe-only monolith that speaks solely 3270, contrary to the mental image of it still savored by many members of the IBM world. CICS is now a cross-platform

TABLE 6.1   Major application-specific Web-to-SNA solutions.

Product	Host Applications Supported	Operating System Gateway Server	Distributed Approach		Server Approach		
			Client Applet	Client-to-Server Protocol	Web Server APIs	Protocol/API to Host	Rejuvenation
Blue Lobster Mako Server	CICS	Windows NT, OS/2 UNIX	Java	IIOP over TCP		ECI over SNA or TCP/IP	Programmatic
IBM CICS (with integrated 3270 bridge and Web interface)	CICS	OS/390			ICAPI, GWAPI	Internal	AutoGUI
IBM CICS Gateway for Java	CICS	Windows NT, OS/2, UNIX	Java	ECI/EPI sockets over TCP		ECI/EPI over SNA or TCP/IP	Programmatic
IBM CICS Internet Gateway	CICS	Windows NT, OS/2 UNIX			CGI	EPI over SNA or TCP	AutoGUI
IBM IMS Web	IMS	Windows NT, AIX, OS/390			CGI, Net Data	IMS TCP/IP OTMA	IMS Web Studio
IBM IMS WWW Templates	IMS	OS/390			CGI, ICAPI	APPC	AutoGUI or programmatic
IBM MS Client for Java	IMS	—	Java			IMS TCP/IP OTMA	Programmatic
IBM MQSeries Client for Java	MQSeries	—	Java			MQSeries messages	Programmatic
IBM MQSeries Internet Gateway	MQSeries	Windows NT, OS/2, UNIX			CGI	MQSeries message	AutoGUI
IBM Net Data	DB2, Oracle, Sybase, IMS, other databases	Windows NT, OS/2, UNIX, OS/390, OS/400	Java		CGI, NSAPI, ICAPI, ISAPI	Various, specific to database	Net data Tools, JavaScript, VisualAge
Interlink Active CICX	CICS	Windows (3.x, 95/98, NT)	ActiveX			Winsock over TCP	Interlink CICS Programmer's Toolkit
Interlink Active IMX	IMS	Windows (3.x, 95/98, NT)	ActiveX			Winsock over TCP	Interlink CICS Programmer's Toolkit
Sterling VM:Webgateway OfficeVision Interface	OfficeVision/ VM	VM			CGI	IUCV	AutoGUI
Sterling Vision:Webaccess	Oracle, DB2, SQL Server	Windows NT	Java	Proprietary over TCP		Various, specific to database	Vision: Clearaccess

solution with an ingrained client/server architecture that supports a wide range of clients. Its server components, which perform the classic transaction-monitor functions that are synonymous with CICS, are now available for mainframes, AS/400s, NT servers, Sun Solaris systems, Hewlett-Packard hosts, Compaq/Digital UNIX environments, and more. CICS client software is available from IBM for PCs and workstations running DOS, Windows 3.1, Windows 95, Windows NT, OS/2, Apple Macintosh OS, AIX, Sun Solaris, HP-UX, Siemens SINIX, and so on. This client software permits the development of GUI front ends to traditional CICS applications, PC/workstation software that performs local processing, and programmatic solutions that work by exchanging data between a CICS server and a desktop application such as Excel.

CICS clients can interact with CICS servers in at least four very different ways:

1. External Presentation Interface (EPI). This 3270 data stream interception and conversion scheme permits new user interfaces to be developed on the PC or workstation without changing the server-side CICS application or the original 3270 data stream. It is essentially a screen-scraping technique, where the API permits the client software to read the image that would be painted on a 3270 screen and to write data into designated input fields.

2. External Call Interface (ECI). This programmatic interface is available for developing highly optimized client/server applications where the heavy-duty, business-specific processing occurs on the CICS server with the CICS client handling the user interface. ECI enables customer or third-party client software to interact with a CICS program synchronously (that is, interactively in real time) or asynchronously (that is, with results being checked later in batch mode). To the CICS application running on a server, CICS calls made over the ECI look as if they were coming across via a Distributed Program Link (DPL) from another CICS application running on another system.

IBM has positioned ECI as the strategic means for developing new CICS client/server applications. Its structure permits easy and flexible demarcation of the application's business logic from its user interface component. Thus ECI facilitates client/server designs where the business logic part of a CICS application can run on a CICS server and the user interface, or a programmatic emulation of such an interface, can run on a PC/workstation client. The client software interacts with the CICS program running on the server by using a data area known as the COMMAREA. The client places input parameters to the server program in this COMMAREA and waits for the server program to return the appropriate output to that same area. The client software can then retrieve this output and process it further or display it for end-user consumption. Note, however, that all CICS programs, and especially very old ones, are not ECI-compatible (or enabled). Programmatic interaction with such programs would be possible only using 3270 emulation.

3. Traditional 3270 Terminal Emulation. This approach uses a full-function, fat-client, with the client/server interactions being conducted in unadulterated 3270 data stream form.

4. SNA LU 6.2 Program-to-Program communications. The CICS client is linked with the appropriate CICS server via a traditional SNA gateway, such as IBM's CS/NT. In addition, some UNIX-based CICS clients and CICS servers support **Remote Procedure Calls (RPCs)** based on the **Distributed Communications Environment (DCE)** standard.

The communications path between a CICS client and a CICS server can be created through a variety of different transport schemes, including LU 6.2, TCP/IP, NetBIOS, and IPX/SPX. Note that the CICS Internet Gateway and CICS Gateway for Java described later use CICS client software as a gateway component running on an intermediary server rather than on the actual client PC or workstation. Although somewhat unorthodox, this configuration permits IBM to reuse the CICS client software as a means of expediently realizing server-to-CICS communications, where the client in this case comprises the intermediary server.

The CICS Web Interface (CWI) is a mainframe-only, mainframe-resident, CICS-specific, 3270-to-HTML conversion solution. It was first announced in September 1996 as a no-charge option for CICS for MVS/ESA version 4; it became generally available in December 1996. This option is available on the follow-on releases for mainframe CICS (CICS Transaction Server for OS/390 releases 1 and 2). The CWI functionality is wholly contained within the mainframe and does not require any external gateways. This option is, however, contingent on having TCP/IP on the mainframe, as it relies on receiving and transmitting HTML pages over HTTP. Figure 6.20 shows the CWI architecture.

The CWI feature in CICS Transaction Server for OS/390 release 2 supports any CICS terminal-oriented transaction that uses either CICS's intrinsic Basic Mapping Support (BMS) or CICS's Terminal Control SEND and RECEIVE commands to interact with 3270 terminal users. On the i•net side, CWI accepts input in the form of Web pages in HTML format delivered across HTTP from a standard Web browser; it delivers transaction output to Web browsers using HTTP/HTML. A component within CWI, referred

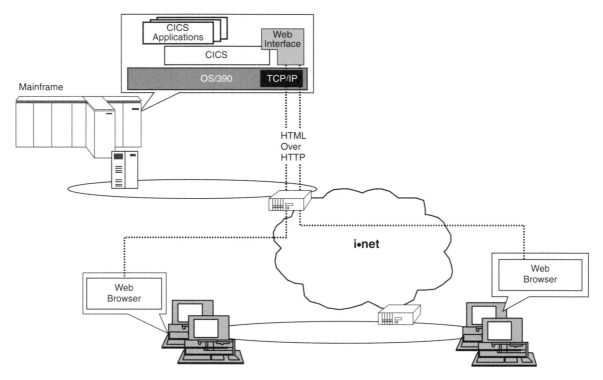

FIGURE 6.20   CICS-to-HTML conversion via the mainframe-resident CICS Web Interface.

to as the Template Manager, handles the 3270-to-HTML transformations. The Template Manager produces HTML output from existing BMS map definitions. Customization options available within this HTML generation process permit some user interface facelifting—in particular, the addition of background textures, screen colors, and named buttons.

In addition to requiring TCP/IP on the mainframe, CWI has some other, albeit relatively innocuous limitations. The main constraint is that it cannot currently deal with HTML pages larger than 32KB. With a typical 3270 screen unlikely to exceed 4KB, this limitation is not yet a major showstopper. In addition, CWI may not work with CICS applications that use both BMS and SEND/RECEIVE to interact with terminals. Such applications may need to be redesigned to use either one or the other of these approaches. To ensure optimal security, CWI should be used in conjunction with the mainframe-based IBM Internet Connection Secure Server for OS/390 (ICSS/390) or the IBM/Lotus Go Web Server (LGWS). Both of these servers provide security functions such as basic authentication and SSL functions.

CWI interacts with ICSS/390 and LGWS to obtain these security services by using a CICS-supplied Dynamic Link Library (DLL) that supports both the Internet Connection Application Programming Interface (ICAPI) and the Go Web Application Programming Interface (GWAPI).

The CICS Internet Gateway (CIG), in marked contrast to the totally mainframe-bounded CWI, is a server-based, "off-board" 3270-to-HTML conversion solution. This gateway is a component of the IBM CICS Client version 2.0 software product for Windows NT, AIX, and OS/2. Because it is an external server-based solution, as shown in Fig. 6.21, the CIG can be used to achieve browser-based access to any CICS application running on a mainframe, AS/400, AIX system, OS/2 server, or NT box. This ability to facilitate browser-based access to all of the key CICS server platforms is a redeeming strength of this solution, differentiating it from the mainframe-only CWI.

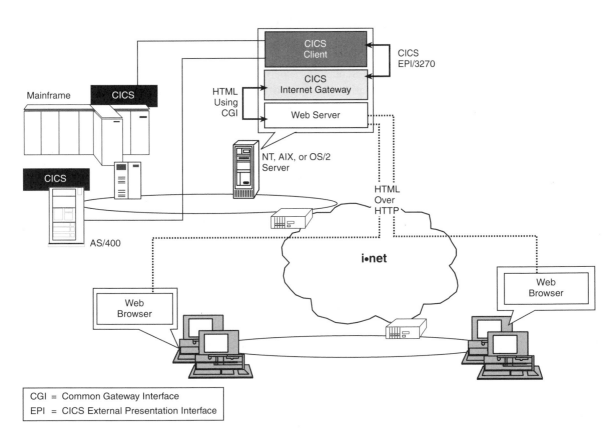

CGI = Common Gateway Interface
EPI = CICS External Presentation Interface

FIGURE 6.21   Architecture of IBM's CICS Internet Gateway.

IBM claims that CIG's 3270-to-HTML conversion will also work with any CICS 3270 application. The multiplatform CICS support possible with CIG, as well as its ability to support any 3270-based CICS application, can also be realized with general-purpose 3270-to-HTML solutions, such as Eicon's Aviva for Java. The CIG (as shown in Fig. 6.21) interacts with its colocated CICS client using the standard EPI. It communicates with its adjacent Web server using the CGI. IBM currently recommends the following Web servers for use with the CIG: IBM Internet Connection Server for OS/2 or Windows NT, Netscape Communications Server for NT, or the widely used Microsoft Internet Information Server (IIS) version 2.0 or greater.

In addition to 3270-to-HTML conversion, CIG performs state management for every CICS session passing through it, thereby ensuring that the fidelity and reliability of CICS transactions can be maintained on an end-to-end basis. General-purpose solutions, such as Novell's HostPublisher and Sterling's VM:Webgateway, address this session integrity issue by using hidden session ID and sequence numbers (as was discussed in Chapter 5). The HTML output of the CIG is currently based on HTML 2.0. IBM provides a user interface rejuvenation option, whereby the HTML flows output by the CIG can be intercepted and augmented using any standard HTML editor, such as Allaire's HomeSite. In essence, this scheme is not dramatically different from the script-based rejuvenation schemes offered by the general-purpose 3270/5250-to-HTML conversion solutions.

The CICS Gateway for Java (CGfJ), much like the CIG, is an integral component of the CICS Client version 2.0 package for Windows NT, AIX, OS/2, and Solaris. It differs fundamentally from the two previously described approaches in that it is based on a Java applet, whereas the other two were based on 3270-to-HTML conversion. The applet used by CGfJ, however, is not a tn3270(E) emulation applet, like the applet used with general-purpose solutions such as IBM's Host On-Demand, Eicon's Aviva for Java, and WRQ's Reflection EnterView. Instead, CGfJ expects the applet to use ECI as its communications protocol, as shown in Fig. 1.11. IBM supplies a Java applet that permits ECI requests and responses to be exchanged with a CICS client. Enterprises can use this IBM-supplied applet as a basis for building customized applets to suit their particular CICS access needs. The ECI-based interactions performed by the applet will be relayed to the appropriate CICS server by the CICS client. Unlike in the CIG configuration, where all server components must be colocated, CGfJ permits the CICS client and CGfJ to reside in a box that is physically separate from that running the Web server.

With CICS Transaction Server for OS/390 release 2, which started to ship in late 1997, IBM made available a mainframe version of CGfJ. The CICS client CGfJ component has been ported for execution under OS/390, as an OpenEdition (that is, UNIX) application. With this mainframe-based CGfJ component, enterprises can eliminate the intermediate PC server if they prefer.

Blue Lobster's Mako Server is another Java applet-based solution that uses the ECI as its means for interacting with CICS server applications. Figure 6.22 illustrates the overall architecture of the Mako Server approach. Mako Server differs from CGfJ in that it is highly object-oriented and relies extensively on the **Common Object Request Broker Architecture (CORBA)** to facilitate integration between objects written in different languages and located on diverse platforms. Mako Server permits developers to write platform-independent Java applications that can freely exploit previously written objects.

Blue Lobster provides a Mako client that is written in Java. This client is integrated into the custom Java application to provide the required support for objects via CORBA. Both CGfJ and Mako Server could be effectively used to develop highly customized applets for dramatically rejuvenating the user interfaces of CICS applications. In many instances, this approach might

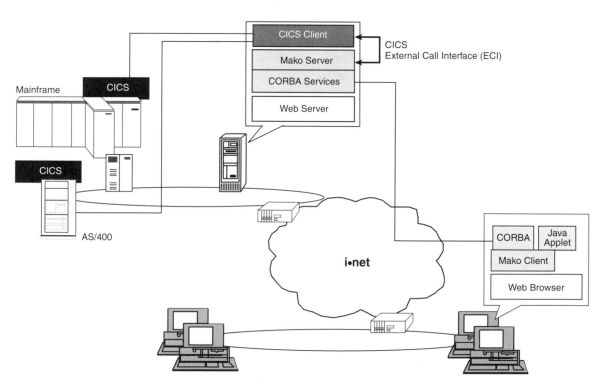

FIGURE 6.22 The high-level architecture of Blue Lobster's Mako Server-based, object-centric solution.

be overkill—akin to using a sledgehammer to crack open a nut. Both approaches are better suited for developing new twenty-first-century client applications, with very contemporary GUIs that have transparent access to CICS resources via the programmatic ECI interface.

Like the CWI, the CICS 3270 Bridge became a standard feature within the CICS Transaction Server for OS/390 release 2. Although it supports browser-based access (in marked contrast to the CWI), Web enablement is not the 3270 Bridge's primary raison d'être—it is essentially a subset of its overall capabilities. The 3270 Bridge provides a generalized data stream remapping capability to facilitate unencumbered access to 3270-based CICS transactions, without the need for a 3270 terminal or a 3270 emulator on the PC or workstation. The goal of the 3270 Bridge, much like that of the ECI, is to enable the business logic of a CICS application to be separated from its user interface handling. The bridge achieves this presentation interface decoupling by intercepting the programming commands used to interact with the terminal. Much of this interception involves actually parsing the source code of the CICS **Basic Mapping Support (BMS)** maps that describe the format and content of the terminal interactions. For situations where the original BMS source code may be unavailable, IBM supplies a Reverse Compiler tool that allows the maps and corresponding macros to be regenerated from the existing runtime load module. A 3270 Bridge-specific bridging transaction module, as well as a user-developed, message-driven program module, can be used to intercept and convert the 3270 data stream flows.

Whereas the Web-specific CICS solutions mentioned to this point have all been 3270-to-HTML or Java-oriented solutions, Interlink's ActiveCICX is based on ActiveX. ActiveCICX enables a Windows application to invoke and transparently exchange data with a CICS application. It was designed to handle, and has been tested with, applications developed using Visual Basic, VBScript, JScript, Visual C++, PowerBuilder, and Delphi. ActiveCICX supports both synchronous and asynchronous modes of operations, similar to the CICS ECI; it also offers optional user authentication and connection timeout management.

ActiveCICX works in conjunction with Interlink's CICS Programmers Toolkit (CPT) for mainframes running MVS and OS/390. CPT was initially developed to permit seamless interactions between TCP/IP applications and CICS applications. This toolkit provides a set of mainframe-resident modules that interact with CICS applications using send and receive queues. An API (supported in S/370 Assembler, COBOL, PLI, and C) is available so that CICS programmers, if necessary, can write modules that will enable their applications to be integrated with CPT. Figure 6.23 illustrates the overall architecture of ActiveCICX.

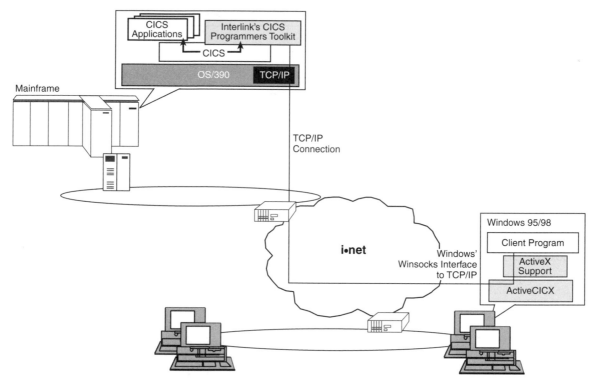

FIGURE 6.23   The high-level architecture of Interlink's ActiveCICX access to CICS across TCP/IP.

6.2.2   The Pros and Cons of Application-Specific Solutions

If an enterprise has only one mainframe or AS/400 application that must be Web-enabled, and if a compelling, relatively tightly integrated application-specific solution exists for that application, then an application-specific solution should certainly be considered as the prime candidate for achieving the necessary Web-to-data center integration. It would also help if the candidate for Web enabling happens to be based on CICS, IMS, or DB2, as most of the application-specific solutions available address only one of these three applications. If the application that needs to be Web-enabled is not based on CICS, IMS, or DB2, or if multiple applications must be Web-enabled, then application-specific solutions are not the way to proceed. Implementing multiple application-specific solutions (say, for CICS, IMS, DB2, and Oracle), as opposed to a single-general purpose solution is difficult to condone because each solution must be individually supported, administered, customized, and maintained. Table 6.2 outlines the pros and cons of application-specific solutions.

TABLE 6.2   Pros and cons of application-specific Web-to-data center solutions.

Salient Characteristics

- Exclusively targeted at Web-enabling one of the widely deployed SNA applications, such as CICS, IMS, and DB2
- Solution may be based on 3270-to-HTML conversion or applet-centric programmatic approaches
- Solutions may be mainframe-resident or server-based
- IBM is by far the primary purveyor of such solutions
- Direct alternative to general-purpose solutions if only one application—ideally CICS, IMS, or DB2—needs to be Web-enabled

Pros	*Cons*
✓ Possibility of rapid, turnkey Web, enablement (for example, with the CICS Web Interface)	✗ Danger of proliferating multiple solutions if more than one application needs to be Web-enabled
✓ Some solutions, such as the 3270 Bridge and CICS Web Interface, are tightly integrated and available as built-in features of the application	✗ Solutions not available for all SNA applications
✓ Some solutions, such as the CICS Gateway for Java, Blue Lobster's Mako Server, and Interlink's ActiveCICX, provide extensive facilities for developing new client applications that access CICS resources in the background, using programmatic and possibly object-oriented means	✗ Impractical as a means of Web-enabling a typical mainframe-based data center, where each mainframe may host multiple SNA applications
	✗ Most of the tightly integrated solutions use 3270-to-HTML conversion and do not offer any applet-based alternatives
	✗ Tighter "lock-in" to a particular solution/vendor than would be the case with the general-purpose solutions, where the same type of solution is available from multiple vendors
	✗ Evolution and competitiveness of a given solution is not as assured as with a general-purpose solution, where the competition is far greater

6.3   PROGRAMMATIC OR APPLICATION SERVER-BASED WEB-TO-SNA ACCESS

Programmatic access relative to SNA is a multifaceted and many-tiered proposition with a star-crossed heritage—and a bewildering array of promising solutions. Although programmatic access to SNA became possible in the late 1970s, when minicomputer vendors began offering APIs on top of their nascent 3270 and RJE emulators, few would argue that programmatic access to SNA has been a resounding success to date. This situation is bound to change, and quite dramatically, once the IBM community recovers from the trauma of the Y2K issue. For nearly a decade and a half, one has heard the ongoing refrain of how SNA applications will change or even disappear; today, however, some potent factors promise to make a big difference. These factors include the following:

1. The Y2K issues have brought into sharp focus the fact that SNA mission-critical applications remain the life-blood of most mid-size to large corporations but are ancient by any standard. At a minimum, companies recognize that these applications should be front-ended with a new genre of applications that are based on modern programming methodology, leverage i•net technology, and fully exploit the capabilities of today's powerful, multimedia-capable PCs and workstations.

2. High-profile, client/server-oriented, "total-business" information systems—in particular, SAP R/3 with its more than 1000 proven, industry-specific business modules—are beginning to usurp, or at least front-end, SNA mission-critical applications. For example, SAP R/3 is now installed at more than 4000 IBM mainframe shops.

3. The standardization on intranets as the in-house corporate networks of choice will boost the use of Web server-oriented applications.

4. Windows NT and, to a lesser extent, UNIX are becoming the preferred platforms for application development and deployment; mainframes appear destined to become high-capacity data servers to applications running on NT or UNIX servers. Figure 6.3 depicted the three-tier client/server architecture, with the mainframe as the third-tier data server, that is now gaining increasing popularity. This type of configuration is readily supported by the new breed of corporate business applications from the likes of SAP, PeopleSoft, and BAAN.

5. The Internet is an inescapable role model regarding what is now possible with i•net technology.

6. Java, JavaBeans, ActiveX, and object technology, in cahoots with visual application development tools such as Visual InterDev, Visual J++, and Visual C++, are making it easier than ever to quickly develop client-side applications.

7. A surfeit of compelling solutions is available today in the form of JavaBeans, applets, middleware, and ODBC-type direct database access technology to facilitate programmatic Web-to-data center access.

Given these factors, one must admit that, by 2006, most of today's venerable SNA applications will likely be front-ended, or be in the process of being "end-gamed," by a new breed of applications. The current trend toward user interface rejuvenation of SNA applications is merely a precursor to these

Programmatic, application server-based access to SNA is the final frontier in the three-decade-long saga of SNA. Programmatic access will rapidly become the preferred means for interacting with today's mission-critical SNA applications once MIS budgets and resources can be restored after the rigors of the Y2K compliance campaign.

applications being pushed into the background, where they will act as transparent data servers to applications that will perform expanded business logic functions and interact with the users via a Web-inspired user interface. The SNA applications and the data accessible through them will also become back ends to the Enterprise Resource Planning (ERP) and Online Analytical Processing (OLAP) applications that are now in vogue to help enterprises extract as much knowledge as possible from their data. Today's user interface rejuvenation techniques, which permit one to capture the keystrokes required to establish an SNA session and then navigate through various 3270/5250 screens, will be expanded; this access logic will be made into reusable JavaBeans. Many of the new front-end applications will use such JavaBeans to obtain the mainframe or AS/400 data they require via SNA applications.

In any event, programmatic access to SNA applications from browser-oriented clients will represent the final chapter in the eventful, three-decade-long evolution of SNA access. User interface rejuvenation, even when it involves considerable screen consolidation and rationalization (as with FedEx's Free Bird application), nevertheless relies on the original SNA application to perform all of the business logic. Programmatic access takes the next logical step—synthesizing the data accessible through, and the business logic inherent in, an existing mission-critical application or even multiple applications into the body of a brand new application.

Consider the rejuvenated screen shown in Fig. 6.8. This user interface to an AS/400 application calculates ground-transport freight costs for a freight-shipping company based on the source and destination cities involved, the total weight, and any special shipping priority. With programmatic access, this SNA-based program could become a subroutine for a new browser-based Java or ActiveX applet—for example, one that handles Internet-based, "mail-order" shopping for furniture. After the user selects the items required, the freight cost calculation subroutine might be automatically and transparently invoked across the Internet, quickly determining and displaying the shipping costs beneath the total costs for the selected goods. With this type of programmatic access, the user will remain unaware that another application—an AS/400-resident SNA application—was used in the background to calculate the shipping costs. This scenario illustrates the realistic mid-term future of today's SNA applications: becoming behind-the-scenes commodities for new Web-centric applications.

Programmatic Web-to-data center access implies that some client software will reside on the client PC or workstation, whether it takes the form of a browser, applet, or application that interacts with a data-center-resident application or a database across an i•net. Some form of intermediary software, which may or may not be in the class of software deemed to be "middleware," will always be required to achieve this goal. Today, a very wide range of options exists for this intermediary software. These options include the following:

- 3270 data stream-oriented schemes, such as IBM's Host On-Demand HACL; Host On-Demand JavaBeans; Blue Lobster's Stingray 3270 Software Development Kit (SDK); Attachmate's Enterprise Access Class Libraries (EACL); the Open Host Interface Objects (OHIO) endorsed by both IBM and Attachmate; and the HLLAPI interface, which is universally available with tn3270(E) and ip3270 solutions

- LU 6.2-based program-to-program schemes through the APPC or CPI-C interfaces available with some ip3270 emulators, such as Attachmate's EXTRA!, Wall Data's RUMBA, and IBM's PComm

- Traditional, pre-Web, middleware solutions, such as IBM's MQSeries and CNT/Apertus's Enterprise/Connect, which can be used with browser-based or browser-invoked clients to realize programmatic Web-to-data center access

- New wave, Web-oriented, middleware solutions, such as Bluestone's Sapphire/Web Application Server, OpenConnect's Integration Server, BEA WebLogic, and Novera jBusiness, which provide high-end database management features such as two-phase commit to facilitate secure updating of distributed databases

- ODBC- or DRDA-based capability, such as that available within Microsoft's SNA Server or Cisco/StarQuest's StarSQL, for directly accessing data located with DB2-like relational databases

- IBM VSAM file ("flat file")-resident data access schemes, such as that available within Microsoft SNA Server version 4.0

- Application-specific solutions, such as IBM's CICS Gateway for Java, Blue Lobster's Mako Server, and Interlink's ActiveCICX

Because programmatic solutions, by definition, rely on linking programming elements to each other, a detailed exposition of some of these options is really outside the scope and mission of this book; it would require detailed descriptions of APIs and programming conventions. The goal of this book relative to programmatic access is to highlight the tantalizing possibilities and describe the options available. To this end, an actual case study involving 3270 data stream-based access is appropriate at this juncture, as it provides a glimpse of the possibilities inherent with programmatic access.

6.3.1 Case Study of Programmatic SNA Access in the Insurance Sector

Fort Wayne, Indiana-based Lincoln National Reinsurance Companies, which has offices from Manila to Mexico City, is one of the world's largest and most respected life and health reinsurers. Reinsurance is the process whereby a company accepts a part of another insurance company's risk on a policy in

The Lincoln National application relies on a 3270-based Software Development Kit (SDK) and provides a hint of the tantalizing possibilities inherent in programmatic access solutions.

return for a percentage of that policy's premium. It is now an integral component of the global insurance industry, most often cropping up in the fields of aircraft and oil-tanker insurance. Lincoln National entered this business when it was in its infancy, in 1912. The company now provides life/health insurance risk management offerings to a worldwide clientele that includes insurance companies, HMOs, self-funded employer groups, and other risk-accepting organizations.

Most of Lincoln National's information about its far-flung client base is maintained on a mainframe—a Hitachi Data Systems' S/390 plug-compatible. Lincoln uses two applications on the mainframe for this purpose:

- A CICS application, written in COBOL, that keeps track of client contact information
- A FOCUS application from Information Builders that maintains accounting summaries for each client (FOCUS, which includes a wide range of application development and reporting tools, is used on many platforms to develop decision support applications, especially when there is a need to access data from disparate databases)

Account representatives in Lincoln National's relatively large sales organization need regular access to the information managed by these two applications so as to track client information, client status, and client profiles. To expedite and streamline access to these data, the client information maintained on the mainframe is replicated on an NT/SQL server database. The presence of this NT/SQL server ensures that account reps can gain quick access to well-structured account profiles without logging on to the mainframe. The only problem with this setup, when it was first instituted, was that there was no automated system to routinely synchronize updates between the NT/SQL server and the mainframe. This potential for disagreement, as can be appreciated, was not optimal.

A laborious, error-prone, and multistep process was used to overcome this problem. Client information was first updated on the mainframe, then the NT/SQL server was updated manually. A rep would update the mainframe database and receive an extract of this transaction as a confirmation of the update. The rep would then submit this extract to a program running on the NT/SQL server. This program would read through the extract line-by-line, determining which updates had been performed on the mainframe databases. It would then replicate these updates on the database managed by the NT/SQL server. These database synchronization operations were performed daily in batch mode, with reruns often required to handle errors and other problems.

This manual process was fraught with pitfalls—chief among which was the fact that account reps were never sure whether the data on the NT/SQL server were completely up-to-date. Because the process was not automated, database synchronization would sometimes be pushed to the sidelines when other pressing tasks loomed. With no automatic error checking, errors were frequently propagated to the NT/SQL database. Obviously, Lincoln National was very anxious to find a scheme that would eliminate these problems and maintain the veracity of the client information, at all times, across all databases.

Blue Lobster Software and HDS came to Lincoln National's rescue. Developers at HDS created an application called Relationship Management System (RMS) that would enable the client databases on both the mainframe and the NT/SQL server to be updated simultaneously in real time. At the heart of RMS was Blue Lobster's Stingray Software Development Kit (SDK). The Stingray SDK is a general-purpose, 3270 emulation toolkit carefully designed to expedite the development of Java-based mainframe access solutions. It includes a Java-based 3270 emulator and session interaction recorder, a set of Java-based tn3270 classes, and JavaBeans for 3270 terminal emulation. The Java applets created with the Stingray SDK include a Stingray Runtime component that supports standard tn3270 connections to a tn3270(E) server. A trademark feature of Stingray is its ability to easily record the data flow on 3270 sessions and then automatically generate Java code that can emulate the transaction flow on these sessions. (This feature is commonly offered by user interface rejuvenation tools.) This capability was leveraged by HDS to create the RMS application.

The three-tier architecture of the RMS/Stingray solution used at Lincoln National is shown in Fig. 6.24. Client updates entered by account reps on their PCs are intercepted by RMS, which converts the updates into business objects that are sent to a Visigenic Object Request Broker (ORB). These objects are passed up to the RMS server component that resides on the NT server using the Internet Inter-ORB Protocol (IIOP). The RMS server applies the client updates to the SQL server and simultaneously sends them to the Stingray Runtime applet for transmission to the mainframe. A successful database update at the mainframe triggers CICS and FOCUS to send confirmation messages back to Stingray Runtime, per standard SNA conventions. Stingray Runtime relays the confirmations to the RMS server, which then commits the database updates to the NT/SQL server. This commit-based updating process ensures that the NT/SQL server database and the mainframe databases are always synchronized, as the NT/SQL commit occurs only when RMS knows that the update has been successfully performed at the mainframe.

This Stingray-centric example at Lincoln National gives a hint of what one could expect from programmatic access in the future. It is also worth noting that this application is just one of a multitude of ways that a Java-based 3270 emulation SDK, like Stingray, can be gainfully used to achieve

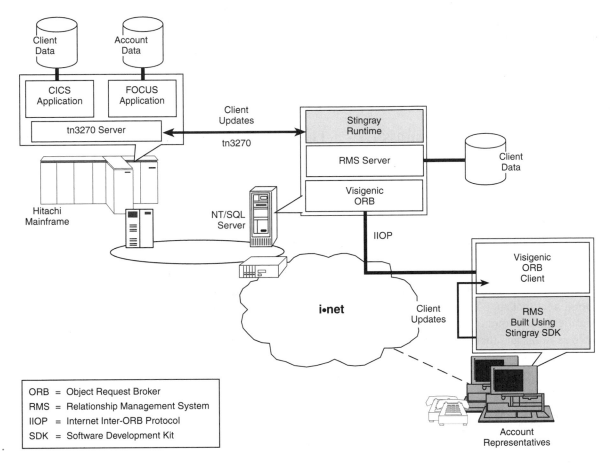

FIGURE 6.24   The architecture of the Blue Lobster Stingray-based solution being used by Lincoln National Reinsurance. (Source: Blue Lobster.)

effortless and transparent access to data center resources from within new client applications. The JavaBeans available with IBM's Host On-Demand version 3 and later offer another Java-based 3270-centric approach to programmatic access.

6.3.2   Host On-Demand JavaBeans

Host On-Demand is IBM's highly touted Java applet-based 3270 emulation solution. A hallmark feature of version 3, which became available in beta-test form in June 1998, was the inclusion of a set of JavaBeans. These JavaBeans essentially duplicate the session establishment, 3270 emulation, and keyboard support functions performed by the standard Host On-Demand applet. Using these JavaBeans, Java application developers can easily gain programmatic access to data center applications or data by incorporating the necessary beans within their new applications. The incorporation of these beans into new Java-oriented applications can be realized using visual drag-and-drop methodology, as is possible with development tools such as IBM's VisualAge for Java.

The following JavaBeans are available with Host On-Demand version 3.0:

The Host On-Demand JavaBeans clearly illustrate how today's applet-based emulation solutions will be extended over time to cater to the needs of programmatic access.

- **Session Bean**: Contains the logic for configuring, establishing, and querying the status of a tn3270(E)-based mainframe session. This bean will trigger events if changes occur that are related to the communication link, presentation space, or the status-line Operator Information Area (OIA). Figure 6.25 depicts how the various Host On-Demand Beans interact with each other, with the Session and the Screen Bean always remaining in the center of the action.

- **Screen Bean**: Provides the GUI functions for displaying the 3270 terminal presentation space. The screen bean works in conjunction with the session bean and waits for notification of presentation space, communication link, or OIA events from the session bean. It monitors and triggers events related to keyboard activity. It also contains the logic for cut-copy-paste functions via a Clipboard.

- **Terminal Bean**: A hardwired composite bean made up of the session and screen beans that provides all functions related to mainframe communications and presentation space management.

- **KeyPad Bean**: Contains the functions necessary to convey function key events to the session bean via the screen bean.

- **KeyRemap Bean**: Contains the functions required to map PC/workstation keystrokes to a SendKey event and data string.

- **FileTransfer Bean**: Embodies the logic for transferring a file between a mainframe and a PC or workstation and monitoring the progress of this file transfer.

- **Macro Bean**: Includes the functions for recording and playing back a single macro, where the macro comprises a script containing commands to be issued relative to a mainframe session.

- **MacroManager Bean**: Provides record, play, load, and delete functions to enable multiple macros to be defined and managed.

3270-centric approaches, such as these beans and Blue Lobster's Stingray SDK, lie at one end of the spectrum of programmatic access solutions. The other end of the spectrum includes heavy-duty, Web-oriented middleware solutions such as Bluestone's Sapphire/Web Application Server.

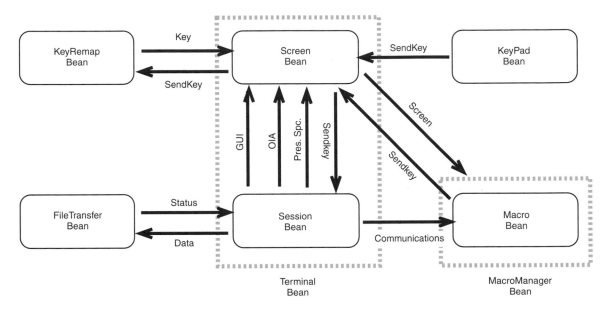

FIGURE 6.25   The IBM Host On-Demand JavaBeans. (Source: IBM.)

6.3.3   Bluestone's Sapphire/Web: An Example of a Web-Oriented Application Server

Sapphire/Web is a classic example of a Web-oriented application development platform—with strong back-end interfaces to data center resources—that will start to play an increasingly strategic role in programmatic access after Y2K efforts cease.

Bluestone's Sapphire/Web Application Server 5 offers an open, unconstrained architecture as well as a complete set of functional modules that correspond to building blocks of that architecture. The goal of the architecture and the associated building blocks is to provide developers with a solid platform, emphasizing industry standards, for expeditiously implementing, deploying, and integrating object-oriented, next-generation corporate applications. The architecture pays particular attention to issues related to system availability, load balancing, distributed database management (for example, two-phase commit), scalability, and manageability. OpenConnect Systems, a pioneer in applet-based host access with its OC://WebConnect product, is working with Bluestone to add transparent data center and asynchronous terminal access (for example, VT220, VT100, and VT52) support to the back end of Sapphire/Web.

The Sapphire/Web framework includes five components.

Sapphire/Universal Business Server (UBS)

The UBS is the cornerstone application deployment architecture around which all other elements of this platform are arrayed. In addition to the features mentioned earlier, UBS advocates the notion of applications that can run on any viable platform—whether a Web server, an NT server, a UNIX system, or even a mainframe. The architecture deals with the possibility of generating server-side business logic in either Java, C++, or C and with directly accessing databases using ODBC or Java Database Connectivity (JDBC). UBS also addresses the needs of state management and specifies how CORBA and IIOP can be used for object-based distributed computing across a client/server configuration. It includes a scheme, referred to as "optimal-weight client," to detect the type of browser being used by a user and the browser's level of support for Java and the amount of bandwidth available to that user (for example, for intranet or Internet access).

Sapphire/Developer

This rugged, feature-rich, highly visual, productivity-enhancing IDE supports the drag-and-drop application development methodology as well as wizards and templates to expedite application creation and Web page generation. In keeping with the UBS's precept of openness, this IDE enables developers to quickly integrate their favorite development tools into the IDE framework. Particular emphasis is given to ensuring that developers have the means to easily associate any type of contemporary GUI with back-end data resources. Other features offered by this very powerful development platform include the following:

- Source code control and integration with support for products such as Microsoft's Visual Source Safe
- Flexible and systematic merging and integration of application development components developed by autonomous project teams
- Automatic HTML- or Java-based GUI generation that relies on SQL objects and certain applications such as SAP or PeopleSoft
- Effortless integration with all popular Java GUI development packages, including Visual J++, Visual Café, VisualAge for Java, JavaWorkShop, and JBuilder.
- Total resource and object management for all non-Sapphire-generated files (such as GIF images and sound clips), including rules-based manipulation

Sapphire/Enterprise Development Kit

The EDK is a state-of-the-art, object and component integration facility that supports all major object paradigms, including CORBA, JavaBeans and Microsoft's COM (which is related to ActiveX). EDK can automatically detect objects that conform to any of these schemes and link them to the Web-oriented applications under development. Moreover, EDK gives developers the option of invoking an object dynamically or precompiling the object into the application.

Sapphire/Integration Modules

SIMs are prebuilt, data integration modules that extend the scope of Sapphire/ Developer and UBS by permitting new applications to transparently interact with existing data systems. At present SIMs are available for the following applications:

- Transaction systems such as CICS, MQ Series, Tuxedo, and Microsoft Transaction Server (MTS)
- SNA applications running on mainframes or AS/400s via OC://Web-Connect
- ERP applications such as SAP and PeopleSoft
- E-mail and directory access

Additional SIMs will become available in the future for security, electronic commerce, and data modeling. In addition, a SIM Builder is available to enable third-parties to develop other appropriate SIMs.

Sapphire/Application Manager

SAM is an agent-based control and management system for monitoring, controlling, and collating the status and performance of various Web infrastructure components. It can be easily integrated with popular management platforms, such as IBM's TME 10 NetView, Hewlett-Packard's OpenView, and Computer Associates' Unicenter. SAM allows corporations to determine, in real time, whether the i•net infrastructure meets the performance expectations envisaged for the network.

Bluestone's Sapphire/Web Application Server epitomizes what one expects in the future in terms of twenty-first-century development platforms that permit easy integration with data center resources. Sapphire/Web is not the only Web-oriented application development framework in today's red-hot Web software industry. Competing packages include NetDynamics 4.0, Netscape's Application Server 2.1, BEA WebLogic's Application Server 3.1, EveryWare Development's Tango Enterprise 3.0, Haht Software's HahtSite Application Server 3.1, and SilverStream Software's SilverStream Application Server 1.5. At present, Sapphire/Web happens to have more IBM-oriented capabilities. Other platforms will, indubitably, bolster their data-center-specific features in the near future as the IBM world begins moving toward new Web-oriented applications following the Y2K trials and tribulations.

6.4 THE LAST WORD

The adage, "old soldiers never die, they just fade away," could now be applied to the veteran SNA applications that have served the corporate world so well and for so long. With the plethora of compelling user interface rejuvenation options now available with browser-based access, especially AutoGUI schemes, the hallmark green-on-black façade of these SNA applications will be the first to fade away. By 2000, millions of users will be routinely interacting with SNA applications, primarily across the Internet, as if they were dealing with standard Web pages. These users will remain completely oblivious to the fact that they are dealing with mainframe applications that were probably developed when their parents were toddlers!

Extensive interface rejuvenation, including the consolidation of the functions performed by multiple 3270/5250 screens into a single page, is now possible with both 3270/5250-to-HTML conversion solutions and applet-based emulation schemes. The only real drawback is the lack of any standardization; all the various solutions advocate a different paradigm for realizing the interface reengineering process. In practice, this diversity is likely to represent less of an impediment than it first appears during the product evaluation process, as a corporation is unlikely to adopt more than two rejuvenation schemes. The need for two schemes will arise only if the enterprise needs one approach for 3270-to-HTML conversion applications geared mainly for Internet access and another method for applet-based emulation schemes for mission-critical intranet applications. The bottom line is that no excuses remain as to why the dated 3270/5250 user interface cannot now be easily and economically rejuvenated.

Application-specific Web-to-data center solutions tend to run the gamut between powerful general-purpose solutions and the "world is your oyster" possibilities offered by programmatic approaches. Understandably, programmatic solutions are now available for only a handful of the most widely installed SNA applications—in particular, CICS, IMS, DB2, and Oracle. The tightly integrated solutions, such as the CICS Web Interface, set out to streamline the effort involved in Web-enabling a mission-critical application. The major problem with application-specific solutions is that they are practical only if one or perhaps two SNA applications must be Web-enabled. Otherwise, the effort of implementing separate solutions for each application would be totally indefensible—in terms of both the initial implementation and ongoing maintenance.

Programmatic Web-to-data center access in the end, however, will be the final frontier when it comes to SNA access. New Web-oriented applications, developed using techniques such as JavaBeans on platforms such as Web/Sapphire, will finally relegate SNA applications to the background. There, these applications will act as behind-the-scenes data servers to the new applications. Like the Internet users who access SNA applications via a "Webified" user interface, corporate users dealing with the new applications will be oblivious to the presence of these SNA applications.

Most SNA shops will not pursue the development of new applications until they have successfully cleared all of their Y2K-related hurdles. By 2002, however, SNA applications, though they probably still have another five to six years of active productive life remaining, will start to fade away into the background, where their presence and continued contribution will be known and acknowledged only by a few data center specialists.

Network Infrastructure, Management, and New Mainframe Gateways

The bandwidth, security, and management requirements of SNA-capable i•nets are markedly different from those of SNA-only networks or even the bridge/router-based multiprotocol networks that have been widely used in the 1990s to transport SNA/APPN traffic. The perennial IBM 37xx Communications Controllers that were the cornerstone of SNA networking and the accepted means of attaching SNA networks to mainframes are no longer the optimal or obvious way to provide SNA-capable i•nets with mainframe connectivity.

Although the very-high-margin 37xxs remain dear to IBM's heart and can still positively influence the bottom line, IBM is nevertheless precipitating a major reevaluation of mainframe gateway options. The company is including an **Open Systems Adapter 2 (OSA-2)** as a built-in option with all of its strategic CMOS-based S/390 Parallel Enterprise Server mainframes. In addition, it is making the channel-attachable 2216 Model 400 Multiaccess Concentrator bridge/router extremely compelling by offering an extremely low-cost, highly scalable tn3270(E) server option. The OSA-2 adapter can support 155Mbps ATM, 100Mbps Fast Ethernet, 4/16Mbps Token Ring, 10Mbps Ethernet, and 100Mbps FDDI ports. At an all-inclusive price of $66,250 for the hardware and the software, the 2216-400 provides in excess of 15,000 tn3270(E) server sessions at a total cost of $4 per concurrent user. A new Gigabit Ethernet OSA will be available in mid-1999 that will support 2Gbps, full-duplex data transfers, and will be interfaced directly to the 333MBytes/sec (2.6Gbps) internal bus of the latest S/390 mainframes. Given the changes in bandwidth, security, and management needs, coupled with the new enticing mainframe gateway options, one really has no choice except to totally gut the existing networking infrastructure and reconstitute a new i•net-specific network to the data center, including a new strategy for connecting this network to the mainframe.

The composition, feel, and texture of an SNA-capable i•net will differ from that of an SNA-only network much like chalk differs from cheese. The same magnitude of disparity will apply to the security and management issues and concerns, with the new network requiring considerably more access control safeguards and most likely mainframe-based TCP/IP and SNA management in addition to a standard, "off-board" SNMP management system for monitoring and controlling the overall LAN/WAN infrastructure. The venerable IBM 37xxs FEPs, although still marginally viable, will not be the optimal choice for connecting the new networks to the mainframe, with IBM itself offering better solutions such as the 2216-400, OSA 2, and the new Gigabit Ethernet OSA.

The bandwidth demands of SNA-capable i•nets will inevitably exceed those of the networks they will be superseding. One primary reason for these greater demands will be a marked increase in the user population being served given that the new TCP/IP-centric network will, by definition, support much more than just SNA/APPN applications and users. In most instances, this network will also act as the corporate intranet and support Web- and TCP/IP-based applications, and possibly even voice and video traffic in the form of voice-over-IP and video-over-IP. Hence the volume and intensity of traffic on this network will be significantly greater than those on an SNA-only network. Furthermore, these demands will likely grow steadily for quite a few years as the scope, reach, and penetration of the intranet and its applications continue to increase. The new network will therefore require additional bandwidth to satisfactorily deal with the higher volume of traffic. If any extranet activity is associated with the new network, whether it be intranet-to-intranet or remote access over the Internet, the traffic volumes—and hence the bandwidth demands—will be even greater. Public access to any of the SNA, Web, or TCP/IP applications for e-commerce, home banking, home investing, online travel reservation, and other purposes will further increase traffic volumes, in most cases quite dramatically, on the Web servers and to and from the data center.

An increase in the user population and the applications accessed, although pivotal and most pronounced, are not the only factors contributing to the increased bandwidth demands of SNA-capable i•nets. The bandwidth requirements of SNA-capable i•nets will normally exceed those of an SNA-only or even a multiprotocol network even if the number of users supported by the new network is no greater than that supported by the older network. This situation could very well arise, at least initially, when a corporation transitions its in-house, corporate network from being a multiprotocol network with IPX/SPX, NetBIOS, DECnet, AppleTalk, and similar protocols to a TCP/IP-centric SNA-capable intranet.

Multiple reasons explain the need for additional bandwidth even when no great increase occurs in the user population. First, the delivery of the highly graphical Web pages used by the intranet applications, within acceptable response-time thresholds, will require quite a bit more LAN, campus, and WAN bandwidth than was required in the past to handle primarily textual display screens. The bandwidth demands will increase even more if the Web pages contain extensive animation, high-resolution photographic images, or video clip annotation.

Second, the 40-byte TCP/IP headers and Layer 2 headers that will now prefix most of the message units transmitted across the network will invariably be longer than those used in the past by other protocols, such as Source Route Bridging, Transparent Bridging, and RFC 1490/FRF.3, for multiprotocol networking. This increase in header lengths, which will increase as much as 50% with the introduction of IPv6, adds up over the course of a day when tens of thousands or even hundreds of thousands of message units are sent over the network. To eliminate any degradation in response times due to the additional traffic caused by this header overhead, one has few options except to increase overall network bandwidth. Widespread use of TCP/IP-based encapsulation schemes such as DLSw or even ip3270 will further tax bandwidth as these encapsulation schemes introduce their own headers (for example, the 16-byte header used by DLSw). HPR-over-IP, which uses UDP rather than TCP as its Layer 4 transport protocol (as discussed in Chapter 2), benefits marginally from the fact that UDP's 8-byte header is 12 bytes shorter than TCP's header. The HPR headers—in particular, the Network Layer Header, will nevertheless eliminate this small, initial advantage.

Third, many internal, housekeeping-related protocols used within TCP/IP networks—for example, routing table updates and "keep alive" messages—increase the overall volume of traffic within the network and often necessitate the incremental addition of bandwidth to guarantee that the response times of production-use mission-critical applications are not impacted. The need for additional bandwidth to compensate for ongoing, dynamic, housekeeping protocols may seem an alien notion to network professionals who grew up with SNA networking. The essentially static configurations in subarea SNA networks minimize the need for elaborate network upkeep-related protocols. The Transmission Group Sweep protocol that occurs each time 4095 message units are sent across a multilink transmission group comes to mind as the exception that proves the rule.

The additional bandwidth that may be required to successfully implement an SNA-capable i•net should not be viewed as detrimental or undesirable. An SNA-capable i•net, even if one discounts its strategic importance relative to issues such as e-commerce, will do more and, in the long term, support more users. The additional bandwidth is therefore justifiable. In some instances, an SNA-capable i•net might even reduce overall networking costs by gracefully consolidating and rationalizing what were disparate networks, such as SNA, multiprotocol, remote access, and even voice, each with its own set of bandwidth, operational, and management costs.

An important factor that should be taken into account is that bandwidth, although unlikely to ever be totally free, will become more cost-effective, efficient, and prevalent. The ability to profitably use the burgeoning Internet, whose backbone is being systematically revamped with digital, broadband bandwidth, with impunity for in-house corporate applications through browser-based access or Virtual Private Networks (VPNs) provides a virtually free source of hitherto unavailable bandwidth. Concerns about the need for extra bandwidth therefore will not prevent corporations from standardizing on SNA-capable i•nets as their single, strategic multipurpose, multimedia (that is, voice, video, and data) network for the twenty-first century. The only real challenge lies in obtaining the required and optimal bandwidth as efficiently and cost-effectively as possible.

7.1   SATISFYING THE BANDWIDTH DEMANDS OF SNA-CAPABLE I•NETS

The increased bandwidth that most likely will be required to successfully implement an SNA-capable i•net should be neither a deterrent nor an excuse to procrastinate, as increasingly cost-effective bandwidth is readily available for all aspects of the new network.

When transitioning to an SNA-capable i•net from an SNA-only or multi-protocol network, one needs to diligently evaluate the bandwidth demands, vis-à-vis performance expectations, on a global end-to-end basis. This assessment must always factor in the additional traffic volumes due to new users, new applications, TCP/IP headers, housekeeping protocols, and so on. Consequently, bandwidth requirements need to be checked at the following levels:

- LAN and desktop campus backbone
- WAN
- Mainframe gateway

In parallel, one needs to check the throughput, capacity, and scalability of the following components:

- Routers or switches used to realize the WAN backbone
- Bridges or LAN switches used at the LAN level
- Web servers
- Firewalls
- tn3270(E) servers
- SNA-Web gateways used in conjunction with browser-based access for 3270-to-HTML conversion or applet augmentation
- VPN routers or switches, if VPN will be used

Given the many levels and components involved, it is best to analyze bandwidth requirements at the LAN, campus, WAN, and data center levels. The remainder of this chapter will be structured along these lines. Prior to doing so, however, it is wise to identify three major bandwidth-related mega-trends in the IBM world:

- The gradual but certain demise of Token Ring
- The rampant popularity of Fast Ethernet, including IBM's now whole-hearted backing of this LAN methodology as well as Gigabit Ethernet
- The paring down of ATM's role to only embrace campus and some wide area networking

The cataclysmic disintegration of the supposed importance of ATM as the ultimate panacea for end-to-end, desktop-to-data center bandwidth had been aggressively advocated by IBM in the 1993 to 1996 period along with its 25Mbps ATM initiatives, its much vaunted 2220 Nways BroadBand Switches, and the much hyped Networking BroadBand Services (NBBS) architecture that was labeled the "SNA for ATM networks." Although ATM remains a strategic means of realizing highly scalable, multimedia-capable bandwidth at the campus and WAN levels, it is no longer seen as the be-all-and-end-all when it comes to networking "fabrics." ATM to the desktop, although viable, is rarely mentioned as a strategic option either.

With its beloved 25Mbps ATM initiatives, IBM for much of the mid-1990s ardently believed and furthermore led the world to believe, that Token Ring would eventually be superseded by ATM. Well, this is certainly not going to be the case. In fact, the 16 million-plus installed base of Token Ring end stations (as of the end of 1997) is now shrinking. Its loss does not mean a gain to ATM, but rather to Ethernet and especially 100Mbps Fast Ethernet. Although IBM and others such as Olicom and Madge belatedly developed the 100Mbps **High-Speed Token Ring (HSTR)** standard and NIC adapter cards in mid-1997 to 1998, the momentum and mind share had begun to erode. HSTR has some very attractive technical strengths vis-à-vis Fast Ethernet, such as its much larger block size. Nonetheless, most corporations when wiring new buildings or procuring new equipment inexorably opt for Ethernet or Fast Ethernet given these factors; lower costs—and the fact that no real technical impediments exist to supporting SNA over Ethernet, especially with desktops transitioning to ip3270, tn3270(E), or browser-based TCP/IP clients.

7.2 OPTIONS FOR LAN BANDWIDTH

Since their advent in 1986, Token Ring LANs have gone hand-in-hand with SNA networking. With a very few exceptions brought about by highly enlightened networking cognoscenti who appreciated the innate robustness and scalability of Token Ring LANs compared with Ethernet, Token Ring was adopted only by IBM, and therefore SNA, shops. Even at the start of 1998, despite a marked swing toward Ethernet, one would not have been wrong in claiming that most SNA desktops were based on the Token Ring architecture. This situation will change dramatically over the next few years, however, as most of these desktops transition to TCP/IP-based clients for SNA access.

With the demise of SNA at the desktop, Token Ring will lose its loyal constituent base and what was in effect its preordained raison d'être. Given its relatively high cost compared with Fast Ethernet, most people no longer see a credible justification for Token Ring in the long term despite its indubitable technical superiority (for example, its much larger, performance-enhancing block size) over Fast Ethernet. By mid-1998, the erosion of the Token Ring installed base was small but noticeable. The pivotal issue was that most decision makers had already made up their minds to move away from Token Ring and toward the readily available and ludicrously low-priced 10/100Mbps Ethernet/Fast Ethernet networking solutions. Thus, like SNA networking in general, Token Ring networking appears to be in an "end-game" mode—albeit with a rather gradual rate of erosion expected to span quite a few years. Despite a sizable installed base that will linger for a few years to come, one now has no choice except to make LAN decisions related to SNA-capable i•nets by assuming that Token Ring is no longer strategic.

Token Ring, although declining in popularity, continues to deliver remarkably good performance to its users, even without the aid of switching or 100Mbps High-Speed Token Ring, thanks to its original, well-conceived architecture.

A very good reason exists as to why the decline in the Token Ring installed base, although inevitable, will be graceful and prolonged. Even in mid-1998, most Token Ring LANs were not saturated and were delivering more than acceptable performance to their users. In general, Token Ring users have fared remarkably well in terms of overall LAN performance and bandwidth availability—particularly so in the case of 16Mbps LANs. As a result, Token Ring LANs will remain a dominant LAN technology within SNA-capable i•nets at least until around 2003.

Four key reasons explain why Token Ring users have continued to prosper long after Ethernet users were forced to resort to Ethernet switching or Fast Ethernet to overcome their bandwidth-related performance woes.

First, the intrinsic token-capture scheme used by Token Ring networking to arbitrate access to the physical LAN media ensures controlled, deterministic, and above all equitable use of the LAN bandwidth. This token-capture scheme is, in essence, a polling mechanism analogous to that used by BSC or SDLC. It ensures that, in marked contrast to Ethernet, the performance of Token Ring LANs remains consistent and crisp even when traffic levels begin to exceed 75% of capacity.

In contrast, the contention-oriented CSMA/CD access used by Ethernet (and Fast Ethernet) results in tangible degradation in performance as traffic levels approach 50% of capacity. This performance degradation ensues because of an increase in the rate of collisions as more and more users try to gain access to the LAN at the same time. Each collision not only invalidates the data on the LAN, but also forces the devices involved in the collision to back off from trying to access the LAN for a predesignated period of time. The data lost due to collisions, as well as the mandatory penalty of having to back off after each collision, results in frequent blackout periods when no productive data transfers take place across the Ethernet network. The accumulation of these blackout periods as the rate of collisions increases, which is proportional to the number of users on the LAN and the amount of traffic that they are trying to exchange, noticeably degrades the performance of Ethernet LANs as usage increases. In contrast, the controlled, deterministic aspect of Token Ring networks precludes both data loss due to collisions and back-off penalties.

Second, both Ethernet and Fast Ethernet do not permit any frames (or "blocks") that are longer than 1518 bytes. In contrast, Token Ring supports frame sizes as much as 18,000 bytes in length, with 4000-byte frames commonly used since around 1994. Ethernet's anachronistically meager frame size dictates that only around 1500 bytes of data can be sent per Ethernet, or Fast Ethernet, frame. Although this limitation is not a major drawback for the typical SNA traffic, which is usually in the range of 1000 bytes from the mainframe and 150 bytes into the mainframe, it represents a major "speed bump" for most other traffic types—in particular, file transfers and Web page displays. With Ethernet/Fast Ethernet, any data block that is longer than 1500 bytes must be broken into multiple 1500-byte frames; each of these frames then has to be separately transmitted with at least the mandatory interframe gap (9.6 μs in Ethernet) between each frame.

Moreover, under the CSMA/CD access scheme, the transmitting station must compete for LAN media access to transmit each frame—with the very real potential of collisions and subsequent back-off penalties at each attempt, especially on a busy LAN. Segmenting the data block into multiple frames, each with its own Ethernet header and trailer (for example, Frame Check Sequence) also increases the overall volume of bits sent across the LAN. Figure 7.1 illustrates the effect of additional traffic volume and interframe gaps when a large data block must be segmented into multiple 1518-byte-long frames. The 1500-byte block size of Ethernet and Fast Ethernet is thus a major and well-recognized impediment to overall LAN performance.

Third, a 16Mbps Token Ring network has at least 2 to 3Mbps more usable bandwidth than a 10Mbps Ethernet. The actual difference between these two schemes is not 6Mbps, however, because protocol- and interframe-gap-related "overhead" reduces the amount of real bandwidth available on the LAN for end-user data transfer.

Fourth, SNA has tended to be the major form of traffic on Token Ring LANs. SNA traffic—in particular, the traffic related to real-time, interactive, transaction processing that typically represents the lion's share of SNA usage—tends to consist of relatively short message units, with rates of 1000 bytes from the mainframe and 150 bytes into the mainframe being well-accepted rules of thumb. The relative brevity of these transaction-processing-related message units means that a single SNA user is unlikely to monopolize the Token Ring network for any significant period of time. Consequently, multiple users can routinely gain equitable and rapid access to the LAN without undue delay. The overall architecture, chip-set design, and integrated "control" mechanisms (for example, the "Address and Copy" bits included in

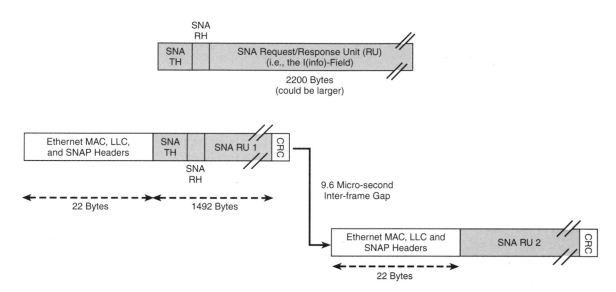

FIGURE 7.1   The 1518-byte Maximum Transmission Unit (MTU) size of Ethernet adds additional traffic in the form of headers and interframe delays when transmitting large blocks of data.

the frame that indicate to the transmitting station, when the frame returns from its journey around the ring and is ready to be removed from the LAN, whether the intended destination was found and whether the frame was copied by the destination) of Token Ring LANs ensure that they are usually more rugged, resilient, and less prone to errors than their Ethernet counterparts. The low incidence of corrupted and spurious frames maximizes the usable bandwidth on the LAN.

In the event that more performance is required on a Token Ring LAN, one can pursue the readily available option of cost-effective, third-generation Token Ring switching. This option can take the form of sub-$250 per port desktop Token Ring switches from Cisco and Olicom that support cut-through mode switching and 32Mbps full-duplex mode operation. LAN switching—whether Ethernet, Fast Ethernet, or Token Ring—is a compelling and highly economical means of enhancing the bandwidth of existing LANs with minimal disruption and little risk. Although the performance improvements possible with LAN switching in general can sometimes be spectacular, Layer 2 LAN switching, irrespective of the LAN type, is really not a very complex technology. In essence, LAN switching takes advantage of two basic premises: dedicated bandwidth to individual users and very fast port-to-port forwarding of frames ideally using cut-through mode, where the forwarding begins as soon as the address of the destination port is determined.

7.2.1   LAN Switching—A Short Tutorial

Token Ring switching leverages the throughput of existing Token Ring NICs to ensure that Token Ring users, in most instances, have adequate bandwidth for Internet access, intranet applications, and emerging multimedia applications such as desktop video-conferencing, voice-over-IP, and real-time news feeds. Token Ring switching profitably extends the productive life of existing Token Ring NICs and maximizes the existing investment in Token Ring, whether it be NIC adapters, wiring, operational procedures, redundant path configurations, or mainframe interfaces. Token Ring switching in particular, but LAN switching in general, can be profitably exploited to realize high-throughput, highly scalable, end-to-end switching solutions that encompass desktop-to-server, desktop-to-mainframe, desktop-to-Internet, or desktop-to-desktop connections.

LAN switching, the nearest thing to a "free lunch" in this industry given its capability of dramatically increasing overall performance at a very low cost and with near-zero disruption, is now an established commodity in the Ethernet world. Third-generation Token Ring switches, which are vastly different from the first-generation switches, offer total functionality, exceptional performance, and sub-$250 per port costs.

Today's hub-based Token Ring LANs do not provide users or even the attached LAN servers and hosts with 4 or 16Mbps of continuous bandwidth. Although seldom recognized as such, conventional hub-based LANs—whether Ethernet, Fast Ethernet, Token Ring, or FDDI—are by design shared-bandwidth transmission schemes. A given LAN station has use of the bandwidth offered by that LAN only when it manages to gain access to the LAN media so as to transmit a message frame. All LAN types provide an arbitration mechanism whereby LAN stations can, in effect, bid to gain access to the LAN bandwidth.

This lack of continuous bandwidth is the root cause of poor LAN performance and unacceptable LAN server access delays. LAN switching in general eradicates this bandwidth deprivation to individual LAN users. With LAN switching, all LAN-attached devices—whether PCs, workstations, LAN servers, FEPs, or mainframes—have continuous, zero-wait-time access to productive bandwidth. Moreover, LAN switching ensures that all LAN servers and hosts can even work continuously in full-duplex mode, which delivers 32Mbps in the case of 16Mbps Token Ring and 200Mbps in the case of Fast Ethernet.

As a rule, LAN switching is not contingent on the use of any special NICs or wiring. LAN switching can provide tangible performance gain through the provision of dedicated bandwidth to individual devices by using existing NICs and LAN wiring. The only exception would arise with full-duplex mode operation. Some Token Ring NICs (in particular, the IBM NIC sold since 1996) are capable of full-duplex operation; others are not. If full-duplex mode operation is required, you must have a full-duplex-capable NIC. Otherwise, all you need to enjoy the performance gains of LAN switching is a solid, proven switch from a recognized vendor.

In Token Ring LANs, access to the LAN media is governed by a LAN station's ability to capture the token that circulates around the ring. A PC, workstation, or LAN server with a 16Mbps NIC, on a conventional Token Ring with other devices with 16Mbps NICs, does not have at its disposal a constant and dedicated bandwidth of 16Mbps. Instead, it has that 16Mbps bandwidth for only certain—relatively short—durations of time. At other times, it has zero bandwidth and must wait until it can capture the token again to transmit data.

This bandwidth constriction becomes further exacerbated if a hub-based Token Ring LAN has some devices with 16Mbps NICs and others with 4Mbps NICs. Such a LAN cannot run at 16Mbps. Instead, hub-based, shared-bandwidth Token Ring LANs with both 4Mbps and 16Mbps devices must run at 4Mbps so that the 4Mbps NICs can read the bits flowing on the LAN. A single "rogue" 4Mbps device on an otherwise all-16Mbps, hub-based Token Ring network will cause the entire LAN to run at one-fourth of its potential capacity. With PCs being continually added to or moved between LANs, it is not difficult to inadvertently connect PCs with 4Mbps NICs to what was a 16Mbps LAN. In some situations, the network administrator may not even realize that sluggish LAN performance is due to the presence of one or two rogue 4Mbps PCs, and may blame increased traffic for LAN congestion and delays.

The bandwidth limitations of hub-based, shared-bandwidth Token Ring LANs increase as the LANs expand. As the number of stations on a LAN grows, each station must wait for longer periods before it can gain access to the media and thus to bandwidth. This sporadic access to bandwidth translates into palpable delays, poor throughput, loss of productivity, and frustrated users.

Dedicated Bandwidth Over Dedicated Media

With LAN switching, each LAN-attached device gets dedicated bandwidth that is equivalent to the speed of its NIC—that is, 4 or 16Mbps in the case of Token Ring, and 100Mbps in the case of Fast Ethernet. If multiple devices are connected to a single port on a switch via a LAN segment, each device obviously cannot enjoy dedicated bandwidth. Nonetheless, the devices on that LAN segment will be able to share the total bandwidth available at the switched port—say 16Mbps—rather than having to compete for bandwidth with all devices attached to the switch. This type of configuration, in which LAN segments with multiple devices are attached to a LAN switch, is referred to as LAN segmenting or microsegmenting, because the presence of the switch divides a larger, shared-bandwidth LAN into multiple, smaller units, each with its own allocation of usable bandwidth. Figure 7.2 depicts the notion of Token Ring segmenting using a Token Ring switch.

Token Ring LAN segmentation using a Token Ring switch can also improve overall LAN performance by segregating the PCs or devices with

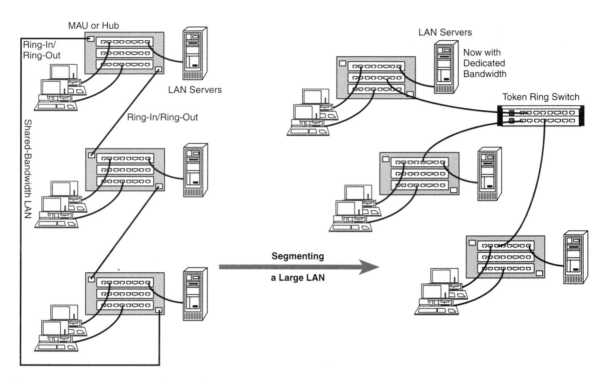

FIGURE 7.2   Segmenting a large Token Ring LAN using a Token Ring switch.

4Mbps NICs from those with 16Mbps NICs. The PCs and devices with 16Mbps can therefore work at the 16Mbps rate without being slowed down to 4Mbps by the PCs and devices with the slower-speed NICs. Highly affordable third-generation Token Ring switches make it very easy and cost-effective to microsegment large LANs (for example, those with more than 60 PCs or devices) so as to dramatically increase the performance experienced by individual LAN users. This microsegmentation could be achieved in two ways: by dividing the original LAN into smaller, shared-bandwidth (hub-centered) segments that are interconnected via a Token Ring switch (as shown in Fig. 7.2) or by directly connecting all of the PCs and devices to switching ports (as shown in Fig. 7.3).

Today, it is no longer necessary or justifiable to share LAN bandwidth. Bandwidth sharing was predicated on the fact that early LAN technology was originally based around shared LAN media—unpowered, "dumb" concentrators in the case of Token Ring. The use of shared LAN media had already become passé by the late 1980s. Hubs that support "hub-and-spoke" star-wiring schemes have now been the standard means for implementing Token Ring and other LANs for several years. With hub-based, star-wired

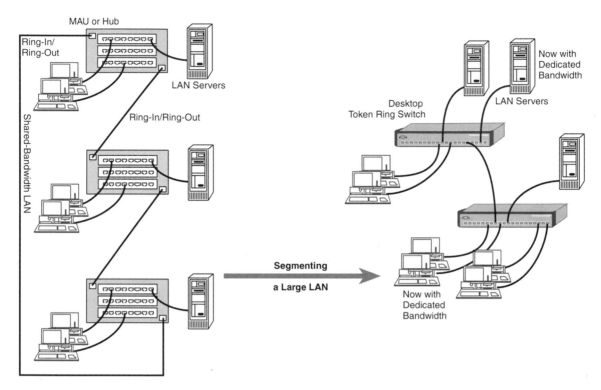

FIGURE 7.3   Providing dedicated bandwidth to all PCs and servers using the new, low-cost Desktop Token Ring switches.

LANs, each LAN station has dedicated LAN media (for example, UTP/STP wiring) between itself and individual ports on the intelligent hub. LAN switching relies on this ready availability of dedicated LAN media.

With LAN switching, each LAN device directly attached to a port on a switch does not have to contend with other devices to access the LAN media. Instead, it must simply make sure that the switch port is not trying to send it a frame, as only two stations reside on that micro-LAN—the switch port and the actual LAN device. When a LAN station has data to transmit, it can proceed to do so at once without any delay—in the case of Token Ring switching, without waiting to capture the token. The effect of having this dedicated LAN bandwidth would be very apparent, for example, if a large file transfer—say of a 10MB file—is conducted between two PCs. Provided that no traffic was attempting to reach these two PCs from other ports, the file transfer would take place at more or less "line-speed" bandwidth, with no delays caused by having to wait to capture the token after the transmission of each frame.

With LAN switching, frames received at one port are dynamically forwarded to the relevant destination port based on the destination MAC address. The forwarding of frames from the input port to the destination port may be performed in Token Ring environments either in on-the-fly, cut-through mode or once the entire frame has been assembled and error-checked in store-and-forward mode.

The switch maintains a directory with entries specifying which port number serves either a particular destination MAC address or a set of destination MAC addresses so as to expeditiously perform the port-to-port forwarding of frames. LAN switches provide adequate buffering for frames that cannot be immediately delivered to the destination port. Such delays in delivery would occur if the destination port is already involved in a data transfer operation (that is, if it is "busy"). This case might arise when two PCs simultaneously attempt to send data to the same LAN server.

Cut-Through versus Store-and-Forward

Cut-through mode is a key performance-enhancing feature of LAN switching. In cut-through mode, the switch starts to forward bits that make up a frame from the source port to the destination port as soon as it reads the destination MAC address that appears close to the start of the frame and determines the required output port. With this on-the-fly bit forwarding from source to destination port, all bits making up a complete frame will pass through the destination port shortly after the final bit was received at the source port. The only delay (the so-called latency) encountered in forwarding the complete frame from source to destination is the time taken to determine the output port and the processing time to move bits from one port to the other across the switch. With cut-through mode, the total latency through the Token Ring switch for a given frame would be in the range of 25 to 40 microseconds.

The alternative to cut-through mode is store-and-forward mode. With this mode, the switch waits until it receives a complete frame—free of errors as denoted by the Frame Check Sequence (FCS) near the end of the frame—before it forwards that frame over the output port. Store-and-forward, understandably, has a higher latency than cut-through, because the first bit of the frame being switched does not hit the output port until the entire frame has been assembled and checked. Consequently, the latency through the switch for a given packet in store-and-forward mode could approximate 100 microseconds.

The higher latency associated with store-and-forward does not, however, mean that cut-through is always the optimal scheme for packet switching. For a start, cut-through carries a danger that erroneous frames may be forwarded—thereby wasting bandwidth on the output port and LAN and possibly delaying the forwarding of other, error-free packets to the destination port. The throughput gains possible with cut-through also depend on congestion and the nature of the traffic. If the output port required to forward a packet is busy either receiving or forwarding another packet, cut-through mode cannot work—and the switch essentially reverts to store-and-forward.

Full-Duplex Mode Operation

32Mbps full-duplex—or dedicated Token Ring (DTR)—mode operation is another vital throughput-enhancing capability of Token Ring switching. Full-duplex Token Ring operation is a natural extension to the dedicated bandwidth-over-dedicated media notion promulgated by Token Ring switches. With dedicated media, the need for arbitrating access to the media, as discussed earlier, is essentially eliminated because only two stations reside on the LAN—the switch port and the actual LAN device.

With dedicated media, it would be possible for a given LAN station—albeit with a full-duplex-capable NIC—to concurrently send and receive frames to and from the Token Ring switch independent of the data transmission status of the other stations attached to the switch. This concept is the basis for full-duplex Token Ring operation. Figure 7.4 illustrates the concept of full-duplex operation à la Token Ring. This mode of operation, however, is contingent on the presence of a switch. Full-duplex operation is not possible with hub-based LANs, even if servers have full-duplex-capable NICs, because the fundamental precept of full-duplex mode operation is dedicated bandwidth across dedicated media. Hubs are incapable of delivering dedicated bandwidth and, by definition, function only in shared-bandwidth mode.

With a full-duplex adapter, a LAN server could simultaneously transmit a file to one PC at 16Mbps and accept a file from another PC also at 16Mbps. Full-duplex operation does not require any changes to existing Token Ring applications. Contemporary LAN server software (for example, Windows NT, NetWare, UNIX, and OS/2 Warp) is designed to operate in full-duplex mode in conjunction with an appropriate NIC and a function-enabling switch. The delays associated with accessing a LAN server could be dramatically reduced if the LAN server could transmit data to one station while concurrently receiving data from another station. This increased performance is exactly what full-duplex mode operation delivers. With full-duplex, LAN servers can operate at their full capacity and minimize LAN access delays. Thus full-duplex mode operation offers an inexpensive, zero-risk, and high-return means of turbocharging LAN server throughput.

Full-duplex mode operation is also a very cost-effective means for realizing additional campus bandwidth, as discussed in Section 7.3. In some cases, multiple full-duplex Token Ring NICs, each attached to a separate port on a switch, might be installed on the same LAN server. Such a configuration will

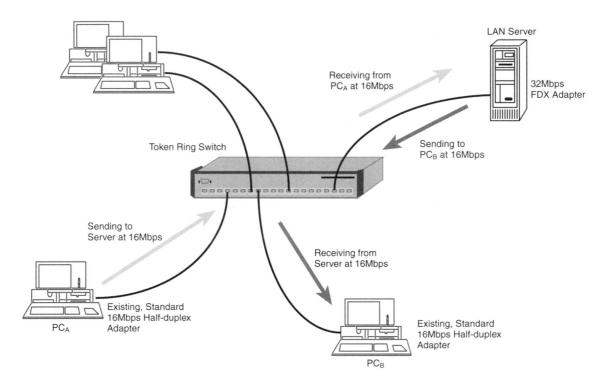

FIGURE 7.4 Full-Duplex LAN server operation in a Token Ring environment with a Token Ring switch.

permit concurrent access to the LAN server by multiple users, further minimizing LAN server access delays and boosting overall response times.

Over the past few years, following the advent of Token Ring switching, the only justification for using shared bandwidth hubs has been their comparatively low price per port compared with switches. First-generation Token Ring switches, with their $750-plus per-port costs, were understandably cost-justifiable only for backbone interconnect applications and occasionally for microsegmenting large LANs. Third-generation Token Ring switches, however, have changed all of the cost points and market dynamics.

Although the per-port price of a Token Ring switch remains higher than that of a typical Fast Ethernet switch, Token Ring switching nonetheless represents a very affordable and attractive option. In addition, third-generation Token Ring switches provides built-in bridging functionality (for example, Source Route Bridging), VLANs (virtual LANs), RMON (remote monitoring), and traffic filtering (for example, filtering out spurious broadcasts). RMON on top of standard SNMP management provides detailed ongoing and historic data on the workings of the Token Ring environment, including individual ports on the Token Ring switch. The VLAN capability available on Token Ring switches minimizes the spread of broadcast traffic, accelerates source-to-destination connection establishment, curtails overall LAN congestion, and improves data security.

Hubs are now passé in the Ethernet world. Low-cost Ethernet switches, including desktop Ethernet switches, made that happen. New Ethernet and Fast Ethernet networks are invariably implemented around switches, including desktop switches.

Source Route Bridging, Transparent Switching, and Other LAN Switching Technologies

With third-generation Token Ring switches supporting all possible Token Ring bridging modes (for example, transparent switching, Source Route Bridging, Source Route Switching), one can use different bridging modes in different parts of the network to maximize performance and minimize complexity. Source Route Bridging (SRB) is not typically required for desktop Token Ring switching per se, or for that matter when a large LAN is microsegmented. Instead, transparent switching can be used in these applications.

In practice, SRB is a requirement only when one must deal with multiple Token Ring ring numbers. Thus SRB is needed for "dual TIC" host attachment configurations, where the same (locally administered) MAC address, on different ring numbers, is used to identify the host interface because it is not permitted to have duplicate MAC addresses on the same ring. Figure 7.5 illustrates a "dual TIC" high-availability mainframe access configuration. SRB is also required if network management practices or procedures rely on users identifying their LAN in terms of a Token Ring ring number.

SRB is not mandatory for Token Ring switching, as was clearly highlighted by IBM when its first entry into Token Ring switching, the star-crossed IBM 8272 Token Ring switch, did not support SRB for nearly the first two years of its existence. Transparent switching invariably delivers better performance and simplifies administration and management. The entries in a Token Ring switch's directory are typically created dynamically. Token Ring switches use a MAC address "learning process" identical to that employed by the transparent bridges used in Ethernet environments. With this learning process, the switch reads and notes the source MAC addresses of frames it receives on each port. It then uses this information to dynamically create and update directory entries. When trying to forward a frame received on one port to its intended destination, the switch can check its directory to see whether it contains an entry corresponding to the destination address. If the

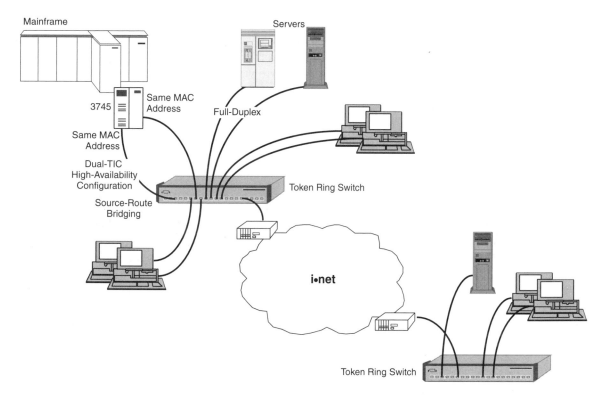

FIGURE 7.5 High-availability, 3745 "dual TIC" configuration using the Source Route Bridging capability of a Token Ring switch.

destination address had been previously learned when the switch encountered a frame with that address as its source address, the directory entry will specify the necessary port number.

If the destination address for a frame to be forwarded does not appear in the directory, the switch will automatically forward that frame to all potential destination ports on the switch. This process of propagating frames whose destination ports have yet to be determined to all potential destination ports is sometimes referred to as "flooding the ports". It is, in effect, an "all routes" broadcast search, which is really no different than what SRB does when it encounters an unknown destination address.

The flooding process ensures that the frame has the maximum possibility of reaching its destination. When the frame eventually reaches its destination, the recipient will issue a response. That response will have the sender's MAC address as the source address. Upon learning this new source address, the switch will create a directory entry for it. The next time this address appears as a destination address, it will be unnecessary to flood the ports. This continual learning process, with its built-in directory update mechanism, ensures that a switch has to do a broadcast search only the very first time it encounters an unknown address, as opposed to traditional SRB, which does not cache the routes learned.

The port flooding search process described above is referred to as transparent switching or transparent bridging, as it matches that performed by a transparent bridge. It tends to be the preferred (and default) mechanism for locating unknown destination addresses in Token Ring switching environments. This approach has the indubitable virtue of being a simple, intuitive, and proven scheme that will work in any networking scenario.

Transparent switching in Token Ring switches works totally independently of SRB. It does not need to know anything about SRB. For its part, SRB relies on a field within the MAC header known as the Routing Information Field (RIF) to maintain a description of the route taken by a particular Token Ring frame. During an SRB broadcast search, each bridge will update the RIF field of a frame before forwarding it. The update will denote the bridge and LAN segment that the frame has just traversed. When a frame eventually reaches its intended destination during such a search, its RIF will contain a complete audit trail of every LAN segment and bridge that it traversed to get there.

The recipient of the search frame will return a positive acknowledgment to that frame to indicate its safe delivery. This acknowledgment reflects the RIF that appeared in the search frame. From then on, all frames flowing in both directions between the original sender of the search frame and its recipient will include this RIF. Source route bridges, on receiving a frame with a "non search" RIF, will read the RIF to determine to which destination port they should forward that frame. SRB is required in Token Ring switching environments only if network managers wish to use the notion of ring numbers for network management or if redundant paths are required for high-availability networking.

Transparent switching remains unaware of RIFs. When trying to locate an unknown destination, transparent switching does not examine, update, or create a RIF, or any entries within a RIF. Although a transparent switching-based Token Ring environment does not necessarily have to have ring numbers, this setup could disrupt existing network management procedures and disorient users and administrators. Not using SRB also precludes redundant (or alternate) paths from being available within the network and eliminates the possibility of using duplicate MAC addresses on separate LAN segments. Both of these features are often used in IBM SNA environments to realize a degree of alternate routing. Networks that rely on ring numbers for network management purposes or have a need for redundant paths should opt for using Token Ring switches with SRB activated.

The Last Word on Token Ring Switching

LAN switching is an ideal, undisruptive, and low-cost approach for significantly maximizing LAN bandwidth, turbocharging LAN server throughput, noticeably accelerating LAN transactions, reducing overall LAN congestion, and improving manageability. Thanks to its performance-boosting and delay-minimizing capabilities, LAN switching can improve user productivity and maximize transaction processing volumes. Moreover, it works with existing NIC adapters and wiring and does not require an overhaul of the overall LAN infrastructure.

The first-generation Token Ring switches that appeared on the market in 1995 lacked functionality (such as cut-through mode, support for all forwarding modes, and full-duplex operation), were not especially fast, and were expensive. By early 1998, things were very different: third-generation switches offered total functionality, without exception or compromise, ASIC-powered near-wire-speed frame forwarding, 100Mbps or ATM uplinks, and affordability. Nonetheless, Token Ring switching has not been as widely exploited as one would expect. Most are not even aware of the existence of third-generation switches and have prematurely dismissed the possibilities of Token Ring switching as a means of extending their investment in Token Ring because of the poor performance of the early switches. In much the same manner as happened with SNA/APPN, a very loyal installed base has been enticed away by lower-cost, open, non-IBM technology—in this case, Fast Ethernet and Gigabit Ethernet.

7.2.2   The Bottom Line on LAN Bandwidth and SNA-Capable i•nets

Token Ring, by default, will prevail as the prevalent LAN scheme of SNA-capable i•nets into the early years of the twenty-first century. Mixed Token Ring and Ethernet/Fast Ethernet environments will become the norm, with corporations opting for Ethernet/Fast Ethernet when procuring new PCs and workstations or when installing or upgrading wiring closet equipment. Where necessary, translational bridging, or translational switching, will be used to achieve Token Ring to Ethernet/Fast Ethernet interworking. This interworking within mixed environments will become even easier as more SNA-related traffic relies on TCP/IP through protocols such as DLSw, tn3270(E), and ip3270, because the Layer 3 routing of IP automatically and adroitly handles the necessary media translations.

Although now available, 100Mbps HSTR is not a serious long-term contender, even though its 18,000-byte maximum block size guarantees that it will invariably outperform Fast Ethernet in i•net environments given that the minimum size of an average Web page tends to exceed 1500 bytes. The same is true of FDDI, or more germanely CDDI, vis-à-vis Fast Ethernet; FDDI/CDDI offers the added bonus of built-in ruggedness and redundancy. Nonetheless, Fast Ethernet outshines both HSTR and FDDI/CDDI in terms of cost, widespread use, and most importantly mind share given that vendors (including IBM of late) and the media have been incessant in their endorsement and praise of Fast Ethernet.

HSTR NICs, which are at least two to three times more costly than 10/100 Fast Ethernet NICs, are not being promoted as a means of providing 100Mbps bandwidth to the desktop. Instead, they are targeted at LAN servers. Even here, however, HSTR runs into competition from 155Mbps ATM—particularly given that most popular switching hubs (for example, IBMs 8260) and Token Ring switches now readily support ATM uplinks. Most corporations will, as a last resort, attempt to imbue some additional bandwidth to their Token Ring LANs via Token Ring switching, rather than HSTR.

ATM to the desktop, at 25Mbps or 155Mbps, remains available from IBM, Olicom, and some other vendors, even though most no longer see a compelling justification for it in the age of Fast Ethernet, Gigabit Ethernet, voice-over-IP, and IP-based QoS. In many ways, TCP/IP and Ethernet/Fast Ethernet are perceived as going hand-in-hand because of their common roots in the UNIX world and their "nothing-to-do-with-SNA" badge of honor. Thus the wholesale move toward IP-centric networking, whether it be for voice, video, faxes, or pizza delivery over IP, coupled with the frenzied attempts by the vendors to ensure that Fast and Gigabit Ethernet can match ATM when it comes to QoS capability, has ensured that Fast Ethernet, rather than ATM, will be the preferred strategic option for desktop and LAN bandwidth.

Fast Ethernet, Gigabit Ethernet, and ATM will be the preferred means of satisfying future LAN bandwidth demands. 100Mbps HSTR, despite its technical advantages, will eventually succumb—even IBM is now an avid fan of Fast Ethernet.

7.3   OPTIONS FOR CAMPUS BANDWIDTH

A campus network in the IBM world is thought of in either of two ways: (1) as a collection of geographically adjacent, interconnected LANs, with one or more LAN servers and possibly a data center, in the case of a corporate headquarters, or (2) a large corporate complex. The bandwidth requirements for campus networking fall into two distinct camps. The first is the bandwidth required to interconnect the various LAN segments for high-speed, LAN-to-LAN communications. The other is the bandwidth required to efficaciously connect various servers, whether they be LAN servers, Web servers, tn3270(E) servers, SNA-LAN gateways, NT-based application servers, UNIX systems, or even mainframes, to the campus backbone such that LAN users can interact with them at high speeds and with minimal delays.

In some instances, the bandwidth requirements for both LAN interconnection and server attachment can be addressed within one box, if one opts for a contemporary switching hub and uses dedicated ATM, Fast Ethernet, full-duplex 32Mbps Token Ring, or HSTR links to the various servers. Given the wide range of options available, however, it is best to look at the bandwidth options for LAN interconnection and server attachment as separate opportunities.

Well into the twenty-first century, the necessary bandwidth for the campus LAN interconnection can be realized in two ways. First, one can use the backplane of a hub or, more strategically, a switching hub, such as the IBM 8260 Nways Multiprotocol Switching Hub or Nortel Networks System 5000, whose backplanes are rated for multi-gigabit throughput per second. In some cases, the backplane of these switches uses an ATM cell-based architecture. The contemporary switching hubs offer the added advantage of supporting all LAN media types, including LAN switching modules.

Figure 7.6 illustrates the notion of using a switching hub as the basis for a campus LAN backbone. The type of configuration shown in this figure is

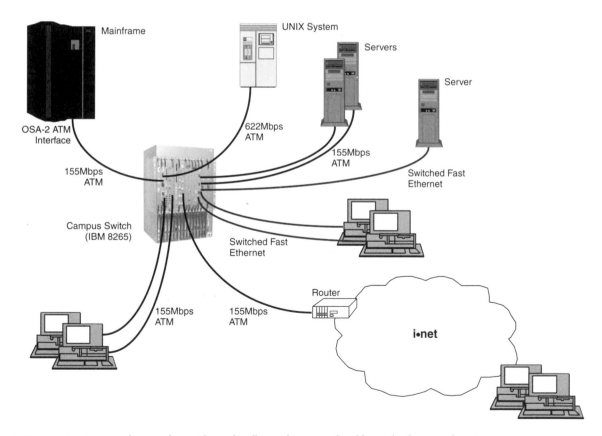

FIGURE 7.6   ATM and Fast Ethernet-based collapsed campus backbone built around IBM 8265.

known as a "collapsed backbone" configuration, because the entire campus backbone consists solely of the switch's backplane. IBM's extremely cost-compelling and feature-rich 8265 ATM Switch, which began shipping in late-1997 and provides a 12.8Gbps backplane and support for 622Mbps ATM ports, is a very attractive option for adding significant campus backbone bandwidth for SNA-capable i•nets—even though the latest version of this switch no longer supports Token Ring ports and has only switched Fast Ethernet ports as its sole LAN capability. The lack of LAN ports in the 8265 can be overcome by using it in conjunction with LAN switches, such as Olicom's OC-8600 CrossFire Token Ring Switch or Cisco's Catalyst 3900 third-generation Token Ring switches with ATM uplinks. IBM's 8272 or 8270 Token Ring switches, though somewhat viable options, are not as cost-compelling or feature-endowed as the Olicom and Cisco offerings.

Another option, albeit a more expensive approach is to use the IBM 2216 bridge/router as a feeder for the 8265s or possibly the IBM 2212 Access Utility, assuming that IBM will offer an ATM module for it in the 1999 time frame. Figure 7.7 depicts a next-generation campus backbone centered around an 8265.

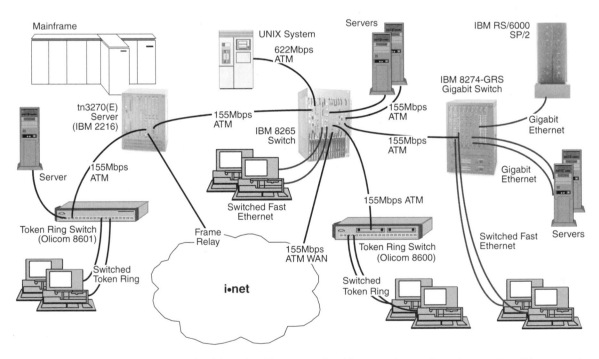

FIGURE 7.7 Representative 2001 high-bandwidth campus backbone with Gigabit Ethernet, Fast Ethernet, ATM, and switched Token Ring.

Second, one can deploy multiple bridge/routers, switching hubs, LAN switches, or a combination of these devices around the campus with high-speed 100Mbps LAN, 155Mbps ATM, or 622Mbps ATM links between them. This setup, for obvious reasons, is called a "distributed campus back-bone" because backbone bandwidth consists of an amalgamation of the back-plane capacities of the switches and bridge/routers as well as the bandwidth of the links used to interconnect them. Figure 7.8 shows the configuration of a typical distributed campus backbone, highlighting how it differs from the collapsed backbone shown in Fig. 7.6. The former architecture includes many peer-oriented hubs, whereas only a single hub exists in a collapsed backbone.

In many cases, ATM is the preferred and strategic means for implementing distributed campus backbones. 100Mbps connections in the form of FDDI/CDDI, Fast Ethernet, and proprietary forms, such as Cisco's Inter-Switch Link (ISL), are also popular and viable. Fast Ethernet and ISL are capable of 200Mbps bidirectional throughput if implemented in full-duplex mode. (In this context, it is very important to remember that ATM is inherently full-duplex-capable and that all ATM speeds quoted—whether 25Mbps, 155Mbps

With muscle-bound ATM switches such as the IBM 8265, LAN switching, and 100Mbps LANs, obtaining sufficient scalable bandwidth for broadband campus backbones is really a breeze.

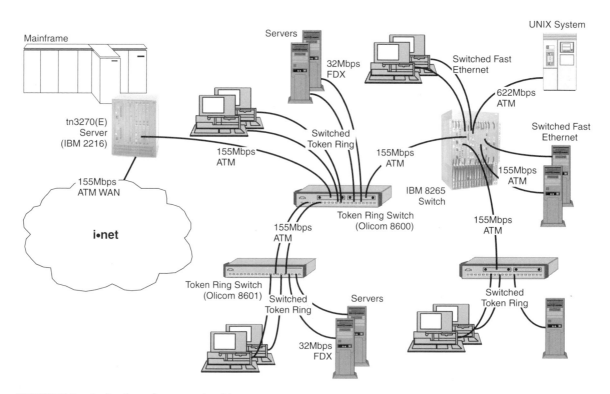

FIGURE 7.8 A distributed campus backbone.

or 622Mbps—should be viewed as having twice that capacity if used in full-duplex mode.) The block size of Fast Ethernet, as discussed earlier will be a speed-bump, and FDDI/CDDI (or ISL with its large block size option) will deliver better throughput even though it works at the same bit rate. Neverthe-less, the best mid- to long-term strategic options for distributed campus back-bones will be ATM and Fast/Gigabit Ethernet.

Multiple viable and attractive ways exist through which servers can be connected to campus backbones, whether collapsed or distributed. It is always possible to have multiple connections between a server and the campus back-bone to both increase bandwidth and provide redundancy in the event of a NIC failure. The options available include the following:

1. Full-duplex adapters are possible—for example, 32Mbps FDX Token Ring as shown in Fig. 7.4.

2. Fast Ethernet, in full-duplex mode if necessary, is an increasingly popular choice given the twin lures of ubiquity and very low cost (less than $50). The 1518-byte block size, however, is a tangible impediment to "pedal-to-the-floor" performance, especially when compared with HSTR or CDDI/FDDI. Fast Ethernet and Gigabit Ethernet, nonetheless, will prevail as strategic means for server attachment.

3. 100Mbps HSTR, with its large block size and robustness, is an obviously compelling choice, especially if much of the LAN infrastructure is Token Ring despite its relatively high cost compared with Fast Ethernet. Some, somewhat myopically, are reluctant to pursue HSTR because their mid- to long-term plans call for transitioning to Fast Ethernet. The $250 to $350 cost of an HSTR NIC, however, is not so great that one cannot look upon it as a disposable, tactical short-term solution that will deliver optimum 100Mbps performance.

4. 155Mbps or 622Mbps ATM, along with Fast and Gigabit Ethernet, will be the dominant and strategic means of delivering scalable, broadband bandwidth in the future.

The bottom line is that although multiple options exist for realizing ade-quate campus bandwidth, ATM and Fast/Gigabit Ethernet will be the clear favorites, at least during the early years of the twenty-first century.

7.4   OPTIONS FOR WAN BANDWIDTH

Compared with SNA-only or even multiprotocol networks, a typical SNA-capable i•net will most likely appear to have a ravenous appetite for WAN bandwidth—given, obviously, the additional volumes of traffic bound to be involved. Adequate and readily scalable WAN bandwidth will thus be vital to making an SNA-capable i•net become a reality. The good news is that multiple, increasingly economical ways of obtaining the necessary WAN bandwidth have become available, including the option of profitably exploiting the Internet as a virtually free font of considerable, though potentially erratic, bandwidth. The options for WAN bandwidth are discussed below.

Frame Relay, X.25, and ISDN

Public Frame Relay services, and in countries where Frame Relay is not available, either X.25 or ISDN could be used to provide the necessary bandwidth. Since 1995, Frame Relay, with its highly efficient RFC 1490/FRF.3 standard for native SNA-over-Frame Relay, has been a widespread success, particularly in North America, as a cost-compelling alternative to SDLC leased lines. The well-justified popularity of Frame Relay as a very affordable and plentiful means of high-quality (that is, with a low incidence of error) bandwidth should prevail with SNA-capable i•nets, especially with some services offering bandwidth as high as 45Mbps. The RFC 1490/FRF.3 encapsulation of SNA, as was widely promoted by many in the mid-1990s (with this author at the front of the pack), is considerably more efficient than DLSw. Figure 7.9 contrasts the relative encapsulation overhead of DLSw with that

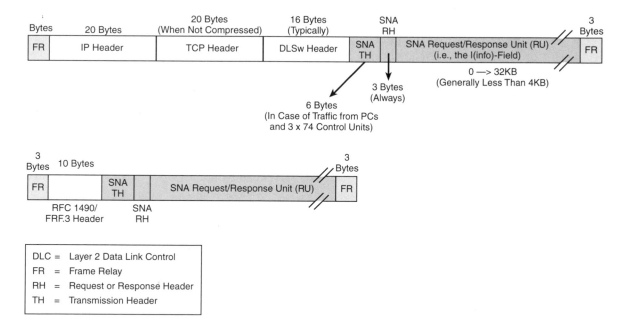

FIGURE 7.9   Comparison of DLSw and Frame Relay RFC 1490/FRF.3 encapsulation of SNA message units (to scale).

of RFC 1490/FRF.3. Although RFC 1490/FRF.3 can be used as an alternative to DLSw within the context of SNA-capable i•nets, especially given that most popular routers support both, most network professionals now want to standardize on TPC/IP-based DLSw encapsulation because their networks are TCP/IP-centric. This preference is understandable, defensible, and even logical. Given the preponderance of TCP/IP traffic within an SNA-capable i•net, it makes sense to eliminate as many non-TCP/IP protocols as possible to simplify network management and administration.

ATM Services

Frame Relay, ATM, and most excitingly the Internet are the strategic means for obtaining the necessary WAN bandwidth for SNA-capable i•nets. Using the Internet as a means of virtually free bandwidth for corporate WAN applications is effortless and highly secure with browser-based access and VPN solutions.

Public ATM services now offer cost-effective bandwidth in the 1.54Mbps (T1 speeds) to 155Mbps range. Even higher speeds, such as 622Mbps, are promised for the future, when a sustained, widespread demand exists for such bandwidth. When thinking of 622Mbps ATM-based WAN bandwidth, which will most likely emerge in the 2004 time frame, it is worth reflecting that this bandwidth is more than 10,000 times greater than most SNA shops now have with their new 56Kbps Frame Relay virtual circuits. Despite ATM's unceremonious fall from grace as the ultimate means for desktop-to-mainframe bandwidth, as it was billed in the past, it remains unparalleled as the only viable means for WAN bandwidth needs beyond 45Mbps.

Ironically, as had been presaged by IBM in 1993, there is growing interest in low-speed ATM (that is, ATM T1 to T3) as a head-to-head competitor for Frame Relay. Indeed, many North American carriers now offer low-speed ATM bandwidth at tariffs comparable to Frame Relay. To exploit such ATM services, Cisco and some other vendors sell ATM-FRADs, such as the Cisco MC3810, which support voice, data, and video traffic across either ATM or Frame Relay circuits at speeds as high as 2.048Mbps.

The Internet

The Internet as a source of WAN bandwidth for SNA-capable i•nets can be harnessed in multiple ways. One obvious approach would be to use browser-based access for applications such as telecommuting, employee/agent remote access, and public access. In earlier chapters, the issues, technology, and security aspects of this approach were discussed at length, with multiple case studies provided of companies that are already profitably using the Internet for remote access. Another popular use of the Internet is to handle some e-mail and file-transfer transactions. One could also perform extranet applications, where a user of an intranet application in one corporation interacts with an application or Web server on another company's intranet, across the Internet; of course, the application in question must be designed for such intercompany use and the appropriate authorization must be in place.

One could also use VPNs. With VPNs, one can take advantage of the Internet with impunity, as if it were providing a series of dedicated point-to-point links. In effect, one employs the Internet as the WAN "cloud" for a part of the corporate network. Consequently, routing or switching functionality must be provided at both ends of the Internet connection, or at least remote access functionality at the remote end (in the form of an appropriate client) and complementary routing technology at the other end. (Compare this approach to browser-based access, where all that is required at the remote end is a browser and possibly an applet.)

VPNs are best suited for interconnecting geographically dispersed offices or campuses to each other on a LAN-WAN-LAN basis, where the Internet serves as the WAN. With this approach, one already has the appropriate campus infrastructure, including the necessary routers or switches, to exploit VPN. Another way to understand this structure is to say that VPN is not optimally geared for single-user remote access (for example, a road warrior) or telecommuting, even though software client-based solutions are available for such applications. Given the need for specialized client software, at a minimum, VPN is certainly not practical for casual public access.

In essence, VPNs synthesize various IP-oriented encapsulation, encryption, and internal IP address "camouflaging" protocols, where the word "tunneling" is often used to describe the encapsulation process, and where an internal IP address refers to an in-house IP address. Some of the protocols involved include **Point-to-Point Tunneling Protocol (PPTP), Secure IP (IPSEC), Network Address Translation (NAT)**, and **Layer 2 Tunneling Protocol (L2TP)**. Although stand-alone, VPN-specific switches are now available, many low-cost routers (including the IBM 2210 and 2212) now offer VPN as an integrated feature. This development is indeed good news and permits relatively easy and very cost-effective implementation of VPN.

The underlying problem with a VPN is that one cannot guarantee the stability of the bandwidth that will be available across the Internet. ISPs, especially those offering differentiated, tariff-based classes of service, will attempt to commit to and guarantee a certain amount of bandwidth for a VPN connection. In reality, the ISP can guarantee this bandwidth only to the point of entry into the Internet. Despite the potential volatility of Internet-based bandwidth, one must acknowledge and applaud VPNs as a strategic, new-wave means of realizing virtually free WAN bandwidth for certain SNA-capable i•net WAN applications.

Leased Lines

One can use leased lines (including satellite or microwave-based lines) to obtain the necessary bandwidth. This option was the norm with many North American SNA networks—at least prior to the advent of cost-compelling public Frame Relay services.

Enterprise Switches

It is possible to implement a private Frame Relay or ATM network using enterprise switches from the likes of Cisco, Nortel Networks, and Ascend. SNA-only networks were the epitome of private networks. In such networks, 37xx Communications Controllers acted as the switches that harnessed and controlled the WAN bandwidth present in the form of leased lines, public X.25 services, or public Frame Relay networks. The overriding appeal of private Frame Relay or ATM networks is that of total and complete control over most aspects of the network—in particular, security, resilience, performance, and bandwidth allocation. Most private networks obviously must continue to rely on public carriers for their WAN bandwidth needs, which reduces the overall level of control they have over the entire fabric of the network. When reliability and resilience are paramount concerns, as is invariably the case with many large, mission-critical private networks (such as a travel reservation network, where the cost of network down time could be $45,000 for the first half-hour, and a credit card network, where the cost of down time could be $45,000 *per minute*), corporations will try to reduce their exposure from resources outside their control by using multiple, parallel sets of resources from different sources. In many cases, they will have contingency backup scenarios that involve using public services.

Deploying private Frame Relay or ATM networks will not be a new, i•net-related phenomenon. Corporations have been implementing such networks since the mid-1990s. Corporations that already have Frame Relay or ATM private networks are most likely to stick with them as they transition to SNA-capable i•nets. The same is likely to be true to some extent for corporations that currently have large, far-flung, mission-critical SNA-networks. For reasons of security and control, they may, quite justifiably, believe that they can transition to an SNA-capable i•net only if it is built around a private Frame Relay or ATM network.

The viable options for WAN bandwidth for SNA-capable i•nets therefore span both public and private networks—with the Internet now on the scene as the most open, egalitarian, and low-cost example of a public network. Although leased lines will remain an option, at least in North America, Frame Relay and ATM, whether in public or private form, will be the strategic technologies for WAN bandwidth for the long term.

7.4.1   IP Switching to Increase WAN Performance

In much the same way that LAN switching can be profitably leveraged to expedite LAN transactions and maximize use of LAN bandwidth, IP switching or Layer 3 switching can be used to significantly increase WAN throughput—especially in networks with very high volumes of IP-based traffic (for example, in SNA-capable i•nets). Although this scheme is quite often used at the campus level, the real impact and beauty of IP switching are best appreciated in context of a WAN. IP switching is a methodology pioneered in early 1996 by a Silicon Valley start-up called Ipsilon Networks. It is now available in many different flavors from most of the leading networking vendors.

IP switching can be envisioned as an amalgamation of traditional Layer 3 IP routing with the fast packet forwarding of Layer 2 LAN switching (for example, Token Ring switching). Just as with LAN switching, the goal of IP switching is to enhance network throughput and eradicate performance bottlenecks. LAN switching, as a Layer 2 technique, works with any protocol, whereas IP switching is restricted to native IP traffic. Rather than being a limitation, this constraint is actually an asset in the context of SNA-capable i•nets, where nearly all WAN traffic will be IP-based. Another difference between these two switching techniques is that IP switching is not restricted to LAN environments. Instead, it can be used in both LAN and WAN modes of operation and across any type of WAN bandwidth, whether ATM, Frame Relay, X.25, or even leased lines.

IP switching eliminates the need for IP traffic to be continually routed at Layer 3 at each node traversed along its end-to-end path. With IP switching, the Layer 3 routing function is performed only once for the duration of an IP connection. Once the route to the destination has been found via the initial routing operation, IP switches correlate the destination IP address with a Layer 2 MAC address for the next hop on the route; they then cache this IP address-to-MAC address relationship in a packet-switching directory.

Subsequent IP traffic to the same destination no longer requires routing. Instead, it is rapidly switched across to the next hop on its route by an IP switch using the MAC address cached in the directory. This avoidance of Layer 3 routing at each stop speeds up the entire data-forwarding process and minimizes traffic buildup at intermediate nodes. IP switching can thus be characterized as a "route once, then reverting to switching" scheme. With this option now readily available on switches, it should be viewed as an obvious means for expediting WAN traffic—particularly in the case of private Frame Relay or ATM networks.

> IP switching can be envisioned as the Layer 3 equivalent of LAN switching. It can significantly expedite IP-based data transfer across WANs via a "route-once, switch-from-then-on" approach.

7.5 OPTIMIZING DATA CENTER BANDWIDTH AND CAPACITY

The bandwidth requirements of a data center, as well as the scalability of the various data-center-resident networking-related components, constitute a multifaceted topic given the wide range of entities involved, and the perplexing range of permutations in terms of how these various components are interconnected. Section 5.2 discussed in great detail the various software components that may be required to implement an SNA-capable i•net as well as how the various server components may be implemented on a single server or distributed across multiple servers. It is also possible, and often essential, to have multiple servers perform the same function—for example, tn3270(E) servers—for the sake of redundancy. Obviously, the way that these server components are deployed in practice and the power and capacity of the hardware on which they run will have a profound effect on the network's scalability and throughput. In addition, some immovable throughput limits need to be circumvented, such as the amount of data that can be exchanged with a mainframe given the relatively slow speed of mainframe channels.

The maximum speed of a mainframe channel at present is 17MBytes/sec—that is, 136Mbps. This speed has not changed since 1991, when IBM introduced ESCON II, just one year after it had first unveiled the ESCON technology at 10MBytes/sec (i.e., 80Mbps). The rate of 136Mbps is just adequate to deal with 155Mbps ATM traffic; the true data throughput of a 155Mbps channel is in the 100 to 130Mbps range, once the overhead of "slicing and dicing" the data stream into 53-byte cells, the cells' eventual reconstitution into packets, and the inefficiencies of LAN Emulation (LANE) over ATM are taken into account. Unlike ATM, however, a single mainframe channel can work only in half-duplex mode. Full-duplex mode operation becomes possible if two separate channels are used in tandem along with the latest IBM channel protocol, **MultiPath Channel Protocol (MPC)**. MPC permits multiple channels to be bonded together, like a true SNA Transmission Group, and thus permits full-duplex operation, the aggregation of the bandwidth on the different channels into a single logical data pipe, and totally transparent protection against channel failures.

The 136Mbps speed of ESCON II mainframe channels can be maximized with the new MultiPath Channel (MPC) channel protocol, while awaiting IBM's new 800Mbps FICON channels that will be available around 1999.

To its credit, IBM has announced that a new type of 100MBytes/sec (i.e., 800Mbps) channel, known as **Fibre Connection (FICON)** channel, will be available as an option on new mainframes announced as of 1998. Just as with ESCON II, three or four years will pass before this new type of channel is supported by a wide range of equipment and therefore before the customer base is willing to commit to it. This new, very-high-speed channel will likely be initially supported by disk drive controllers and possibly just IBM's increasingly formidable 2216 bridge/router. As of mid-1999, the Gigabit Ethernet OSA option will become available; it will bypass channels and instead interact directly with the 333MBytes/sec internal bus of new S/390 mainframes. But don't fantasize about a 3745 FEP with a 800Mbps channel interface. The 3745, which does not even support ATM, is unlikely to have enough muscle to deal with this range of data speeds. The same will be true of the star-crossed 3746-950 Nways controller.

High-speed interfaces, such as ATM and Fast Ethernet, that are advertised as being available on the 3746-950 and the 3746-900 Expansion Chassis for the 3745 are actually implemented by bolting a 2216 to the side of a 3746-9xx through the so-called **Multiaccess Enclosure (MAE)** feature. The channel-attachable 2216, which can also double as a extremely low-cost, 15,000-plus session capacity tn3270(E) server, is an extremely attractive and strategic high-throughput gateway for SNA-capable i•nets. Nevertheless, one must acknowledge that 3745s/3746s are now gentle dinosaurs with a base technology that is nearly 15 years old. Section 7.6 will discuss newer mainframe gateway options, including the now essentially commodity item OSA-2, which is another viable and persuasive option.

7.5.1 Data Center Entities that Need Attention

The following factors need to be addressed to ensure satisfactory performance at the data center:

- The LAN backbone at the data center
- Intranet and Internet connections
- Mainframe gateways(s) and the channel protocols used
- tn3270(E) servers
- Web servers
- Optional SNA-Web gateways

Mainframe tn3270(E) servers, channel-attached routers, and ATM- and UNIX-based high-capacity servers between them can inevitably address the most demanding data center bandwidth and scalability requirements.

Token Ring, especially 16Mbps Token Ring, has historically been the LAN scheme most widely used within the data center given its indelible status of being SNA's handmaiden. Although the 3745 has had an Ethernet interface since 1992, it has never supported SNA across that Ethernet interface. SNA over Ethernet, vis-à-vis a mainframe, was only possible if one used an IBM 3172 Interconnect Controller or a Cisco 7000 with a Channel Interface Processor (CIP). Now both the IBM 2216 and the OSA-2 adapter support Ethernet, Fast Ethernet, and even FDDI—and there is even a nascent Gigabit Ethernet OSA. The move toward a contemporary mainframe gateway and away from a 37xx obviously marks the ideal time to reevaluate LAN options. Fast Ethernet, as ever, will beckon but the small block size could prove a deterrent. FDDI, which can be perceived as Token Ring on steroids, does have the necessary bandwidth, is endowed with renowned ruggedness, and supports large block sizes. It has never been big in the SNA world, however, and this situation is unlikely to change at this late date.

Thus Fast Ethernet and Token Ring will most likely be the mid-term favorites for LAN bandwidth at the data center. In persevering with Token Ring, it is salutary to consider multiple Token Rings and multiple Token Ring interfaces at the mainframe gateway, as well as the use of one or more third-generation Token Ring switches at the data center as means of maximizing bandwidth. Figures 7.5 and 7.8 illustrated how Token Ring switching could be profitably used at the data center to improve overall throughput. Another option is to use an ATM backbone, especially given that the IBM 2216, OSA-2, and Cisco 7000/CIP mainframe gateways support ATM interfaces, as shown in Fig. 7.6.

Figure 7.10 depicts a high-octane, browser-based access scheme that relies on ATM with OSA-2 on a mainframe running OS/390 version 2, release 6, and the latest mainframe Communications Server that includes support for the Host On-Demand applet, a 60,000-session tn3270(E) server, and end-to-end SSL security. Another intriguing possibility is the formidable IBM 8265 ATM Switch, which is channel-attachable via an ESCON II

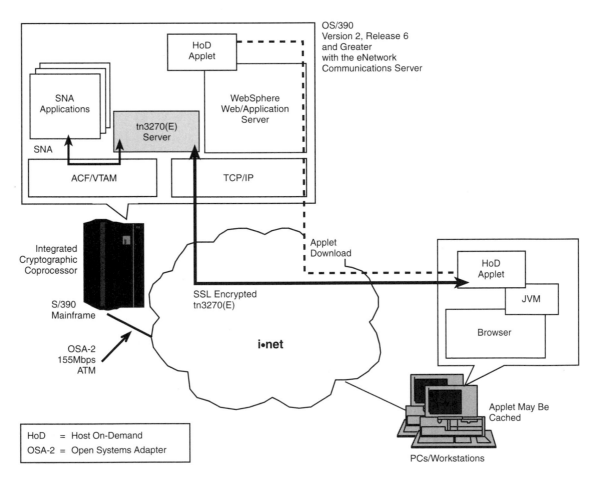

FIGURE 7.10   High-octane, high-throughput browser-based SNA access solution that leverages the S/390 OSA-2 adapter with ATM and OS/390's high-capacity tn3270(E) server.

adapter from Bus-Tech. This channel attachment, presaging future trends, supports only IP traffic. This restriction does not pose a problem if one intends to use a mainframe-based tn3270(E) server, as in the configuration shown in Fig. 7.10. Figure 7.11 takes the configuration in Fig. 7.10 and shows what it would look like with a channel-attached 8265 ATM switch. Given that the 8265 also supports ATM WAN modules, it could be used with an ISP that supports ATM-based Internet access as a high-powered Internet access gateway.

The i•net Connection

The corporate intranet and the Internet will typically be brought into the data center via a high-capacity router, as has been depicted in all relevant figures in this book. This router could obviously be channel-attached. Two performance-related advantages derive from channel-attaching this router

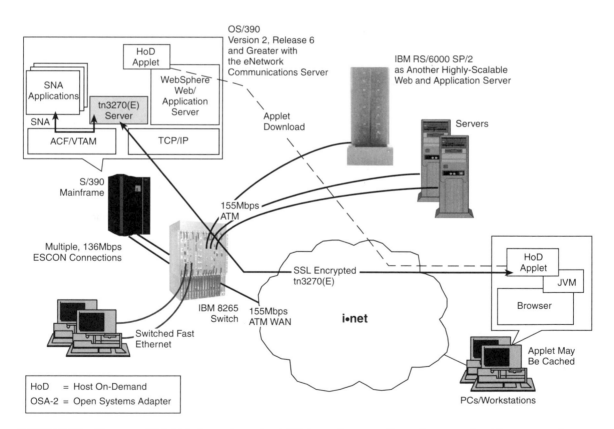

FIGURE 7.11 Using an ESCON channel-attached ATM switch as a collapsed campus backbone, mainframe gateway/network interface.

rather than having it interact with a mainframe gateway via a LAN. First, it eliminates any delays and throughput bottlenecks induced by the LAN due to other devices contending for its bandwidth. Second, it bypasses any delays at the mainframe gateway. These delays can present a real problem if the mainframe gateway happens to be a relatively busy 3745. The 3745's Token Ring interface, the so-called TIC, start to sputter at around 4000 message units per second. In addition, because its processing power is limited by today's standard, it does not forward packets as fast as one might expect with contemporary routers and switches. In other words, its packets per second rating is not in the same league as that of a big, fat router. Hence a channel-attached router or switch, such as an IBM 8265, is indubitably the optimal way to link an i•net to the mainframe.

Cisco pioneered the notion of channel-attached bridge/routers as direct alternatives to the aging 3745 in 1993. Today, channel-attached bridge/routers are no longer a contentious issue, but rather an accepted, highly proven, and widely used data center solution. IBM's wholehearted endorsement of this approach in 1997, when it announced the ESCON II adapter for the 2216, has allayed any lingering doubts. Most SNA shops now realize that they will most likely require one or more channel-attached bridge/routers to initially complement, but in time eventually usurp, their existing 37xx gateways. The issues pertaining to and the options available for mainframe gateway replacement are discussed in the next section.

Channel Protocols

At this juncture, when talking about mainframe gateways it is worth raising the issue of channel protocols. Contrary to a widespread misconception, SDLC was never used as a Layer 2 data link control protocol to exchange data between a mainframe and a 37xx across a channel. Instead, channel-specific Layer 2 protocols served this purpose, such as **Channel Data Link Control (CDLC), Link Service Architecture (LSA),** and **Common Link Access for Workstations (CLAW)**. CDLC, which was developed in the early 1970s, is still used by 3745s and 3174s to support SNA/APPN traffic. LSA was primarily used by the 3172, and CLAW is used when TCP/IP off-load is employed, where "off-load" refers to some Layer 3 processing taking place on the controller without the use of any mainframe resources. Although an IBM protocol, CLAW was popularized by Cisco when it began channel-attaching bridge/routers. CLAW, which permits two subchannels to be used side-by-side for TCP/IP transfers, remains the optimal channel protocol for TCP/IP. It is not supported, at least at present, by the IBM 2216; this device instead uses the non-off-load **LAN Channel Station (LCS)** protocol for TCP/IP transfers.

MPC, as mentioned earlier, is now the undisputed performance champ for transporting SNA/APPN traffic across a mainframe channel. In addition to being able to simultaneously use multiple subchannels, ideally distributed across separate channels, to gain additional bandwidth and resilience, MPC supports very large block sizes and uses a data buffering scheme at the mainframe end that minimizes buffer pointer manipulation. The end result is that MPC can not only use 272Mbps or more bandwidth by taking advantage of multiple 136Mbps ESCON II channels, but it also works highly efficiently. MPC is supported by the IBM 2216, Cisco 7000/CIP, and the Cisco 7200/CPA. The Cisco Channel Port Adapter (CPA) is a single-port, lower-cost CIP for the mid-range Cisco 7200 family of routers. IBM also supports IP across MPC, even though the performance and efficiency advantages in this case are not as great when SNA/APPN is used across MPC.

With ACF/VTAM version 4, release 4, there is now a variant of MPC referred to as **MPC+** or **High-Performance Data Transfer (HPDT)**. MPC+/HPDT is an SNA LU 6.2-based scheme for high-speed, mainframe-to-mainframe bulk data transfer across channels that support MPC. HPDT, which is an ACF/VTAM capability, reduces the amount of data movement within the mainframe during I/O processing, packs the data (that is, aligns the data to required buffer boundaries) into I/O buffers without moving the information around within memory, uses highly optimized code with short path lengths to handle I/O buffer management, and refines the scheduling algorithm for the actual channel programs (that is, START I/O functions) used to execute channel data transfer. With these modifications, IBM claims that HPDT/MPC+ can improve data transfer performance by as much as 40% and reduce mainframe CPU utilization associated with those transfers by as much as 60%. The IBM 2216 and Bus-Tech's PCI bus-based ESCON channel adapters for channel-attaching servers running Windows NT and Novell NetWare, known as EnterpriseExpress Adapter/ESCON, currently support MPC+. Cisco will likely provide support for MPC+ in 1999.

tn3270(E) Server

When evaluating options for tn3270(E) servers, the first question that must be answered relates to the desirability and viability of a mainframe-based tn3270(E) server. Today, proven and highly scalable mainframe-resident tn3270(E) servers are available from both IBM and Interlink. IBM claims support for as many as 60,000 concurrent sessions. The downsides to a mainframe-based tn3270(E) server are the need for TCP/IP on the mainframe and the fact that valuable mainframe cycles will be consumed to perform protocol conversion functions that can just as easily be done off-board. Nevertheless, the unassailable trend is toward TCP/IP on the mainframe.

Thus the need for TCP/IP on the mainframe cannot be claimed any longer as a showstopper. The only real issue is that of using mainframe resources for tn3270(E) serving.

The cost of mainframe computing is decreasing on a yearly basis as IBM continues to churn out faster and less expensive CMOS-based mainframes. One must therefore cogently argue that cost is also a nonissue, particularly given the scalability of the mainframe servers. The mid- to long-term trend appears to favor mainframe-resident tn3270(E) servers, with quite a few enterprises already following this course with considerable success and panache. Some may rail at the notion of mainframe-based tn3270(E) servers, citing the lack of redundancy. This point could be valid. Of course, this "single point of failure" exposure applies to nearly all mainframe entities— unless you have multiple mainframe configurations, as advocated by IBM in its Parallel Sysplex architecture.

Although mainframe-resident tn3270(E) servers promise to be in vogue in the future, most enterprises in the 1998–2000 time frame will opt for off-board data-center-resident tn3270(E) servers as a low-risk, low-cost entrée into SNA-capable i•nets. (This type of server should be installed at the data center, firmly upstream from the i•net, as was stressed in Chapters 2 and 4, to avoid having to transport the SNA output from a tn3270(E) server to the data center across the i•net using DLSw.) When evaluating off-board options, the pivotal issue becomes one of scalability. Many tn3270(E) servers for PC servers are on the market, with Microsoft's SNA Server and Novell's Net-Ware for SAA being the most popular. Unfortunately, a PC-based tn3270(E) server, particularly one running on Windows NT, might not be scalable enough to adroitly support a production network with 10,000 concurrent sessions. For such high capacities, one must turn to a UNIX-based solution, such as OpenConnect Systems' OC://WebConnect SNA Access Server, or a specialized server, such as IBM's 2216 or Cisco's CIP/CPA. The OpenConnect and 2216 servers can be deployed either in LAN-attached or channel-attached mode. The Cisco CIP/CPA, on the other hand, works only in channel-attached mode because the tn3270(E) server software actually runs within the CIP or CPA channel interface modules.

After scalability, the next obvious issue that must be addressed is whether the tn3270(E) server should be directly channel-attached to the mainframe, thereby avoiding the LAN and mainframe gateway-induced delays articulated earlier. In reality, a channel-attached tn3270(E) server is likely to be the optimal solution, until one decides to transition to a mainframe server, because it eliminates all bottlenecks between the server and ACF/VTAM on the mainframe. Currently, the channel-attached IBM 2216, which offers as many as 15,000 concurrent sessions for an all-inclusive hardware and software price of around $67,000, is by far the most cost-effective and compelling of channel-attached solutions. The Cisco 7000/CIP is highly proven and widely used and can support more concurrent sessions—albeit through the addition of extra CIP modules, with each module capable of supporting at least 16,000 sessions.

Other Servers

When it comes to Web servers and the SNA-Web gateway required by some browser-based access solutions, the issue of scalability invariably boils down to NT-based solutions versus UNIX-based solutions. Despite Microsoft's vehement protestations to the contrary, repeated real-life experience confirms that UNIX is inherently more scalable than NT. Obviously, any valid comparison of relative scalability must rely on a common baseline for performance (such as number of processors or processor speed), memory capacity, and bus type of the hardware being used.

Windows NT running on a multiprocessor, RISC-based Compaq/DEC AlphaServer most likely can support more users than a UNIX system running on a low-end box available at one-twentieth of the cost. By the same token, however, if one uses a $5000 PC server, NT will not necessarily be able to support 40,000 users concurrently. Of course, Windows NT-based solutions—in particular, Microsoft's Internet Information Server (IIS)—are extremely popular options for implementing Web servers and SNA-Web gateways. Thus there is little merit in trying to dismiss NT-based solutions by citing scalability problems. Instead, it is important to highlight the potential scalability issues, which may require the use of multiple servers, in stacked configurations, to accommodate the anticipated user and traffic loads. The use of multiple servers, with some kind of IP-based load-balancing scheme (such as Cisco's Local Director and IBM's Network Dispatcher) will obviously protect against server failure and improve overall throughput by distributing the workload.

IBM's strategic OS/390 Operating System, which is positioned as the follow-on to the venerable MVS Operating System, includes Lotus's highly acclaimed Domino Go Webserver as a built-in feature, referred to as WebSphere. Although some corporations may use a mainframe Web server, which will indubitably be highly scalable, this approach is unlikely to be as popular as mainframe-based tn3270(E) servers. Most Web maestros, who tend to view mainframes as ungainly, obsolete artifacts invented long before they were born, will balk at the notion of weaving their Web magic by using a mainframe. Understandably, they will want to continue with the NT- and UNIX-based servers that have served them so well. Mainframe-based Web servers will therefore typically be used in conjunction with nonmainframe Web servers in a multiserver configuration.

7.6 NEW MAINFRAME GATEWAYS

The 37xx Communications Controllers that have served the SNA community so well, for so long, are now approaching the end of their useful life. The move from SNA-only networks to SNA-capable networks sounds a death knell for these controllers, whose architecture and hardware are firmly rooted in mid-1980 technology. The unparalleled forte of 37xxs is handling large numbers of low-speed serial lines (for example, SDLC) and performing SNA subarea routing-related functions. With the move toward SNA-capable i•nets, the need for low-speed serial lines and SNA subarea routing is fast disappearing, as SNA-based WAN and SNA-oriented clients give away to TCP/IP, DLSw, tn3270(E), and browser-based access solutions. Consequently the need for, let alone the merit of, using the anachronistic 37xxs as mainframe gateways is rapidly diminishing.

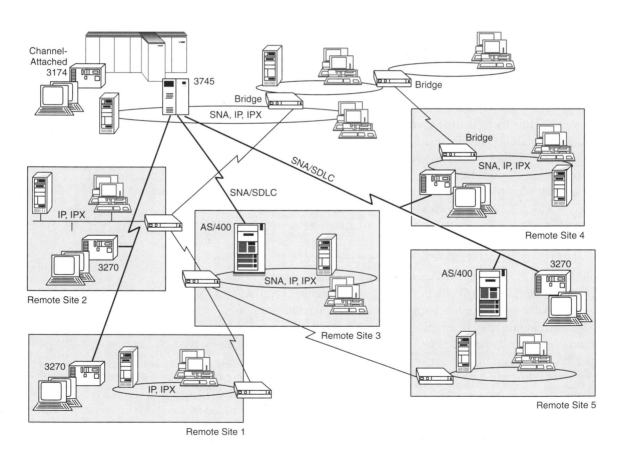

FIGURE 7.12   IBM 3745 and bridging based 'SNA Model' that is now becoming obsolete.

Already 80% of the 37xxs that were deployed as remote link concentrators in **Remote Communications Processor (RCP)** mode at the start of the 1990s have been displaced, with their networking role being assumed by multiprotocol bridge/routers. Even IBM will not spend too much time or effort trying to defend the 37xxs, despite these controllers' status as a high-margin cash cow, now that the company has eagerly endorsed non-37xx gateway solutions such as the 2216-400, OSA-2, and the 8265. Figure 7.12 shows the traditional 37xx-based SNA model, and Fig. 7.13 contrasts that model with the i•net-centric paradigm of the future. Note that DLSw, which is ubiquitously available on all popular bridge/router families, performs the SDLC-to-LAN conversion, as discussed in Chapter 4, to support any lingering SDLC-attached SNA controllers at remote sites.

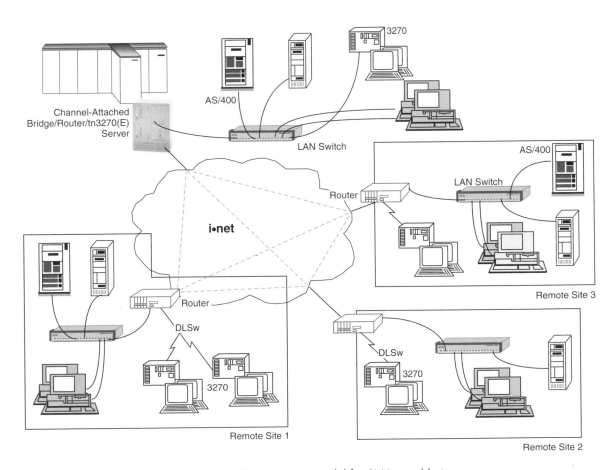

FIGURE 7.13 The contemporary LAN and i•net-centric model for SNA-capable i•nets.

While it may be difficult to discard the venerable 3745s/3746s overnight, the only way to gear up for the bandwidth and IP-centric requirements of SNA-capable i•nets is to complement these old gateways with new-generation gateways such as the IBM 2216 or Cisco 7200/CPA.

Despite the availability of multiple, potential replacements such as the 2216, corporations will not be able to discard all of their 37xxs, even when their leases come due, until the transition to SNA-capable i•nets is well under way. This point is very important to understand and remember. Some SNA-related functions can be performed only by a 37xx—such as the mandatory gateway function required by SNA Network Interconnection (SNI) that is still heavily used for intercompany collaboration, funds transfer, and supply-chain management. Eventually extranets, with suitable new applications, will take over the functions now realized using SNI. This replacement will take a long time, however. The HPR border node might permit some SNI configurations to migrate to HPR, but this trend again will require considerable network reengineering and testing. Thus any corporation that is currently heavily reliant on SNI will have no choice except to hold on to one or more 3745s to act as SNI gateways, even if the mid- to long-term strategy centers on a contemporary mainframe gateway such as the 2216 or Cisco 7000/CIP.

The best option, and in most cases the only option, for most corporations is to install a new mainframe gateway alongside the 3745/3746, ideally on another channel to prevent interference between the two traffic streams. The new gateway can support the SNA-capable i•net-related traffic, and the 37xx can continue to handle any straggling BSC, X.25, or asynchronous traffic until those users or applications are finally transitioned to the i•net. Cisco, in particular, offers support for TCP/IP encapsulation of BSC and X.25, and support for BSC-over-TCP/IP was recently added to the 2216. The bottom line, however, is that a corporation will have to use the new gateway alongside the old and trusted one before all relevant traffic can be channeled in through the new gateway. In some instances, this cut-over period could last for years. One should therefore not be surprised to encounter 3745s humming away merrily in a prime spot at a data center well past the year 2005.

The 2216-based Multiaccess Enclosure (MAE) for the 3746-900 and 3746-950 attempts to address this need for maintaining both the old and the new, working in tandem. In general, however, there is rarely a solid technical justification for keeping the 2216 alongside a 3746 in the form of an MAE—especially given that any SNA or APPN traffic between the two is exchanged across two, full-duplex Token Ring links! Invariably, one can achieve the same results, at a lower cost, by deploying a channel-attached 2216 on its own, on a separate channel to the 3745/3746. This configuration has the added virtue that the 3745/3746 can be more easily decommissioned and removed from the network when all necessary mainframe-related SNA-capable i•net traffic, whether based on SNA/APPN or TCP/IP, can be channeled through the 2216.

Today, essentially three compelling next-generation mainframe gateways exist: the OSA-2, the 2216-400, and the Cisco 7000/CIP (or 7200/CPA). The

3746-950, which specializes in APPN/HPR NN routing, is not a strategic option because of its lack of built-in support for ATM, Fast Ethernet, tn3270(E) serving, and similar protocols. The 2216 and Cisco 7000/CIP are full-function, channel-attached, bridge/router solutions, with full APPN/ HPR NN node routing functionality, comprehensive IP routing, and SNA passthrough support; each also offers a scalable tn3270(E) server. The Cisco offerings offer PU concentration as well, although the need for this capability is rapidly diminishing because move to ip3270, tn3270(E), and browser-based access greatly eliminates the number of downstream SNA nodes within a network.

The OSA-2 does not offer routing functions or a tn3270(E) server. Its redeeming virtue, however, is that one OSA-2 is included as a built-in option with each S/390 Parallel Enterprise Server shipped by IBM as of mid-1998. In essence, IBM is including a gateway that can handle Token Ring, ATM, Fast Ethernet, and FDDI—albeit with somewhat limited capacity—with each new mainframe. A single OSA-2 adapter can support two ports in the case of Token Ring or Ethernet and one port in the case of ATM, Fast Ether-net, or FDDI.

As many as 12 OSA-2 adapters can be installed on a contemporary S/390 mainframe. Additional OSA-2 adapters are relatively expensive, especially compared with the port capacity, functionality, and flexibility of the IBM 2216-400 or the Cisco 7200/CPA. Consequently, the OSA-2 is a real con-tender only in relatively small networks where the traffic load can be handled through two Token Ring ports or one 155Mbps ATM port. In other cases, it would be best to opt for a 2216-400 or a Cisco 7200/CPA rather than trying to justify another OSA-2. In addition, given that the OSA-2 does not provide a tn3270(E) server capability, one must rely on either a LAN-attached off-board server or a mainframe-resident one.

Given these limitations of the OSA-2, the two real contenders as main-frame channel gateways for mid-size to large SNA-capable i•nets are the 2216 and the Cisco 7000/CIP (or 7200/CPA). The Cisco 7000/CIP solution, which pioneered this new gateway technology, is highly proven, widely in-stalled, ardently endorsed by loyal users, and very scalable. The 2216, which is comparatively new, has the advantage of being extremely cost-competitive. Whether one opts for a 2216 as the mission-critical mainframe gateway will depend on the prevailing view of whether IBM has regained its credibility as a networking solution provider. In 1999, all indications suggest that IBM, with the 2216 and the 8265, has demonstrated that it can deliver competitive networking products. Many will require more time and further proof before they trust their networks to IBM networking hardware. The bottom line is that Cisco and IBM, between the two of them, have the only real solutions for next-generation mainframe gateways.

7.7   MANAGING SNA-CAPABLE I•NETS

To successfully manage an SNA-capable i•net, one will need SNA and TCP/IP management on the mainframe as well as off-board SNMP/RMON management and possibly a vendor-specific desktop and server management scheme for contemporary SNA access solutions.

A somewhat hackneyed adage in the industry states that one should not build something that cannot be adequately managed because, in the end, incisive management acts as the glue to keep today's increasingly complex computing world from unraveling at the least unexpected provocation. Fortunately, today's major vendors fully appreciate the imperativeness of good management tools and devote considerable efforts to ensure that their products can be easily but thoroughly monitored, controlled, and administered. Web-based management of many components is merely the latest in a long list of considerable strides made. This case holds true with the technology required to successfully implement a mission-critical SNA-capable i•net. Despite some of this technology being relatively new and evolving quickly, adequate management tools already exist to manage the entire end-to-end fabric of SNA-capable i•nets—albeit not in an all-inclusive integrated package.

Comprehensive management of an SNA-capable i•net involves, by definition, the monitoring and control of both TCP/IP and SNA resources. At first blush, this requirement may appear no different than the management requirements of bridge/router-based multiprotocol networks, which have been widely used within SNA shops since the mid-1990s to support SNA/APPN. There is, however, one pivotal difference. Most multiprotocol networks did not have both mainframe-resident mission-critical TCP/IP stacks and TCP/IP applications that needed to be closely managed, around the clock, along with the SNA applications and ACF/VTAM. Thus SNA-capable i•nets require TCP/IP-based management of mainframe-resident resources in addition to the customary, network infrastructure components such as hubs, bridge/routers, switches, CSU/DSUs, modems, and servers.

Table 7.1 lists the complete repertoire of resources that need to be managed within an SNA-capable i•net and the options for managing them. The table highlights that mainframe-based management, both for SNA and TCP/IP, is crucial to the successful operation of a typical SNA-capable i•net. Those who had assumed that the move to an i•net would enable them to dispose of their mainframe-based management system have little choice but to reconsider. Rather than eliminating mainframe-based management, most will have to expand the scope of this management to include TCP/IP as well.

7.7.1   Continuing Need for Mainframe-Based Management

A mission-critical system will continue to require solid mainframe-based SNA management as long as SNA applications and legacy SNA devices (such as 3174s, 4700 Financial Systems, and ATMs) remain a crucial part of the day-to-day business operation. Not having a mainframe based management scheme would mean that you would lose visibility of these entities and

TABLE 7.1 Resources managed within an SNA-capable i•net.

	SNA Entities	TCP/IP Entities	Hybrid Gateways
Mainframe-resident	SNA applications (e.g., CICS, TSO, DB2) and ACF/VTAM	TCP/IP applications (e.g., FTP, Web server) and TCP/IP stacks	
Data-center-resident	3745s/3746s, 3174s, 3172s, AS/400s	Channel-attached routers, LAN-attached routers, switches, hubs, i•net gateways, AS/400s	tn3270(E) servers, SNA-LAN gateways, SNA-Web gateways
Network	3745s, 3174s	Bridge/routers, switches, hubs, servers, modems, CSU/DSUs	
End-user level	AS/400s, 3174s, 4700s, ATMs, full-stack SNA emulators	PCs, workstations, NCs, servers, AS/400s	
Network protocols involved	DLSw, HPR-over-IP, Source Route Bridging	TCP/IP, tn3270(E), ip3270	SNA upstream to mainframe, TCP/IP downstream across network
Management protocols	SNA	SNMP, RMON	SNA, SNMP
Management platform	Mainframe SNA (e.g., IBM NetView or Sterling SOLVE: Netmaster)	Mainframe TCP/IP (e.g., IBM NetView, Interlink e-Control, or Sterling SOLVE: Netmaster + SNMP/RMON management platform (e.g., Netview for AIX or HP OpenView)	Mainframe SNA, mainframe TCP/IP, SNMP management

would, in effect, be flying blind—and relying on irate calls to help desks to identify problems being experienced by SNA users. This situation is unlikely to be acceptable.

The existence of a TCP/IP-based network between the mainframe and the end devices will not hamper the end-to-end management of SNA devices from the mainframe, thanks to the "in-band" nature of SNA management. With in-band management, all management alerts, requests, and responses are conveyed across the network as standard SNA message units. Consequently, all management-related message units can be transparently moved across the network using DLSw or HPR-over-IP. Network professionals who have experience with multiprotocol networks would readily testify to the fact that the lack of an SNA network does not disrupt or preclude end-to-end SNA management. One can therefore continue to rely on value-added functions such as Response Time Monitoring (RTM) across an SNA-capable i•net, provided that the SNA end devices support the required functions. The presence of the TCP/IP network will obviously not affect the management of the mainframe applications or the channel-attached 3745s or 3746s.

Mainframe-based TCP/IP management schemes are now available from IBM, Interlink, and Sterling. The total set of options for mainframe management are as follows:

SNA's innate in-band management philosophy ensures that end-to-end SNA management, including functions such as RTM, remains possible across TCP/IP networks when one uses protocols such as DLSw, HPR-over-IP, or even Source Route Bridging.

- Mainframe-based SNA management: IBM's TME 10 NetView for OS/390 and Sterling's SOLVE:Netmaster for SNA
- Mainframe-based TCP/IP management: IBM's TME 10 NetView for OS/390 version 1, release 2, Sterling's SOLVE:Netmaster for TCP/IP, and Interlink's e-Control

The mainframe-based NetView, now referred to as TME 10 NetView for OS/390, is obviously the best-known and most widely used SNA management scheme. Version 1, release 2, which became available in mid-1998, reflected the profound changes taking place in mainframe computing by including built-in support for TCP/IP problem management alongside its renowned prowess on the SNA front. This step was indeed historic—a high-profile example of teaching an old dog some dramatic new tricks or a battle-scarred tiger changing its stripes. The ability of this new NetView to provide both SNA and TCP/IP management does not automatically render it the obvious or only option for mainframe management. Life in the fast-changing SNA world of today is not, unfortunately, that simple.

NetView's TCP/IP skills in the initial release are confined to basic problem management. Although this capability is a good start, it is merely one facet of the TCP/IP-related management disciplines required. Other crucial system management-related disciplines are required:

- Performance management (for example, end-to-end response time diagnosis)
- Access control (for example, grant or deny access to mainframe TCP/IP applications based on IP address, user ID/password, port number, or time of day)
- Change (or configuration) management (for example, track and control changes made to TCP/IP-related configuration parameters and files)
- Capacity planning (for example, monitoring and tracking resource usage such as CPU and memory utilization to plan for future upgrades)

Sterling's SOLVE:Netmaster for TCP/IP and Interlink's e•Control both offer TCP/IP-based performance management, with the former having more extensive capabilities. As yet, Sterling has not addressed the other disciplines, though Interlink has. In effect, Interlink's e•Control sets out to provide TCP/IP-based "soup to nuts" system control, à la IBM's 1990 SystemView vision. Naturally, given the depth and breadth of this task, some disciplines are addressed more comprehensively than others. Interlink's TCP/IP-based access controls, so vital to establishing data center security, are outstanding, as are its change management and capacity planning functions. Sterling, at least for now, has the edge when it comes to performance and problem management. This situation creates a dilemma, exacerbated by the fact that Interlink, in marked contrast to both Sterling and IBM, does not offer any SNA management.

Although this situation will change over time, at least in the 1999–2000 time frame the only way to achieve adequate mainframe-based management is to use at least two, and ideally three, products side-by-side. The two-product scenario would be to go with TME 10 NetView and Interlink. This approach would cover most bases but would provide little in the way of performance management. The optimal solution is to use Sterling's SOLVE:Netmaster for SNA, SOLVE:Netmaster for TCP, and Interlink's e•Control. This three-product scenario is not as bad as it initially looks because the two Sterling products, when installed together, work as one; also the combined price of the two is not necessarily that much greater than the price of NetView.

7.7.2 Wrapping Up Management

Adequate SNA cum TCP/IP management at the mainframe level is possible—but at present it requires multiple products. Mainframe management, however, is only one prong of the at least two-prong management required to successfully nurture a mission-critical SNA-capable i•net. The other vital prong is an off-board SNMP/RMON-based management platform, such as IBM's TME 10 NetView for AIX, for monitoring and controlling all TCP/IP-based network infrastructure components. Cooperative interworking between the mainframe SNA management scheme and the off-board SNMP manager is possible with auxiliary products such as IBM's SNA/Manager for NetView and Cisco's CiscoWorks Blue. The need for such interworking is less important than it was with multiprotocol networks, however, because the SNA entities downstream of the data center continue to dwindle as users transition from SNA-based clients to TCP/IP-based clients. Nonetheless, it is good to know that this type of cooperative management remains possible.

In some situations, one may require a third prong to complete the management suite. This prong would be a server and client management scheme, which by nature will be vendor-specific. Some vendors that offer ip3270,

Adequate mainframe-based management, until at least the dawn of the twenty-first century, will require the use of multiple products on the mainframe, with Interlink's TCP/IP-specific e-Control striving to offer SystemView-type total system management replete with impressive security-related access control mechanisms.

tn3270(E), or browser-based access solutions already offer management schemes for centralized configuration of client software, license management, and server management. OpenConnect's OC://WebConnect Management Server is a good example of such vendor-specific management solutions for contemporary SNA access solutions. It should be noted, however, that as of the start of 1999, two IETF-approved SNMP MIBS existed for tn3270(E) servers.

7.8   THE LAST WORD

An SNA-capable i•net will invariably require more bandwidth, across the board, than the network it replaces. Much of this bandwidth reflects the needs of additional users and applications, though some percentage, indubitably, will be consumed by TCP/IP- and Web-related headers and protocols. The good news is that the bandwidth needs of these new networks can be satisfied, at all levels, with relatively cost-effective technology—with Fast Ethernet, switching, ATM, and VPNs figuring prominently as strategic technologies. The small block size of Fast Ethernet represents an impediment, but will not stand in the way of its galloping popularity across the industry.

The 37xxs that once epitomized SNA networking are approaching the end of their useful life, although it will be many years before they are finally dislodged from data centers because of their role in sustaining functions such as SNI, NPSI, and BSC. The bandwidth and IP-centric requirements of SNA-capable i•nets, however, dictate that 37xxs be complemented by new-age mainframe gateways, such as the OSA-2, 2216, and Cisco 7000/CIP; the latter two products offer the most functionality and flexibility.

Managing SNA-capable i•nets will present a challenge—albeit a worthwhile, essential, and eventually surmountable one—given the disparate and distributed entities involved and the multiple management schemes required. For a start, most systems will require both SNA and TCP/IP management on the mainframe. As no single product currently addresses all of the required disciplines (in particular, access control), one will be forced to consider two or even three product offerings to perform this management. TCP/IP management on the mainframe, however, does not obviate the need for a proven off-board SNMP/RMON management platform, such as IBM's TME10 NetView for AIX, for managing the TCP/IP-based infrastructure components. On top of that platform, one may elect to employ a vendor-specific management scheme for desktop and server management. The good news is that the products exist today to provide the necessary end-to-end management. With time, today's initial offerings will no doubt blossom and become more cohesive.

Pulling It All Together

With the approachment of the year 2000, networking in the IBM world is caught, somewhat flat-footed and flustered, between the strong gravitational pull of two counterpoised forces: the huge monetary and labor demands of the Y2K efforts to resurrect aging, mission-critical data center applications, and the tantalizing possibilities promised by Internet-based e-commerce. IBM reckons that e-commerce will account for $600 billion worth of world-wide trade in 2002. Cisco, whose networking equipment handles three-fourths of the traffic traversing the Internet, estimates that this market will reach $1.5 trillion by 2003 and grow exponentially. Companies such as Amazon.com, eBay.com, and Cisco itself, which now does much of its business across the Internet, have demonstrated the glittering potential of e-commerce with great aplomb, with immense rewards going to their for-tunate shareholders. Corporations around the world, irrespective of their size, are understandably highly motivated to ensure that they do not lose out when it comes to the brave new world of e-commerce. The Internet and e-commerce constitute the new nonstop, around-the-clock, global market sans frontiers and boundaries; together, they make up a larger, more acces-sible, dynamic, and unforgiving market than any other trading opportunity in the history of commerce.

A glaring and disturbing incongruity has appeared in the current e-commerce landscape, however. E-commerce is taking root outside the bounds of the traditional data center, while the data center remains caught in the throes of Y2K. In general, 1999 was marked by an inverse correlation between a corporation's dependence on mainframes and the actual progress of its e-commerce initiatives. Unfortunately, this trend will not change until nearly 2002, at which point non-mainframe-centric e-commerce will be well on the way toward being accepted and proven. Unless this trend is

Cisco, by mid-1998, was doing $15 million per day of e-commerce. Although this statistic is an excellent harbinger of the vast potential of Internet-based trade, Cisco is not a mainframe shop. Neither is Amazon.com or eBay.com, two of the other leaders in e-commerce. While mainframe shops have been preoccupied with Y2K, e-commerce initiatives are gaining momentum on NT and UNIX platforms. Much technology exists for mainframe- and AS/400-oriented e-commerce. A concerted effort will, however, be required post-year 2000 to ensure that traditional IBM data centers are not left behind in the pell-mell dash to cash in on e-commerce.

recognized and decisive steps taken to rectify it immediately following the Y2K efforts, a real danger exists that traditional data centers, once the facilitators of much global commerce, could be left out in the cold vis-à-vis the emerging world of e-commerce. This development would be a pity and would cause unnecessary replication of data and applications, because data centers are the current repositories of much of the information required for successful e-commerce, such as customer lists, account information, credit ratings, manufacturing schedules, stock inventories, and shipping manifests. Moreover, mainframes and AS/400s are ideally placed to provide the proven scalability, reliability, and resilience imperative for the ongoing success of a thriving, high-volume e-commerce operation.

No technical reasons prevent mainframes from playing a dominant role in e-commerce. IBM has ensured that OS/390's built-in **WebSphere** Web and application server has all the necessary features, in an unparalleled scalable form, to facilitate e-commerce. For example, WebSphere includes a Payment Gateway option as well as support for the **Secure Electronic Transaction (SET)** protocol developed by VISA and MasterCard. The AS/400 is similarly endowed as an e-commerce server, with IBM going to great lengths since late 1997 to aggressively market it as a highly attractive, cost-effective platform for e-commerce. Vendors such as Open-Connect Systems have provided full-function, feature-rich, Web-oriented application servers with comprehensive back-end connections to data center resources and applications.

Effectively integrating data centers with i•nets—in particular, the Internet—is obviously a prerequisite if mainframes and AS/400s are to influence future e-commerce. The technology for achieving this integration, in multiple forms and from a diverse range of vendors, already exists as described in earlier chapters. Large companies around the world, such as GM, FedEx, Lafayette Life Insurance, Lincoln National Reinsurance, The Chickering Group, Royal Jordanian Airlines, and Al Rajhi Banking and Investment, have already successfully integrated their data centers with i•nets, as illustrated in the case studies. This chapter includes four more real-life case studies involving browser-based access to SNA: Del Monte Foods International, Nestlé, Trans World Airlines (TWA), and the Cairo Opera House. Furthermore, an increasing number of renowned IBM shops now offer genuine Internet-based transaction processing, albeit via data replication on NT or UNIX servers or perhaps with in-house-developed host-to-Web tools. Key among the top-tier IBM shops that have wholeheartedly embraced the Internet and the Internet call center methodology as a very economical and essential means of extending their reach to their customer base are Charles Schwab, Fidelity Investments, American Airlines, BankBoston (which recently merged with Fleet Bank), and the Vanguard Group.

The bottom line is that no justifiable doubt or uncertainty exists about the availability and viability of the pertinent technology—including the relevant security and access control, such as Interlink's e-Control and IBM/Tivoli's Security Management—to seamlessly integrate data centers with i•nets and empower data-center-centric e-commerce. What is missing right now, due to the distractions of Y2K, are the focus and commitment to dismantle the current barriers between data centers and i•nets. The remainder of this chapter provides proof of the practicability of the data center integration technology as well as the appropriate inspiration and motivation for pursuing this course of action.

8.1   TWO MORE CASE STUDIES HIGHLIGHTING TRENDS AND SECURITY OPTIONS

Two case studies from the food industry will clearly illustrate how browser-based access to SNA across the Internet or an intranet can reduce business operation costs and minimize overall network complexity, particularly in the realm of remote access.

Del Monte Foods International

Del Monte Foods International is the worldwide market leader in canned fruits and fruit juices. Its U.K. operation, which has revenues of approximately $170 million, is headquartered in Staines, near London's Heathrow Airport. The U.K. office acts as a central business coordination point for Del Monte operations in seven other countries: Italy, Greece, Belgium, Luxembourg, South Africa, Kenya, and the Philippines. A Del Monte office is located in each of these countries. These offices communicate with the U.K. head office and, where necessary, with each other using an SNA/3270-based network. Much of the infrastructure and bandwidth for this far-flung SNA network were provided by IBM's worldwide Global Network Services.

Del Monte, however, was unhappy with the relatively high cost of using this public network for long-haul SNA access, even though the costs were a fraction of what they would have been if the company used a private, leased-line network or an international dial-up configuration. This lament has become an increasingly familiar refrain as corporations begin to realize that remote access costs, even across a public Frame Relay or X.25 network, are still very expensive compared with the costs of using the Internet as a means of near-free bandwidth. Lafayette Life Insurance, as discussed in Section 6.1.3 had exactly this same concern regarding the expense of a public network such as IBM's Global Network relative to the cost-structure pertaining

Compared with the virtually free remote access offered by the Internet, even the once cost-competitive public packet-switching networks (let alone leased-line private networks) now appear to be hugely expensive and indulgent—despite offering a level of control, consistency, and security unattainable on the Internet. Consequently, large corporations like Del Monte Foods International, eager to contain their networking costs, are increasingly turning to the Internet and browser-based access as a strategic and economical means of achieving some of their worldwide SNA-based remote access requirements.

to Internet access, which essentially consists of a relatively small, monthly ISP charge and local access charges to reach the ISP.

Around October 1997, Del Monte decided that the time was ripe to try Internet-based SNA access as a means of dramatically slashing its remote networking costs. The company called upon the market leader OpenConnect Systems to develop a secure but simple Internet-based SNA access scheme. OpenConnect provided exactly what Del Monte sought through its Java applet-based OC://WebConnect Pro offering.

Del Monte UK selected the Philippines operation as a pilot test for the architecture shown in Fig. 8.1. This architecture, which is the same as that used by GMAC and FedEx (as discussed in Chapter 6), was by then widely deployed, stable, and reliable. As might be expected with such a proven solution, the Philippines pilot was a resounding success. The Internet has been used, uninterrupted, on a production basis since late 1998. Del Monte UK is also rolling out this browser-based access scheme to other countries,

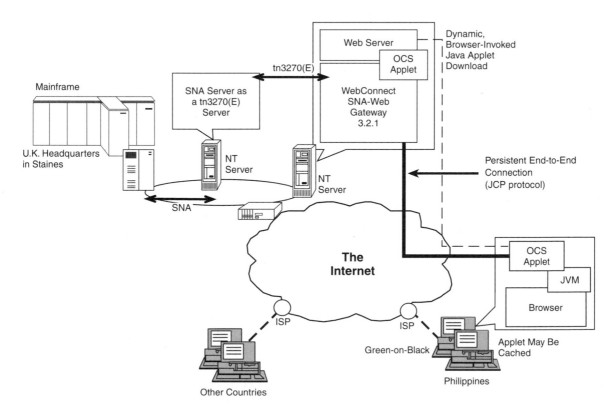

FIGURE 8.1   The architecture of the tn3270(E) applet scheme employed by Del Monte Foods International for SNA access across the Internet.

including some that had never had online mainframe access because of the high cost of remote access.

To satisfy its remote access needs in some European countries, Del Monte intends to use a Frame Relay-based intranet, as opposed to relying on Internet-based access. This choice was prompted by the attractive prices offered for Frame Relay circuits by some European PTTs. With a Frame Relay-based intranet, Del Monte can enjoy a committed and consistent level of service and performance not possible with Internet access. At present, the company is willing to incur the additional costs vis-à-vis European remote access to gain greater control over the network than would be possible when relying on the Internet. Internet access, however, will be the norm for remote access from non-European countries or in situations where the firm cannot get a guaranteed level of Frame Relay service from the local PTT. This theme is likely to be repeated many times over in the next few years, as companies evaluate the merits of Internet-based global remote access.

Despite the unparalleled economy of Internet-based access, concerns over unpredictable response times, stability, and security will cause some companies to shun the Internet and persevere with a public network for their remote access needs, irrespective of the higher costs. Such cost versus control compromises are not new to IBM networking. All SNA shops have already debated the issues of leased lines versus X.25 or leased lines versus Frame Relay at least once during the last two decades. The new twist, in most cases, will be the weighing of the Internet versus Frame Relay.

In the near future, Del Monte UK intends to transition its applications from the mainframe to an AS/400 by relying upon BAAN ERP software. Given that OC://WebConnect Pro supports both 3270 and 5250, this transition from a mainframe to an AS/400 will not affect or require modifications to Del Monte's i•net-based SNA access infrastructure—an added bonus.

Nestlé

Whereas Del Monte's forte is fruits, the Swiss-based Nestlé is the largest food company in the world. Thus Nestlé, like Del Monte, is a huge company with major operational centers in many countries around the world. This case study focuses on Nestlé's operation in Egypt.

Nestlé's Egyptian operation is spread across four major sites, with each site having its own AS/400. To contain remote access costs, this division decided to go with an i•net approach involving both Internet- and intranet-based access. Like some other large companies in the Middle East, such as Royal Jordanian Airlines and Al Rajhi Bank, Nestlé turned to Farabi Technology for its browser-based access needs. Farabi, which supports Arabic with its right-to-left orientation vis-à-vis browser-based access, is now a major player in this part of the world—clearly demonstrating that interest in and deployment of SNA-capable i•nets and browser-based access to SNA are not restricted to only North America and Western Europe.

Nestlé, echoing another trend likely to occur on an increasingly regular basis in the future, wanted both applet-based emulation and 5250-to-HTML publishing. The applet-based emulation was to enable access to existing applications on the AS/400s, whereas 5250-to-HTML conversion was intended for new, Internet-specific applications being developed for the company's traveling users so that they could easily query or submit sales,

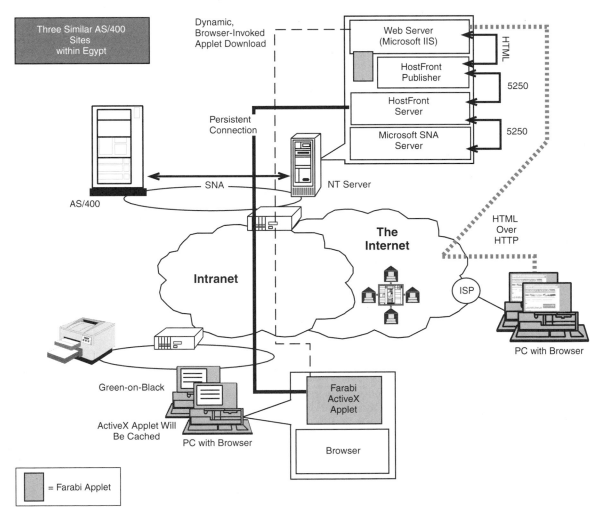

FIGURE 8.2   The architecture of the Farabi Technology-centric applet and 5250-to-HTML-based solution being used by Nestlé in Egypt.

availability, or shipping data across the Internet from the road. Farabi, as discussed earlier, offers both solutions with its HostFront Server offering—in this instance, HostFront Server for AS/400. HostFront Server acts as an SNA-Web gateway to provide applet augmentation, authentication, and encryption, where "applet augmentation" refers to the fact that the server performs certain tasks on behalf of the applet. In addition, it handles the API-based interface with the mandatory and coresident Microsoft SNA Server gateway that manages the SNA/5250-based access with the AS/400. 5250-to-HTML conversion is provided by HostFront Publishing, which sits on top of HostFront Server as shown in Fig. 8.2.

HostFront Server, in common with Attachmate's HostView Server and Wall Data's Cyberprise, supports both Java and ActiveX applets. In this instance, the customer opted for the ActiveX applets primarily because it provided better integration with PC-based printing. This choice, interestingly enough, is another emerging trend. Corporations faced with a choice of ActiveX and Java are opting for ActiveX because of its tighter integration with Windows 95 and 98 and the ensuing advantages, such as seamless local printing. The overriding virtue of Java, on the other hand, is its platform independence. As much of the commercial world is now standardizing on the WinTel platform, however, many companies appear less concerned with choosing a Windows-oriented solution.

Given that Nestlé's sales information, product availability, and shipping data were to be available through this browser-based access scheme, airtight security was imperative. Farabi was yet again in a position to meet this need. A distinguishing feature of HostFront Server is its ability to perform user ID/password-based authentication for both applet-based and 3270-to-HTML-based access. This capability provides an additional level of security to augment firewall, SSL, and AS/400-based security measures. Nestlé uses this Farabi-provided authentication scheme as an integral part of its security strategy. In its applet-based schemes (whether Java or ActiveX), Farabi employs a powerful end-to-end encryption technique, where the encryption key is dynamically altered between transactions to minimize the potential of data interception.

8.1.1 Multiple Levels of Security

The Nestlé's case study clearly highlights how today's browser-based access to SNA solutions can offer multiple tiers of security, in a systematic and hierarchical manner, to ensure an extremely high level of access control, authentication, and privacy—which is generally more than adequate for most commercial applications. The security concerns related to SNA-capable i•nets were initially discussed in Section 3.2 and have been regularly dealt with in later chapters. Given that security remains a preeminent concern related to i•nets, particularly in the IBM world, this point is an ideal juncture to quickly recap the options available and examine how they relate to one another.

The potential security exposure within an intranet that has no interface with the general public is considerably less than that noted when a data center has an explicit interface with the Internet to facilitate two-way public interaction, such as e-commerce. Firewalls are very important in the case of an Internet interface, as is encryption if one deals with any type of sensitive or financial data. On the other hand, encryption, though desirable, may not be imperative within an intranet—assuming, of course, that suitable security measures, such as physical access controls, are in place to safeguard the integrity of the intranet as a whole. Pertinent physical access control mechanisms include measures such as badge-controlled access to buildings and closed-circuit television surveillance to monitor movement in and out of the data center. To this end, however, it should be noted that encryption was rarely used on SNA-only networks, even though ACF/VTAM and devices such as the 3274 control unit provided built-in, SNA-prescribed schemes for end-to-end encryption on LU-LU sessions. The bulk of the SNA traffic flowing across bridge/router- or FRAD-based multiprotocol networks is also not encrypted, even though many of these networks rely on public Frame Relay networks for their WAN bandwidth. Consequently, it is necessary to apply judgment, discretion, and common sense when establishing the security requirements for a given SNA-capable i•net. For example, if implementing a 3270-to-HTML conversion solution to provide the public, via the Internet, with access to public domain information (such as train schedules, flight itineraries, or bank certificate of deposit interest rates), do not add complexity and make the entire process cumbersome by insisting on authentication and encryption, just because the technology is readily available.

With browser-based access schemes, it is possible to have at least six levels of security pertaining to data center access. These six levels of security can provide incisive and proven safeguards at the following levels:

- The session level
- The transport level
- The gateway or server level
- The firewall level
- The host level
- The application level

Figure 8.3 shows where and how these security measures are implemented and how they relate to one another. In the case of applet-based emulation, session-level security is provided through the use of "impenetrable" end-to-end persistent TCP connections, replete with sequence numbers, that

At least six levels of security are possible with browser-based access to SNA. Of these, application-level security realized on a per-application program basis via user ID and password-based authentication is the most sacrosanct and the final barrier preventing unauthorized access. Although single logon schemes may bypass the need to individually log on to each mainframe or AS/400 application, the true merits of such schemes should be carefully evaluated because they essentially circumvent the strong line of defense against breaching traditional data center security.

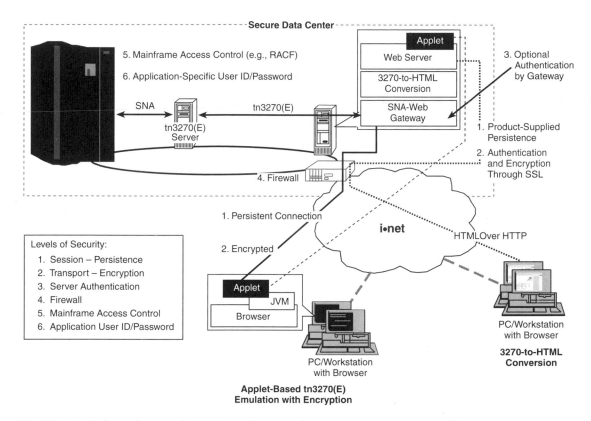

FIGURE 8.3 Both applet-based tn3270 emulation and 3270-to-HTML conversion offer extensive security measures.

ensure that a hacker cannot barge into an existing connection to mount some type of Trojan horse attack to intercept data. Some 3270-to-HTML conversion products, such as Novell's HostPublisher and Eicon's Aviva Web-to-Host Server, provide session integrity by using hidden sessions IDs and sequence numbers (as described in Section 5.5.1 and used by HostPublisher) or the "session-integrity" feature built into Microsoft's IIS Web server via active server page (ASP) technology (à la Aviva).

Transport-level security revolves around encryption. In the case of applet-based solutions, encryption is provided either via a proprietary scheme involving an intermediary SNA-Web gateway (such as the products from Farabi and OpenConnect Systems) or via SSL-arbitrated encryption with a tn3270(E) server (such as IBM's CS/NT, IBM's Communications Server for OS/390, or Novell's NetWare for SAA) that supports SSL-based security.

The role of gateway- or server-level security is to provide auxiliary user authentication even before a browser user comes near the mainframe or

AS/400. Applet-based solutions require an SNA-Web gateway, such as Farabi's HostFront, if they are to offer this capability. 3270-to-HTML conversion products can rely on standard SSL-based authentication by the Web server to provide this security functionality.

Firewall-level security is self-explanatory in this context and will be performed at a minimum by a proven firewall product at the entrance to the data center. In the case of intranets and extranets, some enterprises may also deploy firewalls at the remote sites to preclude the possibility of unauthorized users trying to gain access to the LAN infrastructure at those sites.

Host-level security will typically be arbitrated by a host access control package, such as RACF, ACF2, or Interlink's TCP/IP-centric e-Control.

The final and perhaps most important level of security is that appearing at the application level. To its eternal credit, IBM, dating from the 1960s, has mandated and ensured that each application perform its own user ID and password-based authentication, ideally through a built-in mechanism that forces the password to be changed on a 60- or 90-day basis, irrespective and independent of all other external security measures. This application-specific authentication has paid handsome dividends and stoutly stood the test of time. Compared with other platforms, reports of hackers breaking into mainframe applications are rare.

For some time, various vendors have been offering single logon schemes to eliminate the need for application-specific authentication on an enterprise basis—not just for mainframe applications, but for all applications across all platforms. From a security standpoint, such single logon schemes would be regressive. It is highly recommended that application-level authentication be assiduously enforced within SNA-capable i•nets as the final, time-honored security measure for the data center.

Many of today's browser-based access to SNA solutions can offer all six or at least five of these levels of security. Note, however, that the same does not apply to end-to-end SNA transport across an i•net. With this type of transport, no intermediary SNA-Web gateway or server will exist to afford authentication or encryption. Transport-level encryption may also become product-dependent because encryption is not a mandatory core function within the DLSw standard. Consequently, any encryption performed will be contingent on auxiliary security features, such as VPN functions, offered by the routers being used to realize DLSw or HPR-over-IP. The other four levels of security (session, firewall, host, and application), however, will usually be available and implemented.

This review of security options clearly highlights that contemporary SNA-capable i•nets indeed have the pertinent technology on tap to enforce a very high degree of intrusion protection, privacy, and data integrity. In most cases, a well-implemented SNA-capable intranet is likely to be considerably more secure than the SNA-only or multiprotocol network it displaces. The same is also likely to be true if one compares SNA networks with dial-up or X.25-based schemes for public access with the new networks offering public access through the Internet. For a start, today's solution will include encryption and auxiliary authentication. Hence it is best to be very specific, objective, and rational when evaluating the security needs of SNA-capable i•nets, to avoid becoming distracted and overawed by the sentiment that i•nets are intrinsically insecure and that this issue is insurmountable. In fact, the many security options around ensure that one can implement an SNA-capable intranet that is just as secure as a multiprotocol network, and that the security risks associated with Internet access can be contained and controlled.

8.1.2   Trends Highlighted by the Case Studies

The goal of this chapter is to demonstrate that SNA-capable i•nets are eminently viable and that corporations of all sizes, located around the world, have successfully implemented such networks for gainful production use. To this end, it is helpful to mention some of the key trends that are emerging related to such networks and that are highlighted by the preceding case studies so as to expedite the planning and evaluation phases of future networks.

First, the popularity of Internet-based, in-house remote access (as demonstrated by the Del Monte and Lafayette Life Insurance case studies) to contain and reduce networking costs is growing. This option appears especially attractive when international sites are involved or when the firm has many dispersed agents or field representatives, as in the case with companies involved in insurance, travel, freight, automotive, and heavy equipment (such as farm tractors). In some cases, this access may be provided on an extranet basis if the agents work for separate companies or are self-employed. It may also be achieved using VPN functionality rather than browser-based access or tn3270(E).

Second, in the case of remote access that is restricted to North America or Western Europe, quite a few corporations continue to opt for the control, predictability, and stability provided by an intranet implemented across a public Frame Relay, ATM, or X.25 network despite the tempting economics of Internet-based access. This preference is to be expected. SNA networks were the epitome of private, highly regulated, rock-solid networks that were finely tuned for crisp, predictable, and consistent response times. The potential unpredictability of the Internet is too much of a concern and a risk for many SNA shops, especially when real-time applications such as travel reservations, automated teller machines (ATMs), and currency trading are involved. A public network-based intranet or an extranet is the perfect and easily cost-justifiable compromise for these companies.

Third, use of applet-based emulation and 3270-to-HTML conversion is increasing in tandem. The applet-based solutions are being targeted at intranet

By far the most profound trend is that of the Internet being gainfully exploited as a means of economical bandwidth for global in-house remote access on an intranet or extranet basis. Another crucial trend is the use of 3270-to-HTML conversion to facilitate casual, public access to data center resources across the Internet. Still another hard-to-ignore trend is the emerging interest in ActiveX applets, given that they offer tight integration with the Windows 95/98 environments.

and extranet applications as a replacement for fat client approaches, and the 3270-to-HTML publishing is preferred for Internet applications, especially in the case of public access to SNA applications (for example, online travel, Internet call centers for service scheduling, or status queries).

Fourth, Java by most measures is recognized as the logical and strategic choice for applet-based solutions. It is platform-independent, widely adopted by the programming community at large, and highly endorsed by the likes of IBM and HP. Nevertheless, ActiveX has the uncontrovertible advantage that it is backed by Microsoft and therefore tightly integrated with the Windows 95 and 98 environments, which dominate commercial-sector desktops. Given this tight integration, especially when it comes to local printing and file transfer, increasingly more corporations are opting for ActiveX-based applet solutions—if they have a choice. Notwithstanding the interest in Linux and browser-based Webtops, the stranglehold that Microsoft and Windows have over commercial-sector computing will not diminish soon, even if the U.S. Department of Justice has its way. As long as Windows dominates the commercial desktop, ActiveX will remain a prominent and sought-after solution. It is as simple as that.

Fifth, the overall security of i•nets remains a major concern. Most corporations have had enough exposure to the technology and have seen or heard enough success stories involving large corporations (such as GMAC, Del Monte, National Van Lines, and Lafayette Life) that they are willing to concede that SNA-capable i•nets do, indeed, have formidable security safeguards.

8.1.3   Going Beyond the Remote Access Scenarios in the Case Studies

The Internet- and intranet-based remote access in the Del Monte and Nestlé case studies was restricted to corporate employees; that is, they were in-house remote access scenarios—in essence, private intranets even when the access occurred across the Internet. The GM, Royal Jordanian Airlines, and The Chickering Group case studies discussed in previous chapters, however, allude to what is likely to be a even more cogent application for Internet-based remote access: providing authorized agents or distributors with access to corporate resources via an extranet remote access solution. In the case of GM, the dispersed distributors involved are GM truck dealerships. In the case of The Chickering Group, the remote access is offered to colleges and universities that subscribe to Chickering's student insurance products. With Royal Jordanian, on the other hand, the Internet-based remote access was intended for the convenience of authorized freight handlers scattered around the globe.

GM, obviously, is not the only IBM shop to have a large and widely dispersed network of dealerships that require regular communication with the

Many large IBM shops have large networks of dealerships, agents, or distributors. SNA access from these external entities is typically achieved by using 3270 control units or PCs with special WAN adapters across leased-line, public network, or dial-up schemes. Such remote SNA access is expensive and carries equipment, WAN bandwidth, and maintenance costs. A browser-based solution across the Internet could provide comparable SNA access at a fraction of the cost. Moreover, the remote site installation and activation time will typically be less than one day.

parent company to order products and spares, check on availability of goods, schedule shipments, query the status of deliveries, and so on. The same is true of other automotive manufacturers, as well as manufacturers of boats, buses, heavy trucks, snowmobiles, small aircraft, and farm equipment. Until now, the SNA access requirements of such dealerships were handled, depending on the volume involved, by using leased lines, public networks such Frame Relay, or dial-up connections. Before PCs emerged as a force in the late 1980s, this type of remote SNA access was possible only by having a 3274 or compatible control unit installed at each dealership; multiple 3277 terminals and printers had to be coax-attached off the controller. (If the access could be restricted to just a few terminals, solutions such as the IBM 3275, 3276, and 8775 were possible; these devices were, in effect, terminals with a built-in control unit.)

Because 3174 control units could act as very effective SNA-LAN gateways to enable Token Ring-attached PCs to gain access to SNA applications across a WAN, it was fairly common for dealerships to maintain a 3270 controller even when they moved to a networked PC configuration. In other instances, PC-based dealership access to SNA applications was realized by installing an SDLC or X.25 PC card on one or more PCs. Suffice it to say, this type of SNA remote access was quite expensive, with the actual total costs including equipment cost, WAN bandwidth costs, and relatively steep maintenance costs.

Today, with browser-based access to SNA across the Internet, one can provide distributors and agents with reliable and secure communications at a mere fraction of the cost. The actual cost savings possibilities are dramatic. An Internet-based access scheme could probably pay for itself within months, just by eliminating the leased-line, public network, or dial-up costs, without even taking into account the savings related to equipment, maintenance, and equipment upgrade costs. As if these irrefutable cost savings were not enough, the new schemes offer greater ease of installation and activation. With prior SNA remote access, some amount of lead time was always required either to install the relevant equipment or to obtain the necessary WAN bandwidth scheme. The Chickering Group had run into this hurdle, for example. The rate at which it could sign up and activate new colleges or universities was constrained by the time needed to set up the dial-up configuration at either end. Internet access, of course, can collapse this installation and activation time down to one day—if not to a few hours. In addition to a suitable gateway PC or router at the remote end, all that is really required is a local dial-up connection to an ISP. The software required, which could obviously just be an applet, can be dynamically downloaded from the parent company's Web site.

Thus it is not surprising that companies such as GM and The Chickering Group have already begun to exploit Internet access. What is actually more surprising is that there has yet to be a headlong rush toward this type of access, given that it does significantly reduce costs and complexity. One can only assume that the preoccupation with Y2K has precluded companies from fully appreciating the potential of Internet-based access in the context of networking distributors and agents. If true, then explosive growth could occur in this arena after 2000.

8.2   DATA REPLICATION (WITH AN ILLUSTRATIVE CASE STUDY)

With the ready availability of proven browser-based access solutions from so many vendors, along with the complementary security measures, little justification remains for shunning direct Web-to-host access in favor of an Internet scheme that is contingent on data replication. The Lincoln National Reinsurance case study in Section 6.3.1 illustrated the problems of trying to keep the mainframe and NT server data synchronized before the company adopted its innovative programmatic access-oriented scheme, centered on Blue Lobster's Java-heavy technology, for simultaneously updating the mainframe and NT server databases. Before browser-based technology came of age in 1997, replicating mainframe or AS/400 data on an NT or UNIX server was, in effect, the only way to cogently implement a Web application that involved host data. Safeguarding host access, and hence data center resources, was also a monumental factor in favor of data replication. In reality, lingering security concerns—despite the evidence that browser-based access can offer safe and secure host access—continue to cause many corporations to feel more comfortable with a data replication-based solution than with a direct Web-to-host scheme.

SunGard Trust Systems of Charlotte, North Carolina, is a good example of a company that opted for a data replication-centric Web solution before browser-based access proved its true mettle. This highly successful financial-sector company specializes in providing trust accounting systems for more than 500 mid-size banks around the United States; a trust accounting system is an online computer system that maintains and manages financial data pertaining to trust fund account (for example, personal trust) portfolios. SunGard's trust accounting system is essentially a total MIS outsourcing service for trust account maintenance and management. Trust account management is a complex, sophisticated business. For a start, a huge number of very distinct types of trusts cater to very diverse requirements, ranging from asset protection to inheritance administration. In addition, many of these trust categories permit funds associated with the trust to be invested in multiple ways, including individual stocks, bonds, mutual funds, or even real estate holdings. Keeping track of the holdings of various trusts in terms of their status and current value is a very involved process.

Prior to browser-based access to SNA becoming truly viable, host data replication on an NT or UNIX server was the only way to deliver mainframe- or AS/400-resident data over the Web. This situation is no longer the case. The option of delivering host visibility via data replication nevertheless continues to appeal to many, because it neatly addresses the perennial security concerns related to hackers trying to break into mainframes and AS/400s across the Internet. The SunGard Trust and Lincoln Reinsurance examples demonstrate that replication-based solutions are effective and a pragmatic alternative to browser-based access. Despite the entrenchment of browser-based access schemes, replication will continue to play a role in the IBM world as a technique that mitigates access control fears.

At SunGard Trust Systems, the customer account details and the financial performance data required to provide the trust account information, such as the latest stock and mutual fund prices, reside on a Hitachi Data Systems (HDS) mainframe. Prior to the availability of Internet-based, online systems, trust account owners could obtain trust account information only by contacting the trust manager at the appropriate bank by telephone and having the trust manager query a PC-based system that would contain account information updated overnight from the mainframe. (This prior system relied on mainframe data replication on individual PCs as opposed to a centralized NT or UNIX server.) This process was slow, cumbersome, fraught with delays (for example, the manager might be serving another client), and very expensive for the bank in terms of personnel costs.

SunGard, which was an IBM shop at the forefront of recognizing the immense potential of Internet-based information delivery, decided to augment its PC-based system for banks with a highly secure, 24×7 online system, whereby trust portfolio owners or administrators could check on their portfolio's current value and status over the Internet. The Web-based system adroitly avoids the shortfalls of the old process—in particular, the high cost of servicing telephone requests for account information. Because SunGard was not convinced that browser-based technology was proven enough for its needs in 1997, the company implemented a data replication-based solution involving NT servers. Figure 8.4 depicts the data center configuration at SunGard, where the mainframe is front-ended by two Compaq ProLiant 2500 PC servers running NT to provide Internet access.

SunGard developed an NT application known as the Portfolio Access Link to handle the Web-based queries from trust fund clients. This application, as shown in Fig. 8.4, runs alongside the company's Web server (Microsoft's IIS). The mainframe data required by this Web application are replicated on Microsoft SQL Server, which runs on a different, but adjacent, Compaq ProLiant 2500 server. The mainframe data are downloaded into the SQL Server via a Bus-Tech DataBlaster. The DataBlaster is a highly proven and widely deployed IBM-channel-to-SCSI data transfer system. This high-performance, mission-critical, and cost-effective solution provides high-speed bulk data transfer between mainframes and any system with a SCSI interface. Consequently, the DataBlaster (as well as other mainframe-to-NT server solutions from Bus-Tech, such as the PCI bus-based EnterpriseExpress Adapter/ESCON, which permits NT servers to be directly attached to a mainframe 17MBytes/sec ESCON II channel) can play a pivotal role in the data replication-based Web solution.

The DataBlaster system originally used by SunGard supported a 4.5Mbytes/sec (36Mbps) bus-and-tag connection to the HDS mainframe channel and SCSI interface to the NT server. Initially, SunGard did not need the full 36Mbps capacity of the DataBlaster's mainframe connection.

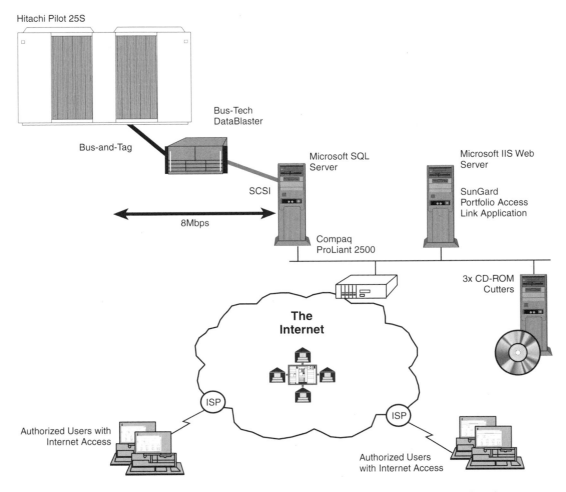

FIGURE 8.4   The solution used by SunGard Trust Systems to provide trust fund clients with online access to account information over the Internet.   (*Source:* Bus-Tech.)

Instead, its NT application required a data transmission rate of 1Mbytes/sec (8Mbps). This mainframe data transfer rate will be increased as more and more banks start offering SunGard's Web-based Portfolio Access Link service to their customers. Bus-Tech's second-generation DataBlaster, known as DataBlaster 2, can support bulk data transfers at speeds approaching 32Mbytes/sec (250Mbps). SunGard Trust, therefore, is no danger of running out of capacity when it comes to mainframe-to-NT data transfer.

A SunGard-developed application running alongside the SQL Server reads the data being transferred through the DataBlaster and loads it into an SQL database. This mainframe-to-SQL Server data transfer is performed once a day, during the middle of the night, in unattended mode. Approximately 1.5GB of data is transferred in this manner each night. The Portfolio Access Link system obtains the pertinent account and financial data required to satisfy a given customer query from the SQL Server, across a 100Mbps Fast Ethernet LAN, on an as-required, on-demand basis.

The Web-based, online trust fund accounting system has been an unqualified success. Replication-based systems such as this one and the system at Lincoln Reinsurance aptly demonstrate that Web solutions based on host data replication work and can be very effective. Obviously, replication has a cost element associated with it—if nothing else, in terms of duplicate data storage and the need to regularly transfer data between the host and the external server, not to mention potential "lost opportunity" costs because the data are outdated. Some will persuasively argue that this price is a small cost to pay for the peace of mind when it comes to ensuring mainframe security. It is hard to vehemently argue this point, especially if the career prospects of an MIS professional are contingent on ensuring that mainframe resources remain protected at all costs.

Thus, when it comes to Web solutions based on replication, the issues boil down to a classic case of choice and compromise. Browser-based access obviates the need for data replication and ensures that one always has the latest data. Despite the multiple levels of security available, some remain leery of the whole world, via the Internet, gaining easy physical access to the mainframe. The bottom line is that replication cannot be dismissed; it will continue to represent an option for those who remain unconvinced that TCP/IP-based security measures, however sophisticated and refined, will be potent enough to safeguard their mainframe.

8.3   A CASE STUDY ON MAXIMIZING EXISTING INVESTMENT THROUGH REJUVENATION

TransWorld Airlines (TWA), a pioneer in transcontinental air travel, remains an evocative name that conjures up visions of sleek, four-engined, three-fin Lockheed Constellation planes and sumptuous in-air service in an era when flying was a luxury. Although sadly no longer in the top tier, TWA, after a somewhat bumpy ride in the 1980s, is now steadfastly on an upward trek. In early 1999, in fact, it won the highly coveted J. D. Power & Associates award for being the number one airline in terms of customer satisfaction.

These days, TWA has some 22,000 employees worldwide, of which some 4300 have access to e-mail via IBM's OfficeVision office automation solution. OfficeVision, which was unveiled by IBM in 1989, is essentially a mainframe-oriented product intended to provide e-mail, calendar, word-processing, library management, and file-archiving services to 3270 terminal

A senior technical manager at TWA provides what is the ultimate endorsement of the viability and appeal of Web-to-Host solutions: *"Everybody is clamoring for Web technology. It is colorful. It is point and click. It is pretty. And it works."* Mainframe-based 3270-to-HTML conversion (as provided by Sterling Software's VM:Webgateway) was a resounding success at TWA, enabling the company to maximize its existing investment in IBM's OfficeVision/VM services, while drastically reducing its remote access costs and dramatically rejuvenating the interface used for e-mail and other personal productivity applications.

users. In the case of TWA, OfficeVision runs on a mainframe that uses IBM's Virtual Machine (VM) as its operating system. Figure 8.5 shows the highly dated, 3270-centric, function-key-driven, green-on-black textual user interface still used by OfficeVision/VM.

With a steadily increasing worldwide operation, TWA was anxious to find a surefire means to contain, if not reduce, its escalating remote access costs. The Internet was the obvious and optimum choice. TWA thus started looking at browser-based access to SNA solutions. During this process, it made a serendipitous discovery. Browser-based access would enable the company, with essentially no effort and no real additional cost, to replace the anachronistic OfficeVision user interface with a contemporary, PC-oriented and user-friendly GUI.

Strict budget constraints, dictated by today's highly competitive and cost-conscious airline industry, meant that TWA was not in a position to totally revamp its global network to provide its highly dispersed user base with LAN server-centric office automation tools and e-mail. The browser-based solution, at a stroke, provided them with a compelling work-around. By invoking rejuvenation, it could deliver, essentially for free, a contem-

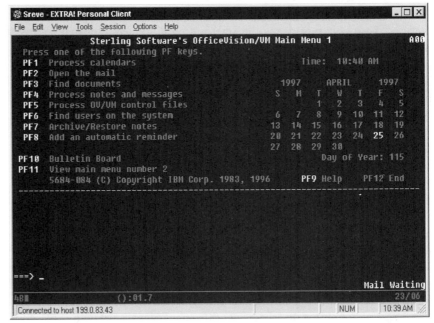

Source: Sterling Software

FIGURE 8.5 OfficeVision/VM's anachronistic, 3270-centric textual user interface. (*Source:* © Copyright Sterling Software, Inc. All rights reserved. VM:Webgateway is a trademark of Sterling Software, Inc. All other trademarks are the property of their respective owners.)

porary user interface to the users without reengineering the overall networking infrastructure, deploying new LAN servers, or installing new client software on all remote PCs.

Having a VM-based operation helped TWA home in on what proved to be a tailor-made solution: Sterling Software's VM:Webgateway product with its optional OfficeVision interface. VM:Webgateway, which is a mainframe-based and VM-specific 3270-to-HTML conversion product, was described in Section 6.1.3 in the context of the Lafayette Life Insurance case study. Lafayette, however, was not an OfficeVision user. The OfficeVision interface of VM:Webgateway is a potent "out-of-the-box" solution for Office-Vision customers such as TWA. It dramatically rejuvenates all OfficeVision/ VM screens automatically, without the need for any customer-provided scripts, customization, or programming. Figure 8.6 shows "before and after" images of the main OfficeVision/VM screen: the original green-on-black

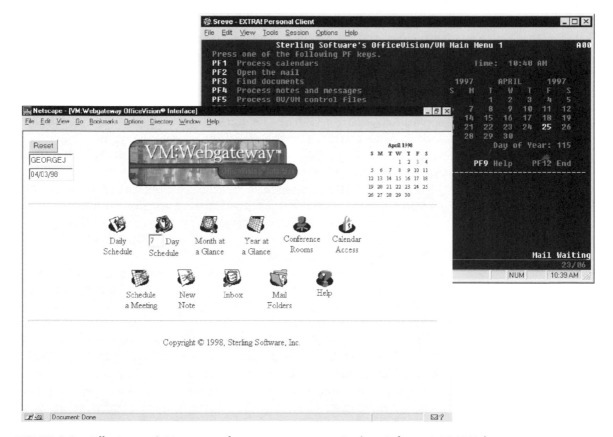

FIGURE 8.6 OfficeVision/VM user-interface rejuvenation via Sterling Software's VM:Webgateway OfficeVision Interface. (*Source:* © Copyright Sterling Software, Inc. All rights reserved. VM:Webgateway is a trademark of Sterling Software, Inc. All other trademarks are the property of their respective owners.)

form, as shown in Fig. 8.5, and the rejuvenated screen created by VM:Gateway's OfficeVision option. This Sterling solution gave TWA everything it wanted—browser-based Internet access plus automatic OfficeVision/VM user interface rejuvenation, in a totally integrated, highly scalable, VM-based package.

The VM:Webgateway was an instant and resounding success at TWA. The implementation was simple. Even more importantly, the solution, as is imperative for e-mail and for a mainframe application, has proved to be highly robust and resilient. This mission-critical availability was very important to TWA, especially given that the company has limited data center support resources to handle problems. With more than 4000 users, even if only one-third are online at any time, this solution is one of the largest 3270-to-HTML conversion-based systems in operation today. It clearly demonstrates that the scalability of this technology is limited only by the potency of the processor employed.

Figure 8.7 depicts the mainframe-centric architecture of TWA's VM:Webgateway-based solution. Note that VM:Webgateway comes with a built-in Web server. Consequently, there is no need for an external Web server such as one based on NT, NetWare, or UNIX. Given that this Web server uses HTTP just like any other server, TCP/IP on the mainframe is a prerequisite. This requirement does not present an impediment or even an issue, as the ongoing trend calls for mainframes to have TCP/IP so as to natively support applications such as FTP-based file transfer. VM:Webgateway's mainframe-resident Web server supports SSL-arbitrated data encryption, which provides the same level of security as is available with traditional Web servers. At this juncture, it is important to remember that VM:Webgateway is a generic 3270-to-HTML solution; the OfficeVision interface is merely one of its features. Also, recall that 3270-to-HTML conversion via VM:Webgateway is not restricted to VM applications—a point not lost on TWA.

VM:Webgateway can be used as a 3270-to-HTML gateway for mainframe applications based on MVS, OS/390, VSE, or even TPF. All that is required is an SNA connection between the VM host running VM:Webgateway and the other non-VM mainframes running the subject applications. Consequently, VM:Webgateway can be envisioned as a general-purpose 3270-to-HTML solution, where the conversion takes place on a VM-based server rather than an NT, NetWare, or UNIX server. Figure 5.13 on page 204 depicted how VM:Webgateway can act as a 3270-to-HTML gateway for non-VM applications. Many IBM shops have used a small VM machine as a platform for testing new releases of mainframe software (including operating system releases, given that the abiding beauty of VM is its ability to allow other operating systems to execute seamlessly on top of it). With the cost of mainframes steadily declining, thanks to IBM's aggressive CMOS processor-based S/390 initiatives, it is indeed possible to justify the use of a

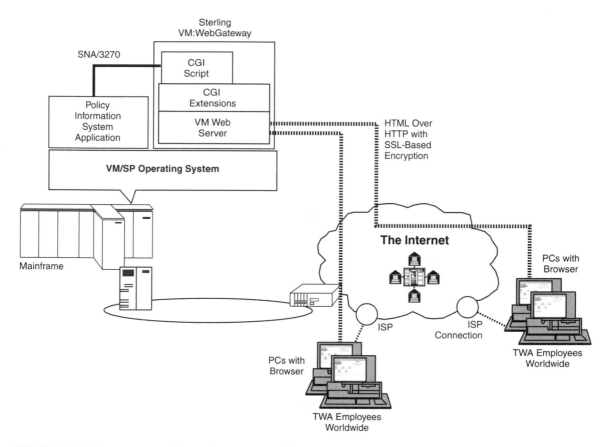

FIGURE 8.7   TWA's VM-specific, Sterling's VM:Webgateway-based Web-to-host solution.

small mainframe as a highly scalable and robust 3270-to-HTML server capable of supporting a few thousand concurrent users without figuratively breaking into a sweat.

Spurred by the very visible success of the OfficeVision conversion project, TWA is now in the process of Web-enabling other VM applications using VM:Webgateway. As described in the Lafayette Life case study, this process requires the development of application specific Common Gateway Interface (CGI) scripts, which are typically written in IBM's ubiquitous REXX scripting language. (The OfficeVision Interface is, in effect, a Sterling supplied CGI script for VM:Webgateway.)

A senior technical manager at TWA was eloquent and emphatic in his praise of the possibilities opened up by VM:Webgateway: "Everybody is clamoring for Web technology. It is colorful. It is point and click. It is pretty. And it works." This unequivocal endorsement of Web technology clearly summarizes the promise and potential of browser-based solutions within tra-ditional IBM environments. In addition to providing an unparalleled means of realizing economical remote access, they usher in the possibility of easily replacing the stark, productivity-sapping 3270 user interface with a contem-porary GUI.

8.4   TCP/IP ON THE MAINFRAME

By 2001, most mainframes running MVS and OS/390 will have TCP/IP installed on them. This development does not automatically signal the demise of SNA applications. Instead, SNA applications will coexist with TCP/IP applications. TCP/IP on the mainframe facilitates FTP-based end-to-end bulk file transfers as well as the possibility of using the mainframe as a highly scalable, high-capacity Web server. Mainframe-based tn3270(E) servers, capable of supporting 60,000 or more concurrent sessions, will start to gain strategic recognition. By mid-1999, IBM will start ensuring that TCP/IP applications have native support for Parallel Sysplex functions such as workload balancing. By 2005, it will be difficult to find a mainframe that is not heavily TCP/IP-oriented.

The TWA case study highlights another fairly predictable trend in IBM net-working—the growing presence of full TCP/IP software stack, or even mul-tiple stacks, on the mainframe. The current consensus is that at least 95% of mainframes running MVS or OS/390 will have TCP/IP on them by 2001. Installing TCP/IP on a mainframe is no longer a difficult, nerve-wracking, or laborious undertaking. Extensively proven, extremely efficient, highly scal-able, and extremely reliable TCP/IP stacks for mainframes are now available from IBM and Interlink. In fact, IBM's highly strategic OS/390 operating system already includes both TCP/IP software and a full-function Web serv-er (WebSphere) bundled in as part of the standard offering. The presence of TCP/IP and a Web server within OS/390 amply illustrates IBM's think-ing on this issue. IBM has recently been an avid proponent of end-to-end TCP/IP-based solutions, with TCP/IP on the mainframe being a pivotal aspect of such solutions. Significant strategic and tactical advantages follow from installing TCP/IP on a mainframe and moving toward a TCP/IP-centric computing environment. For example, this tactic provides a solid basis for e-commerce related initiatives.

Installing TCP/IP on a mainframe facilitates its integration with i•nets, permits fast, high-speed bulk data transfers with TCP/IP clients or other sys-tems, and positions the mainframe as a data server for Web-based applica-tions. There is a burgeoning demand for file transfers based on FTP (or NFS) between mainframes and the various NT- and UNIX-based servers, includ-ing Web servers, that now play an increasingly important role in corporate MIS solutions. TCP/IP on the mainframe greatly simplifies the performance of such file transfers and eliminates the need to first stage the data at an exter-nal server using SNA (for example, via the LU 6.2-based AFTP protocol) and then use FTP or NFS to download the data to its final destination.

The volume of data being transferred to and from mainframes using FTP is becoming so large that many corporations have little choice but to regu-larly search for the fastest and most efficient mainframe-based TCP/IP stacks so as to maximize data transfer rates and minimize data transfer times. IBM and Interlink have been locked in combat over which can deliver the fastest and most efficient FTP solutions, with each trying to outdo the other with each new software release. This competition has proved a great boon to IBM shops because the scalability, efficiency, and performance of mainframe TCP/IP have increased at a near-exponential rate since the mid-1990s. Thus, when considering implementing TCP/IP on a mainframe, it is imperative to obtain the latest capacity and throughput statistics from IBM and Interlink rather than relying on figures obtained even a year ago, as the latest numbers will invariably be considerably more favorable and compelling.

Having TCP/IP on the mainframe also permits it to be used as a highly scalable, high-capacity Web server—not just for 3270-to-HTML conversion applications, but also for disseminating other non-SNA-related data to browser users. Another attractive application for mainframe TCP/IP involves the use of a mainframe-resident tn3270(E) server, as opposed to a channel-attached (for example, IBM's 2216, Cisco 7500/CIP, Cisco 7200/CPA) or PC server-based (for example, Microsoft's SNA Server, Novell's NetWare for SAA, OpenConnect's OC://WebConnect SNA Server) tn3270(E) server. Some earlier case studies (such as the Ohio State University case study in Section 5.5.2) demonstrated that some IBM shops are already using mainframe-based tn3270(E) servers. Mainframe-based tn3270(E) servers are now available from both IBM and Interlink. In early 1998, IBM claimed to be able to support at least 60,000 concurrent sessions. This type of scalability is obviously the primary lure of a mainframe-based tn3270(E) server solution. The number of concurrent sessions supported will continue to grow as IBM and Interlink introduce new releases of their TCP/IP and tn3270(E) server software.

When a need exists for 30,000 or more concurrent tn3270(E) sessions, as would increasingly be the case as large SNA networks are transitioned to SNA-capable i•nets, a mainframe-based server is likely to be the most cost-effective and straightforward solution. It will, after all, eliminate the need for multiple external servers, as external servers rarely attempt to support much more than 30,000 sessions per instance of the server. The fail-safe, redundancy argument of deploying multiple separate servers, as opposed to a single large server, to guard against the failure of one server does represent a downside to the totally mainframe-centric scenario. The counterpoint is that the mainframe per se is a single point of failure, and having multiple external servers cannot guard against hardware or software failures at the mainframe. Thus it is safe to assume that mainframe-based tn3270(E) servers will be the strategic direction for large SNA-capable i•nets as of 2001. Figures 8.8 and 8.9 show two configurations where applet-based tn3270(E) emulation schemes are used with mainframe-resident tn3270(E) servers.

Security concerns can no longer be used as a valid excuse for not implementing TCP/IP on a mainframe. IBM, with its Tivoli Security Management Server, and Interlink, with its e-Control, set out to provide TCP/IP-specific access control to mainframe resources. Interlink's e-Control, for example, can grant or deny TCP/IP-based access or connections to a mainframe according to

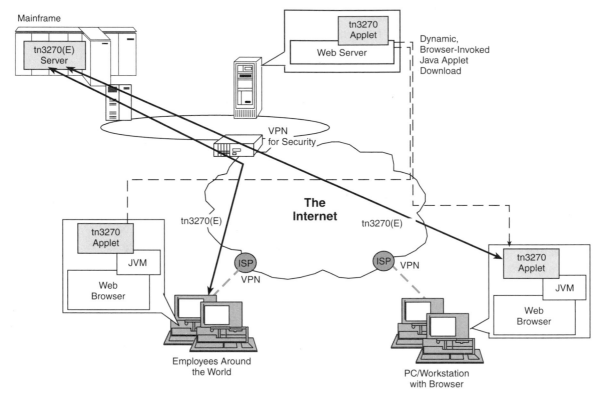

FIGURE 8.8   An applet-based tn3270(E) emulation permutation made possible with a mainframe-based tn3270(E) server. In this instance, encryption is provided via VPN technology.

IP address, time of day, port numbers, or user ID/password criteria. Mainframe-based TCP/IP management is also no longer an issue, as IBM, Interlink, and Sterling are all vying to deliver increasingly feature-rich offerings (see Section 7.7).

The inability to natively support S/390 Parallel Sysplex functions such as workload balancing, Multi-Node Persistent Sessions (MNPS), and Generic Resources was once the last criticism that could be leveled against mainframe TCP/IP. This situation is also changing. The Communications Server software that will be available with IBM's OS/390 version 2, release 7, shipping as of April 1999, for example, includes support for TCP/IP-based workload balancing in Parallel Sysplex environments. Furthermore, the lack of native support has never precluded TCP/IP from being implemented in Parallel Sysplex configurations. Instead, the Parallel Sysplex functions were available only to SNA applications that used APPN or HPR network node routing through ACF/VTAM. TCP/IP clients could still avail themselves of the Parallel Sysplex functions through the use of ip3270 or tn3270(E).

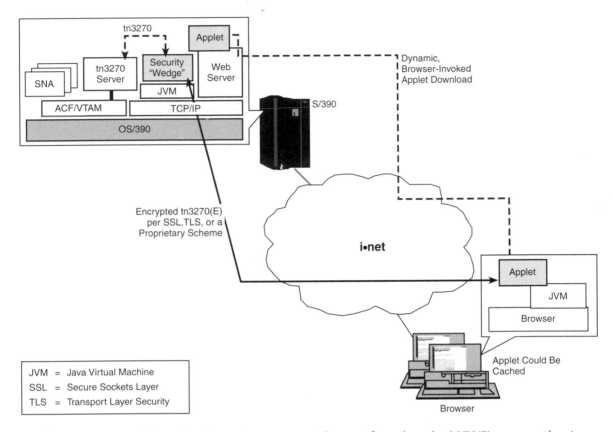

FIGURE 8.9 A tn3270(E) applet scheme that interacts with a mainframe-based tn3270(E) server, with a Java-based module providing security.

Thus the bottom line is that TCP/IP on the mainframe is clearly strategic and that no genuine excuses exist for shying away from embarking on this essential step toward long-term, end-to-end TCP/IP solutions, including mainframe-oriented e-commerce. By 2001, 95% or more of all MVS and OS/390 mainframes will be using mainframe TCP/IP applications on a production basis.

8.5 IMPLEMENTING MISSION-CRITICAL SNA-CAPABLE I•NETS—A FINAL CHECKLIST

When evaluating the merits and implications of transitioning to an SNA-capable i•net, it might help to reflect on the tale of the Great King Canute of England and Denmark (c. 1016). King Canute tried to demonstrate to his adoring subjects that there were powers that even he, as great as he was, could not control by showing that he was utterly powerless to stop the tide from coming ashore. Just as it was in the case with PCs and LANs before, TCP/IP is now an unstemmable technological tide for IBM networking—possibly even a tidal wave. Whether one likes it or not, relishes it or fears it, TCP/IP, intranets, and the Internet are here to stay—and will dominate worldwide computing for at least the next two decades. Consequently, enterprises that rely on mission-critical SNA applications on mainframes or AS/400s really have no choice except to start thinking, and thinking fast, about implementing a robust and secure SNA-capable i•net.

All of the technology required to implement a highly reliable and secure, full-function SNA-capable i•net is here, is proven, and is widely available from multiple established vendors. Preoccupation with Y2K is the only valid excuse for not embarking on a concerted effort to quickly transition to an SNA-capable i•net. Such i•nets, in addition to offering strategic integration with data centers, will reduce networking cost and complexity in multiple ways.

The technology for successfully implementing SNA-capable i•nets is plentiful, varied, proven, and highly economical. In addition to the invariably lower cost of the individual constituent components compared with those that they replace (such as an applet-based tn3270(E) client versus SNA/3270 fat client, or a $60,000 channel-attached bridge/router at the mainframe gateway as opposed to a $250,000 IBM 3745 Communications Controller), SNA-capable i•nets can reduce overall cost and complexity in other ways.

For example, remote intracompany or extranet access over the Internet, as has been repeatedly demonstrated with the case studies, is essentially a "nearly free" proposition. Internet-based remote access not only slashes remote access costs, but also ensures that new users or locations can be brought online with hardly any lead time or effort (as was shown with The Chickering Group case study in Section 5.6.2). Highly secure (that is, authenticated and encrypted) remote access to SNA applications over the Internet can be realized using either a browser-based access solution or VPN. Either applet-based emulation or 3270-to-HTML conversion would work in the case of the browser-based remote access with an applet-based scheme, with built-in encryption being preferable if one must manage sensitive data or wants maximum performance for heads-down, high-volume transactions.

In addition to remote access over the Internet, browser-based access schemes can be gainfully used for the following purposes:

- To replace SNA/3270 fat clients in intranet and extranet scenarios.
- To enable the public to transparently access SNA applications over the Internet for online investing, home banking, online travel reservation, online package tracking, or other applications.
- To effortlessly Web-enable SNA applications so that they can be freely accessed across any i•net.
- To easily rejuvenate and modernize the dated 3270/5250 user interface via AutoGUI schemes such as IBM/AT2's ResQ!Net, OpenConnect's AutoVista, Eicon's Web-to-Host Server, or Attachmate's HostSurfer. Figure 6.6 showed the AutoGUI rejuvenation prowess of ResQ!Net, and Fig. 8.10 demonstrates the capabilities of AutoVista.

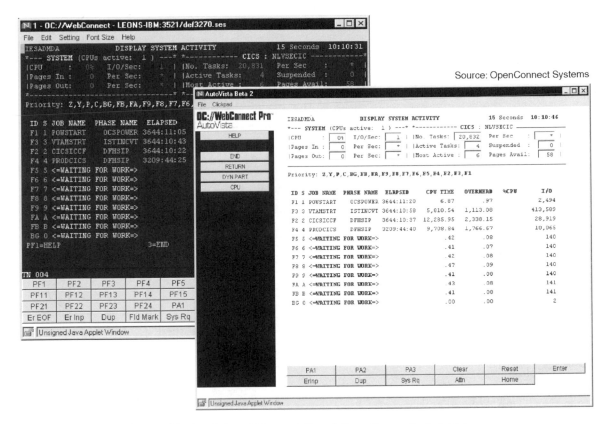

Source: OpenConnect Systems

FIGURE 8.10 "Straight-out-of-the-box" AutoGUI capability of OpenConnect's AutoVista. (*Source:* OpenConnect Systems.)

- To seamlessly synthesize mainframe and AS/400 data with external data sources, especially in the context of Web-oriented application servers with strong data center interfaces, such as OpenConnect's new OC://WebConnect application server. Figure 8.11 shows the generic architecture of a Java-based application server.

- To provide authentication and encryption for all 3270-based SNA access given that most fat clients and tn3270(E) clients do not provide built-in encryption as a standard feature.

Browser-based access can also reduce networking cost and complexity in the following ways:

- By eliminating the need to install, maintain, and upgrade SNA-related client software on individual PCs and workstations.

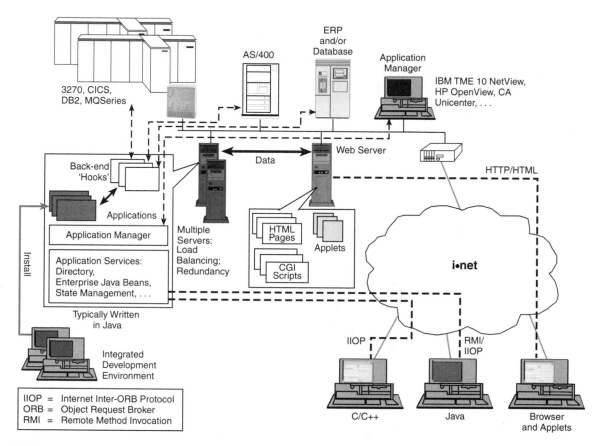

FIGURE 8.11   The generic architecture of Java-based corporate application servers.

- By enabling corporations to profitably exploit the "concurrent user"-based pricing models now widely available, where one pays only for the maximum number of users who are likely to use SNA at any one time rather than buying a license for every user that might potentially use SNA. One could easily have a 1:4 or even greater ratio between the maximum number of concurrent users likely to be using SNA and the total number of users that require SNA access, particularly in multinational corporations operating in different time zones, whose entire SNA population is unlikely to be active at the same time.

- By facilitating effortless user interface rejuvenation, which will enhance user productivity, minimize data entry errors, and improve user satisfaction.

Although browser-based access is indubitably strategic when it comes to implementing an SNA-capable i•net, in many instances it will be merely one of the technologies that will be required to realize a full-function, end-to-end network. Some scenarios may require the continued use of ip3270 or tn3270(E) to accommodate a highly customized GUI running on top of a specific 3270 emulator, the need for undistracted, heads-down data entry, a 3270 emulator-specific customization feature, or possibly a highly specialized graphics (or light pen) capability not supported by the browser-based scheme. It is also important to note that, after 2001, SNA access will inevitably start to gravitate toward programmatic solutions aided by application servers.

In addition to the possible need for multiple SNA access schemes to handle non-SNA clients, a need will arise to cater to true SNA devices, such as IBM 4700 Financial Systems, 3x74 control units, and automated teller machines. End-to-end SNA transport in the context of SNA-capable i•nets can be achieved by DLSw or HPR-over-IP (Enterprise Extender).

DLSw is proven and ubiquitous, supports LU 6.2, and appears quite scalable with version 2. In a majority of situations, it should be chosen without hesitation as the optimal end-to-end SNA transport scheme. HPR-over-IP, as described in Section 2.4, has the edge over DLSw in only two scenarios. The first scenario arises when there is a genuine need to ensure shortest-distance, optimal routing when remote users are switching between SNA applications resident in geographically distant data centers. The second scenario occurs when there is a valid reason for wanting uncompromised LU 6.2 COS-based traffic prioritization end-to-end across the network—from the desktop to an SNA application. If either or both of these scenarios apply, then HPR-over-IP should be used instead of DLSw. HPR-over-IP is now available on IBM's 2216, 2212, and 2210 families of bridge/routers.

A complete checklist of the technologies potentially required to implement a full-function SNA-capable i•net, in addition to the obligatory Web servers, Web browsers, routers, and switches, would include the following items:

1. SNA access scheme(s): ip3270, tn3270(E), applet-based emulation, 3270-to-HTML, application-specific, and programmatic

2. SNA transport scheme: DLSw, HPR-over-IP, or VPN

3. tn3270(E) server (for example, channel-attached IBM 2216) or SNA-LAN gateway for TCP/IP-to-SNA protocol conversion

4. Optional 3270-to-HTML server if host publishing is to be used

5. Optional application server(s) for programmatic solutions

6. Optional SNA-Web gateway with some applet-based emulation schemes for authentication, encryption, and possibly applet function augmentation

7. Firewall(s): definitely one or more at the data center-to-i•net interface and possibly at each remote location to guard the remote site network against intrusion from the i•net

8. Network management schemes: ideally a mainframe-based system that can manage both SNA and TCP/IP resources in parallel with an off-board SNMP/RMON-based management platform (for example, IBM's TME 10 NetView or Hewlett-Packard's OpenView) for managing the TCP/IP infrastructure of the i•net

9. A contemporary LAN- and TCP/IP-oriented mainframe gateway, such as the IBM 2216, Cisco 7500/CIP, or Cisco 7200/CPA

10. TCP/IP-specific access control mechanisms at the mainframe, such as Interlink's e-Control

All of these technologies and actual products are now readily available and quite affordable. Moreover, most of the core technology, such as DLSw, tn3270(E), applet-based emulation, and firewalls, is available from several credible vendors. Thus one cannot legitimately claim that any of this technology is untested, unproven, or unavailable. Y2K-induced distraction is the only valid excuse for postponing the inexorable march toward TCP/IP-centric, SNA-capable i•nets. If any doubt exists, it is always good to reflect on good King Canute and realize that it will be futile to resist the force of the onrushing TCP/IP and i•net tide.

8.6   AN OPERATIC CASE STUDY AS THE FINALE

The Cairo Opera House provides another scintillating example of how the Internet can be profitably harnessed to provide virtually free WAN bandwidth for SNA applications. In this instance, a move from dial-up connections to browser-based access over the Internet made it cost-justifiable to have opera tickets printed at remote ticket agencies. It is easy to see how such an application can be effortlessly extrapolated into a full-blown, credit-card transaction-processing, e-commerce application.

Befitting the highly popular adage, that nothing is truly over until the large, female soprano has had her say on stage, it is appropriate that this book concludes with a case study involving an opera house—the Cairo Opera House, to be precise. Even better, its application, which involves the remote printing of opera tickets, can in some ways be construed as an e-commerce application. After all, it does involve credit-card transactions over the Internet and the delivery of products (in this case, the tickets) across the Internet.

Egypt's Cairo Opera House uses an AS/400 for its back-office functions, including reservation tracking and issuing tickets. Given the very large and geographically scattered community being served, the Cairo Opera permitted opera lovers to make reservations through local travel agents. In some instances, ticket agents might have to telephone the Opera House in Cairo to make these reservations. Other agents, however, were able to make online reservations using 5250 emulation on PCs and a dial-up connection to the AS/400 in the Opera House. Nonetheless, due to high dial-up costs and poor line quality, the Opera House did not provide for the remote printing of opera tickets at the ticket agents' offices. Instead, opera tickets had to be picked up at the theater. This setup resulted in long lines at the box office prior to each show. Given that bandwidth availability and costs were the main impediments to remote ticket printing, the Cairo Opera House (like Nestlé, as discussed earlier in this chapter) turned to the Internet as an obvious solution to its dilemma.

Farabi Technology, as noted earlier, has a very high profile in the Middle East due to a large operational presence in that region and its support of right-to-left languages (such as Arabic, Hebrew, and Farsi) within browser-based solutions. Thus it is not that surprising that the Cairo Opera House asked Farabi to help implement an Internet-based remote ticket printing application. The company's standard Farabi HostFront family of solutions supports applet-based 5250 emulation, and its ActiveX-based applets can further facilitate PC-oriented printing. (Note that Nestlé also opted for ActiveX applets in preference to Java to obtain tighter integration with Windows-based PC printing.) The architecture used by the Cairo Opera House is shown in Fig. 8.12, and Fig. 8.13 shows images of actual opera tickets issued over the Internet.

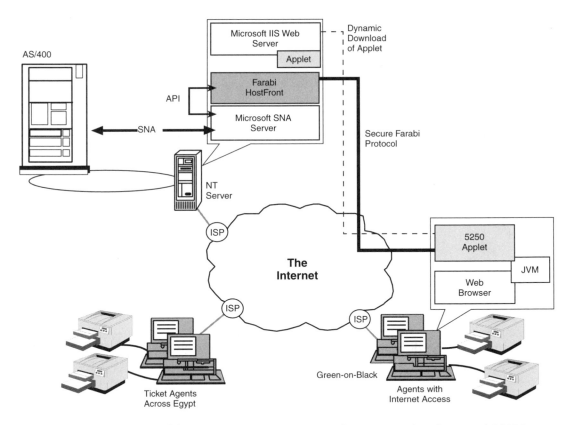

FIGURE 8.12 The architecture of the Cairo Opera House system for printing tickets from an AS/400 across the Internet.

FIGURE 8.13   Examples of the opera tickets that will be printed by the Farabi HostFront-centric solution adopted by the Cairo Opera House.   (*Source:* Farabi Technology.)

This final case study, in addition to yet again validating that SNA-capable i•net technology is ready for prime time, amplifies upon the trend of the Internet becoming a strategic means for remote access and, in this instance, for remote printing applications. Given that ticket agents appear in the loop, this situation is an extranet application like that discussed in Section 8.1.3. It is not difficult to see how this ticket reservation and ticket issuing application could be extended to become a true public-sector e-commerce application, however, whereby opera lovers from around the world could at least make online reservations via the Web. The printing of tickets would obviously be slightly more difficult given the diversity of printers involved and the safeguards that would be necessary to prevent the forging of expensive opera tickets.

In the case of online reservations, the same architecture being used today in the extranet configuration could be easily extrapolated to cater to public access—possibly with some additional application-level modifications to handle online credit-card processing and validation. Security per se is not an issue, because the Farabi scheme provides server-level authentication and encryption. The one disadvantage is that this scheme requires the downloading of the 5250 applet. As bandwidth is not as plentiful and relatively economical in the Middle East as it is in North America, many users in the Middle East may not have access to 56Kbps or even 33.3Kbps ISP connections. Indeed, 28.8Kbps or even slower connections are still quite prevalent. With such a slow-speed ISP connection, an applet download, even if it is comparatively small, could take a few minutes. The way to circumvent this issue would be to use 5250-to-HTML publishing.

Interestingly, the Farabi architecture handles both applet-based emulation and HTML publishing through the NT server-resident HostFront Server component. Thus the architecture shown in Fig. 8.12 could be extended to support 5250-to-HTML by adding the HostFront Publishing component. Figure 8.14 shows the architecture of a HostFront-based scheme that will

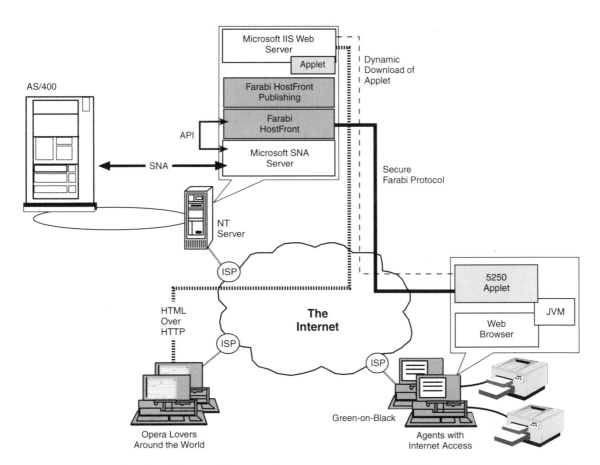

FIGURE 8.14 Extending the scheme at the Cairo Opera House to support 5250-to-HTML conversion so that Internet users around the world will have ready access to its program schedule.

support applet-based emulation for extranet users (that is, agents) and 5250 publishing for public access. Note that 5250-to-HTML conversion, through the Microsoft IIS Web server, also supports authentication and encryption via SSL.

This type of Web server-based SSL encryption of HTML is the primary security scheme being used by e-commerce leaders such as Amazon.com and e-Bay. The same is true for Web-based stock trading companies such as Charles Schwab, Fidelity, and e*Trade. The last word on security, a very valid and perennial concern, is that the technology is already available to provide it. SNA-capable i•nets offer as many, if not more, security measures and safeguards than those now routinely used to conduct e-commerce and online stock trading over the Web. Ongoing concerns about security should not be an excuse for holding back on SNA-capable i•nets.

8.7   THE LAST WORD

By 2003, SNA will be 30 years old! For an architecture that was crafted when 9.6Kbps was considered the ultimate in broadband communications and the notion of a PC was just a gleam in someone's eye, it has done amazingly well. Resilience and adaptability have been its hallmarks. SNA-capable i•nets, in effect, will be SNA's final and most spectacular metamorphosis. Change in the SNA world, much more so than in other arenas, is always difficult, laborious, and traumatic. Conservatism—forced by the need to safeguard the availability and integrity of mission-critical applications that have a direct bearing on the bottom line of most mid-size to large corporations—remains deep-rooted. Nonetheless, the noteworthy longevity of SNA reflects its astonishing ability to adapt, assimilate, and metamorphose.

It took a long time for SNA to accept PCs. Supporting LANs took even longer. Bridge/router-based multiprotocotol networking was a challenge at first, but today much of the world's considerable volume of SNA/APPN traffic flows across multiprotocol networks. Thus SNA has slowly but surely kept up with all prior technological innovation. In reality, i•nets are merely the latest set of networking methodologies that SNA must accommodate. The good news is that the necessary enabling technologies are already in place, proven, and even being used on a production basis by many IBM shops around the world.

In addition to suffering from the inertia induced by conservatism born of mission-criticality concerns, the forward motion of SNA networking was impeded for the better part of five years, during the mid-1990s, due to the fuss about ATM. IBM's strident claims during the 1993 to 1996 time frame, that end-to-end ATM, from the desktop to the mainframe, was the ultimate solution for next-generation networking caused many IBM shops to put their long-term network evolution plans on hold to determine how and when ATM could benefit them. ATM, although still the strategic means for obtaining highly scalable, multimedia-capable campus backbone and WAN bandwidth, no longer appears to be the panacea that it was portrayed to be. Instead, i•nets and Fast Ethernet are now as strategic and significant as ATM. Enterprises that planned to reengineer their SNA networks to base them on ATM now need to do a double-take. Networking reengineering in the IBM world will now strive to implement SNA-capable i•nets rather than another networking technology.

SNA-capable i•nets, with their proven capacity to reduce cost and complexity while simultaneously providing much-needed additional functionality, such as automatic user interface rejuvenation, is indubitably the way forward and the optimal framework for SNA in the twenty-first century. After the setback with ATM, SNA-capable i•nets now provide IBM shops with the first real opportunity in more than a decade to reshape and modernize their overall network infrastructure. The turn of the new millennium is indeed the time to abandon the old, optimize the essentials, and embrace the new. There will not be another chance. The future of SNA will be within the context of SNA-capable i•nets.

Transitioning from an SNA-only or multiprotocol network to an SNA-capable i•net is not a trivial undertaking. It is, however, eminently feasible. Several corporations have already made the transition very successfully. Rather than dwelling on the inevitable challenges, focus on the opportunities and possibilities. This technology is exciting. The Internet and i•nets are forging an entirely new and very invigorating era of commercial and social change. This is the start of the Information Revolution. Not since the creation of the printing press has there been such a pivotal change in how information is disseminated and consumed. We should consider ourselves extremely lucky to actively participate in this process. Don't look back. Step up to the mark, embrace i•nets, and take time to enjoy being an architect of change and progress.

Acronyms and Abbreviations

A&C	Address and copy in Token Ring
ACF2	(Computer Associates') Access Control Facility
ACF/NCP	Advanced Communications Functions for the Network Control Program
ACF/VTAM	Advanced Communications Functions for the Virtual Telecommunications Access Method
AIW	APPN(/APPC) Implementers Workshop
AIX	(IBM's) Advanced Interactive Executive
ANR	Automatic Network Routing
ANRF	ANR routing field
API	application program interface
APPC	Advanced Program-to-Program Communications
APPI	(Cisco's) Advanced Peer-to-Peer Internetworking
APPN	Advanced Peer-to-Peer Networking
ARB	Adaptive Rate-Based Congestion Control
AS/400	(IBM's) Application System/400 and now Advanced Server/400
ASCII	American Standard Code for Information Interchange
ASP	(Microsoft's) Active Server Page technology
ATM	Asynchronous Transfer Mode; automated teller machine; Adobe Type Manager
AWT	Abstract Windowing Toolkit
BAN	(IBM's) Boundary Access Node
BMS	(CICS) Basic Mapping Support

bps	bits per second
Bps	bytes per second
BSC	Binary-Synchronous Communications
B-STUN	(Cisco's) Binary Synchronous Tunneling
CGI	Common Gateway Interface
CICS	Customer Information Control System
CIP	(Cisco's) Channel Interface Processor
CIR	committed information rate
CLAW	Common Link Access for Workstations
CM/2	OS/2 Communications Manager/2
CMOS	complementary metal oxide semiconductor
COM	(Microsoft's) Component Object Model
CORBA	Common Object Request Broker Architecture
COS	Class-of-Service
CP	control point
CPA	(Cisco's) Channel Port Adapter
CPE	customer premises equipment
CPI-C	Common Programming Interface for Communications
CRC	cyclic redundancy check
CS	(IBM's) Communications Server
CS/NT	(IBM's) Communications Server for Windows NT
CSMA/CD	Carrier Sense Multiple Access with Collison Detection
CTC(A)	Channel-to-Channel (Adapter)
CTS	Common Transport Semantic
CUA	common user access
DCE	Distributed Communications Environment; Data Circuit-Terminating Equipment
DDDLU	Dynamic Definition of Dependent LU
DDLSw	Desktop DLSw
DES	Data Encryption Standard
DHCP	Dynamic Host Configuration Protocol
DLC	Data Link Control
DLCI	Data Link Control Identifier
DLL	Dynamic Link Library
DLSw	Data Link Switching
DLU	Dependent Logical Unit
DLUS/DLUR	DLU Server/DLU Requester

DNS	Domain Name Server
DOS	Disk Operating System (PC or IBM mainframe)
DOS/VSE	(IBM's) Disk Operating System/Virtual Storage Extended
DRDA	Distributed Relational Database Architecture
DSL	Digital Subscriber Loop
DSPU	Downstream Physical Unit
DTE	Data Terminal Equipment
E1/E2/E3	2.048Mbps link/8.448 Mbps link/34.37Mbps link
EBCDIC	Extended Binary Coded Decimal Interchange Code
ECI	(CICS) External Call Interface
EDK	Enterprise Development Kit
EHLLAPI	Extended HLLAPI
EJB	Enterprise JavaBeans
EOR	end of record
EPI	(CICS) External Presentation Interface
ERP	Enterprise Resource Planning
ESCON	Enterprise System Connectivity architecture
FCS	Frame Check Sequence
FDDI	Fiber Distributed Data Interface
FDX	full-duplex
FEP	Front End Processor
FICON	Fiber Connection
FIFO	first in, first out
FR	Frame Relay
FRAD	Frame Relay access device
FRF	Frame Relay Forum
FSL	Farabi Script Language
FST	(Cisco's) Fast Sequenced Transport
FTP	File Transfer Protocol
Gbps	gigabits per second (billions of bits per second)
GIF	Graphical Interchange Format
GM ·	General Motors
GUI	graphical user interface
HACL	(IBM's) Host Access Class Library
HDLC	High-Level Data Link Control
HDX	half-duplex
HFS	Hierarchical File System

HLLAPI	High-Level Language Application Program Interface
HoD	(IBM's) Host On-Demand
HPDT	(IBM's) High-Performance Data Transfer
HPR	High Performance Routing
HPS	(Attachmate's) HostPublishing System
HSTR	High-Speed Token Ring
HTML	HyperText Markup Language
HTTP	HyperText Transfer Protocol
HTTPS	Secure HTTP
i•net	intranet, extranet, or the Internet
IAC	interpret next octet as command
ICSS/390	(IBM's) Internet Connection Secure Server for OS/390
IDE	integrated development environment
IETF	Internet Engineering Task Force
IIOP	Internet Inter-ORB Protocol
IIS	(Microsoft's) Internet Information Server
ILU	Independent Logical Unit
IMS	Information Management System
IOS	(Cisco's) Internetworking Operating System
IP	Internet Protocol
IPL	Inital Program Load
IPsec	Secure IP (or IP Security)
IPX	(Novell's) Internetwork Packet Exchange
ISA	Industry Standard Architecture Bus
ISDN	Integrated Services Digital Network
ISO	International Standards Organization
ISP	Internet Service Provider
ISR	Intermediate Session Routing
J1/J2	1.586Mbps link/6.312Mbps link
JCP	(OpenConnect's) Java Control Protocol
JDBC	Java Database Connectivity
JDK	Java Development Kit
JES	Job Entry System
JVM	Java Virtual Machine
Kbps	Kilobits per second (thousands of bits per second)
L2TP	Layer 2 Tunneling Protocol
LAN	local area network

LANE	LAN Emulation
LCS	LAN Channel Station
LDAP	Lightweight Directory Access Protocol
LLC	Logical Link Control
LPAR	Logical Partition
LSA	Link Service Architecture
LU	Logical Unit
MAC	Media Access Control
MB	megabytes
Mbps	Megabits per second (millions of bits per second)
MMMTG	Mixed-media, multilink transmission groups
MNPS	Multinode persistent sessions
MPC	MultiPath Channel
MPOA	Multiprotocol over ATM
MPTF	Multiprotocol Transport Feature
MPTN	Multiprotocol Transport Networking
MTS	Microsoft Transaction Server
MVS	Multiple Virtual Storage
NAP	Network Access Point
NAT	network address translation
NC	network computer
NCCF	Network Communications Control Facility
NCF	(IBM's) Network Computing Framework
NCP	Network Control Program
NetBEUI	NetBIOS Extended User Interface
NetBIOS	Networking Basis Input/Output System protocol
NFS	Network File System
NHDR	Network Layer Header
NIC	network interface card
NLP	Network Layer Packet
NLPID	Network Layer Protocol Identifier
NMVT	Network Management Vector Transport
NPDA	Network Problem Determination Application
NPM	NetView Performance Monitor
NPSI	NCP Packet Switching Interface
NRF	Network Routing facility
NSI	Non-SNA Interconnection

NTO	Network Terminal Option
NVT	Network Virtual Terminal
OAF	Origin Address Field
OC3	155Mbps link
ODBC	Open Database Connectivity
OHIO	Open Host Interface Objects
OIA	Operator Information Area
OLAP	Online Analytical Processing
OLE	(Microsoft's) Object Linking and Embedding
OLTP	Online Transaction Processing
OMG	Object Management Group
ORB	Object Request Broker
OSA(/2)	Open Systems Adapter (version 2)
OSF	Open Software Foundation
OSI	Open System Interconnection
OSPF	open shortest path first
PComm	(IBM's) Personal Communications
PF	program function key
PIR	Protocol Independent Routing
PIU	Path Information Unit
PLU	Primary Logical Unit
POP	Post Office Protocol
POWER	Performance Optimization with Enhanced RISC; Priority Output Writers, Execution Readers
PPP	Point-to-Point Protocol
PPTP	Point-to-Point Tunneling Protocol
PU	Physical Unit
PUCP	Physical Unit Control Point
PVC	permanent virtual circuit
QOS	quality of service
RACF	Resource Access Control Facility
RAS	remote access server
RCP	remote communications processor
RFC	Request for Comment
RH	Request or Response Header
RIF	Routing Information Field
RIP	Routing Information Protocol

RMI	remote method invocation
RMON	remote network monitoring
RNR	Not Ready to Receive (Receive Not Ready)
RPC	Remote Procedure Call
RR	Receive Ready
RSRB	Remote Source Route Bridging
RSVP	Resource Reservation Protocol
RTM	Response Time Monitor
RTP	Rapid Transport Protocol
RU	Request or Response Unit
SAA	Systems Applications Architecture
SBA	Set Buffer Address
SCS	SNA Character Stream
SDH	Synchronous Digital Hierarchy
SDK	Software Development Kit
SDLC	Synchronous Data Link Control
SET	Secure Electronic Transaction
S-HTTP	secure HTTP
SLIP	Serial Line Internet Protocol
SLU	Secondary LU
SMDS	Switched Multimegbit Data Service
SMTP	Simple Mail Transfer Protocol
SNA	Systems Network Architecture
SNAP	Subnetwork Access Protocol; SNA portable software
SNF	Sequence Number Field
SNI	SNA Network Interconnection; Subscriber–Network Interface
SNMP	Simple Network Management Protocol
SONET	Synchronous Optical Network
SPX	(Novell's) Sequenced Packet Exchange
SQL	Structured Query Language
SRB	Source Route Bridging
SRT	Source Route Transparent
SSCP	System Services Control Point
SSL	Secure Sockets Layer
STP	shielded twisted-pair
STUN	(Cisco's) SDLC Tunneling
SVC	switched virtual circuit

SVN	switched virtual networking
Sysplex	system complex
T1/T3	1.536Mbps link/44.7Mbps link
TCAM	Telecommuincations Access Method
TCP	Transmission Control Protocol; terminal control program
TCP/IP	Transmission Control Protocol/Internet Protocol
TDM	time division multiplexing
TDU	topology database update
TG	transmission group
TH	Transmission Header
TIC	37xx Token Ring Interface Coupler
TLS	Transport layer security
TPF	Transmission Priority Field
TR	Token Ring
TSO	Timesharing Option
UA	Unnumbered Acknowledgment
UDP	User Datagram Protocol
URL	uniform resource locator
UTP	unshielded twisted-pair
VB	Visual Basic
VC	Frame Relay virtual circuit or virtual connection; ATM virtual channel
VM	Virtual Machine
VPN	Virtual Private Networking
VR	virtual route
VSAM	Virtual Storage Access Method
VTAM	Virtual Telecommunications Access Method
WAN	wide area network
WWW	World Wide Web
XCA	External Communications Adapter
XID	exchange identification
XML	Extensible Markup Language
XRF	Extended Recovery Facility
Y2K	year 2000

Glossary

2210 IBM's low-cost bridge/router family.

2212 IBM's midrange bridge/router family.

2216 IBM's strategic channel-attachable bridge/router family replete with tn3270(E) server, VPN, and HPR-over-IP functionality.

2217 IBM's now-defunct AnyNet Gateway, which permitted multiprotocol networking across a single-protocol APPN/HPR backbone.

3172 Interconnect Controller, whose primary role is to act as a low-cost, LAN-to-mainframe gateway.

3270 Generic name for a once ubiquitous family of terminals, printers, and control units for accessing mainframe-resident applications.

37xx IBM Communications Controllers (e.g., 3745, 3746, 3725).

3x74 3270 Control Unit, which can now be used in a variety of other roles, including that of an SNA-LAN gateway.

5250 The equivalent of 3270 for accessing applications on AS/400s and other IBM minicomputers such as the S/36 or S/38.

7200 Midrange, channel-attachable Cisco bridge/router.

7500 Cisco's high-end, channel-attachable bridge/router family.

7xxx Generic term for the Cisco 7500 and 7200 family of bridge/routers.

8265 IBM's channel-attachable, highly scalable ATM switch.

ACF/NCP IBM-supplied SNA software that runs on a 37xx Communications Controller. Version 7, release 1, available as of February 1994, supports SNA over Frame Relay per RFC 1490.

ACF/VTAM IBM-supplied host software that is a prerequisite for implementing a host-centric SNA network.

ActiveX Microsoft's strategic object-oriented component technology that is tightly integrated with Windows and is seen as a competitor to Java.

AIW   APPC/APPN Implementers Workshop, an IBM-sponsored forum that ended up as the de facto guardian of DLSw. AIW is not a recognized standards body.

ANR   Agile Layer 2 connectionless protocol employed by HPR.

AnyNet (gateway)   Family of IBM software products that perform protocol conversion. This software can either reside within a product or be deployed within a stand-alone gateway (e.g., IBM 2217). It can be used to convert SNA to TCP/IP, or vice versa. The gateway can also encapsulate IPX and NetBIOS traffic within LU 6.2 message units.

APPC   Marketing term for LU 6.2-based interactions.

applet   Java- or ActiveX-based software that can be dynamically downloaded from a Web server for execution on a PC or workstation.

application server   Server-side, Java-heavy systems to facilitate the implementation of object-oriented, Web-centric applications.

APPN   Advanced Peer-to-Peer Networking—the born-again, peer-to-peer, plug-and-play replacement for SNA that has been around since 1986.

APPN end nodes   Smart APPN peripheral nodes that establish a CP-to-CP session with an APPN NN. This session allows you to obtain services, such as directory services, from the NN. It can dynamically register LUs with the NN.

APPN network nodes   Smart APPN nodes responsible for intermediate node routing, directory services, route selection, and network topology management.

ARB   HPR's anticipatory congestion control mechanism.

AS/400   IBM minicomputer.

ASP   Microsoft's server-side technology for creating dynamic, highly interactive, high-performance Web server applications.

ATM   Strategic Layer 2, CCITT data transfer standard that combines the constant bandwidth and consistent delay characteristics of circuit switching with the resource sharing and "bursty" traffic to accommodate features of packet switching. The basis of ATM is the very fast switching of fixed-length, 53-byte cells.

BAN   IBM's variant of RFC 1490 for encapsulating SNA/APPN traffic within Frame Relay. It uses the same encapsulation scheme as utilized by bridges rather than the SNA/APPN-specific native scheme specified by RFC 1490/FRF.3.

bandwidth   The data transfer capacity of a link in terms of bits per second.

Boundary Function   SNA: a set of services, including address conversion, provided by a subarea node to the peripheral nodes attached to it. HPR: ensures interoperability between HPR and APPN nodes.

browser   Client software, such as Netscape Navigator or Microsoft Internet Explorer, that is used to view Web pages.

BSC   An IBM link protocol from 1967 that is still used by devices such as automated teller machines.

bus-and-tag   The original scheme for channel-attaching devices to an IBM mainframe. It uses two bulky cables per attachment and transfers data 8 bits at a time in parallel form. The maximum bandwidth is 4.5MBps (36Mbps).

cache (directory) Directory containing dynamically created entries for objects typically located through a search process. Old entries that have not been recently referenced may be overwritten with new entries.

channel-attached Locally attaching a device to an IBM mainframe via a high-speed bus-and-tag or ESCON connection.

CICS IBM's widely used subsystem for transaction-processing applications.

CIP Two-port, channel interface processor, with optional tn3270(E) server functionality, to directly attach the Cisco 7500 family of bridge/routers to mainframes.

CMOS The low-cost, ubiquitous semiconductor chip technology that is now the basis of IBM's S/390 Parallel Enterprise Server mainframes.

CORBA Object Management Group standard for robust, transparent, network-type-independent interworking of objects distributed across heterogeneous platforms.

CP Component in T2.1 and APPN nodes that provides local directory and configuration services.

CPA One-port variant of the Cisco CIP for channel-attaching the 7200 family of bridge/routers to mainframes.

CSMA/CD Contention-based access scheme used by Ethernet.

CTS IBM-developed, Layer 4-based, protocol mapping and conversion scheme. Basis of AnyNet.

cut-through A forwarding mode in LAN switching where the switch starts to forward bits that make up a frame to its destination as soon as it determines the relevant destination port without waiting to receive the end of the frame and checking whether it is error-free. The opposite of store-and-forward.

DB2 IBM's strategic relational database manager.

desktop DLSw A scheme whereby SNA/APPN traffic is encapsulated within TCP/IP packets at its source (e.g., PC/workstation) even before it reaches the LAN. It is justifiable only in dial-in scenarios for mobile users.

DHCP Scheme to dynamically allocate IP addresses to end users on-demand.

DLSw A core set of facilities now available on most multiprotocol bridge/routers for supporting SNA/APPN and NetBIOS traffic across a TCP/IP backbone. It embraces TCP/IP encapsulation, SDLC-to-LLC:2 conversion, local LLC:2 acknowledgment, and more.

DLU LU resident within a traditional SNA node that is able to establish LU-LU sessions only by depending on an SSCP to provide it with directory services.

DLUS/DLUR Technology required to ensure that traditional SNA traffic can be freely supported across an APPN or HPR network without any restrictions on the locations of the SNA devices.

domain The set of SNA resources controlled by a single SSCP.

DSL New technology for high-speed data communications over existing, copper telephone wiring.

DSPU   LAN-attached SNA node supported by an SNA-LAN gateway.

e-commerce   Electronic commerce across the Internet and extranets.

Enterprise Extender   IBM's marketing term for HPR-over-IP.

Enterprise JavaBeans   Server-side JavaBeans.

ESCON (II)   The now strategic means for mainframe channel attachment that is based on a multimode fiber connection and serial transmission of data. The maximum bandwidth is 17MBps (136Mbps) and channel distances can be as great as 36 miles. The latest version is referred to as ESCON II.

extranet   Business-to-business or agent-to-corporate interactions between intranets or across the Internet.

FICON   IBM's new 800Mbps channel technology.

firewall   Security technology used to control and monitor external access to a network.

Frame Relay   New generation, high-performance, low-overhead, connection-oriented, Layer 2 packet-switching standard prescribed by both the CCITT and ANSI. It can be thought of as a slimmed-down and streamlined X.25. It supports speeds as high as 45Mbps, although it is used only at less than 4Mbps at present.

FRF.3   Addendum to the RFC 1490 standard that specifies how to natively (i.e., without TCP/IP or MAC/LLC headers) encapsulate SNA/APPN traffic within Frame Relay frames.

home page   Either the opening or start page of a Web site, or the initial Web page that a browser displays when it is invoked.

Host On-Demand   IBM's Java applet-based SNA access solution.

HPDT   Mainframe-to-mainframe, LU 6.2-based bulk data transfer scheme.

HPR   Successor to SNA and APPN.

HTML   The language used to describe the format and content of Web pages.

HTTP   Connectionless, Layer 4 protocol used on top of IP for data transfer between Web servers and Web browsers.

HTTPS   Security in the form of SSL used over HTTP on a transaction-by-transaction basis.

IETF   The august group responsible for, among other things, setting i•net industry standards.

IIOP   Object interworking across TCP/IP-based i•nets à la CORBA.

ILU   LU 6.2s resident in T2.1 or APPN nodes that can establish LU-LU sessions without depending on an SSCP for any services.

IMS   IBM's large-scale database management scheme that first saw the light of day in 1963.

i•net   Collective term for the Internet, intranets, and extranets.

Internet   The huge collection of interconnected TCP/IP networks that now make up the new information frontier.

intranet   A private, corporate-specific network based on Internet technology.

IP   Layer 3, connectionless, unreliable protocol that is the lifeblood of all i•nets.

ip3270   Conventional SNA-LAN gateway model with Novell's NetWare for SAA or Microsoft's SNA Server, where TCP/IP is used for all communications between the gateway and the client-side 3270 emulator.

IP switching   See *Layer 3 switching*.

IPX/SPX   Internetwork Packet Exchange (IPX), which Novell NetWare's Layer 3 protocol, and Sequenced Packet Exchange (SPX), which is NetWare's Layer 4 protocol.

ISDN   Digital telephone service that permits multiple voice and data channels to be shared across one line.

Java   Highly popular, widely endorsed, platform-independent, object-oriented programming scheme introduced by Sun Microsystems circa 1995.

JavaBeans   Client-side Java objects to facilitate the reuse of program components between different applications.

JDBC   Java equivalent of ODBC.

JDK   Software development kit from Sun consisting of a Java compiler, a debugger, standard Java classes, and a JVM for UNIX.

JVM   Platform-specific environments for executing Java applets.

LAN switch   Internetworking device that rapidly forwards LAN frames from one of its ports to another.

LAN-over-SNA   Encapsulating TCP/IP, IPX/SPX, and NetBIOS traffic within LU 6.2 message units so that these protocols can be transported LAN-to-LAN across an SNA network.

Layer 3 switching   Route once, switch thereafter (LAN switching scheme) to expedite end-to-end delivery of IP-based data.

LLC   Logical Link Control—the upper portion of the OSI Layer 2, Data Link layer, as defined by the IEEE 802.x standards. It provides data link control functions, such as flow control and error recovery. LLC:2 refers to a connection-oriented (i.e., session-like) version of LLC that uses a superset of the commands offered by SDLC and is often employed to support SNA, APPN, and NetBIOS LAN traffic.

Local LLC:2 acknowledgment   Precludes LLC:2 acknowledgments having to be transported across a WAN.

LU   Ports through which end users gain access to an SNA network.

LU 6.2   Strategic means for program-to-program communications in SNA, APPN, or HPR networks.

Media Access Control   The lower portion of the OSI Layer 2, Data Link layer, as defined by the IEEE 802.x standards. It provides controlled access to a LAN.

MPC   IBM's strategic Layer 2 channel protocol.

MPTN   The formal architecture for CTS and AnyNet.

multiplexing   Sharing the bandwidth of a link between multiple users.

NBBS   An IBM architecture for value-added, ATM-centric networking.

NCF   IBM's heavily Java-biased client/server paradigm for Web-centric application development.

NCIA   Cisco's version of Desktop DLSw.

NetBIOS   LAN protocol widely used by IBM LAN applications, most notably IBM's OS/2 LAN Server.

NetView   Name of IBM's family of network management products.

Networking Blueprint   A framework put forward by IBM in 1992 for network-neutral applications that could be run across a variety of network types. AnyNet is a manifestation of the CTS technology postulated by this blueprint.

Nways   IBM's brand name for strategic, multiprotocol products that perform Layer 1–3 functions.

ODBC   Open standard for transparent database access.

OS/390   IBM's flagship mainframe operating system, replete with TCP/IP and a Web server.

OSA-2   Integrated I/O adapter on S/390 mainframes that supports Gigabit Ethernet, Fast Ethernet, Token Ring, ATM, and FDDI.

pacing   An SNA congestion control mechanism that permits a receiver to control the rate at which data are forwarded to it.

Parallel Sysplex   IBM's strategic mainframe processor clustering technology.

peripheral node   SNA type 2 or type 1 node.

PIR   CrossComm's proprietary routing mechanism.

PIU   Path Information Unit—the technical term for an SNA message unit.

PPP   Point-to-Point Protocol, which is widely used to transport TCP/IP across asynchronous/synchronous links.

PU   Software component within an SNA node that controls and manages the physical entities (e.g., links) associated with that node. Does not refer to actual devices.

PU Concentrator   Type of SNA-LAN gateway that aggregates the LUs in multiple SNA nodes into a single virtual node so that a mainframe does not have to support as many DSPUs.

remote polling   A technique that eliminates the need to continually transmit BSC or SDLC polls across a backbone network.

reverse multiplexing   Aggregating the bandwidth of multiple low-speed links to realize a high-bandwidth channel. Similar to an SNA TG.

RFC   The process for formulating i•net-related standards, where the ratified and proposed standards are referred to by their RFC numbers.

RFC 1490   A generic IETF standard for transporting alien traffic end-to-end across a Frame Relay WAN. It specifies an encapsulation scheme and a means for segmenting frames. FRF.3 extends RFC 1490 to embrace SNA/APPN traffic.

RH   SNA request/response header, which prefixes the data portion of an SNA message unit.

RIP   One of the popular routing protocols used by IP.

Routing Information Field (RIF)   A field in the Layer 2 MAC header used by Source Route Bridging to specify the LAN-to-LAN route that should be traversed by an inter-LAN packet.

RSRB   Cisco's proprietary scheme for encapsulating SNA/APPN traffic within TCP/IP.

RTP   Connection-oriented, full-duplex, end-to-end protocol used by HPR on top of ANR.

RU   SNA request/response unit that carries the data being transported within an SNA message unit.

S/390   IBM's new family of mainframes based on CMOS technology.

S/3x   S/36 or S/38 minicomputers that were the precursor to the AS/400.

SAA   Once highly touted IBM master plan introduced in 1987 for platform-independent, client/server application development.

SDLC   Synchronous Data Link Control—an IBM link protocol introduced in 1974 along with SNA that is widely used to support link-attached SNA devices.

SDLC-to-LLC-2 conversion   A technique used to integrate SDLC link-attached SNA devices into a LAN/WAN internet, where a modified remote polling process is used to make the link-attached devices appear as if they were LAN-attached.

SET   A security standard advocated by major credit-card companies for e-commerce over the Internet.

SLIP   Internet protocol used to run IP across serial links.

SMDS   Switched, high-speed, connectionless public service. It will support speeds as high as 155Mbps.

SNADS   LU 6.2-based, store-and-forward mail and data delivery service.

SNA-LAN gateway   Gateway that permits LAN-attached PCs/workstations to access mainframe- or AS/400-resident SNA/APPN applications.

SNA routing   SNA's native, subarea-to-subarea routing scheme based on network addresses and VRs.

SNMP   TCP/IP's network management protocol.

sockets   Widely used API for TCP/IP-based interactions.

Source Route Bridging (SRB)   The default technique in Token Ring environments for realizing communications between devices on different LANs.

spanning tree   Algorithm to prune a network with alternative paths so that only one active route exists between any given pair of nodes.

SRT bridge   A bridge that supports both SRB and transparent bridging.

SSCP   SNA centralized control point function that provides directory, configuration, and management services.

SSL   Authentication and encryption method negotiation technology from Netscape that is now widely used as a proven security scheme between browsers and Web servers.

store-and-forward   A forwarding mode in LAN switching in which the switch waits until it has received a complete error-free frame before it starts forwarding it to the destination port. The opposite of cut-through.

subareas/subarea nodes   The SNA type 4 or type 5 nodes that support peripheral (or end) nodes and are capable of performing SNA routing. A subarea node and all peripheral nodes attached to it form a subarea—the basis of SNA network addressing and routing.

SVN   IBM framework for implementing and managing switched, as opposed to routed, networks.

TCP/IP   Layer 3 and Layer 4 protocols in the internet community.

TCP/IP encapsulation   Encapsulating of traffic using alien protocols, such as SNA/APPN or NetBIOS, within TCP/IP packets.

TH   SNA transmission header that prefixes all SNA or APPN message units.

tn3270(E)   Strategic, client/server-based methodology that permits a TCP/IP-based client to gain access to SNA applications using a 3270 data stream through a tn3270 server. The "E" refers to enhanced functionality such as support for color, highlighting, and so on.

transparent bridging   Bridging scheme used by Ethernet.

transparent switching   Transparent bridging as it applies to LAN switches.

TSO   Interactive application execution system for MVS and OS/390 operating systems.

UDP   Connectionless, Layer 4 counterpart of TCP.

URL   The address of a Web site or Web page as specified to a browser in the format "http://*www.xxx.yyy*".

VPN   Encryption and tunneling technology that permits Internet bandwidth to be securely and profitably exploited for intracompany data transfer. VPN in effect enables a corporation to create an intranet inside the public Internet.

Web   World Wide Web.

Web browser   See *browser*.

Web server   Server-side software that services Web users' requests for Web pages and applets.

WebSphere   IBM's application/Web server.

World Wide Web   Although now used as a synonym for the Internet, in reality the HTTP/HTML-oriented graphical portion of the Internet.

XML   Flexible, next-generation HTML.

Bibliography

IBM Multiprotocol Networking

Anura Gurugé. *Reengineering IBM Networks*. New York: John Wiley, 1996.

SNA: Detailed Description of Traditional SNA Components and Protocols

Anura Gurugé. *SNA: Theory and Practice*. New York: Pergamon, 1984, 1989.

Key SNA/APPN Specifications from IBM

IBM. *Systems Network Architecture Formats and Protocol Reference Manual*. Document SC30-3112.

IBM. *Systems Network Architecture Formats and Protocol Reference Manual: Architecture Logic for LU Type 6.2*. Document SC30-3269.

IBM. *Systems Network Architecture: APPN Architecture Reference*. Document SC30-3422.

HPR-Over-IP

APPN/HPR in IP Networks. IETF RFC 2353. May 1998.

Data Link Switching

IETF RFCs 1434, 1795, and 2166.

tn3270 and tn5250

IETF RFCs 1576, 1647, 2355, and 1205.

Overview of TCP/IP

W. Richard Stevens. *TCP/IP Illustrated: Volume 1—The Protocols.* Reading, MA:
Addison-Wesley, 1994.

Introduction to Intranets

Lynn M. Bremner et al. *Intranet Bible.* Las Vegas: Jamsa Press, 1997.

Web Technology

Nancy J. Yeager, Robert E. McGrath. *Web Server Technology.* San Francisco:
Morgan Kaufmann, 1996.

HTML

Chuck Musciano, Bill Kennedy. *HTML: The Definitive Guide.* Cambridge: O'Reilly,
1996, 1997.

Security and Firewalls

William R. Cheswick, Steven M. Bellovin. *Firewalls and Internet Security.*
Reading, MA: Addison-Wesley, 1994.

Java

Paul Týma et al. *Java Primer Plus.* Corte Madera, CA: Waite Group, 1996.
Aaron E. Walash. *Java for Dummies.* Foster City, CA: IDG Books, 1997.

Index

Addison-Wesley Computer and Engineering Publishing Group

How to Interact with Us

1. Visit our Web site

http://www.awl.com/cseng

When you think you've read enough, there's always more content for you at Addison-Wesley's web site. Our web site contains a directory of complete product information including:

- Chapters
- Exclusive author interviews
- Links to authors' pages
- Tables of contents
- Source code

You can also discover what tradeshows and conferences Addison-Wesley will be attending, read what others are saying about our titles, and find out where and when you can meet our authors and have them sign your book.

2. Subscribe to Our Email Mailing Lists

Subscribe to our electronic mailing lists and be the first to know when new books are publishing. Here's how it works: Sign up for our electronic mailing at http://www.awl.com/cseng/mailinglists.html. Just select the subject areas that interest you and you will receive notification via email when we publish a book in that area.

3. Contact Us via Email

cepubprof@awl.com
Ask general questions about our books.
Sign up for our electronic mailing lists.
Submit corrections for our web site.

bexpress@awl.com
Request an Addison-Wesley catalog.
Get answers to questions regarding
your order or our products.

innovations@awl.com
Request a current Innovations Newsletter.

webmaster@awl.com
Send comments about our web site.

cepubeditors@awl.com
Submit a book proposal.
Send errata for an Addison-Wesley book.

cepubpublicity@awl.com
Request a review copy for a member of the media
interested in reviewing new Addison-Wesley titles.

We encourage you to patronize the many fine retailers who stock Addison-Wesley titles. Visit our online directory to find stores near you or visit our online store: http://store.awl.com/ or call 800-824-7799.

Addison Wesley Longman
Computer and Engineering Publishing Group
One Jacob Way, Reading, Massachusetts 01867 USA
TEL 781-944-3700 • FAX 781-942-3076